Bleisure

Bleisure

Adventures of International Business Travel

EDDY GUARASCIO

RESOURCE *Publications* • Eugene, Oregon

BLEISURE
Adventures of International Business Travel

Resource Publications
An Imprint of Wipf and Stock Publishers
199 W. 8th Ave., Suite 3
Eugene, OR 97401

www.wipfandstock.com

PAPERBACK ISBN: 979-8-3852-7114-6
HARDCOVER ISBN: 979-8-3852-7115-3
EBOOK ISBN: 979-8-3852-7116-0

VERSION NUMBER 050626

Dedicated to my beautiful wife Susie and loving daughters Bridget Rose, Kaitlin Leigh, and Tierney Anne.

I am so blessed and happy to be traveling through this life with my amazing women!

Also dedicated to Rick and Beverly Guarascio,
my father who left us way too soon
and my mother who sadly passed away more recently . . .
both are greatly missed by all.

Whatever intellectual curiosity, adventurous nature, joy, and lifelong zest for learning I have I owe to them!

I look at things with a traveler's mindset . . .
with curiosity, joy, and positivity.

—*Rick Steves*

CONTENTS

PREFACE

Travel is not reward for working, it's education for living.

—*Anthony Bourdain*

"Oh, let's hear from the world traveler." "We don't care where you've been." "Oh, you're a real one-upper." These are common refrains I hear when I occasionally discuss my international business travel experiences. And I emphasize "occasionally" as I seldom discuss my travels or business doings. I've taken photos, and I share a few interesting stories along with the trials and tribulations of international travel, but little else. Over the years my wife has asked that I create a collage of photos taken around the world. She would like for me to display these in a hallway or elsewhere as a conversation piece. I've never really considered doing so though I have kept many photos, ticket stubs, restaurant cards, and maps accumulated throughout the years.

From time to time, my mother-in-law proclaimed that I really needed to write a book about my experiences, tales from all the exciting cities I've visited. This is a bit funny as my wife (her oldest daughter) has actually written a wonderful book—deep insights relative to her journey of faith. It was never my desire to write anything at length, though I was certainly inspired by her example.

So . . . from the beginning, how is it that I experienced business travel? After nearly twenty years working for a Pittsburgh-based government contractor, I made an interesting job change. I joined a small, fast-growing medical device manufacturer as head of procurement. By all accounts, I was way out of my league. The company was global, commercially driven, healthcare focused, and owned by a large German pharmaceutical enterprise. This was all very new to me and, fortunately, "I didn't know what I didn't know." In addition to our Pittsburgh operations, a small European headquarters was operated in Maastricht, Netherlands, and a comparable Asian site in Osaka, Japan. Accordingly, via baptism by fire, I came to understand, in the words of British author John le Carré, "A desk is a dangerous place from which to watch the world."[1]

Although our German parent company was generally "hands off," I would be invited to join various groups for corporate reviews and team-building. I quickly learned that there were two annual Global Procurement team meetings. Each fall, the global team would meet throughout Germany, oftentimes in Berlin. And each spring, the team would meet near a rotating European office location, primarily in very dynamic capital cities. So, here I was at the age of forty-three, having never traveled outside the United States or Canada. Further, I had never even applied for or obtained a passport. Funny . . . it really is never too late to start traveling!

Next, you might wonder: What is "bleisure"? Bleisure is a *portmanteau* (port-man-toe) or a "blend of words," i.e., business and leisure. Bleisure refers to a trend of people adding onto or enjoying sightseeing (leisure) as part of business travel. It's estimated that almost 10 percent of business trips can be categorized as "bleisure" trips.[2] That figure is much higher in many companies where team-building and "work-life" balance are understood and promoted. The phenomenon has been studied for years and has exhibited steady growth. In fact, the pandemic recovery (and increased hybrid work) has resulted in offerings of "bleisure travel" as a necessary perk to employees. The stories that follow can all be classified as "bleisure" or leisure activities pursued in association with my own business travels. Many resulted from scheduled flights providing a day on the ground. Others, from a relentless pursuit to seek fun and knowledge in lieu of recommended rest and sleep. And many others were layover weekend activities on my off days abroad.

While writing this book, I revisited a few saved cartons of old photos, collected brochures, torn ticket stubs, restaurant business cards, maps, and more. Much of the same is stored on my iPhone. I also reviewed my company's SAP Concur travel and expense management tool as a concrete reminder of my specific business trips, dates, and activities. These also include specific detailed receipts and expenses. Finally, know that every effort was made to ensure any shared information is accurate and still current. No doubt I have a few facts misstated, confused, unsubstantiated, or otherwise

1. Le Carré, *Honourable Schoolboy*, 65.
2. Jet, "Are Bleisure Trips."

in error where information is debated, changed, or is outright incorrect. I apologize in advance for any such errors.

I hope you enjoy my unique recollections and insights. Ideally, you too will be motivated to consider your own "bleisure" travel if given the opportunity to do so.

ACKNOWLEDGMENTS

On the road again
Goin' places that I've never been
Seein' things that I may never see again.

—*Willie Nelson*

First and foremost, I am grateful to my wife, Susie, who had published her first book and strongly encouraged me to write about and share my business-related travel experiences. Her book is a much deeper, personal, and spiritual memoir titled *Love Was There: A Testimony of Faith*. Nonetheless, she inspired me and showed me first-hand how to "stay at it." Along the way, she also taught me the ropes as to the world of book publication. I am also grateful to my mother-in-law, Mary Pat (O'Grady) Soltis, who prodded me, anxiously awaited, and quickly and thoroughly read and *seemingly* enjoyed each new chapter. She provided steady encouragement throughout.

I consulted nearly a thousand online magazine articles, stories, and travel brochures while writing *Bleisure*, far too many to cite here. One excellent book series that I had purchased over the years and that proved especially helpful is the *DK Eyewitness Travel* collection. These outstanding, well-organized books are filled with colorful, interesting pictures and plenty of invaluable tips and information. I relied on the Eyewitness series in preparing for past travels and, more recently, revisited them to aid and validate my recollections. I have often gifted these books to friends and family in advance of their own international travels. *Rick Steves' Europe* books are also an excellent in-depth resource with incredible insights and a wealth of information. Thanks also to our local Norwin Public Library and their "Travel" bookshelves.

I cannot thank Beth Bevis Gallick enough for her outstanding, comprehensive editing.

I'd be remiss if I failed to mention my wonderful "bleisure" colleagues throughout the United States, Germany, and all four corners of the world. Few are lucky enough to have worked in two highly interesting, always challenging, fun-filled, diverse, and respectful enterprises—businesses that proudly advanced world peacekeeping, global life science, and overall healthcare.

Last and most important, I am blessed with a large loving family of brothers, two sassy sisters, and numerous in-laws. I thank all of them who fill my life with endless love, laughter, and adventure. I've read and fully understand that the best part of life is the people we love and any good we might do along the way. That is certainly followed by all the beautiful places we've traveled . . . and the cherished, lasting memories we've made.

INTRODUCTION

The world is a book and those
who do not travel read only one page.

—*Saint Augustine*

I imagine most everyone dreams about visiting exciting and exotic locations. I am no exception. Amusingly, it started when I first discovered James Bond 007 as a youth. I recall playing a James Bond board game as a very young boy. The game's board featured several intriguing locations, including a mountain cabin, a casino, a deserted mine, a cemetery, a warehouse, and, of course, a back alley. As a result, I was fascinated with 007's movie locations, such as the Furka Pass in the Swiss Alps, the Monte Carlo Casino in Monaco, underground coal mines on the Japanese island of Hashima, and the "Red Alley" in the Al-Darb al-Ahmar outskirts of Cairo.

For a long time . . . travel was nothing more than a dream. I grew up in the Western Pennsylvania steel town of McKeesport, very near Pittsburgh. McKeesport was a thriving industrial city of national importance during most of the twentieth century. It was the center of US steel manufacturing and pipe making. However, in time, the city faced decline as steelmaking gradually left the region and general economic malaise set in. McKeesport's strength was always its unique "salt of the earth" people, a highly diverse mix of races and many nationalities. McKeesport's population was proud, supportive, hardworking, and tough. Conversely, most families were not largely afforded great means and opportunity for world travel. In fact, few families left the area as they strived tirelessly to simply build a better life for their children. That said, many from McKeesport overcame hardship and adversity, excelled, and have made worldwide contributions.

As for me, when finally given an opportunity to travel through business, I was well prepared to optimize my international travel experiences. I would research known attractions, explore modern-day guides and current activities, and strategically book hotels in walkable city centers or notable old-town districts. Work activities were always paramount and never shortchanged. However, whenever possible, I would also plan and allocate time for sightseeing, exploration, and learning, aka "bleisure" travel. Foremost, I always maintained a personal objective to deliver a healthy business return on trip expenses. Years of relationship building, and the following of meeting action items, has easily and greatly enriched both my *business* and *leisure* outcomes.

This book represents "snippets" from my international bleisure travel experiences. I have been blessed to admire the Sistine Chapel, visit the Sydney Opera House, study the Mona Lisa, toss a coin in the Fountain Trevi, pray in Fatima, explore Kyoto's Golden Pavilion, attend London theater, investigate Checkpoint Charlie, tour Anne Frank's house, admire the statue of David, scale the Cliffs of Moher, stroll the Champs-Élysées, and so much more. The book's aim is solely to provide entertaining and educational anecdotes and insights based on a sampling of my personal international business travel experiences. The book is cross-genre, with short story elements of travel, business, history, religion, food, art, a bit of how-to, memoir, and more. Really, it's both all of that and none of that! In the end, it's just a storybook, with countless entertaining "fun facts" and adventures, not intended as a travel guide. In a nutshell, the book is a labor of love to share my joy and gratitude in everyday living and my travels along the way. Ideally, I hope you enjoy a short, firsthand, personal account of a few of the world's greatest locations, sites, and treasures offered from my unique "bleisure" point of view.

CHAPTER 1

MILAN

I love Milan, and I'm not just saying that. It's a city that gives me a great sense of euphoria. I can't explain why, but I feel a special energy there.

—*Shawn Mendes*

Milan HOLDS A SPECIAL place in my heart, much like the feelings of young Mr. Mendes. In fact, my very first visit to Europe was to Milan for a Global Procurement Conference. I also returned more recently to help facilitate a significant office relocation. For this reason, I will start my stories in Milan.

The thriving city of Milan, Italy, is not your typical northern Italian metropolis, town, or village. Milan is one of the leading fashion capitals of the world, with notable strengths in commerce, design, education, literature, media, finance, performing arts, and tourism. It's the capital of the Lombardy region and the second most populous city in Italy after Rome. The city proper has a population of 1.5 million while the metropolitan area has over three million residents. The wider Milan area has a population more than ten million. Milan is considered a leading alpha global city. And, of course, Milan is one of four world-recognized fashion capitals, along with London, New York, and Paris.

Milan's history goes way back to 600 BC, when Celtic inhabitants appear to have first founded a settlement. In 222 BC, the Romans captured the settlement, and Milan has been a capital city for over two thousand years. From 1277 to 1500, Milan was ruled by two aristocratic families: Visconti and Sforza. These family dynasties introduced classical learning and brought about a refinement and grandeur associated with the Renaissance period.

Every invader in European history has taken turns at ruling the northern Italy region. Partial destruction occurred after conflicts in AD 539 and 1157 and again in 1944 post–World War II. Thus, unlike other capitals, little of Milan's antiquity has survived.

From my perspective, Milan is also Leonardo da Vinci. Although born just outside Florence, Leonardo lived in Milan between 1482 and 1499. It is believed he came to Milan to study anatomy, though during his time in Milan, his influences were broad. For example, Leonardo engineered the city's canal system. He also designed a flying machine (four hundred years before the first sustained flight). More importantly, while in Milan, Leonardo drew thousands of sketches related to flight, weaponry, musical instruments, mathematics, botany, etc. These drawings and writings are preserved in the famous twelve-volume, 2,200-page Codex Atlanticus notebook.

This is just a very brief overview of the city, and I urge you to read more. What follows next are a few specific stories related to major sites or activities I personally experienced and enjoyed via bleisure travels. These are certainly not a comprehensive guide to the cities themselves. A similar format is used throughout.

The Last Supper

Most notably, while in Milan, Leonardo da Vinci painted. And though his *Mona Lisa* may be the most famous portrait ever painted, Milan is home to Leonardo's magnificent *Last Supper*. This masterpiece is one of the most celebrated artworks in all the world. Accordingly, *The Last Supper* is surely one of Italy's must-sees, though you should book in advance. Of course, I did not, and only through the grace of God, along with some good fortune and Italian generosity, did I finagle, I mean secure, a pass—not once but twice. First, the painting is not in a museum. *The Last Supper* is painted on the smallish dining-room wall of the Santa Maria delle Grazie (Holy Mary of Grace) convent in a quiet neighborhood a short distance from Milan's city center. Visitors' entry is very restricted to groups of just twenty-five fortunate guests every fifteen minutes.

Many supposed mysteries and enigmas surround the iconic painting, one of the most studied paintings of all time. *The Last Supper* has also been the subject of countless novels, movies, and songs. It has inspired numerous wild theories and popular fiction. *The Last Supper* is not a traditional fresco painted on wet plaster but an attempted experimental wall painting. The painting took three years—largely attributed to the painter's procrastination and da Vinci's many other competing and interfering interests. Further, the painting has had an unbelievable history of unfortunate bad luck and neglect. Shortly after it was completed in 1598, Leonardo's paint-on-stone technique had failed. The colorful paint had started to flake and decay. Restoration has been largely ongoing, with marginal success. Also, unimaginable site construction and destruction have occurred. Most noticeable, in 1652, a doorway was added to the painting's wall, eliminating the lower central part of the masterpiece. Jesus's feet were lost! The fragile painting was also said to have been used by Napoleon's troops for target practice, and the convent itself withstood World War II bombings.

As a Catholic, I appreciate how the painting captures several climactic, successive moments of the church's highest teachings. It's a dramatic scene described in connected accounts throughout the various Gospels. *The Last Supper* depicts the precise moment in which Jesus declares that one of his apostles will betray him. For these reasons, American novelist Henry James declared the mural "the saddest work of art in the world."[1] It also depicts the moment where Jesus institutes the Holy Eucharist. The bread and the cup of wine within Jesus's reach are key symbols of the holy sacrament.

The Last Supper is quite large at approximately 15 by 29 feet. Specks of silver and gold were used to enhance human characteristics. Real life models were used to capture each apostle's personality in the exact moment of betrayal. Talk about attention to detail. Even the jails of Milan were searched as Leonardo sought to locate the perfect scoundrel to portray traitorous Judas. Prior years of detailed, macabre anatomical study helped da Vinci master the illusion of three-dimensional space on a flat surface. Most striking, as experienced firsthand, is its single-vantage-point perspective, which draws any viewer to step into the scene. Regardless of personal religious beliefs, viewing *The Last Supper* is a memorable experience that extends far beyond art appreciation.

Milan Cathedral (Duomo)

One of the true joys of traveling to Europe is experiencing the majestic Gothic cathedrals. Soaring domes, mystical stained-glass windows, towering spires, ethereal art, religious artifacts, and unreal sculptural detail result in some of the most loved and admired architecture in the world. Uniformly, all cathedrals were passionately created to the glory of God. The given understanding is that the cathedrals should be as grand and beautiful as wealth and inspired otherworldly craftsmanship permits. Cathedrals traditionally and proudly function as the given, long-standing ecclesiastic and social

1. Duggan, "Can We Ever Restore."

meeting place for the entire region. Often, the remains of an acknowledged local, regional, or adopted patron saint are interred behind the high altar.

Along my travels, I have been fortunate enough to have visited many of the world's most renowned cathedrals. These include Rome's Saint Peter's Basilica, Notre-Dame de Paris, Cologne Cathedral, Venice's Saint Mark's Basilica, Paris's Sacré-Coeur Basilica, Florence's Cathedral of Santa Maria del Fiore, London's Westminster Abbey, and Antoni Gaudí's Sagrada Família in Barcelona. However, the very first such cathedral I saw was *Milan Cathedral*, or the Duomo, as it is better known. More properly, it is known as the Basilica of the Nativity of Saint Mary, and I was rendered speechless by its size and ravishing beauty.

For anyone visiting Milan, it would be nearly impossible to miss the magnificent Gothic Duomo in the main piazza. Construction of the cathedral began in 1386 and took thousands of workers, a new canal transport system, and nearly six centuries to complete. The sheer size and appearance of the cathedral are daunting. Yet, in Italian fashion, it is warm and inviting as well. The Duomo's capacity is estimated at forty thousand, though mostly it sits relatively empty and reserved for solitary reflection and adoration. Astoundingly, every inch of the edifice, including the roof, is decorated in a forest of precious Candoglia white marble cladding. The marble came from a wonderful lake cave at the nearby Swiss-bordering Lago Maggiore.

In addition to admiring the cathedral's interior, it's important to experience the rooftop and terraces. The rooftop is only accessible via a seventeenth-century elevator or by ascending 180 narrow steps. Here you will also find the Madonnina spire crowned by the polychrome "golden" Madonna statue. The colossal Madonna (protectress of Milan) was erected on the Duomo's tallest steeple in 1794. By tradition, no building in Milan was to exceed the 356-foot-raised Madonna. However, several Milan corporate buildings subsequently exceeded this height. The corporations circumvented the church's scorn only by adding their own replica Madonna statues atop.

Another item of great interest to me is the *Rite of the Nivola* ancient tradition. Each year on the Saturday closest to September 14, Milan's archbishop ascends to the apse near the Duomo's high altar. There, preserved in a reliquary, is a holy nail from the True Cross from Jesus's crucifixion. The Holy Nail is lowered to the ground for the faithful's viewing for just forty hours before being returned to the tabernacle. The spot is marked throughout the year with a red light.

As my bleisure travel time was always quite rushed, I often abbreviated tours with attention to key sites and activities. There are usually quite fascinating facts of interest surrounding world-renowned cathedrals, and here are just a few relative to Milan's Duomo:

- Cathedral construction generally coincides with ascension to power. This was the case in Milan, where the new archbishop set out to reward both nobles and working-class people who had long suffered under a previous tyrant.
- Construction was regulated under the Fabbrica del Duomo (dedicated factory), which had three hundred employees and lead engineers.
- In 1488, Leonardo da Vinci and Donato Bramante created models in a competition to design the central cupola. Leonardo would subsequently withdraw his submission.
- The Duomo's most famous sculpture, the gruesome marble figure of glorious martyr Saint Bartholomew, who was flayed alive, was installed in 1562. There are said to be more statues in the Duomo than any other Catholic cathedral.
- In 1786, astronomers from the academy placed a sundial on the Duomo's floor. A ray of sunlight from a hole on the opposite wall strikes the clock. Though quite ancient, the sundial is surprisingly precise and is still used today to regulate clocks throughout Milan.
- In 1805, Napoleon Bonaparte, about to be crowned king of Italy, ordered the cathedral's façade to be finished. All expenses were to fall to the French treasurer, though the reimbursement was never paid. Napoleon was crowned king of Italy at the Duomo.

The Duomo remains the sixth largest and one of the mightiest Catholic cathedrals in the world. Its rich spires extend heavenward and embolden it as the truest crowning symbol of Milan.

Milan Galleria

For sheer Milanese splendor, there's no better place than the Galleria Vittorio Emanuele II, or *Milan Galleria*, landmark. The spectacular glass-topped, four-barrel-vaulted nineteenth-century building is possibly the world's earliest and most extravagant shopping mall. The glass and metal roof consists of 350 tons of cast iron and was the most innovative, daring, and unprecedented project of its time. The Galleria is named after the Kingdom of Italy's first king and was built in 1865. For perspective, this was the same time as the United States Civil War. Construction of the whole Galleria was the result of considerable international collaboration.

The Galleria is in the city's heart, midway between the majestic cathedral and the famous La Scala opera house. The Galleria's space forms a four-story octagon-shaped arcade. The great glass dome provides an ethereal effect and a splendid sight. As intended, the design and location of the Galleria allow it to fulfill a variety of social functions. In true Italian fashion, the Galleria is just as functional as it is aesthetically pleasing.

The Galleria is full of symbols, and not to be overlooked are the beautiful and symbolic mosaics on the ground floor at the center of the octagon. As I personally discovered, the mosaics are an underrated source of fun. I recall one memorable evening in Milan when I learned the legend of the "lucky bull." The Galleria contains four distinct mosaic designs on the floor. Three of the designs portray the coat of arms of the three capitals of the Kingdom of Italy—namely, Roma, Florence, and Turin—and the fourth mosaic contains the symbol of Milan. Representing Rome is the she-wolf together with founding brothers Romulus and Remus. Florence is simply the lily flower. Milan is a red cross on a white background. As for Turin, the symbol is a little dancing bull or, in Italian, *torino*. The bull of Turin is represented with big genitals and became quite popular. People came to believe that touching the bull brought good luck. Men spin around three times with their heel on the testicles of the bull. Women touch the testicles thinking that the gesture could improve fertility. Unfortunately, over time, that part of the little bull has been damaged in the process. Nonetheless, the mosaic still attracts hundreds of curious and superstitious visitors daily. I've kept a favorite photo of myself in front of dozens of global colleagues. I'm depicted twirling and feverishly spinning my heel in search of some good luck!

Visiting Europe for the first time was an entirely new and exciting travel experience. I returned for a second visit when a decision was made to relocate the Italian (Milan) office to a new under-construction location. I had an important role in overall design and furnishing of the new office in accordance with many corporate global directives. Most fortunately, from a “bleisure” perspective, I was also able to briefly visit both nearby Venice and Florence.

CHAPTER 2

VIENNA

When will you realize Vienna waits for you?

—*Billy Joel*

My first visit to beautiful Austria was to its enchanting capital city of *Vienna*. My father-in-law always claimed Austria was the most beautiful country in the world. Consequently, I was very excited to visit. My visit to Vienna became a bleisure experience in the truest sense of the phrase. The trip entailed a relatively quick two-day visit to validate and purchase a specialized, quite expensive injection molding machine. The machine was needed for a process to develop a unique catheter invented by an enterprising Mayo Clinic cardiologist in his garage. It was our responsibility to successfully build a prototype that could also be mass produced. Fortunately, work was concluded early on the second day of our visit, freeing up the afternoon. We were scheduled to fly home the following morning. The supplier's salesman happened to be an extremely proud central Viennese native who very much wanted to show us his beloved city . . . and boy did he ever!

Vienna is located on the Danube River within range of the stunning, distant Alps. It is home to approximately two million residents and has been occupied since 500 BC. It is no surprise that Vienna was named the most livable city in the world as recent as 2019 (just prior to the COVID pandemic).[1] The esteemed rating is largely based on Vienna's location, beautiful parks, world-class museums, delicious food, and its MUSIC! For the past 250 years, Vienna has justifiably earned the moniker "The City of Music." There's

1. *Economist*, "Vienna Remains."

a reason that many of Europe's finest composers, i.e., Beethoven, Haydn, Mozart, Schubert, and Strauss, all lived and worked in Vienna.

We had just a brief autumn afternoon with our young, passionate tour guide. During this time, he delighted in sharing an abbreviated insider's view to just a few of Vienna's must-see, lesser-known attractions.

Saint Stephen's Cathedral (Stephansdom)

Our guided tour commenced at Vienna's iconic, nine-hundred-year-old city-center cathedral dedicated to the first Christian martyr, Saint Stephen. There is considerable lore associated with Saint Stephen's cathedral. And, although our time was limited, I learned that the cathedral was started in the year 1137. Like many of Europe's beautiful cathedrals, it was essentially destroyed during World War II and rebuilt afterwards. Nonetheless, daily services are held there to this day. The cathedral was built on an older pagan site of worship with some degree of deference to the old pagan gods, while replacing the ruins with a Christian cathedral. Elements of the earlier Roman construction were respectfully integrated. In terms of folklore, it is rumored that master mason Hans Puchsbaum made a deal with the devil in exchange for his artistry. Consequently, Puchsbaum sadly fell to his death from the scaffolding.

It's unfortunate that we did not allocate an additional day to explore the cathedral and Vienna's many other attractions. You always believe you will someday return to destinations but should plan as if you might not. Nonetheless, we were lucky to visit the church and marvel at its history and beauty. Adding historical perspective, inside is the Gothic pulpit from which Saint John of Capistrano preached a 1546 crusade against the Ottomans. We were also shown the unusual site of a Turkish cannonball and symbols of later Nazi resistance; this is what I recall most. As we rounded the church's exterior, we were asked to gaze upward. Here we could see a small cannonball embedded in the tower's buttress. We were told the cannonball is one of thousands catapulted at the cathedral (from nearly a mile away) in 1683 during the second Turkish Siege. That date is inscribed on the cathedral beneath the cannonball. There are also several reminders of Austria's dark days of World War II. One is a lantern denoting the reconstruction of the cathedral in 1945. Another is a blackened stone honoring the securing of the cathedral and liberation of Vienna. The Austrian resistance aided the Allies in a manner I immediately associated with patriotic Captain von Trapp of *Sound of Music* fame.

Saint Michael's Church (Michaelerkirche)

With an insider's knowledge of Vienna, our enthusiastic guide took us to one the most unusual sites I ever visited: the catacombs at Saint Michael's Church. First, understand that Saint Michael's, the parish of the imperial court, is very old, dating back to 1220. For context, this was an age when Genghis Khan, King Henry III, and Saint Francis of Assisi were living. There is an eerie, medieval, and mystical aspect to this church I've not experienced elsewhere. Our time exploring the church interior was brief, though there is an overwhelming sense of enduring history through the centuries. I also learned that Saint Michael's Church is famous for presenting the premiere of Mozart's Requiem in D Minor in December 1791 shortly after his death.

Saint Michael's is notable also for its Michaelergruft, a large crypt located beneath the church. The crypt was created in the sixteenth century with the closure of a surrounding graveyard in 1508. It began as individual burial vaults for noble families. Access to the crypt was later opened to the middle class in 1678. In 1783, the emperor decreed that no further burials were to be carried out in Vienna's inner city. Astonishingly, our guide was able to gain special access to the crypt. We entered the underground crypt within the church off the choir area. Upon entering, a cold, chilling air greets you. There are an estimated four thousand bodies in the crypt but only a few hundred coffins. Many could not afford a wooden coffin or, it's said, coffins were later retrieved and burned for firewood. In any case, scattered human bones entirely composed the crypt floor. Additionally, due to the catacomb's unusual climatic conditions and constant cool temperature, many bodies had not decomposed. Several mummified bodies, within open coffins, are perfectly preserved with fingernails and garbed in fine outfits, shoes, and wigs of the time. Some coffins are adorned with flowers and rosaries and are decorated with baroque paintings or symbols. Teeth are evident on many skulls. To my further surprise, I was advised that skulls with teeth are, in fact, the poor who could not afford cakes and other sweets. Conversely, the wealthy usually lost their teeth due to sugar consumption and a lack of modern dentistry. Visiting old Saint Michael's underground crypt was a gruesome, chilling experience for certain. It was a fascinating, thought-provoking memory I'm not likely to ever forget.

Prater Park and Schweinsstelzen

Following a busy morning of meetings and our impromptu tour of Vienna, it was time to consider a late-afternoon meal. Our guide knew exactly where to go to further share his love for Vienna. A short distance from the city center is *Prater Park*. Originally this area was an imperial hunting ground preserved for nobility. The Prater area borders the Danube River and was opened to the public in 1766. By the nineteenth century, a corner of Prater became a funfair with rides, games, food stands, beer gardens, and sideshows. One of Vienna's most famous landmarks is the giant Ferris wheel constructed in Prater Park in 1896.

We visited the park's legendary Schweizerhaus restaurant. The restaurant is situated in one corner of Prater Park and will fully meet your need to check off an Austrian beer garden, one with exceptional atmosphere and food. With the park's Ferris wheel in the background, Schweizerhaus is Vienna's biggest beer fest, seating over one thousand guests both indoors and outside in a lively parklike setting. And while it's estimated that over ten thousand beers are sold and consumed daily, the *Schweinsstelzen* (leg of pork) is the garden's real star. The leg is served upright on the bone with a knife and cutting board as your only aids. The Schweizerhaus is a high-energy, joyful restaurant packed with both locals and visitors to experience the famous "Stelze." Their trademark pork dish is generously coated with salt, pepper, and garlic, then spit-roasted to perfection. The crispy skin is crackling in texture and sweetly coated. Inside, the meat is moist, soft, juicy, plentiful, and so delicious. A memorable meal indeed! Just recalling this visit and the crispy leg of pork is making my mouth water even now. In fact, I am looking into Austrian or German-themed beer gardens within the Pittsburgh area in search of Schweinsstelzen.

Sachertorte

Following lunch, we returned to the heart of Vienna where the afternoon could not have ended on a "sweeter" note. This would include a visit to the famed, upscale *Hotel Sacher* café. Here we experienced Austria's extraordinary coffee and Vienna's most famous culinary specialty: the "original Sacre Torte." *Sachertorte* is a rich chocolate cake, or torte, invented by Franz Sacher in Vienna in 1832. It's reported that Franz Sacher, then an apprentice, was required to create a novel cake on a day that the chef was ill. Franz's son claimed the torte was invented for a crowned prince, though this appears to be an embellishment, mere nostalgic appeal to past Viennese imperialism. The cake has multiple variations, though the "original" has two layers of apricot jam between the dark chocolate icing and the dense chocolate sponge cake. The desirability of the original torte is said to lie in its delicious icing composed of three separate specialty gourmet chocolates. The torte is traditionally served with unsweetened whipped cream and always with Viennese coffee or mélange (espresso with steamed milk topped with foam). Even today, the original Sachertorte, sold only at limited European locations and online via the Hotel Sacher shop, remains immensely popular in Austria and worldwide.

What a wonderful way to end a perfect, productive bleisure visit to Austria. Fortunately, I would return to Austria on a future date to visit beautiful Salzburg.

CHAPTER 3

PARIS

Paris is always a good idea.

—*Audrey Hepburn*

I'm often asked, "What is your favorite visited city?" My response: Rome is fascinating, London is entertaining, Sydney is cool, Florence is beautiful, Mexico City is lively, and Venice is magical; however, to me, *Paris* is *all* of the above. For this reason, I was always thrilled to visit my favorite city, Paris. I recall that one visit pertained to our European fleet contract negotiations and another visit was to our French office located outside Paris. On a few other occasions, I would visit Paris on weekends en route elsewhere via then-direct Pittsburgh to Paris international flights. Over the years, I have even had my wife and daughters individually join me when possible. Consequently, I have confidently mastered a very exciting, exhilarating, action-packed three-day tour of Paris.

Paris is an electric city . . . a place that sends a charge through you the moment you arrive at Charles de Gaulle Airport. The airport has an exciting, hip 1960s vibe and design. It is also celebrity-packed with politicians, musicians, athletes, and film stars always passing through. A train from the airport station delivers you to the heart of Paris in just thirty minutes. The old Paris train stations, such as the Gare du Nord, are equally beautiful (as featured in many movies, like the *Bourne Identity*). The Gare du Nord is the busiest station in the world outside Japan.

Paris is a very large city of nearly 2.5 million people, with 4.5 million on the outer ring and nearly ten million in the region. Paris is made up of twenty districts, known as *arrondissements*, and is divided by the Seine River, resulting in a Right Bank and a Left Bank. Each district is relatively small and has its own unique charm. My favorite is the sixth arrondissement on the Left Bank and in particular its historic *Saint-Germain-des-Prés* quarter. It's a lively area full of cafés, book shops, cinemas, and jazz clubs, with narrow cobbled streets off the main boulevard. Some streets date back to the thirteenth century. The area is also very near the Seine River, where you can stroll to and easily board a *bateau mouche* (a hop-on, hop-off water taxi). A river ride is a great way for an introduction to Paris's beautiful architecture and surroundings, with stops at popular places, e.g., Notre Dame Cathedral, Avenue des Champs-Élysées, Eiffel Tower, Musée du Louvre, etc. I love to stay at the small, boutique *Crystal Hotel*, conveniently located in the heart of Saint-Germain. I find it the quintessential Paris spot given that the Café de Flore, Les Deux Magots, Le Procope, and Brasserie Lipp are just steps away. Further, the *Ladurée* macaron shop and a delicious crepe vendor are just around the corner.

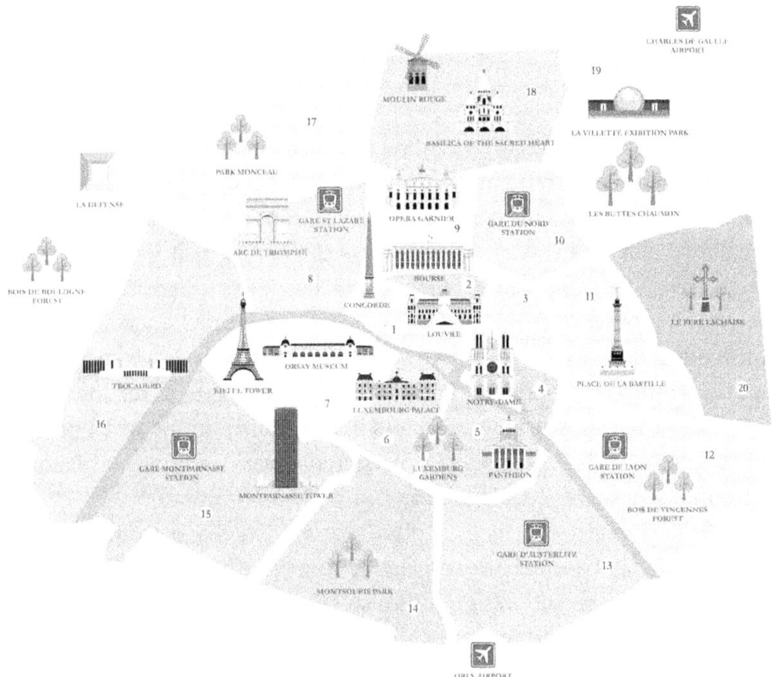

Paris District/Attractions Map
Adobe Stock | Image 138702617

My second favorite Paris district is charming *Montmartre* in the eighteenth arrondissement, which is furthest north on the Right Bank. Offering sweeping views of Paris from the steep, winding streets, small terraces, and tiny squares, Montmartre maintains a lively, artsy village atmosphere. It is also home to the majestic Sacré-Coeur Basilica, Moulin Rouge cabaret, and Place du Tertre (artists' square). When visiting, my daughter identified the square as a magical village reminiscent of *Beauty and the Beast*.

Having provided guidance on Paris in the past, here are the activities I most enjoy when on a limited, few-days stay.

Wander the Left Bank: Latin Quarter and Saint-Germain-des-Prés. This is an older, historic district favored by artists, revolutionaries, writers, and thinkers and is where I prefer to stay. It was the regular haunt of a younger Napoleon, philosopher Jean-Paul Sartre, Ernest Hemingway, Colette, F. Scott Fitzgerald, Gertrude Stein, Robert Wagner, and more. Many of their apartments are still marked. I like to stop at one of the very old cafés—

you never know who will be sitting around you or passing through. Order a crepe and coffee or a carafe of wine and return to 1920s Paris. Stop in the old Saint-Germain-des-Prés Church (location of the tomb of French philosopher Descartes) or Saint-Sulpice Church, featured in Dan Brown's *The Da Vinci Code*. Both medieval cathedrals are notably fascinating and worthy of visit. Lastly, the nearby beautiful Ralph's (Lauren) Restaurant is wonderful, high-brow Americana abroad.

Visit the Musée du Louvre and the Musée d'Orsay. No trip to Paris would be complete without a visit to two of the greatest, most visited art museums in the world. I make it a point to visit the museums, albeit briefly, on every trip to Paris. Besides unimaginable art, the grounds and buildings are eye popping. The Louvre is housed in an extended, block-long fifteenth-century royal palace. The scale of the Louvre is astounding; high drama and excitement abounds. In contrast, the Orsay is housed in a former beaux-arts railway station. You must plan well ahead or brave long lines. Lacking time, my personal "non-ideal strategy" is to go at five o'clock in the evening, near the six o'clock closing, and target certain floors, rooms, and art of most interest. Bear in mind that the Louvre has ancient through nineteenth-century art, whereas the Orsay features post-nineteenth-century art. This means the Louvre has the statues Winged Victory (Nike) from 200 BC and Venus de Milo from 130 BC, while also displaying the world's most famous painting, the *Mona Lisa,* from 1503. The *Mona Lisa* started as a standard commission to paint a wealthy merchant's wife; the merchant never received the painting. Leonardo spent the subsequent sixteen years working and reworking the *Mona Lisa*. He carried the painting from Florence to Milan and on to France, where he died still in possession of the *Mona Lisa*. In contrast to the Louvre, the Orsay's focus is on more recent French art, including beautiful impressionist paintings of Monet, Degas, Renoir, Manet, Cézanne, Gauguin, and van Gogh.

Tour Notre Dame Cathedral. On April 15, 2019, flames and smoke billowed from the roof of the spectacular Notre Dame Cathedral. Parisians, and all the world for that matter, responded with an outcry of disbelief, horror, and grief. The fire destroyed the spire and the oak roof beams supporting the lead roof. The aftermath left devastating destruction to the cathedral's interior. Fortunately, the main structure remained intact. Over five hundred firefighters were employed to save the façade, towers, walls, buttresses, and stained-glass windows. The great eighteenth-century eight-thousand-pipe organ was also saved but suffered considerable water damage. The cathedral is owned by the state and self-insured. Nonetheless, immediately after the fire, French President Emmanuel Macron vowed that Notre Dame would be fully restored. The president called for the work to be completed in 2024, and a festive grand reopening did indeed occur on December 7, 2024.

The world-famous Notre Dame Cathedral, with its sheer Gothic beauty, stands majestically on the Île de la Cité (island) floating mid–Seine River in the cradle of Paris. The cathedral was built between 1163 and 1345. Notre Dame features golden walls, ornate windows, and its famous gargoyles, hobgoblins, devils, and birds of prey. Throughout history, Notre Dame also suffered great turmoil. Most notably, after the French Revolution of 1789, Notre Dame was seized and made public property. Religion was banished and it briefly transitioned to a temple to the Cult of Reason. The great cathedral was even temporarily used as a warehouse for the storage and sale of food and wine. Shortly thereafter, in 1804, Napoleon restored Catholicism and declared himself emperor of France at Notre Dame. However, after the Napoleonic Wars that followed, Notre Dame was in such a state of disrepair that Paris city officials even considered its demolition.

At that time, in stepped Victor Hugo, famed French poet, novelist, author, playwright, and dramatist of the Romantic movement. Publication of Victor Hugo's 1831 "smash hit" novel, *The Hunchback of Notre Dame*, is largely credited with saving Notre Dame from imminent destruction. Hugo thought of Notre Dame as a work of art authored by humanity itself, with no individual artist. The sentiment was that Notre Dame surpassed anything an individual could do and, therefore, became the best of what all of us can do. For that very reason, the *Hunchback* reminded us that Notre Dame Cathedral must be rebuilt again. The worldwide fanfare with the eventual reopening of Notre Dame Cathedral was enormous. Every trip I've made to Paris includes a personal visit to the cathedral. Possibly my favorite Paris activity is attending six-thirty Mass at Notre Dame on Saturday evening. Those attending Mass can circumvent and bypass tourist queues and seek an open pew. I always make my way up front on the side. It's a known, comical critique that Catholics tend to avoid the first few rows. Consequently, I always locate an excellent open seat near the expansive altar. On several occasions, I enjoyed the same outstanding young female cantor, the renowned organ, and the world-class acoustics. Of course, when exiting, it's always a good idea to light a votive candle for a specific personal intention.

Visit the Luxembourg Gardens. They say the best way to get to know a city is to walk its neighborhoods. Nowhere is this truer than in Paris. With each trip, I greatly look forward to visiting the Jardin du Luxembourg or Luxembourg Gardens. It's a short stroll from my usual outpost. Merely cross tony Boulevard Saint-Germain onto Rue Bonaparte. In short order you'll arrive at the gardens, which are also located in the sixth arrondissement of Paris. The leisurely walk on charming Rue Bonaparte will take you past the Place Saint-Sulpice square as well as an obscure, intriguing bronze statue of a beautiful young peasant girl. The girl is sitting on a bench, glancing downward beneath a large floppy hat, with hands cupping her chin. After several visits, I finally discovered that the statue sits outside the Balassi Institute, a worldwide, long-standing nonprofit cultural organization funded by Hungary. There's space on the bench next to the girl inviting someone to sit down. As was intended, many who notice the statue do just that. I have photos of my daughters emulating the young girl's pose.

It is said that Luxembourg Gardens is one of the most successful parks in the world. This is primarily because it is so well integrated into the fabric of Paris all around it. The gardens are easily accessible and welcoming to one and all. The Luxembourg Gardens came about following the assassination of King Henri IV in 1610. It is believed that his second wife, Marie de Médicis, could not continue living in the Louvre Palace with his memory. As a result, commencing in 1615, she had the Palais du Luxembourg and the surrounding gardens built in what was then a pastoral countryside. The palace was to replicate her larger childhood home, Palazzo Pitti and the Boboli Gardens, in Florence, Italy. The pristine palace (now a senate building) appears as if it was only recently constructed.

Paris's most captivating park has been open to the public since the seventeenth century. The gorgeous gardens are best described as serene and ideal for people watching. Daily occupants present an image of an unhurried Parisian existence from a simpler time. Its many attractions include shady chestnut trees, under which old men meet to play chess. There's also potted orange and palm trees, spacious open lawns, fountains, tennis and basketball courts, beehives, puppet theaters, playgrounds, pony rides, and motorized toy sailboat rentals (in the central octagonal grand basin). The toy boats often display the national flag of the worldwide visiting renter. Statues of France's queens (including Marie de Médicis herself) and famous French artists and writers, and even a model replica of the Statue of Liberty, are located about the park's many adjoining terraces and avenues. All year round, joggers circle the garden's circumference as sunbathers and bookworms fill the park's iconic steel green chairs. Simultaneously, card-playing seniors seek shade near the palace, music resonates from the band shell near the Boulevard Saint Michel east entrance, and supervised children run throughout the park. Others may visit to momentarily take pause and enjoy one of the cafés. The sheer variety of enjoyable things to do can consume hours. The beautiful "City of Love" gardens serve as the perfect background for cinema and one of the most famous and romantic scenes in literature. Specifically, fans of Victor Hugo's famous novel *Les Misérables* are very aware that it was in the beautiful Luxembourg Gardens where the glances of Marius and Cosette first met.

Stroll up to Montmartre. There's a magical hillside village (the *Butte Montmartre*) located just above Paris. Montmartre may be one of my favorite places in the world. It's the one Parisian district that I think about returning to the most. Montmartre is north of Paris on the Right Bank in the eighteenth arrondissement. It's a whimsical, charming, bustling neighborhood filled with countless cobblestone streets, artists, bistros, gardens, tiny squares, and vintage shops. There's even a couple of windmills remaining from days past. Then, like a cherry on the top, you arrive at the graceful and grand white-domed nineteenth-century Romanesque-Byzantine *Sacré-Coeur Basilica*. The entire hillside has retained its stunning village vibe and offers spectacular views of Paris below. And for me, getting to and strolling through Montmartre is half the fun. I am not a great fan of structure and conformity so, admittedly, my jaunts to Montmartre have varied every time. Happily, each visit has allowed me to observe, experience, and learn more. For those with time who don't mind being lost, I highly recommend this approach. Though I must warn you that the streets and stairways up the approximate one-kilometer-high hill are quite steep and testing. Others should chart out a favored tour route up the sandstone butte or consider a guided walking tour, take the funicular, or simply hop on the village's exclusive *Montmartrobus* (bus) to avoid all the uphill walking and steps.

There are five primary metro stations offering access to Montmartre that are well connected to the rest of the city. Four stations that I am most familiar with include Pigalle, Blanche, Abbesses, and Anvers. Each area is quite unique and offers different experiences and certainly proximity. At the bottom of the hill is Place Pigalle and the Blanche stations. The Abbesses and Anvers metro stations are further up the Montmartre hillside and a shorter walk to Sacré-Coeur Basilica. In fact, the Anvers station is just a two-minute walk to the to the bottom of the basilica. Even from there, you have the choice of considerable stairs or the funicular. For this reason, I look to use the Abbesses station or, preferably, wind my way up the hill through the Place des Abbesses square (named to commemorate the nearby Benedictine nuns). Two reasons for this route: First, the lively little square is one of the most charming and picturesque in all of Paris. While looking like a Hollywood set, it offers a great glimpse into everyday Parisian life. There's a colorful small carousel in the square and the famous forty-foot enameled lava wall panel where "I love you" is written in nearly three hundred languages. The second reason is the masterpiece Abbesses metro station itself. The station is one of just three remaining original Hector Guimard Art Nouveau designs. Opened in 1913, it is also one of the deepest metro stations in Paris and delivers you directly to the Montmartre-spirited maze of streets. The station's glass roof entrance with its unusual green wrought iron arches and amber lights are iconic.

The two other aforementioned stations, Blanche and Pigalle Place, are at the foot of the Montmartre hill in a somewhat depraved, but oh-so lively, area known as Pigalle. Gentrification efforts of Napoleon and then the monarch led to eviction of the poor from central Paris. Many homeless residents and struggling artists moved to the outskirts; Pigalle and Montmartre were popular destinations. Pigalle is commonly known as the sleazy, sequin-infested Paris district filled with bordellos, cabarets, cancan revues, peep shows, and other exotica. Though in European fashion, it is also a residential district with slices of everyday life. There are some wonderful bakeries, churches, and schools on the main boulevard and across the side streets heading up the hillside. Most notable, and just outside the Blanche metro station, is the historic, world-famous Moulin Rouge cabaret. It's here that wild, colorful, high-kicking cancan dance shows were memorialized. Opened in 1889 and rebuilt after a 1915 fire, the cabaret continues today. Moulin Rouge (or Red Windmill) was an instant success and even today captures an atmosphere reminiscent of the turn-of-the-century optimistic Belle Époque period. Its extravagant setting, most-unique architecture, new dance, and famous dancers were loved by all. Here you could see clowns, singers, acrobats, tightrope walkers, and erotic cabaret. Moulin Rouge appealed to both resident artists and the upper crust looking to "slum it" in the fast-evolving, fashionable Montmartre district. While the notorious Pigalle area is not for everyone, it is a very cool place to catch a glimpse of Moulin Rouge and commence the steep climb to Sacré-Coeur. I have taken my grown daughters there via the Blanche station for a quick photo shoot at the small square across the street.

Montmartre has been associated with art for over two hundred years. Many world-renowned painters such as van Gogh, Monet, Toulouse-Lautrec, Renoir, Picasso, Dalí, Modigliani, Degas, and Matisse lived and worked in Montmartre, often roaming the squares, meeting up in cafés, and painting in their respective artists' studios. This artistic vibe remains abuzz, having never left Montmartre. No place is art more evident than in the storybook-like *Place du Tertre*, the village's vibrant central "artists' square." Constructed in 1133 and opened to the Parisian public in 1635, "the place is," in the words of my daughter, "magical." The Place du Tertre is the beloved tourist center of Montmartre. It is lined with cafés, bars, and creperies and bustling with portraitists, painters, poets, and other artists. The artists paint "en plein air" (open air) throughout the square. It's said that nearly three hundred painters are licensed to paint in Place du Tertre and there's a ten-year license waiting list. Artists are allocated just a square meter of space, often sharing the 150 daily available spaces by working shifts. The Place du Tertre should not be missed when visiting Paris. On one such visit, my daughter and I stopped at the red-painted Chez la Mere Catherine. Besides "Catherine" being that daughter's quasi namesake, the restaurant is the oldest in the square, dating back to 1793. It is rumored that the word "bistro" was coined in this restaurant during the Russian occupation in 1814.[1] The Russian Cossacks would often bang their fists and bellow "bystro" (meaning quick) to hurry along the staff and their drinking comrades alike. Consequently, the French started to use the word "bistro" to describe their less formal restaurants. For its enchanting, picturesque beauty, creative artistic vibe, and fond memories, Place du Tertre is one of my favorite spots. Next, just a short five-minute walk from the square to the summit and the focal point of Montmartre, is one of the most visited sites in all of Paris, the monumental Sacré-Coeur Basilica.

I would certainly never miss an opportunity to visit the majestic Basilica of the Sacred Heart of Jesus otherwise known as *Sacré-Coeur Basilica.* Sacré-Coeur holds a special place in my heart, as I attended elementary school at Sacred Heart Parish in McKeesport, Pennsylvania. The basilica has a most fascinating origin and was specifically dedicated to the Sacred Heart of Jesus. Started in 1875, and located on the highest point in Paris, Sacré-Coeur is considered a post-war political and cultural landmark. Its conception originated at the onset of the 1870 Prussian War when two influential Catholic businessmen made a religious vow. If the men lived to see France spared and Paris should survive, the men would build a church dedicated to the Sacred Heart of Christ. Despite the onslaught of war, fifty-eight thousand resultant tragic deaths, and a lengthy siege, a decree of public interest authorizing construction was enacted. It was decided that at Paris's highest point, with its panoramic city views, the divine love of the Sacred Heart must reign. As further reassurance, above the basilica's narthex, set inside a

1. Kracklauer, "Parisian Tradition."

niche, a large Jesus statue reveals his heart to the entire city of Paris. Maybe it was the outstanding weather I experienced each visit or the surrounding atmosphere that made my visits to Sacré-Coeur so uniquely special. Locals and visitors alike attest that Sacré-Coeur is a true beacon on the hill that elicits both deeper insights and a certain inner peace. There are so many interesting facts related to Sacré-Coeur, and here are just a few:

- Construction of the basilica was largely funded by generous donations of faithful Parisians. Parisians could purchase one to three stones for a cost up to 500 francs. In turn, names of the investing donors are engraved over the church walls.
- Sacré-Coeur is the youngest of Paris's many churches, with completion in 1914. Unlike the familiar Gothic style of so many older cathedrals, the basilica's architectural style is Romanesque-Byzantine. For this reason, Sacré-Coeur is often compared to Saint Sofia in Constantinople and San Marco (Saint Mark) in Venice.
- The shiny, bright white Sacré-Coeur Basilica exhibits eternal youth. It is unlike most monuments that tend to darken over time and require constant maintenance. Credit the architect who chose a white stone from nearby quarries. The same stone is used on the famous Arc de Triomphe. In wet weather, the stone is resistant to water infiltration. In fact, when it rains, the stones release a calcite substance that acts like a bleach and cleans the stones.
- Lastly, one of the most astounding facts is that since 1885 (before construction was near completed), Sacré-Coeur has hosted an "uninterrupted prayer" or perpetual adoration to the Blessed Sacrament. Every evening after the 10:30 p.m. closing to the public, a prayer relay continues. Faithful worldwide churchgoers register in advance for *Night Adoration*, where they pray and spend the night at the Sacré-Coeur Basilica Guest House. All guests are then invited to join a continental breakfast after the basilica reopens at 7:00 a.m. Consequently, a continuous, uninterrupted prayer has been ensured over 140 years.

Finally, there's so much more to see both outside and inside the basilica including a Saint Joan of Arc equestrian statue, a great mosaic, bronze doors, a crypt, and the bell tower with one of the heaviest bells (nearly twenty tons) in the world. One thing is for certain, Sacré-Coeur Basilica is a peaceful, blessed Parisian sanctuary and a bright jewel for all of France.

Tour the Palace of Versailles. The weather was picture perfect on the Sunday afternoon that my oldest daughter and I visited the royal château in Versailles. The cloudless September sky was the deepest cornflower blue shade that I had ever seen. So much so that the surreal photos we took resemble a painted French impressionist masterpiece. It's a short twelve-mile train ride from Paris to Versailles with a clear sense that you are leaving the city. Back in the mid-seventeenth century, Versailles was just a distant country village, a two-hour ride by horse from Paris. Today, Versailles is a wealthy southwest suburb of Paris. My daughter had suggested that we carve out time to visit Versailles. I believe her interest was spurred by Sofia Coppola's 2006 highly stylized hit movie *Marie Antoinette* starring Kirsten Dunst.

I imagine that there are few places in the world that can rival this colossal French landmark in terms of opulence, splendor, and excess. In addition to the 2,300-room château, the surrounding gardens of Versailles are also the largest and most spectacular in the world. The gardens contain six hundred fountains, nearly four hundred statues, fifty-five water features, and over twenty miles of water hydraulics. The gardens also contain hundreds of worldwide botanical species, including palms, pineapples, vanilla, coffee, oranges, lemons, pomegranate, oleander, and more. Versailles's huge gardens, along with its extensive menagerie, allowed for many botanical, agricultural, and zoological studies and even led to the creation of veterinary schools. The palace's "absolute monarchy" origin along with its mind-blowing extravagance is early indication that it was so wrong and unsustainable. Despite its breathtaking beauty, its excess would be the eventual downfall of the people who coldheartedly ruled it. Along the way, the magnificent palace has had a long, wild history of amazing facts, unbelievable stories, bizarre behavior, and incredible quirks.

In total, Versailles was the center of political power in France from 1682 until the start of the French Revolution in October 1789. The palace started as a humble hunting lodge when Louis XIII bought the land and built a château to stay at if he had no time to return to Paris after dark. He gradually expanded the château and acquired more land. His heir, Louis XIV, became king at just age five. In 1661, having reached age twenty-one, Louis XIV had begun to detest and distrust Paris. Instead of the Louvre, then a royal palace, Louis XIV decided to move France's power base to the family's shoddy hunting lodge in Versailles. Wanting to establish himself as a strong king, he began grand-scale, complicated, unsafe construction of the palace with thirty-six thousand workers. Conditions were deplorable from the start, and thousands of workers faced strict discipline or died. Versailles was initially not a favorable place to be for the royal court. After several decades, the palace was completed to great grandeur.

There were strict protocols as to meeting the kings that are evident when visiting the palace even today. For example, the closer one could get to the king's bedchamber, the more important and favored you were. An audience to observe the king getting undressed at bedtime or his ceremonial dressing upon waking were highlights for the nobles. Every hour of the king's day was well organized, and dinner times were strictly observed, with a bevy of formal guests clamoring to be near the king. Louis XIV also imposed a very strict dress code on his guests, insisting on the finest materials and often bankrupting the nobles. Much of France's fashion, dinner etiquette, and culture is derived from the many palace rules of Louis XIV, who ultimately ruled for seventy-two years. Succeeding king Louis XV, known as Louis the Beloved, was king of France from 1715 until 1774, a lengthy fifty-nine-year reign of his own. Louis XVI and the Viennese beauty Marie Antoinette were the last king and queen of France before the French Revolution. As you likely know, it did not end well. Marie Antoinette remains a most iconic character in the rich history of Versailles and a key symbol of its wanton extravagance. As an example, Marie Antoinette had a love of hot chocolate, a delicacy of the time and the exotic choice of the king and royals. As such, Marie Antoinette brought her own chocolate maker, titled Chocolate Maker to the Queen, to Versailles. Further renovations to the palace were stalled as France was slowly going bankrupt. Considerable money was allocated by Louis XVI to the American revolutionaries to fight the common British foe. Efforts to raise even more taxes upon the now starving Parisians were refuted. On October 5, 1789, the people marched upon Versailles. This was the end of the French monarchy until restored at the end of Napoleon's control in 1830. The palace suffered decline and restoration throughout the following years. It also served as the location of many important world history events. Most notable was the 1783 Treaty of Versailles signing where Britain conceded to France and Spain that the United States of America was an independent nation.

Lastly, there are countless features to see while passing through the palace's rich and vast interior, including the gilded furniture, though nothing is so dramatic as the iconic Hall of Mirrors gallery. The remarkable 270-foot corridor adorned with 357 Italian-cut mirrors is a work of art in and of itself. At the time, mirrors were one of the most expensive items to possess. The hall was primarily a main thoroughfare but was surely designed for spectacle. The king would sit in his throne at one end with seating installed in the corridor for the public. Venice had a monopoly on luxury mirror making in the late seventeenth century, although France was suddenly rivaling Venice. To the chagrin of Venice, France had enticed Venice mirror makers to defect and come to Versailles to create the beautiful specialty mirrors. For all these reasons, Versailles remains one of the most popular attractions in France, with throngs of annual visitors.

Climb the Eiffel Tower, Visit the Arc de Triomphe, Stroll the Champs-Élysées. Three of the most obvious, fun, "must-do" activities in Paris include the above. No trip to Paris is otherwise fully complete. I have had the pleasure to visit these sites on my own and to share the experience with my wife and daughters. Each time, I have captured a photo of them on the identical Champs-Élysées bench with the Arc de Triomphe towering in the background. Given most everyone's familiarity with these well-known monuments, I want to provide just a few limited facts and a handful of related personal bleisure weekend experiences.

The *Eiffel Tower* is undoubtedly the most synonymous Paris symbol. The tower was built in 1889 by Alexandre Gustave Eiffel (of Statue of Liberty fame). Astoundingly, the Eiffel Tower is said to weigh seven thousand tons but only exerts the same pressure on the ground as an average-sized man sitting in a chair. And, although it's a beautiful, timeless, architectural marvel, the tower was originally meant to be temporary and was soundly denounced by the Parisians. Seeing the tower in person and walking underneath and all around the surrounding park is truly a cherished lifetime memory. If possible, climb the 1,665 steps or patiently ascend the double-decker elevators. For magnitude, the top, third-level tower is 905 feet above ground and its viewing gallery can hold eight hundred people at a time. It's great to visit the tower at sunset as all of Paris lights up below. Inside the tower are cafés, bars, memorabilia, the Eiffel bust, and the very pricey, famous Jules Verne restaurant. It is a short walk outside the Eiffel Tower on the Seine River landing that many of the most skilled portraitists reside. There are various groups, e.g., Chinese, Russians, etc., and an ongoing debate as to who is best. When visiting, my daughters each had a portrait drawn, and they were outstanding. Lastly, always be mindful that it's equally thrilling to periodically spot the skyward Eiffel Tower when exploring various neighborhoods.

Back in 1805, following the Battle of Austerlitz, Napoleon promised the soldiers that they would march home beneath triumphal arches. In keeping with his word, the *Arc de Triomphe* was commissioned by Napoleon in 1806. However, due to Napoleon's loss of power, the Arc was not completed until 1836. The Arc is located at the Place Charles de Gaulle, with twelve expansive, bustling avenues radiating from the center of the Arc. The

Arc in this huge traffic circle can best be reached via marked underground passages; don't try to cross the circle and the constant French "bedlam-like" traffic. Symbolism abounds on the Arc's many captured military-victory scenes, with a tomb of the unknown soldier and a listing of Imperial Army officer names as well. From the 164-foot roof's viewing platform, there's a great view straight down the grand Avenue de Champs-Élysées . . . wonderful both day and night. Many great victory parades have marched through the Arc de Triomphe. Most notable celebrations were the World War I Allied armies in 1919 and Charles de Gaulle–led liberation of France after World War II in 1944. Could there be any better reasons for such exuberant, joyful celebration?

Paris's most famous and spectacular thoroughfare is unquestionably the *Avenue de Champs-Élysées*. My daughters loved it! Beautiful, tree-lined, extra-wide pavements are dotted with flower beds and accommodate throngs of people. "Luxury" is the operative word here as visitors look to see and be seen. The broader Champs-Élysées area, bordering the Seine River to the south, is known as the "Golden Triangle" of Paris. As known, the area contains many of the world's most famous "haute couture" fashion houses, five-star luxury hotels, theaters, clubs, and fine restaurants. Additionally, gorgeous radiating chic avenues contain palaces, museums, town mansions, and several international embassies and consulates. For even more stunning "Golden Triangle" street fashion, turn off Avenue de Champs-Élysées onto posh, glamorous *Avenue Montaigne*. Avenue Montaigne is the crème de la crème of glitzy couture shopping in Paris. Chanel, Gucci, Versace, Dior, Valentino, Fendi, Louis Vuitton, Armani, Prada, Ralph Lauren, Saint Laurent, Jimmy Choo . . . they are all housed here. And while shopping is not an option for most visitors, it is highly worth visiting Avenue Montaigne to view the extravagantly decorated window displays and discreetly people watch. My one "let's splurge" exception with my daughters has been lunch at the Champs-Élysées French restaurant *L'Avenue*. This celebrity hot spot and well-known rendezvous destination is highly elegant but never boring. With its prime corner location and usual buzzing scene, L'Avenue is one of the best and understandably expensive Champs-Élysées restaurants. At any moment, guests might include international designers, heads of state, artists, and authors, as well as a Kardashian or Rihanna. Most of the fun comes from leisurely sitting on L'Avenue's outside terrace among stylish Parisians sipping a cold glass of champagne. Just try not to think about the looming bill!

Those are my personal favorite things to do in Paris, though obviously there is so much more. I hope you can now better understand why Paris is always a good idea!

CHAPTER 4

AMSTERDAM

Some tourists think Amsterdam is a city of sin, but in truth it is a city of freedom. And in freedom, most people find sin.

—*John Green*

Amsterdam is a unique and beautiful city. Moreover, it is relatively small and compact and always a welcomed joy to visit. Notwithstanding my many visits to Cologne in Germany and Limerick in Ireland, I probably made more visits to Amsterdam than to any other European city. For one, Amsterdam was the primary layover destination for my travels to headquarters in Germany. Amsterdam was also very near our European office in Maastricht and the Netherlands office in Mijdrecht. I also recall direct visits to Amsterdam to negotiate European freight and courier contracts with DHL Express and to align with a newly acquired subsidiary office location. Despite its small size, population 750,000, Amsterdam offers a wide range of varied attractions and is home to some of the world's finest art museums. Amsterdam is also known as the "Venice of the North" for its elaborate canal system. Juxtaposed, the natural serenity of Amsterdam peacefully coexists with its notorious, seamy "Red Light" district underside. I can neither admit nor deny that I quickly walked through the district just to see what all the fuss was about. The small, contained area is easily avoidable and should not deter you or your family from experiencing all the beauty and wonder of Amsterdam. In fact, Amsterdam is a top European travel destination with over 7.5 million foreign visitors annually.

First, Amsterdam is a really cool city. My wife, with a somewhat limited sampling to date, has stated that Amsterdam is her favorite European city! I think it was the scenic canals and all the beautiful flowers. Throughout the years, my wife, an elementary school teacher, was able to accompany me on a European business trip just once. It was an extended weeklong, four-country trip that took us to Amsterdam, Brussels, Cologne, and Paris. Our first stop was Amsterdam, and as I had daily business, I strategically booked us at the *Grand Hotel Krasnapolsky* on Dam Square in the center of Amsterdam. The large, historic, bustling main town square borders the royal palace, has fantastic shopping, and is teeming with markets and street entertainment. I know my wife had a fun day being abroad for the very first time and exploring the area. Conversely, on many occasions when I traveled to Amsterdam alone, I would stay at the majestic Victoria Hotel. This older hotel is just a short walk from the beautiful Amsterdam Centraal train station and has attracted celebrities such as Louis Armstrong, Fats Domino, and more recently Katy Perry. In any event, based on my wife's abbreviated visit, she soundly declared Amsterdam her favorite European city. I have a saved photo of my wife on a small, picturesque, seventeenth-century-stone humpback bridge on the Keizersgracht Canal where she looks so pretty and happy. I cherish the opportunities we had and continue to have to travel together.

The origin and global evolution of Amsterdam is quite fascinating. It first emerged as a quiet fishing settlement from the mist of the watery Austrian-ruled Low Countries along the Amstel River. The medieval settlement was defined by its long-standing dynastic and religious-based feuds. The Dutch fought long and hard against Spanish domination for religious and political tolerance. They strongly support that no one should be harmed by the actions of others. The little fortified village grew rich quickly due to a method for curing and preserving herring for export of the fish. It also was a growing port for importing beer from Germany. Amsterdam's population soared in the seventeenth century Golden Age. Three great canals were constructed in a triple ring around the city defining the spirit of Amsterdam. Architects and painters added elegant gabled houses, charitable institutions greatly assisted the poor, and a sort of peace was reached with Catholic Spain. Many famous artists worked in Amsterdam during this period most notably Rembrandt.

Success at home in the Netherlands led to supremacy overseas for the industrious Amsterdam people. Colonization of Indonesia resulted in the Dutch East India Company and a highly profitable spice trading empire. Ships from China, Japan, and elsewhere provided spices, e.g., peppercorns, cloves, cinnamon, and ground nutmeg, throughout Europe. At the time, the

Dutch largely ruled Brazil and, as known, even purchased Manhattan (New Amsterdam) from its Native American owners for just $24. Subsequently, war with England crippled Dutch sea power and the empire, though the Netherlands remained wealthy. Immigrants from around Europe, including many Jews, settled in the tolerant, financial-capital nation. An alliance with France resulted in Napoleon's takeover and his brother Lewis was established as king of the Netherlands. His rule was short-lived, and the country regrouped. The Netherlands remained neutral during both World War I and II only to be invaded by Germany. Most Jewish citizens were deported or forced into hiding, like famous thirteen-year-old Anne Frank. Following the difficult 1940s, a social unrest subculture occurred, and eventual redevelopment followed. Today, Amsterdam remains a major business hub and a city of great beauty and culture.

Amsterdam is a very walkable, though non-grid, town well worth exploring on foot. And, of course, the Dutch love their bicycles. You must always remain mindful of the nearly one million bikers navigating endless networked miles of Amsterdam's flat dedicated bike lanes. Consider renting a bike and exploring the city as the locals do. You should also consider viewing the city by canal boats. Such tours are particularly suited for those with limited time or ability to explore by foot. Given my somewhat limited time when visiting Amsterdam, below are just a few of the main attractions that I've experienced, enjoyed, and consider "must dos." Of course, as with the other noted cities, there is so much more to see and do based on your personal preferences and time allotment. Whenever traveling, it's helpful to be flexible and plan and schedule activities in advance when possible. For certain, Amsterdam is a most exciting, conducive bleisure destination!

Amsterdam's Famous Museums

There are countless museums of great international renown throughout the world, each with breathtaking art collections of unimaginable historic importance and value. Many are readily located throughout the United States in cities such as New York, Chicago, and Washington, DC. However, when traveling abroad and given limited time, it is usually difficult to allocate sufficient time to properly explore museums. That said, there are certain cities, e.g., Paris, Florence, Rome, Barcelona, etc., where a brief, focused museum visit is mandated . . . even for non–art lovers! And Amsterdam, the envy of most cultural cities, is near the top of this list. A visit through the bustling lanes and vibrant plaza of the Amsterdam Museum Quarter is essential. Herein reside two museums generally regarded as among the *top 10* worldwide. Here, fountained landscaped pathways lead to both the stunning, gargantuan *Rijksmuseum* and the avant-garde *Van Gogh Museum*.

First, the red-brick Rijksmuseum is the "national museum" of the Netherlands, presenting eight hundred years of Dutch history. If you have time for only one museum visit while in Amsterdam, it should be the landmark Rijksmuseum. Designed by Pierre Cuypers in neo-Gothic style, the Rijksmuseum opened in 1885 on what was previously farmland. Influenced by French architects, Pierre Cuypers also designed and restored many churches and the beautiful Amsterdam central train station. Today the vast museum has over one million pieces in its collection with over eight thousand, dating from the 1200s, on display. The collection primarily features the Dutch masters with over two thousand Golden Age paintings, including Rembrandt van Rijn, Johannes Vermeer, and many others. The two "must-see" showpieces are *The Night Watch* by Rembrandt and *The Milkmaid* by Vermeer. Also, *The Threatened Swan* by Jan Asselijn is the very first piece acquired by the museum. If time is particularly short, focus on the wing of incomparable seventeenth-century paintings. Undoubtedly, Rembrandt is the most famous of the many artists who lived in or near Amsterdam and produced masterpieces during this period. When not being restored, there are twenty-two Rembrandts and four rare Vermeers on exhibit at the Rijksmuseum.

Rembrandt's striking *Night Watch* was painted in 1642 and is a colossal painting at 12 by 14.5 feet in size. It is so large that the varied figures are nearly life-size. The painting was commissioned by and depicts a militia company known as the Shooting Company or the "Night Watch." There are thirty-four characters in the painting, including Rembrandt himself in a cameo role. Unlike the typically static paintings of the times, this incredibly complex painting depicts the company in motion, marching and on the move. Included is dramatic use of light and shadow, sunlight and shade. Symbolism abounds, with a child mascot in yellow, a dead chicken, a militia goblet, and an oak leaf, all representing recent victory over an adversary. There is speculation as to where exactly Rembrandt completed a painting of this large size. The painting initially hung in Amsterdam's Musketeers' Meeting Hall. Many believe the painting was commissioned to greet the French queen Marie de Médici who escaped France in exile. The painting was removed, rolled, and stored in a special place for a four-year period during World War II. It has been mistreated, attacked, repaired, and restored several times. Many millions have viewed this masterpiece, including most every school-age child in the Netherlands. The second most famous painting and attraction in the Rijksmuseum is Vermeer's imaginative *Milkmaid*. Unlike Rembrandt's *Night Watch*, Vermeer's *Milkmaid* is roughly a mere foot-and-a-half square in size. Likewise, there is not a great militia on the move but rather an ordinary, working milkmaid made immortal. Vermeer's painting is simple with very few objects. Vermeer is said to have completed *The Milkmaid* in 1658; he was quite famous for capturing middle-class moments of everyday life. His *Girl with a Pearl Earring* painting is another such example. There is a slight "Mona Lisa effect" with Vermeer's painting given the mysterious woman and her own faint smile. Uncharacteristically for the time, the attractive maid is seemingly treated with dignity and empathy. Yet she simultaneously oozes sexuality and romance. The painting is done in exceptional detail with a brilliant color scheme. Consequently, the beautiful, busy, working milkmaid remains forever frozen in time at the Rijksmuseum.

Just a few steps from the Rijksmuseum, also in the museum district, is the *Van Gogh Museum*. Dutch artist Vincent Willem van Gogh is Holland's most famous and influential artist. The Van Gogh Museum is implicitly dedicated to the works of art of this fascinating, deeply troubled, world-renowned artist. Most people know the story of Vincent van Gogh. He was born in the Netherlands in 1853 and died at the young age of thirty-seven. During his short, productive life, van Gogh made over 2,100 works of art, including 860 oil paintings and over 1,300 watercolors, drawings, and sketches. Most of van Gogh's artwork was created in his final ten years of his life, beginning in 1880. Van Gogh longed struggled with physical and mental illness and lived and studied under the love and patronage of his younger brother, Theo. As is widely known, about a year before his death, following a fierce argument with fellow artist and house guest Paul Gauguin, van Gogh severed part of his own ear. He was temporarily forced into an asylum in Saint-Rémy, France. Releasing himself, he relocated to Auvers-sur-Oise near Paris. Psychotic episodes, delusions, heavy drinking, and depression continued. Then in 1890, a few days after an apparent self-inflicted gunshot wound, Vincent van Gogh died in the arms of his brother Theo. Considered a madman by most, van Gogh sold little of his artwork in his lifetime. On the verge of greatness, van Gogh died a perceived failure. Unfortunately, fame came only after the death of the now idealized tortured artist. In the ensuing decades, thanks to his sister-in-law, global commercial success followed. Today, van Gogh's paintings remain among the world's most expensive. His great legacy is surely honored by Amsterdam's unparalleled Van Gogh Museum.

Unlike the Rijksmuseum, the Van Gogh Museum is considerably compact, though no less difficult to gain entry to. The museum first opened in June 1973. Housed within the museum is the world's largest collection of van Gogh art. Included are over two hundred stunning paintings, five hundred drawings, and seven hundred handwritten letters and manuscripts of van Gogh. Many of van Gogh's works of art are self-portraits as he battled tirelessly to be recognized and understood. Also included are paintings of several famous, well-known contemporary artists and friends, including Henri de Toulouse-Lautrec, Claude Monet, Auguste Rodin, and even Paul Gauguin. The most legendary of van Gogh's paintings at the museum include *Sunflowers*, *The Bedroom*, and *The Potato Eaters*. *The Starry Night* is not at the museum, as it was first sold by Theo's widow back in 1900. It was subsequently obtained in 1941 by the Museum of Modern Art (MoMA) in New York City. In 2019, the Van Gogh Museum introduced a technology-driven, 3D "Immersive Van Gogh Experience," which has since toured globally. I had the opportunity to experience the amazing immersive event in Pittsburgh. From Amsterdam to Paris and beyond, Immersive Van Gogh has become the number-one selling show in the world.

Van Gogh's impact on modern art is immeasurable, as today he is widely and generally regarded as the most popular Postimpressionist painter. His bold brushstrokes, exaggerated forms, and wild use of color and emotion were considered maddening yet massively influenced all aspects of twentieth-century art. His fascinating lifestyle and free spirit have inspired many, and his work continues to alter the way mankind views beauty and style. While others routinely saw ugliness in the poor and ordinary, van Gogh saw beauty and joy.

The most dazzlingly famous and recognizable van Gogh painting on display at the Van Gogh Museum is *Sunflowers*, painted in Arles, France, in 1888. A series of large canvases with various shaded yellow sunflowers in a vase were rapidly painted by van Gogh, each with unique eloquence. Van Gogh realized immediately that he had created art of distinct importance; the *Sunflowers* would eventually be his signature pieces. The intent of his *Sunflowers* series was initially an experiment in bolder still life colors than typically used. By this time, van Gogh had moved to the south of France in hopes of starting an artist community. When he heard that the avant-garde painter Paul Gauguin would be visiting him, he painted several sunflowers to brighten and decorate the guest bedroom. His friend was quite impressed by the sunflowers, which delighted van Gogh. The paintings held a very special meaning for van Gogh, communicating happiness and gratitude. Again, while most viewed sunflowers as course and unrefined, van Gogh believed just the opposite. Nonetheless, the visit of fellow artist and hero Paul Gauguin did not go well, culminating in van Gogh's further instability and the severed ear incident. And, although the *Sunflowers* failed to sell in van Gogh's lifetime, today *Sunflowers* remains one of the most instantly recognizable artworks in the world. Sunflowers would remain synonymous with the artist from those early paintings. Following his death in 1890, many friends knowingly brought sunflowers to van Gogh's funeral and grave site. The value of these once overlooked paintings is unimaginable. In 1987, nearly one hundred years after its creation, one of the unsigned paintings, *Still Life: Vase with Fifteen Sunflowers*, sold to a Japanese businessman for a then record price of $39.85 million. The likely worth of a van Gogh sunflowers painting today is estimated in the hundreds of millions of dollars. This incredible value prohibits them from traveling outside museums, including the Van Gogh Museum. Singing of Vincent van Gogh, Don McLean's highly inspired 1971 song "Vincent (Starry Starry Night)" frames it best, suggesting that van Gogh was, in some sense, too beautiful for this world.

Anne Frank House

A signature experience that may best define Amsterdam is a sobering visit to the historic *Anne Frank House*. It's one of the most visited sites in the Netherlands. Anne is the well-known teenage diarist who documented Nazi World War II persecution. Consequently, she is one of the most discussed Jewish victims of the Holocaust. Her *Diary of a Young Girl*, first published posthumously in 1947, has received widespread critical acclaim. The diary provides vivid poignant insight into a young Jewish girl living in German-occupied Netherlands. The book was written while Anne hid from Nazis, for over two years, in a sealed-off area of an Amsterdam warehouse. It has since been published in over seventy languages and has sold over thirty million copies.

The Anne Frank House is a museum dedicated to Anne's short life, her writings, and those who hid in the Amsterdam warehouse. The building's preservation and museum's formation are primarily through the effort of Anne's beloved father Otto Frank, the only family member who would survive the Auschwitz extermination and concentration camp in German-occupied Poland. The museum, first opened on May 3, 1960, preserves the famed hiding place as a permanent exhibition. The fifteen-year-old Anne and her family were unexpectedly discovered, based on an unrelated tip, on August 4, 1944. Anne and her sister Margot both died in the concentration camp from the effects of typhus several months later in February 1945.

The historic seventeenth-century channel house is located on a canal in central Amsterdam. The well-known channel is known as the Prinsengracht. Most notable is the house's hidden room known as the Secret Annex. It was here, beginning in July 1942, that Anne and four others hid for two years. The house's owner had built a hinged false bookcase or rotating bureau to hide the room's entrance. Staff from the warehouse business provided the Frank family with daily food, water, and war news updates. Unfortunately, the space was ultimately discovered by the gestapo, and all of those hiding there were sent to German concentration camps. Today, visitors enter the Secret Annex through the movable bookcase's narrow opening. Also, inside the house is Anne's bedroom and diary room where she received the famous red checkered diary on her thirteenth birthday. Anne had understood that public officials were going to preserve wartime journals and longed to tell others of her World War II experiences. Oddly, Anne Frank's diary is addressed to "Kitty" though it remains a mystery today as to who Kitty was. After the discovery and arrest of the Frank family and others, the hiding place was cleared of all remaining contents. The clothes, furniture, and personal effects of those hiding were seized and distributed to families in need in Germany. However, just before the building was cleared, those who had helped hide the families returned, against Dutch police orders, and retrieved important books and papers that would eventually be compiled into *The Diary of a Young Girl*, also known as *The Diary of Anne Frank*.

Just outside the house was the famous chestnut tree. Anne would gaze at the tree and documented it in her diary. In February 1944, Anne beautifully wrote, "From my favorite spot on the floor I look up at the blue sky and the bare chestnut tree, on whose branches little raindrops shine, appearing like silver, and at the seagulls and other birds as they glide on the wind."[1] The tree provided a powerful contrast to the unfolding Holocaust. For Anne, it provided needed hope and a reminder of a better world. In later years, the chestnut tree would become sick and hollowed. In 2007, the city fought unsuccessfully to chop it down, though it survived till 2010 when a storm

1. Frank, *Diary of Anne Frank*, 519.

felled the tree. Prior to its demise, the museum had collected chestnuts to grow seedlings and allow the original tree to flourish elsewhere. Its saplings have been distributed to numerous international parks and schools, including the official Holocaust memorial in Jerusalem.

For those unable to visit Amsterdam and the famous Anne Frank House, you can read books, watch movies, or visit virtually with YouTube episodes. All of these are based on the diary letters of the young Anne Frank. Perhaps no one better captured the unfathomable trials and tribulations that young Jewish girls and boys faced during World War II than young Anne Frank.

Rembrandt's Home (Rembrandthuis)

A trip to Amsterdam, as possible, should also include a visit to the Rembrandt House Museum. The museum is just a fifteen-minute walk from the central station. From 1639 to 1656, the house was home and studio to the legendary painter Rembrandt Harmenszoon van Rijn. He was born in nearby Leiden in 1606. Built in 1607, the house was in a lively settlement of rich Amsterdam artists and merchants, presently known as Jodenbreestraat. The wealthy neighborhood was home to the A-list of the Amsterdam art world and the ruling class. Rembrandt had a long stay in the house, spent his most formidable years there, and created some of his best work there, including the legendary *Night Watch*. He lived at this house until he went bankrupt from unexplained exuberance and years of cheerful, lavish spending. This former residence of Rembrandt van Rijn allows for viewing of several of his estimated three hundred paintings, 290 etchings, and two thousand lifetime drawings as well as the painter's personal memorabilia, including weapons and seashells. There are also several important paintings by others, including several by Rembrandt's mentor Pieter Lastman. Most haunting and beautiful is *The Crucifixion* (1616) depicting Christ's crucifixion at Golgotha, the "Place of the Skulls." As an aside, Rembrandt painted *Christ in the Storm on the Sea of Galilee* (1633), his only known seascape. However, you won't see this painting on display! The infamous painting, along with twelve others, was stolen from the Isabella Stewart Gardner Museum in Boston in 1990. Also included were works by Manet, Degas, and Vermeer. The Rembrandt painting was one of his earliest, rarest, and most valued. Two men posing as police officers made off with artwork estimated at $500 million. Despite intense investigations, and an offered $10 million reward, the paintings were never recovered. The heist remains one of the most prominent unsolved art crimes in history.

Rembrandt was born on July 15, 1606, the ninth child of a wealthy Dutch family. Rembrandt's mother was a Catholic, whereas his father belonged to the Dutch Reformed Church. It was a religiously fraught period in Europe and, though not religious himself, Rembrandt's works reveal a deep Christian faith. Rembrandt was well tutored and became a highly successful painter at an early age. He was an acclaimed portraitist and earned a great deal of money as a result. He also quickly earned a world-class reputation as both an artist and a teacher known in artistic circles stretching to Florence, Italy. Despite international renown, Rembrandt never actually traveled outside the Dutch Republic. However, in 1631, Rembrandt moved to Amsterdam. At the time, Amsterdam was the center of the world, having experienced a period of unprecedented wealth and flourishing culture. Rembrandt was known as a rather cocky, enterprising, and self-assured young man bound for greatness. His heightened success as a young artist enabled him to buy the impressive merchant house on the developing canal ring. Rembrandt worked and taught at this house for nearly twenty years. He lived on the ground floor with his family and many of his most famous paintings were created in the first-floor studio. Due to consequences of his very lavish lifestyle, a drastically declining market, and a reduced list of wealthy clients, Rembrandt was faced with bankruptcy. He was forced to sell the significant house and move to a modest rented house.

By the nineteenth century, the Rembrandt house fell into a state of severe dilapidation. Surprisingly, few knew or realized that the great Rembrandt had lived there in the seventeenth century. It was only later that the people of Amsterdam realized this was the house of the famed Rembrandt and a unique cultural inheritance. Consequently, restoration completed between 1908 and 1911 saved the building from demolition. In 1911, the house was converted into the museum. The interior had been restored, to the extent possible, to its former seventeenth-century glory. Likewise, it has been astonishingly furnished with objects and art utilizing the original inventory drafted upon Rembrandt's sale of the house over 250 years earlier, in 1656. The museum is a powerful creation that preserves Rembrandt's fascinating image. Fittingly, today the Rembrandt Museum both honors the celebrated Dutch master and serves as a showcase of magnificent seventeenth-century Dutch architecture.

CHAPTER 5

ROME

When in Rome, live as the Romans do;
when elsewhere, live as they live elsewhere.

—*Saint Ambrose*

Nothing could have properly prepared me for visiting the timeless, eternal city that is *Rome*! Most ages of recorded history live on in Rome and, without a doubt, it is the most fascinating city I ever visited. For nearly three thousand years, pilgrims have come to explore Rome, whose character is simply unfazed by the thronging crowds. I had no idea that the entire city of Rome is a vast, unparalleled indoor and outdoor museum. Every step reveals astonishing surprise with timeless relics from all ages. There are unimaginable art treasures, magnificent fountains, Egyptian obelisks, palatial baroque buildings, and opulent architecture, galleries, and ancient ruins at every turn in every quarter. Rome is also truly unique in that in many churches you can see endless artwork by famous masters, such as Caravaggio and Raphael, at absolutely no cost. Further, echoes from the past—names such as Cicero, Caesar, Cleopatra, Marc Antony, Marcus Aurelius, Augustus, Nero, Charlemagne, and Michelangelo—linger in everlasting fashion. For nearly thirty centuries, travelers have been captivated by the striking beauty of this eternal city of seven hills. Characterized by historic ancient ruins and a fabled colosseum, Rome is full of bustling life with its many breathtaking piazzas, charming narrow streets and alleyways, hurried Vespas, and majestic avenues with stately monuments. Rome's history is laid open for all to see. It's very easy to understand why all roads lead to Rome . . . the treasure trove of Italy.

Even the debated historic origin of Rome in 753 BC and the associated legends are most fascinating. According to early Roman folklore, the heroic founder of Rome was Troy war hero Aeneas. The fact that Aeneas was said to be the son of the love goddess Venus only gives further credence to Rome's grandiose destiny. As the story goes, at the fall of ancient Troy to the Greeks in 1184 BC (in the famous Trojan horse episode), the city was left in flames. Aeneas and a few other survivors fled Troy and wandered the Mediterranean Sea, finally settling in Italy at the mouth of the Tiber River. There Aeneas founded the state that, over four hundred years later, would become the great city of Rome. Subsequently, Aeneas had a very extensive and impressive family tree. For these reasons, Aeneas—and thus his mother, the goddess Venus—is considered ancestor of the Roman people. Even Julius Caesar and Augustus traced their lineage to Aeneas and the goddess Venus. However, two very important descendants in the eighth century BC were the twin brothers Romulus and Remus, who, according to legend, suckled a mythical she-wolf. Their father was said to be Mars, the Roman god of war. The twins were the nephews of then-King Amulius who believed that the twins were destined to kill him. He ordered the twin babies be cast into the Tiber River. However, the servants took pity on the twins and merely floated them down the river in a basket. The basket came to a rest on the bank and the twins survived, nursed by a wolf, and ultimately raised by local shepherds. Once the twins reached adolescence, they reinstated their just grandfather Numitor on the throne. Next, in consultation with the birds, the twins left to develop a new city at the sentimental place of their childhood. Romulus and Remus had marked and divided sacred grounds on which to build the new city. Sadly, Remus violated the boundaries and Romulus, or possibly his supporters, killed Remus. According to Roman annalists, this event occurred on April 21, 753 BC, and a new city of Rome was formed, taking the name of Romulus.

Today, the metropolitan city of Rome has a population of over 4.3 million residents. Rome is located within the western-central part of the Italian peninsula along the shores of the Tiber River. Rome is often referred to as the cradle of western civilization and the cornerstone of Christian culture. It remains the center of the Catholic Church. In fact, Vatican City, the world's smallest independent country, resides entirely inside the city boundaries of Rome. It's the only existing example of a country within a city. The Roman state was repeatedly attacked and plundered by barbarians throughout the Middle Ages. Decadence and war led to the fall of the Roman Empire, which fell under control of the papacy. However, in time, the Papal States era would restore Rome to its former splendor and glory. Specifically, during the fifteenth century Renaissance, many famous artists, painters, sculptors, architects, and craftsmen made Rome their home and center of activity. They created endless masterpieces throughout the city. The church states of central Italy, including Rome, would remain under the sovereignty of the elected popes from 756 to 1870. The unification of Italy into a single state or kingdom occurred in 1861. Rome was finally declared the capital of Italy in 1870. Today, Rome is home to many international businesses and luxury design and fashion houses. Also, Rome and its famed Cinecittà Studios (Hollywood on the Tiber) has been the set of many Academy Award–winning movies, including *Roman Holiday*, *The Barefoot Contessa*, *Ben-Hur*, *La Dolce Vita*, *The Godfather II*, *The English Patient*, *The Passion of the Christ*, and others.

So how did I arrive in Rome for my one and only visit there to date? What is my "bleisure" connection? I can first tell you that I arrived in Rome via Berlin, Germany, on a beautiful Friday night in early April. I stayed through Monday morning. That Saturday (April 5) was my forty-seventh birthday. My meeting in Berlin lasted well into Friday afternoon, so I was to return home on Saturday. However, upon receiving my travel itinerary, I noticed my return flights (Berlin to Rome to New York City to Pittsburgh) would not land until midnight. And that was only if all went well! Rather than miss my birthday, I decided to fly to Rome on Friday evening and stay the weekend. At the time, airfare was oftentimes significantly reduced with a weekend stayover, and company policy permitted, even promoted, such practice. I had no actual business in Rome but was able to visit in the above fashion. Further, the airfare cost savings could even be applied to cover the added hotel nights and transportation as allowable business expenses. This was an offer too good to pass up, and I was off to Rome for an exciting, albeit exhausting, sixty hours. In my typical fashion, I would seldom explore attractions in great length. My modus operandi when traveling alone was to see and do as much as humanly possible. With a little strategic planning, I feel that I truly experienced Rome that weekend. I only wished that the Rome experience was shared with my wife and daughters. I remain confident that we will, one day, return to the Eternal City. Below is insight into my personal Roman holiday.

Piazza Navona

The two best decisions I made when visiting Rome were staying in the historic Piazza Navona area and choosing the beautiful Hotel Rafael. I am not at all familiar with the various quarters of Rome but cannot imagine a more stunning and perfect location. The piazza and nearby hotel are just a stone's throw from Saint Peter's Basilica, the Spanish Steps, and the Pantheon. I was lucky in choosing an ideal starting point to experience the otherworldly elegance and true character of Rome. I arrived in Rome very late Friday night and arranged transportation to my hotel destination. Tip: it's never a good idea to first visit a new city late at night. It was only on the following sunny morning, upon waking, that I first saw the abounding beauty of Rome. The Hotel Rafael bordered a small, quiet square just around the corner from the famed Piazza Navona. The hotel conveyed a certain old-world charm inside, and a fragrant wisteria and bougainvillea vine covered the outdoor façade. Additionally, the hotel's rooftop terrace provided stunning 360-degree panoramic vistas across the many domes and bell towers of Rome's historic center, including Saint Peter's on the near horizon. The hotel's optimal location allowed me to experience all the below sites entirely on foot . . . though I may have walked twenty miles that Saturday!

The thrilling Piazza Navona, or Navona Square, is a spectacular baroque-period public square in the very heart of Rome. It's considered the city's loveliest square, capturing Rome's true spirit, and is one of the Eternal City's elegant showcase attractions. The square is set apart from the noise and sounds of a busy city and seems to be a mystical remnant from another, much earlier time . . . and that it is. The popular square is a pedestrian paradise, busy day and night with crowds of tourists and fortunate locals. It is surrounded by cafés and is commonly filled with colorful street performers and artists, worldwide visitors, children playing soccer, and the sounds of treasured fountains. In fact, during my visit, I purchased a drawing of children playing that we framed and my wife hung in her elementary classroom for many years. If you haven't grasped it yet, the idea of "old" throughout Europe, and most certainly Rome, is quite different than the American perception. The Romans built sites to last with two-thousand-year-old roads straighter and stronger than most of today's American sidewalks. Piazza Navona is an excellent example. Piazza Navona began life as the Stadium of Domitian (Stadio di Domiziano) in the first century AD. Consequently, the oblong-shaped square precisely reproduces the perimeter of the AD 86 thirty-thousand-seat stadium that was used for Greek-style athletics and sporting events of the day. The stadium also hosted gladiator competitions, horse races, and greased poles, and would even be flooded for mock naval battles and weekend water games. Unlike the coliseum, the stadium generally hosted nonviolent contests of wit and physical fitness, including music and poetry. Subterranean remains of the original stadium can be viewed in the basements of certain area buildings. The crumbling stadium was ultimately paved over in the fifteenth century and hosted Rome's main central market. At that time, the popes rejuvenated the area's surrounding narrow, medieval streets. Cardinals, papal officials, ambassadors, and wealthy bankers took up residence. Intellectual life and world-class craftsmen flourished around the square along with booksellers, engravers, and other shops.

Today, the renowned square maintains its carefree air of the earlier days of Roman circus games, medieval jousts, and carnivals. The piazza continues to attract Romans out for their evening *passeggiata* (promenade) as well as fashion photographers and movie makers. Piazza Navona was featured in numerous Hollywood blockbuster films, including *Angels and Demons*, *Catch-22*, and *National Lampoon's European Vacation*. There's nowhere in the world quite like Piazza Navona! As a special bonus, beyond the entertaining atmosphere of Piazza Navona, there are some significant architectural highlights in the square. Specifically, the square is dominated by Saint Agnes Church and adorned by three historic sculpted masterpiece fountains.

Saint Agnes Church

Saint Agnes holds a special place in my heart, as for the last thirty years I have belonged to Saint Agnes Catholic Church in an eastern suburb of Pittsburgh. The story of Saint Agnes is truly a deeply sad account of one young virgin Christian martyr in Roman times. Like many Christian martyrs around the time of AD 300, Agnes (Agnese), being from a wealthy noble Roman family, drew the attention of Roman officials. High ranking families often met the sword when they failed to pledge allegiance by worshiping Roman gods. Agnes was a member of Roman nobility who was born in AD 291 and suffered martyrdom at the age of twelve on January 21, AD 304. She was a beautiful girl who had many suitors of high rank. Her devotion to religious purity resulted in one such rejected suitor submitting her name as a follower of Christianity. The Roman prefect condemned Agnes to be dragged naked through the streets to a brothel. Legend is that as Agnes prayed, her hair miraculously grew long to cover her body and preserve her modesty. Additionally, men who attempted to rape her were immediately struck blind. The pagan son of the prefect, who Agnes refused to marry, was struck dead but revived upon the prayers of Agnes. She was led out to be bound to a stake, but the bundle of wood failed to burn, then the flames parted. At that point, an officer in charge beheaded Agnes with his sword. Her blood was soaked up with cloths from the floor by other Christians. Ironically, shortly thereafter, in AD 313, subsequent Emperor Constantine (a convert) issued the Edict of Milan accepting Christianity and ending government persecution of Christians. Ten years later it became the official religion of the Roman Empire.

In 1652, the baroque church Saint Agnese in Agone was started by then-Pope Innocent X. Saint Agnes Church was built adjacent to the pope's family palace and over the catacombs that housed Saint Agnes's tomb. It was during this period that Innocent was transforming Piazza Navona into today's showcase. It is believed that Saint Agnes performed her miracles and was martyred at the very spot of the church. Saint Agnes is one of the most beautiful churches in Rome and is located, as the very symbol of Rome, in the middle of Piazza Navona. The church was eventually designed but not finished by the great Francesco Borromini, who gave the church his signature ingenious, theatrical, curved (concave) façade. There are domes, Corinthian columns, and classical Renaissance marble detailing. The church features a single statue of Saint Agnes above the façade and a fresco of her inside the rather small interior. The church, owned by the pope's family for three hundred years, fell into disrepair in the nineteenth century, though the family conducted extensive restoration. It wasn't until 1992 that the family finally donated the church to the Diocese of Rome. The church remains active and is used to host classical music concerts. Saint Agnes's bones are conserved in a crypt beneath the high altar of the Piazza Navona church; the crypt is believed to mark the exact spot where the young girl was martyred. Saint Agnes's skull is preserved in a separate chapel of the church. Admittance is free to the public.

Three Fountains of Piazza Navona

One great advantage of staying in the Piazza Navona area is the opportunity to repeatedly stroll through the popular square and experience its three iconic baroque fountains. I found these magnificent sculptures most captivating in the early morning dawn, prior to the daily crowds, and after sunset when the fountains are spectacularly illuminated. The three imposing, historic fountains include the *Fontana del Moro*, which depicts an Ethiopian Moor figure battling a dolphin; the *Fontana dei Calderari*, depicting the sea god Neptune; and the enormous, fitting centerpiece, *Fontana dei Quattro Fiumi* (Fountain of the Four Rivers). Amazingly, these fountains were supplied by an ancient Roman aqueduct. For example, Aqua Virgo, completed in 19 BC, was one of eleven Roman aqueducts that supplied the city of ancient Rome with daily water. Built under the reign of the Emperor Augustus, the aqueduct name is derived from the purity and clarity of the water that originated in distant springs. In time, the aqueduct fell into disrepair until the pope restored it in 1570. Restoration of the urban piped water line permitted construction of several public fountains throughout Rome. At that time, fountains were intended for drinking and washing purposes. The pope used this opportunity to build new aqueducts into the city and beautifully adorn Piazza Navona for visual and political purposes. Missing was a distinctive focal point or fitting centerpiece, so Pope Innocent X decided on an elaborate fountain. In the process, there was great interplay between two of Italy's greatest artistic sons and bitter rivals: Gian Lorenzo Bernini and Francesco Borromini (who designed and built Saint Agnes Church).

Fountain of the Four Rivers: The seventeenth-century Fountain of the Four Rivers is one of the most famous examples of Italian baroque architecture. Bernini was the leading sculptor in Rome but was firmly established in Pope Innocent's black book (denied papal privilege) as he was the favorite artist of Innocent's hated predecessor. Consequently, Bernini was not invited to compete and submit a design. Per legend, a relative of the pope convinced Bernini to create a model design of his own, which was then smuggled into the piazza. The pope saw the preeminent design and was overcome, stating, "Those who do not want to employ Bernini should not look at his work."[1] Given his own good taste, and putting aside his pride, the pope employed Bernini to sculpt the Fountain of the Four Rivers.

Standing in the center of the Piazza Navona, the jaw-dropping fountain is a personification of the most important rivers of the four separate known continents: the Ganges in Asia, the Nile in Africa, the Rio de la Plata in South America, and the Danube in Europe. The fountain rivers also represent the four corners of the world, which symbolically coincides with the Catholic Church's global mission to unify the world. The sprawling rivers recline from the sculpted rocky crag with rushing fountain water. The enormous sculpture supports an ancient 115-foot obelisk, which soars high in the piazza center. The Egyptian obelisk came from the deteriorated Circus of Maxentius. It was part of the early fourth-century Egyptian temple, covered in hieroglyphs, and broken into five pieces, merely lying along Rome's Appian Way. The obelisk may date back to 20 BC. Bernini restored the towering obelisk, which seems to float unsupported as if an illusion above the fountain's basin. Defying terrestrial physics was a calling card of the virtuoso Bernini. The majestic fountain was unveiled at a public festival in 1651 and hailed as a triumph by contemporaries and all others—except for the

1. Through Eternity, "Bernini's Fountain," para. 10.

peasant vendors with displaced stalls. The masterpiece was greeted with great public acclaim, restoring papal privilege, and opened a new chapter in the artist's illustrious career. With this initial fountain, the popular marketplace was officially transformed into a fantastic papal showcase.

Rome Attractions and Landmarks Map
Adobe Stock | Image 446000890

Fontana del Moro: The impressive Fountain of the Moor is the original and oldest of the three fountains and is situated in the square's southern end. This often overlooked fountain is almost a full century older than Bernini's Fountain of the Four Rivers so dramatically located in the square's center. The rose-colored marble basin was constructed by Giacomo della Porta in 1575 under the commission of Pope Gregory XIII. Giacomo della Porta was a great sculptor and architect of the time and had even served as apprentice to Michelangelo. The original fountain was carved from Pietrasanta marble, or "holy marble," as it was also used in construction of Saint Peter's Basilica. In 1909, the original della Porta statues were moved from Piazza Navona to Rome's Galleria Borghese and replaced with replicas. The original fountain had only a dolphin, four tritons or Roman sea gods, dragons, and masks. The fountain had no centerpiece, as the earlier sixteenth-century public fountains weren't meant to be beautiful but rather functional as necessary sources of water. Although the Fountain of the Moor considerably predates the great sculptor Bernini, he got to put his stamp on the fountain when he redesigned it upon the commission of Pope Innocent X in 1648. This story, in and of itself, is rather amusing and really illustrates the unyielding nepotism and power of the popes. Pope Innocent's sister-in-law and confidante Olympia lived in a house in Piazza Navona overlooking the aging fountain. She believed the fountain wasn't impressive enough to be located outside her house and urged the pope to take immediate action. Upgrades were made with a small commission; however, the bossy sister-in-law was still not satisfied. By about 1653, after digging deeper into his coffers, the pope had Bernini produce a beautiful centerpiece statue with a central Moor figure holding the tail of a watering dolphin. Having gained the demanding approval of Olympia, the Bernini-touched fountain now adequately represented an African Moor standing atop a conch shell, surrounded by the triton sea gods.

Fontana dei Calderari: Lastly, the Fontana dei Calderari was also designed by Giacomo della Porta, in 1574. This fountain would be situated in the northern end of the square. The fountain was appropriately named due to its near proximity to a small Roman alley filled with blacksmiths' workshops. These and other metal-based businesses generated considerable radiating heat. For the next three hundred years, the utilitarian fountain existed with no statues. By 1873, following the creation of the Italian state and the diminished need for washing and drinking fountains, a competition for statuary was conducted. Statuary was clearly needed to balance the Moor Fountain at the piazza's south and the magnificent Fountain of the Four Rivers at its center. The *Fountain of Neptune*, as it is known today, was completed in 1878. Awarded sculptors designed the imposing sea god Neptune battling a giant octopus and many other elaborate sculptures based on the Greek mythological theme. The nineteenth-century fountain, in essence, depicts Neptune in a fish-drawn chariot, intensely battling a sea monster surrounded by sea nymphs or mermaids.

The Piazza Navona fountains are a brilliant, eye-popping example of baroque architecture. It's utterly fascinating to imagine these splashing fountains contrived of hollowed, jagged rockwork, carved from the designs of true masters under unimaginable papal and public scrutiny, fed by ancient aqueducts, and built with Egyptian obelisk ruins and the holy marble of a Roman Empire. Consistently, the many marble statues portray fanatical seafaring tales of Greek mythology across the beautiful Italian piazza.

Saint Peter's Basilica (Basilica di San Pietro)

Enclosed within the very heart of Rome is the world's smallest nation, Vatican City. Headed by the elected pope of the Roman Catholic Church, this independent city-state (firmly established 1929) comprises just 121 acres and has less than six hundred citizens. However, within those sacred walls is a world-class sightseeing compound and collection of iconic art, antiquities, and Renaissance architecture beyond comprehension. Most notable are the ornate *Saint Peter's Basilica* and the astonishing *Sistine Chapel*. So excited to experience the Vatican, I awoke extra early on that beautiful Saturday morning and set out by foot for my first stop, Saint Peter's. It was just a short fifteen-minute walk from my Piazza Navona–area hotel and led me past the towering cylindrical *Castle Saint Angelo* (dating from AD 139). I crossed the narrow, historic Tiber River via the Pointe Saint Angelo (bridge) and continued on to Saint Peter's Square. Upon visiting Rome, philosopher and poet Ralph Waldo Emerson eloquently exclaimed that Saint Peter's Basilica is "an ornament of the earth . . . the sublime of the beautiful."[2] Designed principally by many of Italy's greatest artists—Donato Bramante, Michelangelo, Gian Lorenzo Bernini, Raphael, Antonio da Sangallo the Younger, Baldassare Peruzzi, Giacomo della Porta, and Carlo Maderno—is it any wonder that the basilica is the most renowned work of Renaissance architecture? I was dumbfounded as I approached the massive basilica via the very large forecourt, or square. Seeing the façade of the basilica in the distance, you are greeted by statues nearly twenty feet high of Saints Peter and Paul, the first-century apostles to Rome. The square itself can hold three hundred thousand visitors, and the basilica, the largest in Christendom, covers an area of nearly six acres. At its widest point the square measures nearly 650 feet. The basilica can hold twenty thousand seated guests and sixty thousand total guests. The basilica is a staggering 720 feet in length and 450 feet high. It is one of the world's holiest sites of Christianity and Catholic tradition. Accordingly, the basilica is at the very heart of the Roman Catholic Church, whose influence stretches to all four corners of the world. Every day, nearly forty thousand visitors enter the church, accounting for over ten million annually. The basilica is the highlight of any visit to Rome for Catholics and non-Catholics alike. Some consider Saint Peter's Basilica one of the greatest structures ever assembled by divine-driven mortals.

As the name implies, Saint Peter's Basilica is linked to the martyrdom of the apostle Peter (circa AD 64). Simon, called Peter by Jesus, was a simple Jewish fisherman from Capernaum of Galilee. Catholic tradition holds that

2. Camus, "Sublime of the Beautiful," para. 7.

Peter was assigned a leadership role among Jesus's followers and was of great importance in spreading Jesus's teachings and in the founding of the Christian church. Peter is credited as being named (circa AD 30) the first bishop, or pope, of Rome. However, following a huge fire that destroyed half of Rome, then Emperor Nero blamed the Christians. The Christians were perceived as a radical group by some, making them an easy scapegoat to a no-conscience emperor. Holding the Christians responsible, he condemned many Christians to execution; most likely that included the apostles Peter and Paul. Peter is believed to have been crucified on Vatican Hill; however, to distinguish his death from that of Jesus, he humbly begged to be, and was, crucified upside down. After removal from the cross, Peter was taken and buried in a nearby ancient necropolis, or cemetery. A red rock was placed at the location to mark the grave. Tradition had linked Peter's burial tomb to the exact site beneath the high altar within Saint Peter's Basilica. Because the site of Peter's burial was so strongly believed by Christians to be Vatican Hill, the site of Saint Peter's Basilica was erected on the exact site—a location not so conducive to construction. Astoundingly, it wasn't till many centuries later, in 1950, that remains of the ancient necropolis and human bones were discovered buried underneath the basilica's high altar. At the bequest of Pope Pius XII, a concerted effort had been undertaken to systematically excavate, specifically in search of the long-buried necropolis and tomb of Peter. In the early 1960s, upon repeated forensic examination, the bones were found to be those of a sixty-one-year-old male from the first century. The bones were encrusted in earth, as Peter would have been buried directly in dirt. Likewise, the bones revealed remnants of purple thread. Purple cloth was only used in ancient times for someone royal or holy. Italian archeologists and others argued that the bones indeed belonged to Saint Peter. In 1968, Pope Paul VI determined that the bones were most likely those of the apostle Peter. More recently in 2019, as a bold inclusive action born out of prayer, Pope Francis transferred a few of Peter's bones to the Eastern Orthodox Church. Most of Saint Peter's remains are still preserved in Rome at the basilica.

The fascinating history of Saint Peter's Basilica is befitting of the apostle Peter, the "rock" of the Catholic Church. Likewise, the history of the Vatican took on new significance when in 319 the Emperor Constantine the Great, son of Saint Helena, who's attributed with the conversion of Constantine, built a sanctuary on the believed site of Saint Peter's tomb. Some believe Helena and Constantine sought to fulfill holy scripture related to when Jesus first met Peter and proclaimed, "You are Peter, and upon this rock I will build my church" (Matthew 16:18). In any event, Constantine was influential in promoting tolerance towards Christians and in advancing

Christianity towards the mainstream in Roman culture. This original church is referred to as the Old Saint Peter's Basilica. It took nearly forty years to complete the basilica, which gradually gained importance and became a major pilgrimage site in Rome. Papal coronations were held at the basilica, and on Christmas Day 800, Charlamagne was crowned emperor of the Holy Roman Empire there. The early fourth-century church stood for over a thousand years until near collapse by the fifteenth century. Finally, in 1506, Pope Julius II, following a competition, commissioned Rome's most famed architect, Donato Bramante, to raze the collapsing church and build a new magnificent basilica for Saint Peter. By 1546, then-Pope Paul III persuaded the aging seventy-one-year-old Michelangelo to take on the job to complete the building. Michelangelo returned to Bramante's plan, added a splendid dome, and enlisted others to assist until and after his death in 1564 at age eighty-eight. Michelangelo was said to have done all his work for no pay but rather for the glory of God and the honor of Saint Peter. In time, Bernini was entrusted with the final phase of the build. The new Saint Peter's Basilica was finally completed and dedicated in 1626. It was the world's most magnificent church, as intended. From Bramante to Michelangelo to Bernini, ten or more architects in total, the basilica's construction encompassed 120 years over the reign of twenty popes.

There's an epic feeling as you approach the center of Christendom. Bernini was the principal architect of the beautiful oval-shaped *Piazza San Pietro*, or Saint Peter's Square, one of the defining features of the basilica. Bernini's concept was to create two colossal arms of colonnades, forming two open arms to welcome the world, enclosing visitors in the maternal arms of Mother Church and Christianity's embrace. There are 284 Doric columns topped by 140 saints in total that define the piazza. The details in the saint sculptures convey movement and counteract the rigid columns. The grandeur of the construction design provides a perfect frame for the basilica. At the center of the trapezoidal square is an ancient uninscribed Egyptian obelisk (Vatican Obelisk) of red Aswan granite from the ancient Egyptian city of Heliopolis and an unknown pharaoh. The obelisk is believed to be over 4,500 years old. It is eighty-four feet high and supported on later-added bronze lion sculptures. Emperor Augusta had the obelisk first moved to Alexandria until 37 when Emperor Caligula ordered that the obelisk be brought to Rome. The Vatican Obelisk is also referred to as the "mute witness," as the martyrdom of Saint Peter occurred in the area near the monument. Astoundingly, the obelisk has survived in Rome in essentially the same space for nearly 2,200 years.

As wildly impressive as the exterior of Saint Peter's is, the interior is even more amazing. I can only properly provide a high-level, cursory introduction to the basilica's treasures and a few interesting facts. Included is a recounting of three personal basilica experiences: (1) Michelangelo's *Pietà*, (2) a climb to the dome, and (3) "Papa John." My lucky visit to the Sistine Chapel is a separate, humorous (albeit successful) story in itself! First, the magnitude and beauty of Rome's sublime sanctuary are staggering. The basilica is a complex cruciform design of three naves. Its interior is lavishly decorated with architectural sculptures, gold gilding, reliefs, and fine marbles. The middle nave is the largest and is covered by a barrel vault ceiling. Each nave is formed by wide aisles with numerous, variously sized, adjacent chapels. The huge Michelangelo-designed dome, covered in mosaics and the tallest in the world, crowns the entire basilica and will mesmerize your gaze. The dome is visible throughout the Eternal City skyline and serves as a compass when visitors are wandering the narrow surrounding Roman streets and boulevards. Many brave the climb to the dome and are rewarded with unbeatable views of Saint Peter's Square and the empire below. The superb design masks the overwhelming scale of the basilica and its 150-foot gold-coffered ceiling. To accomplish this, a "proportional design" was employed. Statues on both sides appear to be symmetrical in size; however, the statues increase in size from six to twenty-four feet the higher up the wall they go. Note that none of the paintings inside the basilica are actual paintings but rather painstakingly created glass mosaic replicas needed to preserve the original art. Lastly, as was typical of the time, building materials were either stolen from other Roman structures or repurposed from ancient ruins. Three good examples include the use of the base of the old fourth-century Saint Peter's Basilica, repurposed melted-down bronze from the now-bare Pantheon porch, and even thousands of cartloads of stones transported from the deteriorating Colosseum. Lastly, there are over a hundred coveted tombs within and below Saint Peter's Basilica, including ninety-one of the estimated 260 popes, along with several noted emperors, composers, royalty, and martyrs. The most recent interment was Pope Benedict XVI on January 5, 2023. By request, Pope Francis is interred at nearby Basilica di Santa Maria Maggiore.

Saint Peter's Basilica is a glimpse into the history of Christianity and Roman art. There are over 450 statues, five hundred columns, and fifty altars, among other architectural and artistic works, on full display. The most notable of these undoubtedly include the following.

Balcony Showcases: There are four large load-bearing piers begun by Bramante and completed by Michelangelo in the central nape design scheme. It was strongly questioned whether the four piers of the crossing could support Michelangelo's massive dome, though they have. Bernini had the four piers hollowed to create staircases leading to four balconies. On each balcony, Bernini created showcases framed by eight wreathed ancient columns from the old fourth-century Saint Peter's Basilica. Emperor Constantine had donated the Solomonic columns, brought from Solomon's Temple in Jerusalem to the old church. These showcases display the four most precious basilica relics: namely, the spear (holy lance) fragment of the Roman soldier named Longinus that pierced the side of Jesus, the veil of Veronica used on the road to Calvary with the miraculous image of Jesus, a fragment of the True Cross discovered in Jerusalem by Saint Helena, and a relic of Saint Andrew, martyred brother of Saint Peter. In the niches surrounding the central space, Bernini emphatically placed larger-than-life statues of Longinus, Saint Veronica, Saint Helena, and Saint Andrew associated with the four relics.

High Altar Canopy (Baldachin): The marvelous ninety-five-foot, ten-story, four-pillar baroque bronze canopy is positioned under the dome in the basilica's exact center. The sculpted canopy is positioned over both the high altar and Saint Peter's tomb. It is one of the most recognized and admired symbols in the basilica and perfectly frames the high altar used only by the pope. The bronze was said to have been repurposed from the ancient Pantheon roof or portico; others claim it came from distant Venice.[3] The top of the canopy features little carved bumblebees. This reflects the three-bee papal emblem of the canopy's art-loving sponsor, Pope Urban VIII.

Saint Peter's Chair: Any altar of Saint Peter's discussion is incomplete without noting the monumental Saint Peter's Chair, designed by Bernini and installed in Saint Peter's Basilica in 1666. The symbolic structure is fifty feet in height and was built over ten years using 164,000 pounds of bronze. It is housed in the apse at the back of the basilica. Tradition claims that the chair, known as the Throne of Saint Peter, is the actual wooden oak throne relic of Saint Peter, conserved by the pope and enclosed in the sculpted gilt bronze covering. Others believe the relic dates to the sixth century.[4] Bernini created an illusion that the sunlit chair, representing spiritual authority, is somehow suspended in thin air. Statues of four doctors of the Catholic Church support the bronze throne—Saints Augustine and Ambrose from

3. Wikipedia, "St. Peter's Baldachin," sec. "Description and history."

4. Wikipedia, "Chair of Saint Peter," paras. 1–2.

the West and Saints John Chrysostom and Athanasius from the East. The chair is a reminder for visitors to pray for the Holy Father as he ministers to the beloved universal church.

Statue of Saint Peter: Nearing the high altar, there is likely a line forming to the right with visitors hoping to see the statue of Saint Peter. The statue appears to be from the thirteenth century. Tradition throughout the many centuries has been to kiss the right foot of Saint Peter as a holy blessing. Unfortunately over time, as you might imagine, Saint Peter's toes have worn away and visitors now rub the right foot.

***Pietà*:** In 1497, a French cardinal and ambassador to the Vatican named Jean Bilhères de Lagraulas hired the twenty-two-year-old novice, unproven sculptor Michelangelo Buonarroti to create his personal tomb memorial. The project's exact job description provided to Michelangelo was to create the most beautiful work of marble in Rome, one that no living artist could better. By most accounts that is exactly what the confident young Michelangelo did! He created the beautiful, groundbreaking *La Madonna della Pietà* (Our Lady of Piety) sculpture, simply known as the *Pietà*—a mournful image of Jesus and Mary at Mount Golgotha. All throughout Michelangelo's long life, it was difficult to tell if his genius owed more to his art or his great faith.

Michelangelo was born in the Tuscany area in 1475 but had grown up in nearby Florence, Italy's greatest center of arts and learning at the time. Following his mother's death when Michelangelo was just six years of age, he lived with a nanny and her stonecutter husband near a marble quarry. It was there that Michelangelo gained his love for marble and a knack for handling a chisel and hammer. By age thirteen, Michelangelo was also a coveted apprentice to esteemed painters. He attended a Medici-funded academy, working with many great sculptors, painters, and philosophers. Michelangelo's commissions and the ever-changing political climate in Florence, took Michelangelo to Venice and Bologna before he arrived in Rome in 1496, where he lived and continued to work until age eighty-eight.

In the over 525 years since its 1499 completion, the *Pietà* has only left Rome on a single occasion, and it was on that occasion when, prior to visiting Rome, I first saw and experienced the *Pietà* as a very young boy. It left an indelible impression on me. Upon arriving home, I enthusiastically sketched the *Pietà* for my family. That occasion was the 1964 New York City World's Fair. My father had taken my brothers and me to Queens to visit his family.

My mother and younger sisters stayed behind. In 1964 the *Pietà* was lent by the Vatican to the World's Fair to be installed in the international Vatican pavilion. It was the influential Cardinal Francis Spellman, Archbishop of New York, who requested and convinced Pope John XXIII to boldly loan the iconic sculpture. Securing the *Pietà* was a significant coup for the New York World's Fair. The 6,700-pound statue was shipped in a thick, waterproof crate-within-a-crate-within-a-crate and secured to the deck of the well-guarded Italian liner *Cristoforo Colombo*. Ironically, Christopher Columbus was a contemporary of Michelangelo! The crates contained cushioning so thick that it would float in the ocean in case of an accident. Included was an attached emergency locator beacon and a marker buoy. A modern replica of the *Pietà* was even created to determine beforehand if the statue could be successfully transported and installed without damage. The replica remains on display at a New York seminary. After it survived the risky ordeal, a papal law was passed shortly upon the *Pietà*'s return prohibiting Vatican art from ever being loaned. As expected, the Vatican pavilion was one of the most popular exhibits at the fair, and its success was due to the *Pietà*. I specifically recall entering the ominous dark blue room on a large people-moving conveyor belt; there were three such platforms at various heights. The *Pietà* was spectacularly lit with four hundred lights and rested behind floor-to-ceiling bullet-proof glass. It was a mesmerizing experience for most all visitors, including me. Today, the statue's original World Fair's location is remembered with an inscribed marble bench.

The *Pietà*, carved in 1498–99, is an incredibly poignant depiction of the frail, crucified body of Jesus in death, cradled in the loving arms, below the downcast eyes, of his mother Mary. The scene occurs shortly after Jesus's death and his removal from the cross, though this common subject and scene are not exactly part of the biblical narrative of the crucifixion. The *Pietà* is regarded as one of the most tender artistic depictions of grief known. The statue measure 5'9" by 6'5" and was carved out of a single piece of white and blue Carrara marble from the famous Carrara caves in the Tuscany region of Italy. The *Pietà* is pyramidal in shape with the vertex at Mary's head and widening down to the rock of Golgotha's desolate landscape base. It was the first Renaissance effort that sought to balance classical beauty with a haunting naturalism. As Michelangelo himself described, he set out to create a work depicting "the heart's image." In doing so, Michelangelo's interpretation of the *Pietà* also reflects certain artistic license. For one, the figures are quite out of proportion as required to depict a grown man cradled full length across his mother's lap. Second, Mary is sculpted very young and beautiful rather than as a naturally older woman and mother of a thirty-three-year-old son. Her young, exquisite, penetrating face is soft and grieving. Lastly, gruesome signs of the passion are diminished. Marks of the crucifixion are limited to small nail punctures and a subtle indication of the wound in Jesus's side. Shortly after its completion, the young Michelangelo entered the chapel to see a large group admiring and praising his masterwork. He overheard them falsely claim another artist from their own Milan region was responsible for the sculpture. Michelangelo thought it was strange and unjust that his labors were attributed to another Italian artist. Consequently, one night shortly thereafter, Michelangelo snuck back into the chapel and signed the sculpture across Mary's sash. He wrote, as roughly translated, "Michelangelo Buonarroti the Florentine made this." The signature is in the style of ancient Greek artists. Michelangelo later deeply regretted the vanity of this hot-headed, prideful outburst and resolved never to sign another work of his hands. He never would.[5]

On Pentecost Sunday 1972, an unemployed, mentally ill Hungarian-born Australian geologist hurdled over the Saint Peter Basilica railing to attack the *Pietà* as blasphemous. He was able to manage fifteen blows before being subdued by several bystanders, but unfortunately not before he knocked off Mary's left arm and damaged her nose, cheek, and eye. After options were reviewed, a seamless restoration of the *Pietà* was chosen. Master craftsmen picked through the hundreds of bits of broken marble, some as small as fingernails, and puzzled them back together. Onlookers had absconded with some of the marble pieces, though a few returned the fragments. Using invisible glue and marble powder, recoverable pieces (and a few added ones) were affixed back into the *Pietà*. It is now impossible for observers to know the statue was once brutally attacked. Since the attack and the statue's ten-month restoration, the *Pietà* is now displayed behind bulletproof glass. In the end, the destruction of the priceless work of art was not deemed a criminal offense. A Rome court deemed the perpetrator "a socially dangerous person," committed him to a mental hospital for two years, then deported him back to Australia. The history associated with *La Madonna della Pietà* is long and exhilarating. For me, I was once again spellbound when I excitedly discovered the *Pietà* for a second time. The famous, tragically beautiful sculpture has been and remains inconspicuously enshrined in Saint Peter's Basilica's northern nave (first chapel on the right inside the main entrance).

5. Wikipedia, "Pietà (Michelangelo)," sec. "After completion."

Climbing the Dome: It was only by happenstance that I experienced the extraordinary climb to Saint Peter's Basilica's dome, or cupola. I was eagerly exploring the basilica when I noticed an elevator and a stairway leading to Michelangelo's dome above. So, I bought a ticket and up I went! Note that at nearly 450 feet tall, the tallest in the world, the dome could fit the Statue of Liberty inside. There are 551 steps in total, though the climb is divided into two parts. There is an elevator to bypass the first-level climb, or you can ascend the initial 231 stairs. At this level, you arrive inside the dome 235 feet above ground. It is here where you can look down on the basilica interior for a dove's-eye view, marvel at its grandeur, and, on occasion hear celestial choir music cascading heavenwards. The dome's many mosaics are on full, close-up display at this level. You can also venture onto the roof of the basilica from this level for a landscape of Rome's many surrounding domes and towers. I was personally motivated to go to the rooftop to view the large Jesus and twelve apostles statues, which crown the basilica's façade and are visible from the square below. The twenty-foot rooftop statues include Jesus with just eleven apostles along with Saint John the Baptist. The missing Saint Peter statue is displayed below with Saint Paul at the basilica's entrance. The second part of the climb is optional and reserved for those who are a bit more adventurous, energetic, and clearly not claustrophobic. The only way to the very top of Saint Peter's Basilica is by climbing 320 stairs, after the elevator, from the rooftop to the upper balcony of the lantern. This climb is up narrow (single lane), dark, cramped, slanted stairs, ending with a corkscrew stairwell and a dangling rope to hold onto. And there is no turning back. The climb is taxing, as I certainly learned later that night when I fell into bed. This may sound a bit more ominous than it actually was, as I somewhat recall being motivated by a very fit eighty-year-old Italian woman in front of me. There are a few small windows along the climb and, good news, the stairwell down to the basilica floor is different and much easier. If you do make the thirty-minute climb, you will be rewarded with otherwise unattainable, stunning, panoramic views of Saint Peter's Square, the Vatican Gardens, and all of eternal Rome below. Climbing this unparalleled, four-hundred-year-old masterpiece of Italian Renaissance architecture is a must for anyone wanting a fun and full Saint Peter's Basilica experience.

"Papa John"

Not fully aware of all the practices associated with Saint Peter's Basilica, I came to what appeared to be a glass coffin with a body—in full view for all to see inside the church. Dumbfounded, I questioned a few surrounding visitors, "Who is that?" Again, an elderly Italian woman, though not the same one climbing the dome stairs, angrily scolded me, "That's Papa John, Papa John!" She appeared disappointed but quickly resumed her prayers. On more detailed study, I determined that it was indeed Blessed Pope John XXIII, known as "the good pope," who was right next to me.

Pope John was one of thirteen children born to a poor peasant family near Bergamo, Italy. He earned a doctorate in theology and undertook a diplomatic career with the Vatican, culminating in being elected pope in 1958. Given his advanced age of seventy-seven, many expected Pope John to become a temporary, unimpactful pope of minor influence. That was not to be the case . . . though his short tenure as pope did end with his death in 1963. Pope John XXIII was smart and tough enough to tackle the increasingly rigid and dogmatic Catholic Church. He is largely credited with reforming the church and made ecclesiastical history convening the Second Vatican Council. He initiated many radical reforms to bring the church into modern times, including decentralization, boosting relations with other churches and faiths, increasing the participation of laypeople in the Mass, and tirelessly promoting equality. Most memorable to me (as an altar boy) and most others: he approved use of local languages in lieu of Latin in Masses. The pope also strongly rejected the idea that the Jewish people were responsible for Jesus's crucifixion. Not unlike dozens of other popes, the specially treated body of Pope John XXIII was laid in a wooden casket inside a bronze outer coffin, sealed, and buried in a grave in the ancient, narrow, lower-level grottoes beneath Saint Peter's. In 2001, thirty-eight years after his death, the body of Pope John was disinterred as it was decided to move his tomb to a new prominent space inside the basilica, more accessible to pilgrims. In doing so, it was discovered that the pope's body was practically intact, uncorrupted by time, and had not decomposed. He appeared tranquil, and observers commented that it miraculously appeared as if he had died yesterday! The pope's body was then placed in pontifical ermine-trimmed vestments and shoes and placed in a thousand-pound bronze and glass coffin. The coffin processed to Saint Peter's Square before it was moved and rested in the basilica's central nave. Two other popes are also buried, in masks, in full view inside the basilica. It was a great surprise to have the opportunity to pray to Pope John XXIII. He remains one of the church's most admired, respected, accomplished, and greatly beloved popes of recent times. In 2014, Pope John XXIII was canonized a saint in Saint Peter's Square by Pope Francis.

Sistine Chapel

Any trip to Rome without a visit to the Sistine Chapel, its most illustrious and revered historic site, is sadly incomplete . . . and my trip nearly was! I had wrapped up my self-tour of Saint Peter's Basilica, including the climb to the dome, by about 12:30 p.m. that Saturday. I headed outside directly to the adjacent Vatican Museums. Unbeknownst to me were the museums' hours of admittance. In fact, at that time, the museums, including the Sistine Chapel, closed Saturdays at 1:00 p.m. (final entry 12:30 p.m.). Consequently, the Sistine Chapel was closed until Monday morning, and I had an 11:00 a.m. flight back to the states! Undeterred, and confident that I would find a way into the Sistine Chapel, I arranged for a taxi to take me to the Vatican early Monday to park and wait with my luggage while I ran in to see the Sistine Chapel. From there, the plan was to hustle to the airport and return home. Considering a slight language barrier, the Italian traffic, and crowds of tourists, the plan was more than a bit risky, not to mention improbable.

All went according to plan till I arrived at the Vatican Museums, only to learn that the first hour appeared reserved for prepaid tours and tickets. I'm nothing if not resourceful, and my new plan was to buy a ticket for later admittance, work my way into one of the early tour groups, and hope for the best. After considerable explaining and "finagling," that is exactly what happened, and I found myself in the very front of the line to be admitted first. I recognized that I would only have time for a quick shortcut visit to the Sistine Chapel wing and needed to bypass its other twenty-three amazing galleries and all other wings and museums. The rooms border both sides of the long, wide corridor that leads to the very last room—the Sistine Chapel. Entry to each room is heavily guarded by diligent, no-nonsense Vatican officers with military-style rifles. The awaiting group of visitors was smaller and meandering the lobby, not so concerned with time. Thus, I literally became the first visitor to enter that morning. I walked briskly past all the wing's side galleries straight to the Sistine Chapel, never making eye contact with the somewhat-baffled armed guards I passed along the way. Bear in mind that the Sistine Chapel draws about twenty-five thousand visitors each day with up to possibly two thousand visitors in the museums at any given time. Yet here I was . . . standing entirely by myself, completely awestruck in the Sistine Chapel! After fifteen-minutes, I rushed back outside to find my taxi driver and made it to the airport just in time! Now that may be my ultimate, all-time most adventurous bleisure moment.

The Vatican Museums, fifty-four museums in total, are collectively referred to as the "Museum of Museums." Along with the Sistine Chapel, the museums house the world's largest and most precious collection of art, archaeology, and anthropology artifacts that were gathered by the church and papacy over many centuries: Egyptian, Etruscan, Greek, Roman, and Christian. The collected Vatican Museums art exists to welcome, inspire, and evangelize all people. There are 1,400 rooms, chapels, and galleries in total, and the museums employ over 650 people. I learned while traveling that the Vatican Museums' collection of art, the world's largest, encompasses seventy thousand pieces (or nine miles' worth of art), twenty thousand of which are on display. It is also known as the Apostolic Palace and formal residence of the pope.

The Vatican's most cherished and greatest collection of artworks, created by the world's most well-known Renaissance artists, resides in the Sistine Chapel. The large papal chapel was built by Pope Sixtus IV (thus the name) between 1473 and 1481. It measures 118 feet long and 46 feet wide. Its famous flattened barrel vault ceiling is quite high up to sixty-six feet above the main floor. The chapel shares similar proportions in replicating the distinguished Temple of Solomon built in Jerusalem in 966 BC. The chapel continues to serve both a religious and papal purpose, including as the location of the recent papal conclave, or process by which a new pope is selected. The chapel's fame is more derived from the art decorating the interior. Included are earlier works from esteemed Renaissance painters, followed in 1520 by Raphael, who created tapestries of Saints Peter and Paul for the chapel. However, most notable are Michelangelo's Sistine Chapel painted ceiling and his controversial *Last Judgment* fresco. For over five hundred years since its completion in 1512, people have flocked to see Michelangelo's painted ceiling. The Sistine Chapel ceiling is regarded as one of the major artistic accomplishments of human civilization—so remarkable that in 1787 German poet Johann Wolfgang von Goethe was moved to remark, "Without having seen the Sistine Chapel one can form no appreciable idea of what one man is capable of achieving."[6] Twenty years later, the great Michelangelo returned to create the *Last Judgment* fresco on the altar wall. Oddly, daunted by the difficulty of the task, an unsatisfactory commission, and a demanding pope, the thirty-three-year-old Michelangelo never even wanted to paint the Sistine Chapel ceiling and strongly balked. He stated in a poem, "I am not in the right place—I am not a painter."[7] Single-handedly painting the nearly ten-thousand-square-foot ceiling cost Michelangelo four years of great mental and physical anguish. At one point, Michelangelo even secretly fled Rome to return home to Florence. Authorities requested

6. Sidhu, "Welling Up," para. 1.

7. Pinsky, "Labor Pains."

he return to the pope. Finally, Michelangelo did not paint the ceiling in a lying down position, as portrayed in movies, but rather standing.

The Sistine Chapel ceiling is literally a painted Bible. Nine scenes from the book of Genesis form the centerpiece of his artwork. Its focus is the story of humanity and salvation before the coming of Christ. The narrative is divided into three sections that foretell Christ's coming: the Creation of the Heavens and Earth, the Creation and Expulsion of Adam and Eve, and the story of Noah and the Great Flood. They were painted in reverse chronological order, starting with Noah and ending with creation, from the west to the altar in the east, all in bright colors and easily visible from the floor. In total, Michelangelo developed and painted 175 separate pictorial fields and over 300 figures on the ceiling. The most recognizable fresco is *The Creation of Adam*, depicting the outstretched hand of God giving Adam the spark of life, their fingertips nearly touching. It appears, and is theorized, that the angels and clothing surrounding God form a human brain outline, implying that God gave the first man the gift of intelligence and free will. Others believe the very small near-inch gap represents divine perfection's unattainability for man.[8]

After the ceiling frescoes, it took nearly twenty-five years to draw the now sixty-seven-year-old Michelangelo back to Rome and the Sistine Chapel. *The Last Judgment* was painted by Michelangelo between 1535 and 1541 in a very different political climate in Rome. The *Last Judgment* depicts the second coming of Christ on the day of final and eternal judgment of all humanity by God (as described by John in the Book of Revelation). The subject appears to be in response to Martin Luther's expanding Protestant Reformation movement. The pope's narrative to those growing uncertain of the Catholic Church was a clear reminder of Christ's pending return and our atonement for sins. The frightening grand painting spans the entire wall behind the Sistine Chapel altar and is thirty-nine by forty-five feet in size. It too contains over three hundred figures. At the top is Christ surrounded by groups of prominent saints, the Virgin Mary to his left, and the newly saved. At the bottom left is a group of dead people raised from their graves and ascending to be judged. At the bottom right are those condemned to hell being dragged down by demons. There are also many hidden symbols in the painting and self-portraits. The highly controversial *Last Judgment* quickly became an object of bitter dispute. A censorship campaign sought to remove the frescoes as almost all the male (particularly the damned) and angel figures were depicted naked. Michelangelo himself was accused of immorality and obscenity. Many of the nudes were later partially covered up,

8. Angier, "Michelangelo."

after Michelangelo's death, by another artist. In the end, the masterpiece was defended and survived.

Spanish Steps

Leaving Saint Peter's, I came upon the famous *Spanish Steps* . . . a welcomed, beautiful, eighteenth-century architectural respite in the very heart of Rome's most stylish district. Here, at that time, I could simply sit on the steps with a delicious amaretto gelato in *Roman Holiday* fashion and drink in la dolce vita (sweet life). I noticed that the older steps were deteriorating some (aren't we all) but were no less impressive. Subsequently, with funding from Bulgari jewelers, the steps underwent a major cleaning and restoration project. Since then, sitting, loitering, and eating on the steps have been strictly banned, with reactions to the ban varied.

The imposing Spanish Steps (known as La Scalinata, or the stairway, in Italian) were marvelously constructed between 1723 and 1726. The 135 travertine Rococo style steps, built on three separate garden terraces, is in homage to the Holy Trinity. The steps ascend from the foot of the Piazza di Spagna (Spanish Square) to the sixteenth-century French monastery titular church Trinità dei Monti (Trinity on the Mount) atop Pincian Hill. The history of the steps is intriguing, as both France and Spain had interest and coveted territory in Rome. French King Louis XII set out to build the picturesque Trinità dei Monti on the steep hilltop in 1502 as a stronghold for French nationals. Whereas, at the same time, Spain located the Spanish embassy at the foot of the hill. Despite strained relations, it was eventually French King Louis XIV (the Sun King) who proposed the connecting stairway. His plans were intended to showcase the French church but had also included an equestrian statue of himself on top of the stairway. The Roman government would have none of the statue, and plans stalled. It wasn't till years later that the project was green-lighted. I don't believe the French who funded the steps would be pleased that they became known as the "Spanish Steps" in English. It is believed, the name was most likely coined by John Keats, a favorite poet of mine, who lived adjacent to the steps. The surrounding area became known as the "English ghetto," as many visiting Englishmen traveling through Rome at that time often stayed in the area.

The cascade of polished stone stairs forms the longest and widest steps in Europe. The stunning design includes three successive divided flights of both broad and narrow steps, which the French coveted to exaggerate the height and create a graceful ascent to the church above. There are eleven ramps and a series of winding, twisting ornamental stone railings. Perched at the top of the steps is a forty-five-foot obelisk. Although not an original taken from Egypt, the obelisk is a replica of one that Emperor Aurelian duplicated back in the late third century—1,500 years prior to the Spanish Steps. Conversely, at the base of the steps in the Spanish Square is the peculiar Fountain of the Old Boat, which was completed in 1629. Legend is that the Tiber River flooded, cast a fishing boat ashore, and deposited it in the Spanish Square. This inspired the fountain design, which is a half-sunken ship with overflowing water (from sun-shaped human faces) that flows into the basin. The fountain is slightly below street level due to seventeenth-century water pressure issues. The fountain's sculptor was again a Bernini—in this case Pietro, father of the great Gian Lorenzo, who is believed to have assisted his father.

Colorful banked flowerpots adorn the steps throughout the year, including blooming purple azaleas each April. Traditionally, a crib manger is displayed on the first landing over the Christmas holidays. Many movies have featured the steps in film, and the nearby international design houses prominently use the picturesque staircase in photo shoots. Ever since their completion, the Spanish Steps have always been the place for locals and visitors alike to nightly promenade, to see and be seen.

Keats–Shelley Memorial Museum

The cream-colored Keats–Shelley Memorial Museum sits right at the foot of the Spanish Steps. For most visitors to Rome and the Spanish Steps, the house is unknown or an afterthought of little interest. For me, it was a strange romantic quest triggered by a weirdly favorite very old (1940) library book and the 1948 movie based on the book. This in turn led to a temporary fascination with the young poet John Keats. This is strange and weird in that I'm not particularly a fan of old books or old black-and-white movies and surely not an English Romantic poetry buff. In any case, for some unknown reason, I had read a short book (novella) written by author Robert Nathan called *Portrait of Jennie*. I'm convinced it was the story, that of a struggling New York City artist, that likely caught my attention. Years later, thanks to my mother, I discovered there was a subsequent movie adaptation of the book, also called *Portrait of Jennie*, that was produced by Pittsburgh-born David O. Selznick of *Gone with the Wind* fame. The film is superbly cast with the luminous, brunette beauty Jennifer Jones, Joseph Cotton, Ethyl Barrymore, Lillian Gish, and other renowned actors of the period. The underrated fantasy movie is a haunting, esoteric love story of a handsome starving artist and a mysteriously odd, beautiful girl or ghost

(Jennie). From its opening credits, the unique story seems to center around time travel. True love transcending time and space. The movie was beautifully photographed in New York City, depicting the bygone 1930s depression era. There's also a chilling Claude Debussy soundtrack throughout, including the dreamlike "Afternoon of a Faun." It's certainly a romantic, melancholic tale. Not going to apologize . . . I like a good love story.

What does any of this have to do with John Keats? Well, *Portrait of Jennie* opens with ominous, billowing clouds along with serious questions related to time, space, and mortality. This is followed by literary quotes from ancient Greek tragedian playwright Euripides and English poet John Keats. Specifically, the screen flashes the defying final lines from Keats's 1819 "Ode on a Grecian Urn": "Beauty is truth, truth beauty—that is all / Ye know on earth, and all ye need to know."[9] Debate over the ode's worldly meaning is ongoing. No doubt that these questions were meant to be explored in the movie. In any event, the quizzical quote and movie introduced me to Keats's works and tragically short life. Keats was terminally ill with tuberculosis when he arrived in Rome from London in November 1820. His doctors had suggested that another cold winter in England would kill him. Thus, young John Keats came to Rome to recover in a warmer climate. But it was to no avail: Keats died just four months later, at the very young age of twenty-five. Following the poet's death, in accordance with nineteenth-century Roman health laws, Keats's apartment walls were scraped clean of disease and most items were burned. Much like the movie, Keats's fate was doomed from the onset. It's known that he came to Rome to save his life, though he left behind beloved fiancée Fanny Brawne in London. Sadly, it was Fanny that made his life even worth living. Keats was devastated by his separation from his fiancée and suffered greatly from illness over his final years.

The Keats-Shelley Memorial Association purchased the house in 1906. Prior, it was occupied by two American writers who were often interrupted by random visitors wishing to visit inside Keats's house. The tiny, first-floor rooms where Keats briefly lived and died were preserved and are opened as a living museum, also known as the Keats-Shelley House. The beautifully decorated home contains paintings, manuscripts, handwritten letters, literary works, a reproduction of Keats's walnut wood bed, Ms. Braun's engagement ring, and other memorabilia. In addition to Keats, there are works by his friends and fellow British literary figures, including Lord Byron, Oscar Wilde, William Wordsworth, Percy Bysshe Shelley, and Elizabeth and Robert Browning. There is also one of the finest libraries of Romantic literature with nearly ten thousand volumes. The museum went underground during

9. Dieterle, *Portrait of Jennie*, prologue.

World War II, with the most valuable, unmarked artifacts hidden within a nearby abbey and returned post-war.

The Romantic genius, who explored the limits of the imagination and has been a major influence on literature and arts over the past two centuries, left behind a remarkable collection of sensuous, lyrical poetry. It appeared that Keats had special, unique insight into eternal life and a fascination with his own mortality. Keats had felt and wrote that he had left behind no immortal work. So convinced that he had achieved nothing, dying within earshot of the Spanish Square fountain, he did not want his name engraved on his gravestone. As per his final wishes, the tomb gives reference only to the grave of a "Young English Poet" and simply reads, "Here lies one whose Name was writ in Water."

From the Spanish Steps and Keats House, I continued "roaming" Rome in search of the Trevi Fountain, the Forum and Coliseum, Circus Maximus, the Mouth of Truth, and finally the Pantheon back near my hotel. It was a long, exhilarating journey throughout Rome that I'll never forget. I had no tours scheduled, and time was of the essence. Nonetheless, I managed to see and briefly visit all the exciting, historic sites I had hoped—a plan surely not recommended for all.

Trevi Fountain

Talk about making a first impression . . . wow! The *Trevi Fountain* comes completely unexpected into breathtaking view as you enter from one of the three narrow streets surrounding the tiny square. The name itself means "three roads fountain." Considered the world's most spectacular wishing well, the monumental fountain is one of the most familiar, and possibly most romantic, sights in all of Rome. It is very likely the entire world's most famous fountain. The adjacent area provides a festive air of an endless outdoor party with passing locals, photo-snapping tourists, and beautiful couples. At night, the spotlit piazza and grand fountain are even more thrilling. At first glance, the incredible power and aesthetic beauty of this somewhat hidden fountain is overwhelming to the senses.

The baroque Trevi Fountain was started in 1730 and completed in 1762. The design competition was won by a Florentine, but the watchful Romans insisted on the fountain being built by a Roman. Pope Clement XII relented and it was Nicola Salvi whose design prevailed; unfortunately, he died years prior to its completion. However, the story far precedes those dates. Famous general Marcus Agrippa, companion and son-in-law of Emperor Augustus, was returning from battle with dehydrated troops and desperately in search of water. A young, beautiful girl named Virgo (Latin) led Agrippa to an unknown freshwater spring, revitalizing the troops. Agrippa decided to build an aqueduct from that source to feed into bustling Rome (over eight miles away). Its indirect route made the impressive aqueduct fourteen miles in length. Called Aqua Virgo (after the helpful girl), the aqueduct was completed over two thousand years ago in 19 BC. It remains visible today and is the longest continually operated water source in Rome, true marvel of civil engineering and a great Roman feat for the time. Trevi Fountain is built at the endpoint of the ancient Aqua Virgo. The Agrippa scene is proudly depicted in one of the fountain's relief sculptures.

The modern-marvel fountain is an eye-popping 86 feet high and 161 feet wide. Over the course of a day, the fountain astoundingly recycles over twenty million gallons of water. The project to replace the original utilitarian fountain with one more dramatic was first initiated in 1629. It was abandoned and restarted a century later. Much of the fountain is made from white travertine stone quarried near Tivoli outside of Rome. The background of the fountain is the relatively unknown museum façade of Palazzo Poli. Believe it or not, Pope Clement XII had plenty of bills to pay at that time, so he reinstated a lottery (lotto game) to pay for the fountain. The fountain itself appears as a large cliff or triumphant arch, with many sculptural representations and wild cascading flows of water. At its center, not to be confused with Neptune, is the Greek sea-controlling freshwater god Oceanus. He's driving a shell-shaped chariot, with seahorses and mermen for symmetrical balance. Surrounding allegorical figures enhance the beneficial effects of water, namely healthiness and abundance. Lastly, and few realize this, there is a small two-spouted basin to the right known as the fountain of lovers, traditionally long used by lovers to affirm their vows when one must leave Rome for battle or otherwise. Another funny side story is of a boisterous local barber who was constantly annoyed and complained daily to architect Salvi about the noise and debris during construction. To spite the barber, Salvi erected a symbolic sculpture to the left of the fountain so the barber could never look out of his shop and view his completed masterpiece.

The famous fountain has been featured in many films, most notably *Roman Holiday* (1953), *Three Coins in the Fountain* (1954), and *La Dolce Vita* (1960). One resulted in an Academy Award for Best Original Song, while another unforgettably features stunning Swedish actress Anita Ekburg cavorting in the fountain. Don't try jumping in these days! To preserve the integrity of the treasure, a dip in the fountain will cost you a hefty fine. Few if any daredevils go unnoticed by surrounding patrol. Meanwhile, *Three Coins in the Fountain* song lyrics were written last minute by Sammy Cahn to be sung by Frank Sinatra for the film's release. Despite having no access to the guarded script and film, the fitting lyrics and accompanying music were completed in just one hour and recorded by Frank Sinatra the following day! The song was subsequently used in the movie's soundtrack and climbed the charts. In their haste, Twentieth Century Fox forgot to get the parties under contract. Unfortunately for the studio, complete rights and royalties to the hit song passed to the composers.

Lastly, thanks to the world of cinema, *Three Coins in the Fountain* taught the whole world how to make a wish by throwing coins backwards right-hand over your left shoulder into the fountain. Legend has it that you can ensure your safe return to Rome by tossing a coin into the fountain. A second coin will ensure your return is also met with romance. Finally, a third coin guarantees romance and a Roman wedding. Of course, all personal wishes are welcomed. In sum, roughly $2 million in small coins are tossed into the fountain each year. Since 2006, collected money is gifted to Caritas (love and compassion in Latin), a Roman Catholic charity. Donated funds are used to provide food locally and social programs worldwide to those in need. Unfortunately, 2025 has brought changes gaining entry to the fountain square and coin tossing.

Roman Forum

The incredible *Roman Forum* was initially built at the end of the seventh century BC in the very heart of ancient Rome. It was the all-important, spectacular center of public life in Rome and lasted more than a millennium. Even in those days, Rome had an estimated population of over one million people. Roman laws and powerful armies, originating from the Forum, would temporarily banish the barbarian world. Consequently, the Forum is considered the birthplace of Western civilization and the very core of Roman antiquity. It is one of the most celebrated meeting places in all of history. Today, it is a vast, five-acre area of picturesque ruins and fields that transport you to the glory days of Rome. In its heyday, the road to the forum was paved and lined with an impressive array of seemingly endless impressive structures, many a hundred feet or taller—sights never witnessed by visitors and captors to the republic. Then, in the distance, you see the majestic Roman Colosseum with a capacity of fifty thousand people. Adjacent are many sights of the Palatine Hill.

Some may recall the comedic line "A funny thing happened on the way to the Forum" from the Stephen Sondheim musical by that title, though most will find the walk incredibly surreal and fascinating. The Forum is a haunting, sacred ghost of old Rome. One road leading through the stately

Forum to the Colosseum is the ancient wagon-pitted Via Sacra, or sacred way. There are far too many Forum details to provide herein, so here are just a select few I found of particular interest. In the Forum, you will encounter the original *Arch of Titus* built in the first century to commemorate his famed, dark victory quelling the Jewish revolt in Jerusalem. As a result, Titus brought great wealth back from Judea to Rome along with sixty thousand slaves, who in turn built the Colosseum. There's also the massive *Temple of Venus* built by Emperor Hadrian. From here, you can take a great photo of the Colosseum. You can also find a few remaining arches from the *Basilica of Constantine.* Roman soldiers with drawn crosses on their shields are credited with the first ever Christian battle victory. The remarkably maintained *Temple of Romulus* with its original fourth-century green bronze door is also a highlight of the Roman Forum. Amazingly, the door is still operational today and locked each evening with a large ancient key. Remnants of medieval frescoes also remain on the walls. For romantics, there is the *Temple of Antoninus and Faustina*, which remains a functioning church, though only the original portico has been preserved. Legend is that the good Emperor Antoninus Pius, so stricken with grief over the death of his young and beautiful wife Faustina, built her a temple. Nearby are remnants from the seventh-century-BC *Temple of Vesta* and the *Eternal Flame of Rome*, richly and solemnly maintained by the powerful Vestal Virgins. Another highlight is certainly the *Mamertine Prison*, also built in the seventh century BC. This short-term prison briefly held prisoners prior to trial and execution. Other high-profile leaders were embarrassingly imprisoned here and pardoned only after war and surrender to Rome. It is even believed that Saint Peter was imprisoned at the Mamertine Prison prior to his execution by crucifixion. Next, and clearly standing out, is the intact *Arch of Septimius Severus*. Built in AD 203, this edifice is one of the largest arches in Rome. There's also the *Temple of Saturn* built in 497 BC and rebuilt after a fire eight hundred years later in the fourth century. With only eight columns and a podium remaining, the great temple is left to the imagination. It is believed that a major festival each December was the origin of Christmas as known and celebrated today. During this celebration, all slaves were temporarily given and enjoyed rights of full Roman citizens. Of course, there's also the *Temple of Caesar* where Julius Caesar was assassinated in 44 BC and ultimately burned and buried. Think the Ides of March! Those involved in his murder masqueraded as Caesar supporters. Caesar is the only person honorably buried in the Forum for, at the time, Roman hygiene laws prohibited burials within city limits. Little of the temple is preserved, though visitors still locate the area to leave flowers and coins in memory of Caesar. Lastly, one of the most intact buildings in the Roman Forum is the

Caesar-rebuilt *Curia Julia* or *Julian Senate House*. This listing is only a select sampling; numerous other Forum structures have survived in part. It's also easy to visualize all the Roman celebratory parades, or "triumphs," as they were known, passing down the Via Sacra.

The Forum speaks more soundly to the grandeur of ancient Rome than any other place. It was here where they shouted, "Caesar has been murdered," where Mark Antony delivered his eulogy for Caesar, where Saint Paul passed through on his way to meet with the Emperor Nero, where Cleopatra's legend was built, where Cicero was decapitated, and where famed gladiators paraded.

Colosseum

At the east end of the Forum, in the precise heart of Rome, sits the great *Colosseum*. It's not every day that you walk up to one of the New Seven Wonders of the World! Despite its age—it was completed in AD 80—the surprisingly intact Colosseum is the largest ancient amphitheater ever built and still the largest standing amphitheater in the world. Measuring over six hundred by five hundred feet and fifteen stories high, this iconic symbol of imperial Rome had capacity to hold fifty to eighty thousand frenzied spectators. Again, with just a couple days to see all of Rome, I forewent a formal tour but unapologetically hung about a few English-speaking tour groups. Access around the Colosseum and the arena floor was provided. Standing there, I could not imagine the insane fanfare and brutality associated with the Super Bowl–like spectacles of nearly two thousand years ago. Originally known as the Flavian Amphitheater, the Colosseum entertained Romans for over five hundred years with prisoners' executions, exhibitions and hunts of wild animals, recreational battles, chariot races, Roman mythological dramas, and gladiator fights. It is also believed the Colosseum was even filled with water on occasion to recreate naval battles.

The massive amphitheater is an innovative architectural and engineering wonder, though its designer is unknown. The arena's grand stone and marble elliptical design appears fashioned to resemble earlier Greek theaters. To facilitate crowd flow, there were eighty entrances with four entrances reserved for political and religious leaders. Corridors separated ordinary citizens, and seating was hierarchically determined by social status, wealth, and gender, though all seats provided great visibility. I overheard one tour guide state that disliked nobility and guests would be given outstanding front row seats only to find themselves bloodstained from the nearby action. Other innovations included sophisticated drainage and overhead sail-like retractable awnings manned by imperial sailors to protect spectators from Rome's rain and sweltering summer heat. There were complex underground chambers, tunnels, and galleries to house props, scenery, animals, and participants when not in action. And for dramatic special effect there were ingenious freight elevator lifts and thirty-six trap doors, which allowed the gladiators and even colossal elephants to appear as if from thin air. I also heard from a passing guide of a "botanical mystery" surrounding the plants previously grown within the ancient ruins. Of course, there were plants synonymous with Italy including cypress, hollies, capers, and thistles. However, in addition, there were rare flowers and plants not found in Italy or throughout Europe. One explanation is that the rare flowers were brought as seeds in the fur and stomachs of lions, tigers, giraffes, etc. shipped by the Romans from the wilds of Africa and all corners of the empire. It's merely conjecture; nonetheless, for many centuries, the Colosseum was once a wild and tangled garden of great, mysterious variety.

Sadly, as I heard on a tour, it is estimated that over five hundred thousand people died in the blood-sport Colosseum. Inauguration of the newly completed Colosseum under Emperor Titus included one hundred days of games and took the lives of over two thousand gladiators and five thousand animals alone. Additionally, so many wild and exotic animals were captured and killed in the Colosseum that it is believed certain species became extinct. In time, the Colosseum had become a symbol of an international campaign against capital punishment, though capital punishment was not abolished in Italy until 1948. In contrast, every Good Friday, the Pope leads a torchlit living Way of the Cross procession near the sacred Colosseum grounds to remember the many early Roman Christians who died in the arena. By all accounts, the Colosseum and adjacent Forum that still adorn Rome were once the center of the world. After twenty-seven centuries, Romans still maintain a great sense of admiration and pride in the ancient ruins. Day and night, the city frantically burst with activity all around the Colosseum. Further, most visitors will be sure to take a romantic nighttime promenade around the mellow, spellbinding, golden-lit Colosseum.

Circus Maximum/The Mouth of Truth

What a day it had been so far. . . . I was awestruck at the sights and mind-blowing attractions of Rome. But I figured, "Why stop now?" There were two other adjacent sights I wanted to briefly visit. Thankfully, once again, both were within moderate walking distance.

First stop was *Circus Maximus*, the greatest and largest stadium in ancient Rome. It was also the very first stadium built by the Romans, dating back to the sixth century BC. Circus Maximus was specifically designed for chariot racing but also hosted gladiatorial combats, exotic animal hunts, theater, and lots more. Nonetheless, chariot racing was far and away the most popular ancient Rome spectator sport and endured for a millennium. Following a devastating fire, the original, often renovated Circus Maximus was eventually rebuilt and expanded during the first century. It measured over two thousand feet long and nearly four hundred feet wide. Consequently, it had a capacity of 250,000 people, or a quarter of Rome's entire population then. Huge bets were placed on charioteers, who themselves became famous and wealthy. Chariots by design were dangerously lightweight, likely made of leather, and intended to travel as fast as possible, approaching forty miles an hour. The chariots were no more than a basket on wheels pulled by color-coded teams of four, six, eight, or even twelve spectacular horses. The brave charioteers would circle the track's spine seven times for a total distance of approximately seven miles. The most famous charioteer, winner of over two thousand races, was a Spanish-born slave named Scorpus. Scorpus's great earnings and wealth eventually bought him his freedom. However, it was short-lived, as Scorpus died at just twenty-seven years old. I knew, in advance, that these days Circus Maximus was merely a large field repurposed as a public park. Nonetheless, the impression or undeniable shape of Circus Maximus, along with fragments of ancient ruins and a few surviving stands, remains clearly recognizable. Several large events such as national World Cup celebrations and concerts, including the Rolling Stones, Bruce Springsteen, Genesis, Duran Duran, and others, have also occurred at Circus Maximus. In any event, with a keen imagination, you can easily be transported way, way back in time when visiting Circus Maximus.

My next stop was the *Mouth of Truth*. This may not sound familiar to you, but for anyone who saw the 1953 movie classic *Roman Holiday*, it should be. The iconic ancient marble stone carving is said to bite the hand off liars and was a major plot device in that movie. Dating to the first century, the tall stone disc was carved into a gloomy, stern-gazed, unidentified pagan humanoid face. No one is certain where the large medallion originated, though it could have been a fountain decoration or a massive manhole drain cover. There are hollow holes for the beady eyes, along with nostrils and a gaping, whimsical, lie-detecting mouth suitable for inserting one's hand. The associated legend is that the bizarre, stone-faced disc was used during medieval trials where the accused would insert their hand in the mouth. Those determined untruthful were met with a severe and gruesome fate: a hidden axman would sever their appendage. The superstition continues to this day and creates a few unnecessary jitters, as well as a great photo opportunity, for those lining up to risk the Mouth of Truth. The nearly six-foot diameter, 2,800-pound mask was only installed vertically in the seventeenth century. The disc is conveniently set in the portico of the Basilica di Santa Maria in Cosmedin on the bank of the Tiber River. As an interesting aside (and oddly enough), within the basilica is the flower-adorned skull of Saint Valentine. Proof further of absurdly fascinating Rome! Lastly, *Roman Holiday* actor Gregory Peck coincidentally shares my birthday. And it was on "our" birthday that I visited the Mouth of Truth. Of course, I reenacted the famous "truth-be-told" scene that included the beautiful Audrey Hepburn.

Pantheon

After an incredible, jam-packed day of sightseeing, I decided to head back to the hotel with one last nearby landmark stop. I would visit the *Pantheon* and attend Saturday evening Mass at a site where Mass has been historically celebrated for over 1,400 years. The remarkable Pantheon is undoubtedly the best preserved, continuously used, rebuilt structure in all of Rome. This ancient, ornate Roman temple and architectural marvel, first built in 27 BC by legendary general and statesman Marcus Agrippa, is very hard to consider a ruin. Though it was completely rebuilt, as is today, in AD 126 after a lightning strike. The Pantheon sits in the historic center of Rome in the Piazza della Rotunda. The Pantheon was rededicated as a Catholic Church, Saint Mary and the Martyrs, in 609. This was at the request of many complaining Christians claiming that the Pantheon was haunted by pagan ghosts. Being converted to a church at such an early date is likely why the Pantheon is so well preserved. As most Roman buildings could withstand the test of time, the Pantheon's church status prevented it from being looted for recycling materials.

The circular concrete and stone building, faced with brick, twenty-foot-thick walls, a rising concrete dome, and a front portico of sixteen Corinthian columns, has essentially survived intact. The beauty of the matching 145-foot-tall-and-wide building is astounding, though its architect is unknown. It is said that when Michelangelo first saw the Pantheon nearly 1,400 years after its construction, he proclaimed that it must have been built by angels. The building is considered nearly perfect, and thus its genius design and construction is a bit of a mystery. The porch columns are solid stone, each forty-eight feet high. The columns came from Egypt by slow boats across the turbulent Mediterranean Sea. Imported columns would then be dragged from the shore on wooden rollers and are believed to have been lifted in place by elephants. It's speculated that the porch is only disproportional to the cylindrical building's inner drum due to material shortage; possibly a shipwreck caused the loss of a few of the granite columns en route from Egypt.

Once inside the Pantheon, your attention is naturally and intentionally drawn to the magnificent dome above. There is an open twenty-eight-foot oculus (eye) in the middle of the dome that allows for natural light, as well as rain and occasional snow, to enter the Pantheon. The oculus is also believed to allow visitors direct access with heaven. No worries, as the marble floors below were specifically designed to allow any rain to quickly drain in place. There are several royal tombs located in the Pantheon, including Vittorio Emanuele II, who unified Italy in 1861, and his son Umberto I, who was assassinated in 1900. There are also artists' tombs, most notably Raphael, the darling of the Roman Renaissance. Raphael died very young on his thirty-seventh birthday in 1520. His plain stone sarcophagus is on the back left side of the Pantheon under the statue of Mary holding baby Jesus. Raphael's poet-written Latin epitaph translates, "Here lies Raphael. While he was alive, the mother of all things (Nature) feared she would be surpassed by him; when he died, she feared that she too would die."[10]

To this day, standing for over two thousand years, the Pantheon possesses beauty inside and out that is unparalleled. In fact, the Pantheon's unreinforced concrete dome is still the world's largest. It is the consummate testament to world-class Roman ingenuity and engineering. The Pantheon's longevity mystery seems best explained in the only recently discovered compounding recipe of superior, lime-laced Roman concrete. In any event, the Pantheon spearheaded an architectural revolution, leading to the creation of many beautiful cities as well as societal changes, showing humans how to better live, interact, and prosper. In the 1820s, American founding father Thomas Jefferson modeled the rotunda on the original lawn of the University of Virginia after Rome's Pantheon.

Wow . . . that magical April Saturday in Rome is one I'll forever remember. On most of my quick bleisure visits, I can only marginally touch upon the beauty and mystique of these fascinating cities, and Rome was no exception. Consequently, parting is sometimes difficult, though I always leave extremely grateful for the opportunity provided and even paid for

10. Factum Foundation, "Tomb of Raphael."

by my employer. Being far away from home introduces travelers to new cultures, ethnicities, religions, geography, languages, politics, economics, foods, styles, and ideas. With each visit your life is transformed in one way or another, and you are unknowingly changed forever. Experiencing ancient Rome for two full days was far more impactful than most.

CHAPTER 6

SALZBURG

Let's start at the very beginning, a very good place to start.

—*Maria von Trapp (The Sound of Music)*

SALZBURG IS ONE OF my favorite cities in the world. It's quintessential storybook Austria, a timeless mountain village nestled in the bewitching Alps. In the air is a natural, indescribable charm and an infectious easy way of life. The majestic mountains, a quaint flowing river, stunning baroque domes and church spires, rusted copper rooftops, century-old wrought iron shop signs, abbeys, a formidable cliff-top fortress, Mozart, history, edelweiss, and the *Sound of Music* all send your spirits soaring.

Why call my travels "bleisure"? Well, here is yet another perfect example! I had considerable business in Munich, Germany, that would continue into two workweeks. This rarely occurred in my role but surely provided added travel and sightseeing opportunities. I had plenty of time to enjoy Munich both on my own and in the evenings with colleagues. Consequently, I was free Friday afternoon through Sunday evening and considered visiting surrounding cities—easily accomplished throughout Europe. There were two cities of interest that I had not had the opportunity to visit: Prague, capital of the Czech Republic, and Salzburg, Austria. Both cities were of interest, though Prague is a nearly six-hour train ride from Munich. Conversely, Salzburg is only ninety miles from Munich, conveniently less than two-hours away by train. My visit to Prague would have to wait! It was a great decision to visit Salzburg that crisp mid-autumn weekend, and it's *almost* always a great decision to travel by comfortable, panoramic-windowed, high-speed express trains in Europe. The scenic route passed the largest lake in Bavaria, enchanting valleys, green meadows, and even provided occasional glimpses of the Alps. However, as with most international trips, there will be hiccups along the way. I found this out Sunday evening when I returned to the Salzburg central train station only to discover a convoy of buses. Turns out the train track was temporarily closed so we were advised to crowd onto the standing-room-only buses. That said, I joined the happy-go-lucky students, couples, and young families toting backpacks, suitcases, bicycles, strollers, and more. We made the most of the nearly three-hour ride back to Munich by sharing tales as well as food and drinks. We all accepted our fate and there were no complaints. This was so unusual to me. It made for a fun, seemingly quick bus ride back to Munich, even if I stood the entire time. I was just grateful for a wonderful weekend in beautiful Salzburg!

I didn't know a lot about Salzburg prior to visiting; many people think solely of Vienna when considering a trip to Austria. Of course, I was aware of Salzburg as the backdrop to the *Sound of Music* story and as the birthplace of its most famous son, Wolfgang Amadeus Mozart. The city's name is attributed to the many area salt mines and literally translates to "salt castle." I read that the Salzburg area was first settled by the Celts in the fifth century BC and eventually merged by the Romans around 15 BC. Salzburg was formally established as an episcopal see by Saint Rupert in 696. There is a very long and rich history of religious conflict, annexations, the seeking of greater personal rights, Nazi occupation, and eventual freedom and independence. Consequently, this relatively small city (population of just 160,000 residents) is largely considered the meeting point of northern (Germany) and southern (Italy) Europe.

Today, the city is home to three universities, and there is an abundance of young students. Simultaneously, the very special cultural fabric of Salzburg has been developed and remarkably preserved since the Gothic period or late Middle Ages. Until the nineteenth century, Salzburg, known as "Little Rome," was an extraordinary ecclesiastical city-state ruled by a prince archbishop, unusual for the ruling Holy Roman Empire. Much of its ornate baroque appearance, credited to several famed Italian architects and the many artists and craftsmen drawn to Salzburg, remains intact. There's also a melting of Gothic, Romanesque, and Renaissance period architecture spanning centuries. The result is a bustling townscape of great individuality and uniquely preserved beauty. Add to that a few famous squares and a tranquil, rich skyline of spires and domes, nestled on the turquoise Salzach River against a backdrop of magnificent alpine mountains.

Old Town (Altstadt)

My strategy, as possible and business affordable, is always to stay right in the heart of the old city centers. Many of these hotels are quite old, small, and more boutique and might lack some modern amenities. I'm willing to sacrifice that for cool cultural experiences and location. Besides, when traveling solo, relaxation and sleep are not my priorities. That said, it's sometimes a gamble to forego the larger, comfortable, known hotel chains. Although, on occasion, I guess just right! This has been borne out in Paris, Rome, London, and again in Salzburg. In this instance, I selected the *Hotel Elefant*, housed in a beautiful, fully restored thirteenth-century building. The hotel was on a narrow cobblestoned pedestrian-zoned street full of shops and just steps from most all the Salzburg sights. It even had a small elevator and served a wonderful Austrian breakfast. The Hotel Elefant, and the surrounding Old Town area, was the absolute ideal location for my brief visit to Salzburg.

Most "Old Towns" are special, vibrant places dating back centuries. Salzburg's Old Town proved charming, compact, historic, and uniquely stunning—so much so that in 1997 the Old Town of Salzburg proudly earned a designated spot as a World Heritage Site on UNESCO's list. This means Old Town must be preserved as a site of "outstanding value to humanity."[1] Consequently, it's nearly identical to when Mozart strolled the streets 250 years earlier. Salzburg Old Town is the largest, most monumental World Heritage site on earth! Further, unlike many other cities, most of Salzburg's major attractions are in close, easy proximity to its alluring Old Town neighborhood. A sampling includes the fortress, Mozart's birthplace, the Mirabell Palace and Gardens, Saint Peter's Abbey and Cemetery, Salzburg Cathedral, the old city hall, and plenty of shopping. Salzburg is ideal to explore for scenic leisurely strolls.

Salzburg Fortress (Festung Hohensalzburg)

A literal "can't miss" crowning landmark visible from all points in Salzburg is the massive nine-hundred-year-old Salzburg Fortress. The castle towers on a rocky ledge four hundred feet above the serene Salzach River below. Construction of the fortress castle began in 1077, continually expanded, and was not finished until 1681. It consists of various wings and a large gathering courtyard. For over six hundred years, it served both necessary defense and state purposes. Over all these years, no enemies have managed to win the fortress in Salzburg. At eight hundred feet long and five hundred

1. UNESCO, "About World Heritage," para. 2.

feet wide, the dominating fortress remains the largest fully preserved castle in central Europe. There are elegant state and royal apartments, a museum of medieval art, Gothic artifacts, a sixteenth-century open-air barrel organ (Salzburg Bull), arms and armor exhibits, and a beautiful chapel to be seen within the castle. The refurbished castle became a major tourist attraction in the late nineteenth century. Its location, very near Old Town, allows for easy hiking access via one of many escalating paths and lanes. A perfect way to temporarily escape the humming sound of the city and enjoy the chime of the melodic church bells below. Alternatively, from a somewhat hidden station behind Salzburg Cathedral, a funicular railway leads directly from town to the castle in the sky. The funicular was opened in 1892 and has efficiently operated, every ten minutes, till this day. Even those with little interest in history or castles should visit the fortress for its panoramic views. From the castle terrace or bastions, you can enjoy striking views over Salzburg's rooftops, domes, and towers below. And from the fortress watchtower, you are rewarded with a sweeping view of the magnificent surrounding Alps.

Mozart's Birthplace

Undoubtedly, Salzburg's most favorite son is none other than composer and musical genius *Wolfgang Amadeus Mozart*. Mozart's presence is strongly felt throughout Salzburg. Wolfgang is everywhere! Mozart was born in Salzburg on January 27, 1756, on the rented third-floor apartment of a bright canary-yellow-façade house. He was the youngest of seven children, though only he and a sister survived. By the age of five, young Mozart was already displaying prodigious composing and musical abilities and commenced performing for European royalty. Despite a short life, having died mysteriously at age thirty-five in Vienna, Mozart is acclaimed as the greatest, most influential composer of the classical period, if not all of Western music. His composing inspiration is regarded as divine, though he was also a world-class conductor, virtuoso pianist, organist, and violinist. Mozart created over eight hundred musical works in many genres including several successful operas, e.g., *Marriage of Figaro*, *Don Giovanni*, and *The Magic Flute*. Consider also that Mozart was well-traveled, with seventeen documented major trips to Vienna, London, Paris, Brussels, Cologne, Munich, Milan, and beyond. These road trips, primarily by slow, very uncomfortable horse-drawn carriage, cost Mozart an estimated 3,720 days (over ten years) of his eventually shortened life. Lastly, not unlike other renowned artists, Mozart garnished significant fame though little financial security in his lifetime.

Since 1880, the twelfth-century building has housed the *Mozart Museum* in celebration of Wolfgang Amadeus Mozart's lifetime from early childhood. The museum is one of Austria's most visited, drawing the attention of Mozart and history fans alike. The three floors, which include the third-floor birth room, contain selected works of Mozart's musical development, costumes, set designs, autographs, first edition manuscripts, paintings, family letters, and original furniture. There are also fascinating rarities, including the wunderkind's childhood violin and a harpsichord on which he composed *The Magic Flute*. There is no better place, notwithstanding the opera, to best enjoy and fully understand Mozart . . . an incomparable musical genius.

Mozart Square/Monument

Just a short walk from Mozart's birthplace home and current-day museum, in the very center of Salzburg's Old Town, is the Mozart Square of *Mozartplatz*. Originally the square was created by the prince-archbishop in the early seventeenth century in honor of Saint Michael. In 1841, on the fiftieth anniversary of Mozart's death, the square was to be renamed Mozartplatz with a nearly ten-foot statue of Wolfgang Amadeus Mozart erected and unveiled on the site. Due to the Napoleonic Wars, the city of Salzburg was economically depressed at that time. Consequently, the statue was largely sponsored by Bavarian King Ludwig I, who donated the marble pedestal on which the statue stands. The king was a great admirer of Mozart and in love with the city of Salzburg. Unfortunately, the monument unveiling was slightly delayed until 1842, as a valuable Roman mosaic was uncovered in the ground below and its proper excavation took some time. A copy of the Roman mosaic can still be seen at the foot of Mozart's statue. The statue is the square's focal point and was the first sign of public recognition that the composer had received from his hometown. Two of Mozart's surviving sons were on hand at the monument's inauguration, whereas his wife, Constanze, whose home was in the square, had unfortunately died just six months prior to its unveiling. The very active square plays a significant role in the history of Salzburg and is dotted with churches, shopping, museums, and famous cafés today.

Sound of Music

In addition to its connection to Mozart, Salzburg is THE *Sound of Music* city! This is attributed to the enormous success of Rodgers and Hammerstein's

1959 Broadway musical theater premier of the *Sound of Music*. The play was based on the 1949 *Story of the Trapp Family Singers* written by Maria von Trapp. Consequently, the *Sound of Music* production would result in memorable filming locations all throughout Salzburg. The subsequent 1965 film, starring Julie Andrews and Christopher Plummer, was partially filmed in the city for six weeks in 1964. The classic movie was a smashing success, winning five Academy Awards and becoming the highest grossing film ever made at the time. Most everyone knows the music and the *true* love story of the former young novice (nun in training) and governess Maria (Kutschera) von Trapp and the dashing widower Navy Captain von Trapp, along with their seven musically talented children. The movie maintains cult status and remains one of the most successful films in worldwide cinematic history! Coincidentally, the *Sound of Music* is the first movie I recall seeing as a child in a movie theater. My saintly Aunt Mary took me and my brothers to see the movie at the brand new, somewhat ornate two-screen Eastland Theater in the neighboring town of North Versailles. Aunt Mary (really an older cousin) was our church organist for sixty-five years. Aunt Mary and her husband, Walter, were helpful in providing financial support to our large family. To this day, I distinctly remember the experience and the excitement of enjoying that dark, comfortable, larger-than-life theater.

Consequently, over three hundred thousand visitors descend on Salzburg annually to tour and discover the movie's many original, beautiful, preserved shooting locations. Accordingly, *Sound of Music* coach bus, bicycle, and walking tours are abundant throughout Salzburg. Also in the planning is an exciting new Salzburg *Sound of Music* museum. I opted for a Saturday afternoon bus tour with a group of random visitors from around the world—a bit awkward for a middle-aged businessman traveling alone but a fantastic experience, nonetheless. My family would have loved it! I'm glad not to have missed out. I managed to make a few new friends and buddied with our enthusiastic tour guide. The guide was more than happy to share some added insights. There was plenty to view, and now I have enjoyed revisiting the sites each and every time I rewatch the movie at home. A few of the original movie locations I visited include:

Mirabell Gardens and the Pegasus Fountain: Several *Sound of Music* movie scenes were filmed in the lush seventeenth-century Mirabell Gardens. This is in fact where I started the tour and first boarded the coach. Most notable of these is Maria and the seven von Trapp children dancing around the sprouting Pegasus (winged horse) Fountain while singing the classic "Do-Re-Mi." This is where Maria first takes the children in their new "play clothes" (recycled drapes) as they wander and frolic by many famous Salzburg sites. You may recall that Maria ends the well-known song with an iconic fist raised and a hands-to-head pose at the top of the Mirabell Garden steps. The Mirabell Gardens is also where the real-life Mozart would play private concerts as a young child.

Leopoldskron Palace/Mozarteum Salzburg: Most everyone who has seen the *Sound of Music* movie can recall Maria and the children falling off the boat into the lake, meeting the baroness, and the romantic palace gazebo scene where Liesel and Rolf sang "Sixteen Going on Seventeen." It's the rococo style Leopoldskron Palace, built in 1736, that served as the rear exterior location of the von Trapp home. The palace's interior was not used in the movie scenes, as the gold Venetian ballroom and foyer were rebuilt in Hollywood. Likewise, the gazebo scenes were shot in a much larger Hollywood gazebo. The actual movie gazebo was gifted to the city of Salzburg after filming. The house has a long history of owners, was once confiscated (as Jewish property) and occupied by Nazis, fell into disarray, and was ultimately converted into a five-star luxury hotel in 2014. Recent hotel guests include Prince Charles, Hillary Clinton, Bill Gates, Ruth Bader

Ginsburg, and many others. A second yellow home was used to film the front exterior of the von Trapp house. This 1841 building is the Mozarteum Salzburg music and dramatic arts university. It is surrounded by a tall wrought iron gate, which Maria peers through upon arriving at the house. That building is also featured when Captain von Trapp rips down the Nazi flag and when the family escapes by quietly pushing their car out the front gate.

Mondsee Basilica: The coach continued the tour traveling to the charming lakeside village of Mondsee (Moon Lake). It's a short drive of less than thirty minutes and very relevant to the tour. Specifically, in the heart of Mondsee is the beautiful *Basilica Saint Michael*, which is the filming location of one of the *Sound of Music* movie's most famous scenes: Maria and Captain von Trapp's church wedding. In real life, Maria and the captain were married in Salzburg at the historic Nonnberg Abbey. In Hollywood fashion, the beautiful, relatively small but ornate cathedral is way more befitting of a joyous fairy-tale ending. As seen in the film, the extravagant baroque-style, gold-gilded altar offset by original light pink Gothic vaults provided a stunning image.

The impressive mountain background of the Alps, the quaint and colorful town, and the crystal clear turquoise-colored lake are reasons enough to visit Mondsee. Along the way, you enjoy the Austrian countryside and lake district with views as cinematic as the movie's dramatic opening and closing scenes filmed high atop nearby Mount Untersberg. It was noted that real-life Maria enjoyed countryside visits where she would read and pray as a young girl. Although not part of my tour, that filmed mountain is also easily accessed from Salzburg by bus (or enjoy a cable-car ride or two-hour hike to the filming location from Mount Untersberg's base).

There are numerous other original movie locations to visit throughout Salzburg, and the tours vary somewhat in their routes. One thing for certain is that your spirits cannot help but be lifted as you travel through the captivating Austrian hills, with a busload of friends and family, singing all the classic tunes from *Sound of Music.*

Nonnberg Abbey

Also in the movie but not on my coach tour was the *Nonnberg Abbey.* The beautiful abbey is very visible on a hillside terrace just above Salzburg's Old Town. In fact, most mornings at 6:45 a.m., if you're lucky, you can hear heavenly Gregorian Latin chants from the abbey's singing nun's choir. This is the very abbey where the real-life Maria first became a novice nun and eventually married Captain von Trapp in 1927. I made a separate short, winding walking trip to visit the famed early eighth-century Benedictine monastery. The Nonnberg Abbey is the oldest continuously inhabited convent in all of Europe. Founded by Saint Bishop Rupert of Salzburg in 714, the monastery complex is protected today as a UNESCO World Heritage Site. Ministerial life has continued uninterrupted throughout times of war, economic crisis, and destructive fires. It is believed that the Bavarian emperor sponsored the abbey's construction in gratitude following a severe illness. Salzburg has always been a noted champion of the sick and poor. The Gothic complex also encompasses Romanesque and baroque style renovations and additions throughout so many years. Buildings are quite close, as the historic abbey is flanked by a fortress wall and a steep hillside. A collection of medieval documents, Gothic sculptures, and paintings are housed in the abbey.

Despite its over 1,300-year remarkable and storied existence, the abbey is probably best known for being the home of the troublesome novice nun Maria from the *Sound of Music.* For it is at the Nonnberg Abbey that the story, famously told in the 1965 award-winning film production, begins! The nunnery plays a prominent role in the movie's storyline, with four scenes set in the front of the abbey and its cemetery. You may recall these scenes: the nuns singing "Maria" in the courtyard, Maria leaving the abbey to follow her dreams, the von Trapp children visiting Maria, and the Nazis hunting the escaped von Trapp family (thwarted by the mischievous nuns). Conversely, the abbey interior and cemetery scenes were filmed back in Hollywood, as filming within the convent was prohibited. A brief stop at Nonnberg Abbey is a staple for any *Sound of Music* aficionado.

Saint Peter's Abbey, Cemetery, Stiftskulinarium (Nockerl)

Lastly, immediately flanking the western side of Salzburg's historic Old Town city center is a steep mountain, Monchsberg. A very long 430-foot street tunnel with elaborate baroque portals and a city gate were carved through the mountain in 1766. It's a unique and dramatic entrance to beautiful Salzburg. At the very foot of this mountain is *Saint Peter's Abbey.* Even older than the Nonnberg Abbey (both founded by Saint Rupert), Saint Peter's Abbey dates to 696. Consequently, this date coincides with the formal establishment of the city of Salzburg. The abbey and Benedictine monastery stem from the beginning of Christendom in the area and were established to advance missionary efforts. In fact, it is the world's oldest monastery with a continuous history since its inception. As would be expected, Saint Peter's has gone through considerable transformation throughout the years. The present-day Romanesque abbey church was erected around 1130 with considerable enhancements made throughout the seventeenth century. Initially, in the Middle Ages, it was also regarded as an exceptional school. Accordingly, Saint Peter's houses the oldest library in Austria with over one hundred thousand volumes and eight hundred precious manuscripts on church and local history, monasticism, music, devotions, and artworks. The library is accessible only with special permissions. Saint Rupert was originally entombed next to the abbey's high altar.

Equally fascinating to visit is the small yet beautiful flower-filled *Saint Peter's Cemetery*. The unique cemetery was reestablished during the foundation of the monastery and is older than the archabbey itself. It is a serene, walled sanctuary filled with ornate wrought iron crucifixes, monuments, and centuries-old gravestones. This famous Salzburg resting site is nestled just below the looming fortress and very near the abbey's continuously operating twelfth-century bakery. Another astounding feature is its catacombs carved into the mountain, possibly dating to the late antiquity period as a location serving early Christians in secluded assembly. Two chapels were added in the eleventh century, with one being dedicated to assassinated Archbishop Thomas Becket of Canterbury. Many prominent artists, academics, merchants, and personalities—including Mozart's sister, composer Michael Haydn, and *Sound of Music* uncle Max Detweiler—are buried at Saint Peter's cemetery. As the Nonnberg Abbey cemetery proved too small, you may recognize a replica of Saint Peter's cemetery in the movie. The cemetery was rebuilt in Hollywood for the familiar dramatic movie scene wherein the von Trapp family hides behind tombs from flashlight-wielding Nazis.

Finally, not to be missed is a visit to *Saint Peter's Stiftskulinarium*, believed to be the oldest existing restaurant in Europe, if not the world, dating to 803. Located in Salzburg's oldest quarter, the restaurant is built into the walls of Saint Peter's Abbey, which in turn is built into the mountainside. Initially, it served as both a restaurant and an inn. Known past guests of high acclaim include Charlamagne, Christopher Columbus, Johann Georg Faust, Wolfgang Amadeus Mozart, the von Trapp family, and myself! The restaurant's age is based on the writings of a noted English scholar who served then Holy Roman Emperor Charlamagne. Is it possible, as many speculate, that it was at this restaurant, while dining with the Bishop of Salzburg, that Charlamagne decided that his subjects would be Christian?

The large restaurant is not at all visible from the street and only entered via a courtyard that appears exclusive and mysterious. Don't be fooled into thinking it's a small, dark, dusty Medieval eatery and pub; it's anything but. It's huge, with several themed rooms. It's hip, cool, colorful, fun, and outstanding. Very modern enhancements offset historic walls, stone arches, and wooden doors you wish could talk. Many of the restaurant walls and carvings are original. The award-winning restaurant with the modern touch provides an exceptional fine-dining experience of traditional Austrian fare with an atmosphere steeped in history.

Not to be missed at the Stiftskulinarium of Saint Peter's is an icon of Austrian and Salzburg dessert cuisine known as *Nockerl*. The sweet Nockerl confection is derived from French souffle dishes. Salzburger Nockerl is made with just three simple ingredients: egg yolks, flour, and sugar. The golden meringue tips of this tri-tipped souffle represent the three hillsides surrounding Salzburg's city center, with a dusting of powdered sugar serving as snow-covered peaks. Occasionally, the dessert is garnished with the silhouette of Salzburg's favorite son, Mozart, and is served with lingonberry cream. Is it any wonder why Salzburg is one of the world's most beautiful, enchanting cities and a solid favorite of mine?

CHAPTER 7

LONDON

In London, everyone is different, and that means anyone can fit in.

—*Paddington Bear*

When asked about my favorite international cities, I almost always summarize my opinion by noting that London is the most fun. It's a major global city! Consequently, despite America's very tumultuous beginning with Great Britain, I, like many Americans of our generation, grew up fascinated and entranced with all things British. And I believe the Brits are equally fascinated with America. Today, our countries are likely the closest of world allies and friends. I think there is a good argument to be made that a certain "world order" can be attributed to our two countries. There's great cooperation on a range of vital global priorities, our thriving economic relationship, and the deep ties between our people and civil societies. Lastly, unlike many other visited countries, a key cultural connection is obvious: we speak the same language. That said, English is the recognized global business language spoken throughout Europe with most all colleagues, and most other Europeans are minimally bilingual.

The great history of America begins with its establishment as a British colony; every American child is taught this lesson in elementary school. In 1607, British King James I began establishing colonies in America. Next, following a harrowing journey, a documented 105 brave Brits arrived in North America from England to start a settlement.[1] Jamestown, Virginia, was chosen for the first permanent North American settlement, named after

1. Wikipedia, "List of Jamestown Colonists," sec. "Original settlers (May 1607)."

the British king. The Jamestown location was strategically chosen for several reasons. Primarily, the locale was surrounded on three sides by water and was far inland. This position meant Jamestown was easily defensible against possible Spanish attacks. The water was also deep enough that the English could easily moor their three ships on the shoreline. Lastly, although the area was hunting grounds of the Powhatan Indians, the site was not inhabited by the native population. Everything was going to plan. Unfortunately, the settlers were pathetically ill-prepared for establishing a new colony, and the natives were the least of their problems. Shortly after reaching Jamestown, the settlers began to succumb to a variety of diseases. The drinking water from the river, along with famine, were factors resulting in a high death toll. Only thirty-eight settlers survived the first difficult year.[2] Ironically, if not for the early help of the skeptical Powhatan people, the Jamestown settlement would most likely have failed due to starvation and various diseases. It was not until 1612 that colonist John Rolfe successfully introduced tobacco crops to the colony. He subsequently and famously fell in love with and married Powhatan princess Pocahontas, who converted to Christianity. These actions led to a period of peace and prosperity.

Eventually, in 1620, the *Mayflower* set sail to America from Plymouth, England. Unlike the earlier expedition, these passengers were in search of a new life, some seeking religious freedom from the Church of England. Others were merely seeking a fresh start in a different land. These travelers became known as "pilgrims," and their significant influence on the future of America could never have been imagined! Today, more than thirty-five million people (ten million in the United States alone) can trace their ancestry to the 102 passengers and thirty crew members who sailed aboard the *Mayflower*.[3] That ship landed in Plymouth Bay, Massachusetts, on a harsh November day. There's an inscribed rock (known as Plymouth Rock) at the Cape Cod site. My middle daughter and I visited the small, obscure rock once. The arrival of these colonists would also have an enormous effect on Native Americans and the land they had called home for centuries. Nonetheless, once again, it was the Indigenous Wampanoag tribe who taught the colonists food gathering and other survival skills. Even so, after the first year, only fifty-three settlers would survive starvation and contagious diseases. These pilgrims, along with ninety Native Americans, celebrated the colony's first fall harvest, declared centuries later the initial American Thanksgiving. The *Mayflower*, as one of the earliest colonial vessels, remains a cultural icon in American history.

2. Wikipedia, "List of Jamestown Colonists," sec. "Settlers from First Supply."

3. Ancestry.com, "Tracing Your Heritage," sec. "Mayflower Descendants."

By the 1700s, most of the settlements had formed into thirteen distinct British colonies. And, as known, following a series of events, the thirteen colonies would band together to fight and win a war of independence against the British crown. It was a culmination of grave British missteps and brazen heavy-handedness over the years that stirred the colonists to an American Revolution. Principally, these patriots cried out against the colonial government's increasingly heavy taxation without proper representation in British parliament. In April 1775, relatively small skirmishes between British troops and colonial militiamen in both Lexington and Concord (outside Boston, Massachusetts) kicked off the Revolutionary War. (These historic American towns are a short drive from Cambridge, Massachusetts, where my daughter and her husband lived for five years. We were fortunate to visit the important towns.) By the following summer, rebel colonists, at the great risk of treason to the king, were waging a full-scale battle for independence. By virtue of the issuance of the Declaration of Independence, adopted by the Continental Congress on July 4, 1776, the thirteen American colonies severed all political connections to Great Britain. Eventually, the United Kingdom was forced to officially recognize American independence by signing the Treaty of Paris of 1783. A representative of British King George III signed the treaty along with the American delegation of John Adams, Benjamin Franklin, and John Jay.

As you can see, the evidence of English influence on America is obvious and inescapable, from the language we speak to American architecture, literature, education, and even our legal and political systems. Similarities are unavoidable due to our great historical ties. And, although no United States president was born on foreign soil, the first seven American presidents, from George Washington to Andrew Jackson, were born statewide as British citizens. The American colonies had not yet won their independence from the mother country and, as such, remained a part of Great Britain until 1776.

Throughout the years, there's been a mutual and reciprocal imitation and adoption of popular culture between Britain and America. This includes theater (Shakespeare, Keats, Dickens), sports (golf, track, football), intrigue (Sherlock Holmes, Agatha Christie, James Bond), and so on. We are all familiar with English-themed productions such as *Peter Pan*, *My Fair Lady*, *Camelot*, *Mary Poppins*, *Oliver*, *Scrooge*, and *Phantom of the Opera* . . . and shall we include *Hamilton*? The circus was imported to America from Britain, and the American wild west, jazz, motion pictures, and Elvis were exported to Britain. In the 1960s, American rock and roll music was imitated and refined by British groups, resulting in the "British invasion." Of course, there were the Beatles and the Rolling Stones. Also, the Zombies, Herman's

Hermits, the Kinks, the Who, the Hollies, the Dave Clark Five, Petula Clark, Dusty Springfield, the Moody Blues, and so many more. The 1970s brought Led Zeppelin, Queen, David Bowie, Fleetwood Mac, Elton John, and others who helped form the soundtrack of so many American lives. Along with the music came British fashions, e.g., the miniskirt, longer hairstyles, etc. Many well-respected British performers continue to thrive on the American stage and screen. Likewise, British interest in American celebrities and American interest in British celebrities is equally shared. And most everyone remains enamored with Britain's enduring, drama-filled, devoted royal family.

For all these reasons and a lifetime steeped in fascinating British history, I was very excited to visit London on business. Most older Americans fully understand the great importance of our collective allied World War II efforts and feats. America is inescapably intertwined with popular British culture and everyday influences.

I made two visits to London while on business though the first was a mere twenty-four-hour stopover on return from Germany. The second visit was relative to an office relocation, specifically our London-area United Kingdom headquarters. This entailed a new "greenfield" headquarters construction development site west of London in Reading. The relocation provided a unique, albeit expensive, opportunity to design and build a custom new age office complex to meet the ever-changing needs of the business and our six hundred United Kingdom–based employees. Partnering with noted designer Perkins&Will, we set out to enhance work life and create an inspiring and engaging workplace for today and tomorrow. It's vital to create new workplaces to achieve established goals, overcome challenges, and bring values to life. Elements such as people, space, technology, branding, and innovation are all integrated to create a unique overall workplace experience. There's also growing need for increased focus on multigenerational employees, health and wellbeing, ergonomics, sustainability, attraction of top candidates, globalization, connectivity, cyber security, and so on. We would commence three days of meetings with the architects, builders, and Herman Miller furniture manufacturer in London's famed design district. Given the time constraints with my London visits, I had to forgo tours of all the top attractions. Rather, I used any free time to explore the city, mainly on foot, wandering by all the historic sites and enjoying fun activities of a Londoner.

First, a little historical perspective and background on cosmopolitan London, one of the oldest of the world's great cities. London's history dates to the New Stone Age, as there have been settlements and village timbers discovered in the London area. As recent as 2010, foundations to large timbered structures dating to 4800 BC (radiocarbon dated) were found in the river Thames's foreshore. Despite evidence of these scattered settlements, it is considered that London was only founded in the first century by the Romans and spans just two millennia. The Romans named the city Londinium and its medieval boundaries are still maintained. Roman London had a population of approximately sixty thousand residents. The fifth century collapse of the Roman Empire was followed by geopolitical control of the Vikings. London subsequently grew very slowly for centuries. The tumultuous Middle Ages were followed by the Tudor period and the Protestant Reformation, when trade and business accelerated. There was a Great Plague and the Great Fire of London. These were followed by the American Revolution and a prosperous industrial revolution leading to the two European-ground World Wars. The population of London exceeded one million by 1800. The effects of evacuations and bombings during World War II was a somber turning point in London's history. By 1940 Nazi Germany had occupied France, Austria, the Netherlands, and annexed Poland with sights on Britain just across the English Channel. Consequently, beginning September 7, 1940, London was bombed fifty-seven consecutive nights during the German blitz. Over thirty thousand Londoners died, with over fifty thousand injured. Much of London city and over one million British homes and flats were destroyed. America had strongly vowed not to enter another land war in Europe, as the loss of life and cost of World War I were still fresh in memory. Subsequently, only the skilled statesmanship of Prime Minister Winston Churchill, along with the Japanese bombing of Pearl Harbor, convinced President Franklin Roosevelt and the American people that the threat of Nazism on our societies was too great. Following the lead of the Japanese, Germany immediately also declared war on the United States, and America entered the fray. Bolstered by the Americans, despite great death and devastation, the morale of the British people was strengthened. The British were defiant and resolved to "keep calm and carry on." The immense American-British bond was cemented at that time and continues even now.

Today London is an uncharacteristic city defined by many core districts largely rebuilt after World War II. As London originally developed in such a haphazard way, it's more of a collection of villages. Consequently, London neighborhood ties are very strong, though, surprisingly, the London familiar to tourists is a much smaller, concentrated area. For this reason, I found London to be such an interesting and entertaining, walkable city. London is situated in southeast England on the river Thames just fifty miles upstream from the North Sea. Comparable to New York City, London has a present population of nearly nine million people. London is home to many of the highest ranked universities in the world, e.g., the London School of Economics. London is the most visited city in all of Europe. Add to that the world's busiest city airport and the oldest rapid transit system in the world (the London Underground). On this basis and a convenient east-west time zone locale, London serves as one of the world's leading financial capitals. Lastly, London is one of the truly diverse world cities, with cultures encompassing many nationalities and over three hundred spoken languages. Yet somehow London, as known or imagined, maintains its own unique cultural identity.

London is one of four international centers of fashion with all the associated shopping that entails. There are also the exciting West End theaters (thirty-nine in total), which, along with New York City's Broadway, offer the highest-level English-speaking commercial theater. Several surrounding English playhouses date to the sixteenth century and were used by William Shakespeare's company. The Theater Royal Drury Lane (the West End's oldest) was designed by famed architect Christopher Wren and opened in 1663. London has an endless array of well-known landmarks that include Westminster Abbey, the Tower of London, Buckingham Palace, the London Eye, Saint Paul's Cathedral, Piccadilly Circus, Trafalgar Square, Tower Bridge, the British Museum, and more. Given the above, here's a hodgepodge of very random, miscellaneous stories and interesting takes on my limited, greatly enjoyed bleisure time in London.

Heathrow Airport and Paddington Station

It's always exciting to land in a new city for the very first time and to arrive in a world-famous airport such as *London Heathrow*. Heathrow is the busiest European airport, with the world's most international connections. What started in 1929 as a small airfield on Heathrow Farm along Heathrow Lane has been continually expanded since World War II. Each year, nearly eighteen million international passengers pass through London Heathrow. One can almost envision all the famed travelers, from the Beatles to world leaders, who have traveled through Heathrow. I was tired but very excited to board the Heathrow Express (train) to the majestic *Paddington Station* in central London. It's hard to beat the easily accessible, comfortable, fast, and reasonably priced trains from most of Europe's main airports directly into city centers.

London Paddington is one of Britain's best-loved train stations. A temporary Paddington station was first built in 1838 as the grand terminus for the Great Western Railway. The station was lavishly rebuilt in 1850 with wrought iron, glass, and a large three-span roof. The station was brilliantly designed with mindful, anticipated expansion of the railroad over the next fifty years. Paddington was first served by London Underground trains in 1863. The station was built by Isambard Kingdom Brunel. Brunel is considered one of the world's most ingenious and prolific figures in civil engineering history. In addition to the railways, Brunel also built dry docks, bridges, viaducts, underwater tunnels, propeller-driven iron ships, and even transatlantic steamships. Further, at the direct plea of Florence Nightingale (social reformer and founder of modern nursing) to address poor conditions during the Crimean War, Brunel designed and transported needed prefabricated military hospitals. Many of Brunel's projects are still in use today, and he is credited with revolutionizing modern engineering and public transport. Paddington has been further expanded and extensively refurbished throughout the years, though Brunel's original design is still visible. The beautiful landmark train station is filled with history and culture.

I think most everyone is familiar with the friendly, kind-hearted, polite, and spectacled Paddington Bear. The beloved British children's literature classic fictional character was created by Michael Bond and first appeared in October 1958 in *A Bear Called Paddington*. The storyline is that the middle-class Brown family found the bear at the Paddington railway station. The poor bear was sadly sitting on his small suitcase and had an attached note around his neck that read, "Please look after this bear. Thank you."[4] The author said he was prompted to label Paddington based on newsreels of children in trucks evacuating London during World War II (still etched in his memory).[5] Paddington arrived as a stowaway or refugee from Peru. He comically claimed to have traveled by lifeboat and ate marmalade sandwiches. No one understood his given Peruvian name, so the Browns named the bear Paddington after the railway where he was found. The author originally wanted the bear to be from Africa but quickly learned that there were no bears in Africa.[6] Over thirty million copies of Paddington books have been sold worldwide. Paddington Bear has been successfully adapted for television and critically acclaimed films. The loving and kind nature of Paddington made him a favorite of the Queen Mother. In 1994, a Paddington stuffed bear was chosen by the British tunnelers as the first item to pass through to their French counterparts when linking the underwater Channel Tunnel. In 2000, a small bear-shaped bronze statue of the world-renowned Peruvian immigrant was installed in Paddington station and is a welcoming, beloved icon of the city hub.

4. Bond, *Bear Called Paddington*, ch. 1.
5. Midgley, "Paddington Bear."
6. Druckman, "Story of 'Paddington Bear,'" para. 9.

London Black Cabs

From Paddington Station, I boarded one of the stylish and symbolic London black cabs, or hackney carriages, as they are known. Of note is that widespread use of private coaches by English aristocracy began as far back as 1580. Within fifty years, hackney coaches were abundant on the streets of London. Due to the proliferation and pedestrian danger of so many coaches, by the mid 1600s, ordinances and a system for licensing were enacted. Of course, these were horse-drawn carriages, as steam-powered vehicles were not introduced until 1897. Also, not only is the iconic present black cab design famous, but I've learned that the "cabbies" are equally impressive. I was advised that to gain membership into the aptly named Worshipful Company of Hackney Carriage Drivers, every licensed cabbie in London must first pass the Knowledge of London examination. It can take four years to learn the requisite 320 routes through London, including all related points of interest, twenty thousand landmarks, twenty-five thousand street names, and an ordering of theaters. The knowledge test has not changed much since 1865 except for a few newer points of interest. The skill and intelligence of these licensed cabbies certainly make for fascinating, educational, and always entertaining discussion en route.

The Dukes Hotel

I noted earlier that I somewhat research properties and locations in advance of my travels and every now and then find myself in the perfect hotel. This was never truer than in London on my second longer stay. Also, it was only "business travel policy possible" in that the third night was free on a three-night visit. To this day, the *Dukes Hotel* might be one of the coolest places I've stayed while traveling on business. Because I was interested in the nostalgia of old London, the central and dashing St. James's neighborhood proved to be the ideal location for a quick visit. The hotel and surrounding prestigious area offered a glimpse into how I imagined a timeless, bygone London era. The Dukes Hotel defines itself as a quintessential Victorian English retreat in the fashionable heart of London. That it is! The 1908 hotel, with just ninety rooms, sits in a peaceful cobblestone cul-de-sac off St. James's Street. Many of the guests appeared to be regulars, and there was a warm and friendly familiarity throughout my stay. Further, the hotel was considered a favorite royal haunt of Princess Diana and the Queen Mother. It's even rumored that there's a secret tunnel leading from the Dukes Hotel's bar to the nearby St. James's Palace. Interestingly, St. James's Palace was built by order of King Henry VIII in 1536 and was a recent home of then Prince Charles. The Dukes Hotel proved to be an ideal home base near Green Park, close to the exclusive shops of Jermyn Street, and an easy stroll to Buckingham Palace, Hyde Park, Kensington Gardens, and the West End theaters. English charm in droves!

Of important note is the hotel's *Dukes Bar*. The Dukes Bar, famous for their award-winning martinis, was frequented by author and James Bond creator Ian Fleming. And you already know that I am a huge James Bond fan. The bar proclaims to be the birthplace of the famous "shaken, not stirred" line often used by Agent 007 himself. The catchphrase dates to Fleming's 1958 novel *Dr. No* but was first uttered on screen by James Bond (Sean Connery) in the 1964 film *Goldfinger* and numerous films thereafter.

An Unusual Day in London

My first visit to London was merely a one-day Saturday stopover. I arrived late Friday evening from Berlin, Germany, and was to depart for home early Sunday morning. Friday afternoon meetings in Germany meant a weekend return to home in the United States. As mentioned, in the past, airfares were greatly reduced if they included a Saturday night stay. The savings covered any added personal expenses and also saved the company a fair amount. As such, stopovers were not only permitted but encouraged by the booking agency. In any case, this visit did not allow for traditional sightseeing, so I otherwise kept quite busy in London that Saturday! When possible, the best way to truly experience a new city is "feet on the ground" and interactions with the locals (maybe an occasional cab ride). My plan was very aggressive and included an afternoon walk past major concentrated attractions, historic parks, and lively London neighborhoods, followed that evening by Mass (Catholic upbringing), an upscale dinner for one, a very long-running whodunit West End theater production, and finally a visit to a legendary London jazz club for the late show. Crazy, for sure. Back to the hotel by 2:00 a.m. and out by 6:00 a.m. to Paddington Station and back to the airport. Nonetheless, it was manageable given that an approximate seven-hour flight home would provide an ideal sleep opportunity. Here is how I recall that day going!

London Eye

Most probably, the very first attraction you'll notice in London is the Millennium Wheel, better known as the *London Eye*. This is because the London

Eye is a gigantic, 443-foot-high cantilevered observation wheel, or Ferris wheel, perched on London's Thames River opposite the Houses of Parliament. The London Eye is the tallest cantilevered wheel in Europe and, with nearly four million annual visitors, the most popular tourist attraction in Great Britain. The London Eye was designed by the husband-and-wife team of Marks Barfield Architects. Interestingly, the wheel was constructed in sections, which were floated up the Thames River on barges and assembled in the river. The Eye, opened on December 31, 1999, was intended to celebrate the dawn of a new millennium and to serve as a temporary attraction. The wheel features thirty-two oval, air-conditioned, glass pod capsules, which are meant to represent the solidarity between London's thirty-two different boroughs and their inhabitants. Each capsule has a capacity of twenty-five individuals. Capsules are numbered one to thirty-three, excluding number thirteen for superstitious reasons. Passengers are free to walk around the capsules, as they move very slowly; one rotation takes about thirty minutes. The rotation rate is so slow that the capsules do not stop, except for disabled passengers. Passengers merely walk on and off. Theoretically, 1,600 passengers can ride the London Eye each hour, and to date over eighty-five million passengers have safely enjoyed the wheel.[7] The London Eye provides an opportunity for a stunning, unparalleled 360-degree view of London and up to twenty-five miles of surroundings on a clear day. There are captivating views of all the iconic London landmarks, including Big Ben, Saint Paul's Cathedral, Westminster Abbey, the Shard, and even Buckingham Palace. The London Eye is a fun, galvanizing engineering achievement that has become a highly recognizable, world-famous symbol of the modern capital.

Westminster Abbey

Only half kiddingly, a big downside of bleisure travel is the fact that you're visiting a country strictly to work and be productive, and not to be a sightseeing tourist. And I assure you that I never lost focus and always put work first. I worked long, hard hours to ensure my business travel was a success, paying dividends to the company that afforded me travel opportunities—though not having time to tour breathtaking Westminster Abbey, one of the best things to do in London, is certainly regretful. Westminster Abbey is where Britain's kings and queens are crowned, royal weddings occur, and famous folk are buried. Most recently, King Charles III was coronated at Westminster Abbey and, in 2011, it was the site of Prince William and Kate Middleton's royal wedding. Previously, William's grandmother Queen

7. Merlin Entertainments, "London Eye 25th Anniversary."

Elizabeth II married Price Philip here in 1947 and she was coronated in the abbey in 1953. The funerals of both Queen Elizabeth II in 2022 and Princess Diana in 1997 were held in the abbey. Lastly, among the 3,300 people buried in the massive Westminster Abbey are most of the kings and queens of England, Sir Isaac Newton, Sir Laurence Olivier, Stephen Hawking, and Charles Darwin. Geoffrey Chaucer, Charles Dickens, Rudyard Kipling, T. S. Eliot, and more than one hundred poets and writers are buried in the abbey's Poets' Corner.

Westminster Abbey dates to 960 and is the site of England's first abbey, which was home to a community of Benedictine monks. Shortly thereafter, in 1042, Edward the Confessor (my patron saint) grandly rebuilt the abbey as a royal burial church. King Edward was the first to be buried at Westminster Abbey in 1066. Still visible in the abbey is King Edward's chair (the Coronation Chair), which has been used at every coronation since 1308. Today, Westminster Abbey is a renowned Gothic and Romanesque architectural masterpiece, largely rebuilt in the thirteenth and sixteenth centuries. The abbey tower is 225 feet high. The majestic approach to the high altar is the longest in England at 515 feet. Overall, the abbey boasts over thirty-two thousand square feet of floor space.

Westminster Abbey remains a working church with services held daily. In fact, the abbey has been a continuous place of worship since the tenth century. Westminster Abbey is an Anglican church under the Church of England. However, it was once a Catholic church under the authority of Rome. In 1530, Henry VIII seized control of the English monasteries, breaking away to begin the English Reformation. The newer, immediately adjacent Westminster Cathedral, consecrated in 1910, is a Roman Catholic church. It's easy to understand why the over-one-thousand-years-old Westminster Abbey is of great historic and symbolic significance.

Buckingham Palace

The most famous and profound residence in London is undoubtedly the royal *Buckingham Palace*. Of course, I immediately took a short stroll to the palace located in the very heart of London. Considering that the British monarchy has been around for thousands of years, Buckingham Palace is the relatively new home of the royal family. The palace was originally built in 1703 as Buckingham House for a British Earl who later became the Duke of Buckingham. The plot of land was acquired four hundred years earlier by King James I and was meant to serve as a royal mulberry garden. It was sold to the duke in 1698. King George III purchased the house back in 1761 for his wife, Queen Charlotte. Thus, Buckingham House earned the title of the Queen's House. The king reacquired Buckingham House to serve as a comfortable family home located just a quarter mile from St. James's Palace. Fourteen of King George III's fifteen children were born in the Queen's House. The King of England's official residence at that time and for a period of over three hundred years, from 1531 to 1837, was St. James's Palace. The Queen's House went through many renovations over the early years, though it wasn't until the nineteenth century that esteemed architect John Nash transformed the Queen's House into the magnificent Buckingham Palace that it is today. Nash expanded the palace into its large U shape, adding arches, west wing extensions, and north and south branches. That said, if feeling bad about your own personal career direction, note that Mr. Nash's reconstruction efforts greatly exceeded the given budget, and he was consequently fired. It was only in 1837, following the death of then King William IV, that eighteen-year-old Queen Victoria, King William IV's niece, became the first official royal to call Buckingham Palace home. Her father's three older brothers had died without surviving legitimate issue. Queen Victoria's reign lasted over sixty-three years till her death in 1901. Although current King Charles III was born in Buckingham Palace, the monarchy enjoys numerous homes, palaces, and castles that serve as their favored principal residences. Queen Elizabeth II (known as the Queen Mother) preferred staying twenty miles away at Windsor Castle, viewing the palace as her office. Present King Charles III has chosen to remain at Clarence House, where he and Queen Camilla have resided since 2005, and which is just a short walk away from Buckingham Palace.

The Buckingham Palace building is 830,000 square feet in total, with grounds spanning forty acres of beautiful gardens. In total, there are 775 lavishly decorated rooms, forty-two royal and guest bedrooms, 188 staff bedrooms, ninety-two offices, nineteen state rooms, seventy-eight bathrooms, 760 windows, and 1,514 doors! The massive ballroom is the palace's largest room. Over forty thousand light bulbs are used throughout the palace. Over fifty thousand guests are invited to Buckingham Palace annually for receptions, lunches, state banquets, and garden parties. As many as eight thousand guests can attend the garden parties.[8] Additionally, the state rooms are open to the public each year beginning late July through September and on other select dates. During World War II, Buckingham Palace survived nine German bomb attacks, although one bomb destroyed the palace chapel. Footage of war destruction was aired in cinemas throughout the United Kingdom, intended to illustrate that both the rich and poor

8. Thingstodoinlondon.com, "Buckingham Palace Facts."

were greatly suffering. The best-known Buckingham Palace traditional ceremonial pomp, dating back to 1689, is the Changing of the Guard or Guard Mounting. The Royal Guard is easily recognized by their iconic red tunics and eighteen-inch-tall black bearskin hats. The British adopted the bearskin hats from Napoleon's French Imperial Guard, which the Brits defeated in 1815 at the Battle of Waterloo. The French grenadiers wore the bearskin hats to appear taller and more intimidating. The changing of the old guard to new guard occurs at 10:45 a.m. every Monday, Wednesday, Friday, and Sunday. Military bands, playing a mix of both traditional military and popular music, accompany the new royal guards from Wellington Barracks at each ceremony. The guards are strictly volunteers and perform their duty with great honor. Only elite, highly trained British soldiers who have fought with great distinction qualify for the coveted, prestigious guard post position.

Today, the King's official London residence has a very rich history and remains the working royal palace of United Kingdom sovereigns. Accordingly, Buckingham Palace is known and recognized worldwide as the home of the monarch. The shared site of many national and royal celebrations, both rejoiceful and mournful.

Winston Churchill Statue

I came upon a wonderful statue of Sir Winston Churchill. Churchill is readily acknowledged as one of the greatest world leaders in modern history. He was a British statesman, soldier, and writer who twice served as Great Britain's prime minister. Having courageously led Britain against Nazi Germany during World War II, Churchill is widely regarded as one of the most significant figures of the twentieth century. A victorious wartime leader who defended world democracy, Churchill is largely considered the greatest prime minister in British history. Consequently, it's no surprise that a powerful bronze statue of Winston Churchill was erected in London's Parliament Square, the spiritual and political heart of the city. I stumbled upon the sculpture and was struck by the force and global impact of this world leader. The statue recalls equally powerful representations in both Paris and Washington, DC, and, undoubtedly, countless other cities. The Paris statue is located on Avenue Winston Churchill and is one of just a few statues of foreigners in the French capital. Likewise, an American bronze memorial honoring Winston Churchill is located on Embassy Row in Washington, DC. This nine-foot statue stands in front of the embassy of the United Kingdom, with one foot purposely placed on British embassy land and one foot on American land. Its straddling placement was to demonstrate that

Churchill's mother was in fact born in the United States (Brooklyn, New York) and Churchill received honorary American citizenship.

The London statue, designed by Ivor Roberts-Jones, was unveiled in 1973, eight years after Churchill's death in 1965. The Parliament Square main green location, opposite the Palace of Westminster, is the exact spot where, in the 1950s, Churchill supposedly proclaimed, "This is where my statue will go." The statue was unveiled by Churchill's widow, Clementine, while Queen Elizabeth II gave a ceremonial speech. The twelve-foot bronze statue is somewhat grotesque in appearance, with Churchill wearing his recognizable military greatcoat. The pose is of an earlier Churchill photograph of him inspecting parliament's House of Commons after it had been bombed and destroyed in May 1941. The statue sits on an eight-foot-high plinth, making its image all the more ominous and intimidating. The London sculpture is a clear reminder of Churchill's role in saving Britain and the whole of Europe from Nazi Germany.

Nobu London

My first visit to London and sole night (Saturday) would be jam-packed with exciting fun. I had planned some quintessential London experiences, starting with a wonderful dinner. I never mind eating by myself when on travel and chuckle thinking of the French waiter who once commented, "Sometimes no company is better than bad company." If possible and within reason, given meals are a business expense, I would experience a well-known landmark location or *the* exciting new restaurant in town. At the time of my visit, all the buzz was still about *Nobu*! The original Nobu London on Old Park Lane was the very first Nobu opened outside the United States. Today there are fifty-seven Nobu Restaurants (and counting) worldwide, with three in London.

Nobu London, looking out over Old Park Lane and Hyde Park, was a Mayfair heavyweight on London's dining scene and its original celebrity haunt. Home to some of the world's most talented chefs, Nobu serves Japanese cuisine with unique South American Peruvian fusion accents. Fine sake, premium cocktails, and iconic dishes such as yellowtail jalapeno and their famous black cod with miso. My three daughters would be in their glory! Impeccable taste abounds in Nobu, from oak and maple parquet tables to lacquered bowls and bamboo flasks. You don't have to wear Prada, Versace, Louis Vuitton, or Gucci at Nobu, but you'd be well in line with the restaurant's style gurus if you did. Naturally, the first Nobu in Europe was a major attraction for both monied tourists and smartly dressed Londoners.

I found the origin of the Nobu brand equally fascinating. Back in 1987, Nobu Matsuhisa moved to Los Angeles to open the Matsuhisa Restaurant. Nobu had briefly lived in Lima, Peru, where he developed a signature style, melding Japanese cooking with Peruvian ingredients. Fortuitously, famed actor Robert De Niro was an early fan of and regular customer at Matsuhisa. De Niro approached Nobu about opening a restaurant in New York City, though Nobu first declined, choosing to focus on his Los Angeles restaurant. A few years later, De Niro convinced Nobu to join him in creating what became the Nobu Hospitality Group. The initial venture proved wildly successful, expanding to worldwide restaurants and hotels. Nobu experienced such amazing growth that the chain is now valued at over $1 billion.[9] Robert De Niro, an extraordinary actor and savvy businessman with diverse ventures, is now worth an estimated $500 million thanks in part to the ingenious Nobu partnership. The Nobu modern, upscale, trendy atmosphere remains a favorite among celebrities and Japanese cuisine loving foodies. My experience at Nobu London proved special so, to plan, I was off to London's West End theater district next.

The Mousetrap

Over the years, I've learned that it's relatively easy to purchase a *single* seat theater ticket and that they are often available at the same day, half-price TKTS booth. In this fashion, I was excited to snag a great seat to *The Mousetrap*. *The Mousetrap* is the most successful and longest running show of any kind in the world![10] Agatha Christie's murder mystery play first opened in 1952 in London's West End at the Ambassadors Theatre. The play moved to the landmark St. Martin's Theatre in 1974, where it is still running to this day. For over seventy years, notwithstanding a temporary COVID-19 pandemic pause, *The Mousetrap* has continuously run. The performance count recently surpassed thirty thousand shows, with over ten million people having seen the London play.[11] A unique photo opportunity is available in the St. Martin's Theatre foyer beside a wooden counter indicating that night's running performance number. The long-standing "whodunit" play is set in post-war England in what was originally modern-day 1952. The plot entails the spreading news of a gruesome murder in London as seven complete strangers find themselves snowed in and unable to leave a remote countryside guesthouse. To the strangers' horror, a local police sergeant arrives at

9. Donnelly, "$1.3 Billion Secret."
10. Spectrum News, "Mousetrap."
11. Wikipedia, "Mousetrap."

the guesthouse only to reveal that the London killer is in their midst! One by one, the sordid past of each suspicious guest is revealed as theatergoers try to figure out the identity of the murderer. The play's charm is in the twist ending, which audiences have long been traditionally requested not to reveal after leaving the theater so that the end of the play is not spoiled for future audiences. Over the seventy-plus years, nearly five hundred actors and actresses have played the eight cast-member roles—though best-selling novelist Agatha Christie's enduring story remains the play's real star.

A highly unusual aspect of *The Mousetrap* is that, by contract terms of the 1950s play, production of the play outside the West End is limited, and no film adaptation of the play can be produced until London's West End production has been closed for at least six months. I can't help but think of (though also admire) the great opportunity loss to Matthew Pritchard. He is the only grandchild of Agatha Christie and inherited the rights to the play as a birthday present. That said, for the very first time in a limited engagement, it appears there is a serious effort to finally bring the murder mystery to Broadway and American audiences. The apparent plan is to give the 1952 production new life with a loving, authentic recreation. Broadway plans to borrow pieces of the original London set, e.g., mantelpiece clock and wind machine, to regenerate original performance sights and sounds. It has not materialized just yet. As expected, the London theater experience was fun and memorable. Now it was time to hear some fantastic, late night jazz music.

Ronnie Scott's Jazz Club

I've always enjoyed live jazz music, not as a hard-core jazz aficionado, but enough to seek out world-famous jazz clubs when traveling. For this reason, not even knowing who was performing, I was determined to visit *Ronnie Scott's Jazz Club* in Soho, London. The club was everything a premier jazz venue should be. It was dark, noisy, crowded, strangely romantic, and brimming with energy. People are happy and excited to be in a jazz club having a fun time. More so, Ronnie Scott's is regarded as one of the most influential jazz destinations in the world. Since opening in 1959 the legendary basement club has hosted many famous artists, including Ella Fitzgerald, Chet Baker, Nina Simone, Stan Getz, Sarah Vaughn, George Benson, Van Morrison, and Prince, to name a few. Jimi Hendrix's last public appearance was at Ronnie Scott's in 1970. Owner Ronnie Scott himself, with his repertoire of jokes and one-liners, acted as the club's master of ceremonies until his death in 1996. Many albums were recorded live at Ronnie Scott's under their own label, established in 1978. And musicians and patrons alike often claim Ronnie Scott's gigs are the best of their lives.

I had stopped by Ronnie Scott's earlier in the day to grab a ticket to the late show after the theater. Little did I know it doesn't work that way, with most jazz shows sold out weeks in advance. This explained why no tickets were available online. However, after some pleading and skillful negotiation, I was able to purchase a ticket to the late show. That night's act was an eighty-two-year-old American jazz vocalist known as Little Jimmy Scott. Scott was known for his high natural voice and as a crooner of beautiful ballads and love songs. He was from Cleveland, Ohio, and he passed away a few years after I saw him perform. I learned that Jimmy Scott suffered from a rare genetic disorder that limited his height to barely five feet and prevented him from reaching classic puberty. The result was a uniquely high voice and unusual timbre, which made him a verified jazz legend. I learned that Jimmy Scott was the third of ten children and at age thirteen was orphaned when his mother was hit and killed by a drunk driver. Jimmy overcame many obstacles, turned to music, and by his early twenties had risen to prominence as a big band lead singer. A series of successful jazz albums followed until the late 1960s, when his career faded. Consequently, Jimmy Scott returned to Cleveland and worked as a hospital orderly, shipping clerk, and elevator operator. Inexplicably, twenty years later, Jimmy Scott returned to music with a vengeance. He was again winning awards, gaining Grammy nominations, providing backdrops for various television shows, and teaming with numerous current artists who recognized Scott's greatness. He subsequently recorded music until his death in 2014. So separated were Jimmy Scott's two jazz runs that he performed at both the inaugurations of President Eisenhower (1953) and President Clinton (1993). On each honored occasion, Scott sang "Why Was I Born."[12]

That night at Ronnie Scott's, it wasn't very long before I realized that listening to Little Jimmy Scott was different from listening to any other singer. His high pitch voice carried incredible emotion coming from deep within his heart. His tunes of romantic love and broken hearts soared. Singer and actor Ruth Brown noted that jazz clubs in the 1940s were largely packed with pimps, hookers, rough guys, tough gals, and all kinds of criminals. But when Little Jimmy Scott began singing, Ms. Brown claimed that tears would run down the cheeks of cold-blooded killers.[13] That special night I was at Ronnie Scott's Jazz Club, the fading jazz great sang such classics as "All of Me," "Embraceable You," "Pennies From Heaven," and "Someone to

12. Wikipedia, "Jimmy Scott."

13. Jeske, "Q&A."

Watch Over Me" and concluded with a heartbreaking rendition of "Over the Rainbow." It was a thrill to visit the legendary jazz venue but an honor to surprisingly experience an original jazz great.

The second visit to London afforded me just an occasional opportunity to stroll the Mayfair and St. James's neighborhoods that surrounded the Dukes Hotel. I did get to return to the West End and enjoyed some excellent dinners though mostly I walked through the district and surrounding London parks. Here are just a few slightly offbeat, personal observations.

Beau Brummell

Beau Brummell is a funny moniker. I never knew much about Mr. Brummell till one day walking through London and its perennially fashionable historic St. James's neighborhood. The aristocratic high-end design district has been London's premier fashion stop since the days of King Henry VIII. In fact, many exclusive storefront windows are discreetly adorned with a Royal Warrant indicating that the Royal Family patronizes that elegant, long-standing shop. Suddenly, right there on Jermyn Street at the Piccadilly Arcade entrance, in all its splendor, is a statue of none other than Beau Brummell. I had only heard of Beau Brummell from my father, who would call me that as I dressed up for dates while still living at home. I never bothered to ask my father who Beau Brummell was. It was pre-Google so I merely went about my day. I also discovered that there was a 1960s American band hailing from San Francisco that called themselves the Beau Brummels (one *l* only). They had several hit songs, e.g., "Just a Little," "Laugh, Laugh," etc., that I had heard on the oldies radio stations. Not another thought of old Beau crossed my mind until that day strolling London town . . . and I immediately laughed thinking about my father.

In popular culture, George "Beau" Brummell (1778–1840) was known as a famed "English dandy" and a leader of men's fashion. He was both fashionable and witty and enjoyed a friendship serving as a close confidant to the opulent Prince of Wales who would become King George IV. At first regarded as one of England's most refined gentlemen, Beau Brummell enjoyed a place in high society. He was a recognized "fashionista" and a frequenter of all London's social gatherings and events. What he lacked in class and money he made up for in great style and a personality never before seen. Unfortunately, his five-hour grooming regimen along with excessive gambling, unchecked fashion extravagance, and an overall lavish lifestyle eventually exhausted his own small fortune along with the generous support of others wildly under his influence. Eventually, to avoid creditors, Beau Brummell fled to France, was briefly imprisoned for debt, completely abandoned his personal appearance, suffered physically, and died forgotten and penniless in a charitable asylum.

Reflecting on the bright side, Beau Brummell is largely credited with revolutionizing men's fashion of the day and even invented today's modern look of a suit worn with a necktie. He ushered in the wearing of finely fitted, well-tailored garments and essentially invented the modern trousers. Consequently, Beau Brummell's then-unique style and contributions to men's fashion are still very relevant today. More so, his timeless style and approach to fashion is said to have led to men bathing and shaving daily and wearing fragrances to accentuate their appeal. Naturally, such practices were greatly welcomed and quickly spread across England and throughout Europe.[14] Who knew? Looking back, I'm guessing my dad either thought I looked pretty good or, much more likely, was lovingly razzing me on the lengthy time I took getting ready for my dates. All this only came to light as I stumbled upon London's Beau Brummell statue. Ironically, a plaque on the statue's base is inscribed in Beau Brummell's own words and simply reads, "to be truly elegant, one should not be noticed."

Floris

A short distance from the Beau Brummell statue is *Floris* on 89 Jermyn Street. My introduction to Floris began upon check-in at the Dukes Hotel. Permeating the quaint hotel lobby and expanding throughout the hotel was the sweet smell of spring flowers. I discovered that the beautiful scent was not from a floral bouquet but rather a single hyacinth and bluebell scented candle that burned on the check-in desk. The receptionist advised that the candle was from a nearby historic and quite famous long-standing perfume shop. I decided to visit Floris and purchase a candle as a memento and a special gift for my family.

The history of Floris captures the full flavor of the elegant business quarter of London's swanky St. James's neighborhood. The store is not so different from many of the other surrounding shops selling jewelry, art, antiques, clothing, cigars, or chocolates, some of which date to the 1500s. In 1730, Juan Famenias Floris and his wife Elizabeth opened a shop selling

14. Suit Century, "Beau Brummell's Revolution"; Wikipedia, "Beau Brummell."

perfumes, combs, and shaving products. Mr. Floris arrived in London from the Mediterranean Spanish island of Menorca. He missed the aromas and sensations of his youth. That shop, still run by descendants of Mr. Floris, remains very much in business today. Further, Floris's illustrious and fascinating history is highlighted by its many famous stories and patrons. First is a preserved letter from son Robert Floris to his parents in London outlining his efforts to source ingredients from abroad. The letter is "cross-written"—the practice of taking a written page, giving it a quarter turn, and writing vertically along the margin—a popular means to reduce the high cost of paper and postage in the eighteenth century. By 1820, Floris received a Royal Warrant from King George IV. In addition to perfumes, Floris skillfully made smooth-pointed combs, toothbrushes, and mouthwashes. These products were well-known and highly valued by Floris's ever-growing elite clientele. Of course, even the aforementioned Beau Brummell visited the shop; naturally, he would discuss current fragrances at length with Mr. Floris. In 1852, London hosted the world-famous Great Exhibition in nearby Hyde Park. Exquisite Spanish cabinets and glasswork from the exhibition were purchased by Floris and remain in the shop today.[15] In 1863, Florence Nightingale, having just returned from the Crimean War and busy establishing a hospital training school for nurses, sent a letter addressed to Mr. Floris. This treasured letter thanked him for the "beautiful sweet-smelling nosegays"[16] and remains on display at the shop. Additionally, there is a receipted invoice from December 1934 for two fragrances purchased by Winston Churchill. Both fragrances remain available today in the Floris Signature Collection. Not to be missed is Ian Fleming (James Bond creator) who was a regular customer of Floris. Floris No. 89 Eau de Toilette was a favorite of Ian Fleming and was featured in his 1955 novel *Moonraker* (subsequently the eleventh James Bond movie). By the 1950s, Floris products were increasingly exported to the United States, where they rapidly grew in popularity. A December 1959 receipt includes the purchase of Rose Geranium made for and delivered to none other than Marilyn Monroe Miller at the Beverly Hills Hotel. By 1989, due to increasing demand, Floris opened a shop in Devon, southwest England. The shop was officially and ceremoniously opened by Her Royal Highness Princess Diana. More recently, Floris celebrated Queen Elizabeth's 2013 diamond jubilee with the launch of Royal Arms Diamond Edition. The Royal Arms scent was originally created in 1926 to celebrate the Queen's birth. So historical and interesting is Floris London that a back-shop museum space was created during a 2017 restoration. On

15. For these and other details on Floris history, see Floris London, "Our History."

16. Floris London, "Our History," sec. "Florence Nightingale."

display is a collection of many Floris archive items, including century-old customer ledgers with corresponding rerelease of eight fragrances. Today, this oldest English retailer of fragrances and toiletries remains owned and operated by eighth- and ninth-generation members of the Floris family.

Kensington Garden (Peter Pan)

London is home to the most famous natural urban parks in the world. There's Hyde Park, Green Park, St. James's, Kensington Gardens, and more. In fact, there are eight royal parks throughout the city and an estimated three thousand green and blue spaces in total.[17] London's many parks provide an invaluable year-round retreat for those who live and work in the city as well as visitors. Beyond a quiet retreat or picnic, the parks provide countless activities, including open-air cafés, a zoo, playgrounds, horseback riding, boating, cycling, swimming, tennis, and nonstop open-air concerts and festivals. There's even an occasional soapbox for public opinions. It's hard to believe these beautiful parks are in the very heart of London, within walking distance of Buckingham Palace. The London parks, waterways, gardens, and wildlife habitats are abundant and enjoyed by millions annually, so much so that in 2019 London was declared the world's first "National Park City." The goal is that over 50 percent of the city will be green by 2050.[18]

I walked through the surrounding area and came upon *Kensington Gardens*. It is understood that the park and gardens were once the private playground of English nobility. The park was conceived by Queen Caroline in the eighteenth century and was originally part of Kensington Palace. No longer exclusive, the extraordinary park is open to everyone today. The park is filled with tree-lined avenues, blossoming flower walks, and numerous world-famous landmarks. Its beauty has welcomed generations of writers and artists. Kensington Gardens includes the Diana Memorial Playground. Most notably, the park is home to a very famous fictional resident. Specifically, down by the park's Long Water, keeping company with the swans and ducks, is a statue of Peter Pan. It was exciting to see the Peter Pan statue at the exact location where the iconic, imaginative story was conceived a hundred years earlier. The 1912-unveiled bronze sculpture was commissioned by Peter Pan's author, J. M. Barrie, himself. Its location in Kensington Gardens is very close to local resident Barrie's former home. The Peter Pan story was largely inspired by Barrie's frequent garden walks. The statue is at the exact spot where Peter Pan lands after flying out of the nursery in

17. London City Hall, "Parks and Green Spaces."
18. National Park City Foundation, "London National Park City," sec. "World First."

Barrie's 1902 book *The Little White Bird.* The fourteen-foot statue itself is cone shape, topped by a flute-playing Peter Pan about the size of an eight-year-old. Below Peter Pan, the statue is adorned with various small figures, including squirrels, rabbits, mice, and winged fairies. A plaque was added in 1997 that merely and accurately reads, "Peter Pan, the boy who would not grow up."

My two short bleisure visits to London were more business than leisure, leaving no time for any formal sightseeing tours of its many world-famous, richly historic attractions. Someday there may be a better opportunity to tour Westminster Abbey, Big Ben, Parliament, Buckingham Palace, Saint Paul's Cathedral, and the Tower of London (Crown Jewels). You can also visit the Churchill War Rooms bunker, 10 Downing Street, Borough Market, and the Shard. Further afield from the city is Stonehenge, Windsor Castle, Bath, the Cliffs of Dover, Canterbury, Oxford, Stratford-upon-Avon, and even Downton Abbey Village. On the other hand, the mere opportunity to simply stroll the streets and parks of old London town gave me a great understanding of this once embattled city and the resilient strength of Londoners. I greatly enjoyed visiting this fun, enduring capital.

CHAPTER 8

STOCKHOLM

Stockholm is unique in that it's built on islands and surrounded by water, so you get this enormous sense of freedom.

—*Björn Ulvaeus (ABBA)*

Prior to visiting Stockholm, what ridiculously came to my American mind was the fictional character *Pippi Longstocking* (loved by my daughters), IKEA furniture, Swedish meatballs, the Noble Prize, red Swedish Fish candy, reindeer, hockey, and, of course, the band ABBA. *Mamma mia!* However, what I discovered was an extensive Baltic Sea archipelago with a bustling old medieval town of shops and bistros, cobblestoned streets, ochre-colored buildings, many museums, and a fascinating history. A vibrant, intellectual, whimsical, fun global city . . . even in mostly dark wintertime! And who knew that Stockholm is comprised of fourteen interconnected small islands or islets? It's regarded as the best of sophisticated urban living with contrasting lush green forests and countess crystal-clear lakes.

Many of my later business trips pertained to supporting international office relocations or new construction. I had responsibility for a significant category of contracts classified as "Global Office and Mobility." Bear in mind that we were a worldwide healthcare enterprise with over three thousand buildings in nearly 1,200 sites throughout 102 countries. I know this, as I analyzed and helped develop a global strategy to assist in certain aspects of office renovations and relocations. The strategy involved a great deal of planning, teamwork, high-level cooperation, internal cross-collaboration, extensive follow, and partnership with key supply partners. Engaging groups such as real estate, legal, facilities, engineering, operations, etc. was vital to business continuity, cost management, and overall success. Additionally, impacted employees were always engaged for transparency and to ascertain specific cultural needs and preferences. Consideration of safety, ergonomics, and overall work-life balance was paramount. Clear and concise branding guidelines were essential as well. Lastly, the process was highly dependent on major architect design groups, numerous contractors, and world-class office furniture manufacturers. This was the case in Stockholm, where over two hundred employees needed to be relocated. A wonderful colleague from the neighboring Copenhagen, Denmark, site assisted and would remain on the project as "feet on the ground" through completion.

In pursuit of expanding scientific innovation, a trend was started where we had opened dedicated "innovation hubs" in key cities to leverage major thinktank universities and progressive, intellectual communities at large. This was the case in Cambridge, Massachusetts (Massachusetts Institute of Technology), in California (Stanford and University of California), and in Shanghai, China. Stockholm was to be a hybrid of this approach wherein the existing working office would merely be relocated to the university district. With over thirty thousand students and many doctoral programs, outstanding Stockholm University is one of the largest in Scandinavia. Further, the university's mission promotes research anchored in community involvement and society at large. Office relocation to the beautiful, energetic, vibrant Stockholm University district seemed to make perfect sense. Additionally, the move would provide an opportunity to create a new state-of-the-art office and leverage leading Scandinavian designs. My visit to Stockholm was in December, with a deadline to complete the relocation by the following June. As with many European cities, December is often a fun, festive time of the year to visit! I spent just a few busy days in Stockholm but had the entire first day (landing at six o'clock in the morning) to explore the city. I was aware that daylight would be limited, as sunrise is late and the sun sets in early afternoon throughout Stockholm's winter months. With that in mind, despite considerable jet lag, I set out for a fun day in Stockholm!

Sweden is an extremely unique northerly nation. Sweden was the land of frozen seas giving way to reindeer herders, the midnight sun, and of course fearsome Vikings. Over the last hundred thousand years, Sweden was mostly entirely encased in ice. It wasn't till 12,000 BC that the ice finally retreated north. Not sure how this is known? By 6500 BC, new land was discovered and Germanic nomad herdsmen moved into Sweden's region. Contact with the outside world remained very limited until tribal links with the Roman Empire slowly grew six thousand years later. Subsequently, trade with Rome flourished until the fall of that empire. This led to the Vikings taking the world by storm from the ninth till the mid-eleventh century (when Christianity finally reached Sweden). The Vikings raided and plundered throughout Europe to Bagdad in Asia and even America. As you probably imagine, the Vikings were wild and strong barbarians, highly skilled shipbuilders, and experienced sailors with ample weapons and fleets. However, the Vikings were also skilled craftsmen, farmers, fishermen, and savvy traders. Post–Viking era, many prominent families battled for power and control over the area and kingdom now known as Sweden. By the seventeenth century, though continuously steeped in war with regions south, Sweden was the recognized power of northern Europe. Sweden enjoyed an approximate hundred-year Age of Greatness. Significant changes were rampant and impactful, particularly throughout the twentieth century. Sweden, with an estimated population of just over ten million residents, now enters its third millennium with increased globalization and international visibility. The actual age of Sweden, unified in the twelfth century, remains largely unknown. Today, Sweden is regarded as both one of the cleanest and safest countries in the world.[1]

Stockholm is the capital and most populous city in Sweden, with over two million people living in the city and surrounding urban area. The historic though modern and dynamic city was founded in 1252. Despite its thirteenth-century founding, there is evidence that people have lived in the area for thousands of years since the Stone Age. Small farms and villages formed on the rocky island over time. Stockholm means "log island" in Swedish and is based on folklore that early inhabitants reportedly hid gold in a hollowed-out log that floated to the Stockholm islands. Defensive walls were built to protect homes. As such, Stockholm's island location provided numerous advantages as both a stronghold easily defensible against armed gangs and as an ideal locale for trade to and from the Baltic Sea.

Stockholm is situated on Sweden's east coast and consists of fourteen lush islands contiguous with the Stockholm archipelago, a grouping of over thirty thousand small islands that extend nearly fifty miles east. Many of the islands are tiny uninhabited islets, whereas others serve as beautiful, bustling, well-visited holiday resorts. It's no wonder that Stockholm is often referred to as beauty on water! Easily seen is that 30 percent of the city is comprised of waterways with over fifty connecting bridges. To an extent, Stockholm reminded me somewhat of my hometown of Pittsburgh, which is located at the confluence of three rivers. However, between the rivers and steep hillsides, there are 446 known bridges in Pittsburgh! This total

1. For more about the details in this section, see Wikipedia, "History of Sweden"; www.sweden.se (the official site of Sweden).

now surpasses Venice as the most of any city in the world. Despite its high northerly latitude, Stockholm's weather is relatively mild and very similar to the northeast United States. They enjoy all four seasons, though daylight varies from eighteen hours (summer) to just six hours (winter). Additionally, because of its high altitude, on occasion the dynamic flickering aurora borealis, or brilliant northern lights display, is visible in Stockholm.

As I prefer to do, I quickly settled into my hotel in the enchanting Old Town center, referred to as Gamla Stan. Even in the dead of winter the capital city immediately reflected a very calm, inviting, and charming persona. The concierge assured me that Stockholm had plenty to offer visitors on just such a day, including an incredible array of varying world-class museums. Given that it was a cool and cloudy winter day, I was specifically advised to visit the popular nearby "museum island" of Djurgården with its forest-filled Royal National City Park. I was reassured that there was something for everyone in Djurgården. They were not kidding! Djurgården is the city's biggest draw, and for good reason. On my first and only free day in Stockholm, I decided that I'd be best served simply strolling Gamla Stan and visiting Djurgården via a short ferry ride from the quaint Old Town dock.

Gamla Stan (Old Town)

Seeking a special atmosphere of a charming bygone area with historical heritage, venture no further than Stockholm's Old Town, better known as Gamla Stan. Island-based Gamla Stan is compactly situated on three of Stockholm's fourteen islets (though barely a half-mile wide). Old Town is the very nucleus of Stockholm, with original narrow, meandering cobblestoned thoroughfares and buildings dating back to the Middle Ages. Gamla Stan remains one of the world's best-preserved medieval city centers, having been spared bombing during World War II. The back streets and iconic, picture-perfect mustard-color painted buildings themselves are Gamla Stan's main attraction. It's a fantastic place for strolling, exploring, and taking in the views of the surrounding waterways. Gamla Stan is Stockholm's foremost attraction. The bustling streets of Gamla Stan are filled with ancient shops, antiques, cafés, beer halls, bookstores, toy stores, and souvenir shops (lots of moose memorabilia). There are also elegant palaces, churches, and museums all within close walking proximity. Gamla Stan is both historic as well as modern and cool. Most notably, Gamla Stan is home to the Stockholm Palace and Stockholm Cathedral as well as palaces housing the stock exchange, the supreme court, the House of Nobility, and the Nobel Museum. Per the 1895 last will and testament of Alfred Nobel, each year five separate

Nobel prizes are awarded. The awardees are deemed those who (in the past year) conferred the greatest benefits to mankind. Alfred Nobel himself was a Swedish chemist who famously invented dynamite. The peace prize, which advances fellowship, is awarded in Oslo, Norway, while all other Nobel prizes are awarded annually in Stockholm. I was able to pass and see all these sites while strolling through Gamla Stan. I also oddly encountered the then-president of Italy who was visiting Stockholm on that day. Unlike the presidential motorcade in the United States, his small motorcade processed past me on several occasions with very little fanfare. The star of Stockholm's buildings is the baroque Royal Palace. The palace is reminiscent of London's Buckingham Palace with a changing of the guard (in Summer), a blaring military band, and horse parades. It is the biggest palace in the world (over six hundred rooms) still used by a head of state. King Carl XVI Gustaf and Queen Silvia have ruled Sweden for over forty years now (though they have no political power) and reside in the Royal Palace.

Although Gamla Stan is quite touristy, that hardly diminishes its unquestionable charm and rich cultural history. I only wish I had more time to properly explore and get lost in Stockholm's charming Old Town! One day is probably insufficient to visit Stockholm. However, a visit to Gamla Stan along with a ferry ride to nearby Djurgården can provide a great glimpse into the city's heartbeat, history, and beauty.

Djurgården

No visit to Stockholm, even in chilly December, would be complete without taking to its waterways. No doubt the experience in summer months under a midnight sun would be greatly enhanced. Nonetheless, it's always thrilling and adventurous to board a ferry to another time and place. It was with an open mind and little advanced knowledge that I boarded the ferry from Old Town's central quay. The ferry to Djurgården departs every fifteen minutes, and for a low round-ticket fare you arrive in just ten minutes. It's also a beautiful trip through the harbor with Stockholm cityscape views. I had just a few hours to explore Djurgården before a business dinner but was so glad to have made the trip.

The ferry ride validated that in Stockholm you don't need to leave the city to enjoy the famous Swedish countryside. Djurgården is conveniently situated in the city center next to Stockholm's Old Town. The eclectic, tranquil green island oasis can also be reached via car or even by foot via connecting bridges. It's a unique designated cultural-recreational area that has been royal property for centuries. As such, Djurgården is a treasure trove of many of Stockholm's top activities and attractions, including a timeless amusement park, royal parks and gardens, an aquarium, and numerous popular museums. Many Stockholmers go to Djurgården merely to relax in the forests and meadows of the Royal National City Park. However, the biggest draw to Djurgården is the island's incredible world-class museums. So off I went to explore Stockholm's most popular island of Djurgården.

Gröna Lund Amusement Park

To my surprise, as we neared Djurgården via the ferry, an old-fashioned, postcard-ready, pocket-sized *Gröna Lund Amusement Park* came into view. The park was closed for the winter, though the ferry docked at the park's waterfront entrance terminal. I immediately knew that Djurgården was someplace special and that I was in for a fun and interesting afternoon in Stockholm. I learned that the small amusement park (just ten acres with thirty attractions) opened in 1883. The odd thing about the famed park is that it was built to accommodate the existing nineteenth century residential and commercial buildings already in place. It's these old structures that create a nostalgic, turn-of-the-century appearance. In addition to common amusement rides, the park has three entertainment venues that feature serious pop and rock concerts. In 1980, Bob Marley attracted a record thirty-two thousand people (necessary park restrictions followed). ABBA and Deep Purple performed at Gröna Lund, and more recently Sting and Dua Lipa performed in the park. I passed through the fascinating miniature park, imagined it on a warm summer night, and headed down the road in search of the ABBA Museum.

ABBA: The Museum

I am not particularly a huge fan of the Swedish pop supergroup but thought it would be fun to hear the story of Sweden's greatest musical export. And honestly . . . who doesn't like ABBA just a little bit? So, I headed to *ABBA: The Museum*. Most everyone knows ABBA's many hit songs, including "Waterloo," "Dancing Queen," "Fernando," "Take A Chance On Me," "S.O.S.," "The Winner Takes It All," etc. Undoubtedly, international phenomenon ABBA is one of the most successful musical groups and best-selling music acts of all time. They routinely topped the music charts from 1974 through 1982 and their music lives on and on. ABBA has an estimated 350 million worldwide record sales. If you're wondering, the group's name is merely an acronym of their four first names: Agnetha (my favorite, who shares my birthday), Björn, Benny, and Anni-Frid. And talk about a rebirth! In 1999, ABBA's music was adapted into *Mamma Mia!*, a stage musical that continues to tour worldwide. Having ended in 2015, it remains a Broadway top ten longest-running production. Two successful Hollywood films of the same name and story followed in 2008 and 2018, with a third in development. The *Mamma Mia* movie is regarded as the most successful movie musical ever produced, and more than seventy million people have seen the stage production.[2] The movie greatly propelled renewed, increased global fame for ABBA. Among their many international career awards, ABBA was formally inducted into the Rock and Roll Hall of Fame in 2010. It's no wonder there was an entire well-warranted museum dedicated to ABBA in 2013 that is still going strong. ABBA is Sweden's, and one of the world's, greatest and most iconic musical groups.

The ABBA Museum is a quirky, fun, out-of-the-ordinary experience. It's different than anything I've ever seen . . . and I've been to Elvis's Graceland in Memphis and Pittsburgh's own Andy Warhol Museum! To start, the foot-stomping museum is connected to a boutique *Pop House Hotel*. Then there's a piano installation that is rigged to play only when ABBA band member Benny Andersson is literally tickling his own piano keys real-time from his home! There's also many of the band's original flamboyant costumes, their history-laden instruments, gold records, concert footage, interviews, and all kinds of paraphernalia. Add to that an actual helicopter from ABBA's 1974 album cover, a replica of the band's recording studio, and plenty of *Mamma Mia* movie insights. In essence, the museum chronicles the incredible career of the homegrown ABBA band members and has the full backing of the famous group. It even includes their narration as well as revolving private collection materials. If that's not enough, the museum's extensive interactive activities are the best. You can sing and dance with ABBA holograms and have their digital glam-rock costumes projected on you in a video recording. You can also sing and record your own ABBA karaoke. And for those seeking social media photo opportunities, there are plenty of those. At the quirky ABBA Museum, the legendary group lives on . . . and rightfully so. It's a fun experience for all ABBA or music lovers with an hour or two to spare. In addition, you can't help but feel and understand how giddy and appreciative the young ABBA band members must have been with their surprising, extraordinary, far-reaching fame. Be forewarned that at the ABBA Museum, as their saying goes, you'll "walk in," but you'll "dance out"![3]

2. Laeger, "Did You Know?"
3. See www.abbathemuseum.com.

Skansen

After a short five-minute walk from the ABBA Museum through beautiful royal Djurgården islet, I arrived at the *Skansen* (meaning open-air museum). Skansen, founded in 1891, is the world's first open-air museum. It's a favorite to both locals and visitors and, no doubt, a perfect family outing. The Skansen plays a vital role in nurturing Sweden's traditions. Here within Skansen you can stroll through centuries of Swedish history and experience over 150 dismantled and reassembled historical buildings, farms, and dwellings. The structures are from all landscapes and accurately arranged from north to south in geographical order. It's like time traveling, as you also meet many Swedish characters in period dress and personality. Skansen is also home to the Stockholm zoo, with many domestic and wild native Nordic animals including livestock, elk, reindeer, bears, moose, lynxes, and wolverines, along with a corresponding educational children's petting zoo and indoor aquariums. Skansen also holds a Christmas market and celebrates midsummer in high style with decorations and traditional Swedish folk dancing. There's also a quaint historical district with numerous workshops, including glassblowing, weaving, pottery, bookbinding, and handicrafts. Lastly, there are numerous cafés and restaurants that provide great views of downtown Stockholm in the near distance.

A visit to Skansen could easily be an all-day, fun-filled, educational event depending on plans and interests. My time was limited so my visit entailed only a brief walkthrough. I wished I had an added day to visit Skansen, though admittedly I was anxious to get to my next and final stop of the afternoon, the Vasa Museum. As always, bleisure is "business before leisure," and it was necessary to return for a kickoff business meeting/dinner with a few busy days to follow.

Vasa Museum

On August 10, 1628, on its "maiden voyage" from the southern tip of Djurgården, the Swedish warship *Vasa* capsized and sank in the Stockholm harbor. The ship, which was to be the pride of the powerful Swedish Empire navy, traveled for mere minutes just over one hundred yards before sinking nearly intact with sailors onboard. Some meanly joke that even the *Titanic* had more time at sea. It was not until 1956 that a marine archeologist's relentless search resulted in the discovery and recovery of the *Vasa*. A complex operation to salvage the wrecked warship was commenced, including a two-year period to clear space beneath the hull for cables followed by sixteen stages to raise the ship to shallow waters. Finally, on May 4, 1961, after 333 years on the sea floor, the magnificent *Vasa* was successfully towed into dry dock. This was followed by an exhaustive seventeen-year *Vasa* conservation program. Today, less than a nautical mile from the disastrous maiden voyage, the world's best preserved seventeenth-century battleship is housed in the world-renowned *Vasa Museum*. Opened in 1990, the iconic Vasa Museum is one of Scandinavia's most popular and visited attractions.

Thanks to Stockholm's slightly saline, brackish waters, the ill-fated *Vasa* was remarkably preserved even after three hundred years submerged at the bottom of the sea. Add to that the ensuing conservation effort, and *Vasa* astonishingly claims 99 percent originality. Sweden's King Gustavus Adolphus, known as the Lion of the North, commissioned the impressive ship for the ongoing religious Thirty Years' War. In homage to the king, the ship was ornately decorated in carved wood sculptures. With its bronze cannons, *Vasa* was the most powerfully armed vessel in the world. The ship was an expansive 226 feet long and 172 feet in height. It was believed to be unstable due to excessive weight in the upper hull structure. In essence, the center of gravity was too high. The crew on the maiden voyage consisted of approximately 145 sailors and guests. An additional three hundred soldiers were scheduled to board further out in the archipelago. It is documented that thirty crew members died that day. During the 1961 recovery, the remains of seventeen passengers were found.[4] Other items located included sails, weapons, tools, coins, clothing, food, drinks, and cutlery. The ship and artifacts provided invaluable insights into seventeenth-century shipbuilding and naval warfare. Efforts are ongoing today as to how best preserve the *Vasa* into the future.

By 1981, the Swedish government determined that a *Vasa* museum was needed, and a design competition ensued. By 1987, the *Vasa* was towed into a flooded dry dock under a new, only partially constructed building. The beautiful building is dominated by a massive copper roof and stylish masts, which represent the full height of the *Vasa*. The *Vasa Museum* is one of several maritime museums in Stockholm. The mind-blowing sight within is the magnificent sixty-four-gun *Vasa* warship itself, the centerpiece of the museum. The enormous ship can be closely observed from six different levels via panoramic viewing platforms from the keel (underneath) to the stern castle. What was most striking was the elaborate decorative Renaissance-inspired features of the warship. The ship is ornately decorated with over two hundred carved ornaments and five hundred sculpted wooden figures. I learned that this was to glorify the authority and military power of the

4. Vasa Museum, "Skeletons from Vasa."

ruling Swedish monarch. Intended to taunt and intimidate foes, many of *Vasa*'s sculptures depict grotesque and frightening creatures such as tritons, mermaids, and sea monsters. There were also those bronze cannons. A few highlighted features include:

- A thousand-pound, ten-foot springing lion figurehead for the king, the "Lion of the North"
- Carvings of twenty Roman emperors as well as ancient heroes such as Hercules
- Many biblical and nationalistic figures
- Three of the original sixty-four cannons

The museum also offers guided tours, interactive games, and numerous exhibits and models portraying the construction, sinking, and recovery of the ship. There's a theater with a short film that highlights the dramatic and historic recovery and restoration process. Also, there are exhibits of other seventeenth-century maritime activity in Sweden. Several early-twentieth-century ships are moored outside in the museum's harbor. Lastly, it's never a bad idea to stop in the museum's hip café to enjoy afternoon fika, a Swedish custom of cozily relaxing over coffee and cake. The Vasa Museum is hugely impressive and a must-do!

Stockholm is a very beautiful, fascinating, and fun town even in wintertime. I was disappointed that I was unable to squeeze in a visit to the *Viking Museum*; I'm told there's a frightening ride through dioramas depicting an actual Viking adventure. I also had to pass on an evening visit to the original ICEBAR, with everything from walls to glasses and sculptures hand-carved from ice. Nonetheless, the trip to Stockholm was another bleisure success with fantastic work results and a rewarding glimpse into the Scandinavian people and their culture. I never returned to see the finished office in person, but the final designer portfolio portrayed a welcoming, sleek, modern, productive, state-of-the-art office environment. I understand that the needed office relocation was very well-received, with outstanding employee satisfaction and feedback.

CHAPTER 9

LISBON

By day Lisbon has a naïve theatrical quality and enchants and captivates, but by night it is a fairy-tale city, descending over lighted terraces to the sea.

—*Erich Maria Remarque (German novelist)*

The saying is that either you love Lisbon . . . or you are wrong! What's not to love? Portugal's largest city has everything you'd want in a centuries-old sun-kissed European coastal capital. Mostly it's the Mediterranean climate, winding cobbled alleyways, white-domed cathedrals, colorful tile-work homes, Portuguese cuisine, fado music, and a few medieval castles. Lisbon's legend-shrouded seven hillsides occupy the Iberian Peninsula overlooking the Rio Tejo (Tagus River), which feeds the Tagus Estuary before escaping into the Atlantic Ocean. Few know that, following Athens, Lisbon is the second oldest European city. Lisbon has been continuously settled and fought over since prehistoric times. Pre-Celtic tribes, Phoenicians, Hannibal, Julius Caesar, Germanic tribes, and Napoleon all fought to possess the coveted, strategic Iberian Peninsula. Eventually, Portugal and Lisbon experienced a golden era and Age of Discovery throughout the late fifteenth and sixteenth centuries. Lisbon served as the European hub of commercial business between Africa, India, the Far East, and eventually Brazil. Much of the city's rich history and culture is traced back to the daring explorers who set sail from Lisbon, essentially starting globalization, during the Age of Discovery. Vasco da Gama, Columbus, Magellan, and many other explorers lived in Lisbon in the fifteenth and sixteenth centuries. The country acquired great riches exploiting the trade of gold, spices, sugar, textiles, and more. Portugal is regarded as the longest-lived maritime empire, and its seafaring exploration transformed the world. However, by the early nineteenth century, Portugal was invaded by Napoleon Bonaparte, forcing the monarchy to temporarily flee to Brazil. The Napoleonic Wars led to rapid and marked decay of the country's prior opulence. Lisbon was significantly pillaged and destroyed by invaders. A successful urban landscape transformation and redevelopment of industry, commerce, and education followed. Lisbon remained neutral and served as a key open Atlantic Ocean port during World War II. As a result, Lisbon was spared the horrors and destruction of war. Consequently, Lisbon provided a major gateway for refugees to the United States as well as an intriguing haven for wartime spies.

Today, Lisbon is a major European economic center. Lisbon is a captivating city, with a modern liberal vibe, crafted over centuries. Lisbon has a metropolitan-area population of three million people and is mainland Europe's westernmost capital city. Lisbon is rich in various styles of period architecture and home to beautiful parks, wonderful national museums, opera, and countless maritime, political, and religious monuments. Additionally, the cultural and linguistic influence of Portugal is profoundly far-reaching. Including Portugal, there is a legacy of over 250 million Portuguese speakers around the world, most notably in Brazil, Angola, and Mozambique. Lastly, the Portugal-Spain border, which constitutes the longest uninterrupted border line in Europe, is also very culturally impactful.

As a child, never in a million years did I ever dream of visiting Portugal. Yet it was announced that the upcoming spring Global Procurement Conference was planned for Alcácer do Sal, Portugal. Stumped as to its whereabouts, I learned that Alcácer do Sal was a charming old port town (dating back to 7 BC) about fifty-five miles south of Lisbon. I greatly enjoyed the conferences, not only for their exotic locales but for the tremendous global interactions. Specifically, the semiannual global conferences brought together company executives and leads from over twenty worldwide countries. The conferences were a great way to meet and align with colleagues from Germany, Italy, France, Mexico, Canada, Brazil, Australia, Russia, Japan, and all corners of the world. The agenda was primarily corporate updates, best practice sharing, program and system rollouts, planning, goal setting, team building, and recognition. Relationship building, cross-country collaboration and synergies, friendships, and a bit of fun were the natural outcomes and always my biggest takeaways.

Recognizing that my time in the city of Lisbon was extremely limited to just the day of my early morning arrival, my plan was to simply explore Lisbon on foot. As usual, I would focus on the city's historic old core; this included the neighborhoods of Alfama, Baixa, Bairro Alto, and Chiado.

Over its seven mystical hills, Lisbon is divided into many distinct and vibrant neighborhoods. I knew walking would be the best way to experience Lisbon's friendly locals, its sights and sounds, life and color, and the spirit of so many past eras. There was just one big twist, as my appetite for adventure occasionally exceeds reasonableness and better judgment. Nonetheless, I decided that I could not be this close to the town of Fátima, a most important Catholic pilgrimage site, and not make time to visit. So early afternoon, I drove north to Fátima and returned that evening just in time for a delicious Portuguese meal and to hear some haunting fado music. The following morning, I would drive south for the three-day work conference in the ancient Portuguese town of Alcácer do Sal.

An Abbreviated Day in Lisbon

Following a very early hotel check-in, I wandered outside for a morning walking tour of Lisbon. Fortunately, I was staying in the neighborhood known as the Baixa (downtown) in the historic center of Lisbon. The Baixa is an elegant district largely reconstructed after the destructive 1755 Lisbon earthquake. The reconstruction plans were both earthquake-resistant and a superior urban planning model. With little advance planning, there were two significant landmarks I encountered solely by accident.

Elevador de Santa Justa

The first discovered landmark was the *Elevador de Santa Justa*, a vertical elevator or conventional lift in the form of a metal tower with an amazing observation platform and a connecting walkway. The lift is the fastest way to transverse from the lower Baixa neighborhood to the upper Bairro Alto district (one of the steepest hills in Lisbon). The 1902 ornamental wrought iron structure is 148 feet or seven stories high, with two ornate (polished wood, mirrors, brass, and glass) cabins, each with a capacity of twenty-nine passengers. On the rooftop is a stunning lookout deck offering magnificent panoramic views of the city. The views, high above Rossio Square all the way to Lisbon's triumphant waterfront arch, take in the Castelo de São Jorge, the river Tagus, and impressive ruins of Carmo Church. Elevador de Santa Justa clearly offers one of the most popular viewpoints in Lisbon. The lift tower is decorated in a neo-Gothic style, and its design reminded me of the Paris Eiffel Tower. Turns out this is not accidental, as the elevator was designed by Raoul Mesnier du Ponsard, whose parentage was French and who was a disciple of the great Gustave Eiffel, the iron works master. The design flaunts a distinct French turn-of-the-century style and applies the same design techniques of Eiffel. In the late nineteenth century, elevators were considered a major innovation of an oncoming modern age, rendering the lift a huge success. In addition to the vertical Elevador de Santa Justa, Lisbon also has three remaining and operating funiculars to help locals and tourists ascend the long, steep slopes throughout the city. These turn-of-the-century funiculars were also beautifully designed by Portuguese engineer Raoul Mesnier du Ponsard.

It was very cool to see Lisbon's funiculars, though I couldn't help but think of my own city of Pittsburgh and our funiculars, better known as inclines. There are in fact two inclines still operating in Pittsburgh's South Side neighborhood and scaling Mount Washington to Grandview Avenue high above the city. Together, the inclines serve more than one million commuters and tourists annually. Best known is the nearly 150-year-old 1877 Duquesne Incline. Rising four hundred feet at a thirty-degree angle, the incline is an astounding eight hundred feet long and travels at a speed of four miles per hour. The Duquesne Incline was designed by American-Hungarian civil engineer Samuel Diescher, who was based in Pittsburgh. At the top of the incline is a popular observation deck with a spectacular panorama of Pittsburgh's Golden Triangle and its confluence of three rivers. I am proud to note that *USA Today Weekend Magazine* named it one of the "10 most beautiful places in America."[1] Grandview Avenue is dotted with elegant glass-paneled restaurants where you can romantically dine, celebrate, and enjoy the unique city view below.

Lastly, curiosity getting the best of me, I realized that I had never heard of a Saint Justa. Looking into it, I discovered the fascinating though sad legend of the venerated martyred Saints Justa and Rufina. Justa and Rufina were sisters born into a poor but pious Christian family in Seville, Spain, in the third century. Crafting and selling fine earthenware pottery, the young sisters supported themselves and greatly helped many of the town's poor. Like other merchants, Justa and Rufina sold pottery from an outdoor booth where the public could see their pottery. However, they refused to sell their wares at a pagan festival. The cult in Spain was ancient and powerful at the time, and Christians were persecuted. The locals angrily broke all the sisters' fine platters, bowls, and pots on display. In retaliation, Justa and Rufina smashed a pagan image of Venus and were promptly imprisoned. Refusing to denounce their strong Christian faith, the sisters were then tortured and subsequently starved to death.[2] Their resolve was never broken. Even today,

1. *USA Today*, "10 Most Beautiful Places."
2. Wikipedia, "Justa and Rufina," sec. "Legend."

often depicted with clay pots and palms, Saints Justa and Rufina are the patron saints of Seville and potters. A beautiful Lisbon civil parish (neighborhood), the Rue de Santa Justa (street), and the Elevador de Santa Justa (lift) are deserving honors. My only recommendation would be to include younger sister Saint Rufina, though I did learn that both saints are widely commemorated throughout Spain, as well as Rome, Paris, and beyond.

Lucky me . . . turns out my unexpected discovery of the Elevador de Santa Justa, once an invaluable part of Lisbon's public transit network, is one of the truly unique must-see tourist attractions in Lisbon. The views over Lisbon were as advertised and more. It was also a great privilege to ride in the elegant, century-old Mesnier vertical lift, arguably considered the world's most beautiful elevator.

Praça do Comércio

In almost every city in Europe, there are beautiful, timeless, and vibrant squares, plazas, piazzas, forums, or public marketplaces. The squares are often the most important, recognizable place in town, a place to display the city's history and culture and develop a strong sense of community. They are ideal gathering venues to people watch, filled with cafés, churches, and monuments—places where crafts are sold and where citizens can voice and exchange viewpoints. The squares are often social hot spots and the heart and soul of the city. Most squares have small, restricted entrances and are enclosed spaces that suddenly and magically appear before you. Designed for drama, there's usually a surprise element, a contrast in space. In effect, the squares serve as wonderful "outside buildings" with God's sky as the ceiling. This was my experience in Lisbon. Among the city's many beautiful squares, the iconic *Praça do Comércio* is the largest and considered the most famous and grandiose square in Lisbon.

Praça do Comércio (Commerce Plaza) is Lisbon's large, superbly located, harbor-facing eighteenth-century plaza landmark. From Lisbon's tiny downtown cobblestoned mosaic streets, I wandered into the picturesque square by accident and marveled at its distinctive grandeur. First, it's an open 575-foot space with striking and inviting gorgeous sunflower-yellow-façade government buildings. On top of that, the French-style royal square opens southwards to the sea via the huge Tagus River estuary. The square served as Lisbon's welcome center to all visitors arriving by sea, the dock where kings, chiefs, and heads of state would disembark when visiting Portugal. During the Age of Discovery, the vibrant transportation hub was both the symbolic entrance into Lisbon and the literal gateway to the New

World. It was the location where daring sea captains and merchants would plan perilous voyages to Brazil, India, and the Far East. The great wealth of Portugal was channeled through Lisbon's rich plaza and port. Prior to the great 1755 earthquake, the square was known as the Royal Yard (Terreiro do Paço) and was the site of the Royal Palace. Unfortunately, most of Lisbon was destroyed by the devastating earthquake and the powerful tsunami and fires that followed. Over thirty thousand people died that day and many of the housed classic Portuguese historic books and documents were destroyed. The Praça do Comércio name was chosen at that time to honor the merchants and the financial and bourgeois classes who committed so much hard work to rebuild Lisbon.

At the square's prominent center is a large statue of former King Joseph I of Portugal mounted on his horse. The monument was to honor the king's capable response to the 1755 earthquake devastation. The statue was revealed in massive celebration on the king's birthday in 1775. The king discreetly viewed the pomp and circumstance from the customs building window. The statue is one of the first works of public art cast in Portugal by a Portuguese sculptor Joaquim Machado de Castro. On the north side of the square is the triumphal Arco da Rua Augusta leading onto the bustling shopping street. Rue Augusta is the busiest pedestrianized street in Lisbon. From the terrace of the 1873 arch, you can enjoy panoramic views of the Baixa district over the square to the waterfront and beyond to São Jorge Castle. The arch symbolizes the incredible strength, resilience, and achievements of the Portuguese people. The hundred-foot-high arch has a coat of arms, clock, and beautiful sculptures featuring Glory, Ingenuity, and Valor, including, of course, noble explorer Vasco da Gama. Finally, there are also many fine restaurants in the square, including Lisbon's oldest operating café Martinho da Arcada dating to 1782. The surprising Praça do Comércio was most impressive and is another Lisbon must-see.

A Visit to Fátima

Most everyone knows the beautiful story of *Our Lady of Fátima*. However, for most people, Fátima is an unimaginable event in a far-away land. When I discovered that the famed agricultural village of Fátima was just seventy miles north of Lisbon, I knew I had to visit. Second only to Lourdes in France, Fátima is a very famous, important European pilgrimage site—so much so that Fátima's sacred and profound history and culture fascinates and attracts four million religious and nonreligious global visitors annually.

Not even nonbelievers can remain indifferent when confronted by Fátima's spirituality.

The story is both simple and ethereal. During World War I, Pope Benedict XV made repeated pleas for world peace. Finally, in May 1917, the pope made a direct appeal to the Blessed Mother to intercede. One week later, on May 13, 1917, a smiling Virgin Mary appeared before three shepherd children: Jacinta, her brother Francisco, and their cousin Lucia. She appeared in the Cova da Iria (Cove of Peace) near Fátima. The children had taken their flock of sheep out to pasture. The Fátima apparitions initially began the previous spring when the Angel of Peace appeared three times before the children to prepare them for the Queen of Heaven. The children (ages seven, nine, and ten) reported seeing the vision five successive times as the apparitions continued for six months through October 1917. On the sixth and final visit, the Virgin told the children her name was the Lady of the Rosary. Throughout the Virgin Mary's appearances, the children received prophetic messages of prayer, penance, and peace. And the Virgin exhorted the children to pray the rosary for world peace. Word of the miraculous visits spread, and a growing number of doubting residents of Fátima followed the children. In August, the Lady of Fátima told the children that God would perform a miracle on October 13 so that people would believe. On that date, an estimated crowd of seventy thousand gathered in Fátima and witnessed a stunning atmospheric event that became known as the Miracle of the Sun. The event has been described as a terrifying, unexplained, stunning, and miraculous ten-minute solar phenomenon in which the sun appeared to fall towards Earth. Rain and wind blistered, then all was sunny and dry. The event occurred immediately after that sixth and final appearance of the Blessed Mother to the children. The Miracle of the Sun is considered the greatest miracle to occur since the Resurrection and the only miracle precisely predicted by time, date, and location. Also, the miracle gained added fame due, in part, to Fátima's associated secrets, prophecy (the ending of World War I), and revelations related to future global events.

The full meaning of the miracles of Our Lady of Fátima would not be understood for decades. It wasn't until 1930 that the Fátima events were acknowledged by the Catholic Church and were officially recognized as worthy of belief. The Blessed Mother discussed much with the peasant children, though her message was summarized in three powerful invitations: (1) learn to pray the rosary—the prayer that can change the world; (2) get spiritually healthy through penance; and (3) let Blessed Mary guide you to lasting happiness. Based on all the above, how could I possibly forego an afternoon trip to Fátima? There are several ways to make the trip to Fátima. I drove my rental car approximately seventy-five minutes up the A1 motorway, which offered some scenic views along the way. If I had additional time, I would have stayed at a nearby beach town and visited other historic points of interest. Pressed for time, I knew I could reasonably visit Fátima in half a day.

The village of Fátima has a mystic aura and it's immediately clear that this is an important pilgrimage site. It was relatively easy to find parking in the small town, and the varied pilgrimage locations appeared all in proximity. I was able to visit just a few of the sites. Most prominent is the spectacular neoclassical *Basilica of Our Lady of the Rosary*. The church features fifteen altars dedicated to the fifteen mysteries of the rosary. It is here that the tombs of Saints Francisco and Jacinta and Sister Lucia are contained; Sister Lucia's cause for canonization is still ongoing. I rarely pray the rosary, certainly not near as much as I should. I do know that both my Irish mother and Irish mother-in-law were avid, almost daily, rosary prayers. In addition to the basilica, I was also determined to visit the *Little Chapel of Apparitions*. This simple, relatively modern chapel is located on the very site where the Virgin Mary first appeared to the children. It is here where Our Lady requested that the children build a chapel. I witnessed numerous pilgrims who chose to crawl on their knees six hundred feet, praying the Rosary, to the Little Chapel of Apparitions from the minor *Basilica of the Holy Trinity*. I also visited the *Via Sacra* (Sacred Way), which marks the path taken by the children to the first apparition in the Cove of Peace. Pilgrims walk along the path and pray the stations of the cross. When completed, you arrive at Valinhos, which was the site of the Virgin Mary's fourth (August 1917) apparition and the first and third 1916 apparitions of the Angel of Peace. Mass is offered daily and every hour at various locations in Fátima. Fortunately, I was able to attend a small, beautiful outdoor Mass at the very site where the Virgin Mary first appeared to the children. It was a memorable and spiritual experience to attend Mass in Fátima with pilgrims from around the world. I was unable to visit the house of Francisco and Jacinta, as well as the house of Lucia, nor was I able to visit several Fátima museums and shops. Though it was now time to return to Lisbon for the evening, I would be forever grateful that I was able to visit Fátima.

Fado Music

I was advised that in Lisbon a traditional Portuguese dinner by candlelight, listening to moody *fado* music, is unmissable (even if dining alone). A quintessential Portuguese night. Many cultures have traditional music, though worldly fado music, a recognized symbol of Portugal, is more a state of mind. A soulful voice singing of love, feelings, heartbreak, longing, sadness, and life's encounters. The music is contrasted with a cheerful melodic guitar. The contrast makes the spontaneous fado folk music so uniquely special. Fado is renowned for its expressive and profoundly melancholic character. Yet (similar to me) I bet you never heard of fado till just now? Fado genre music is traced to 1820s Lisbon though probably has earlier roots. The word "fado" comes from the Latin word for fate and often relates to the daily struggles of the working class, with mournful tunes and lyrics of the sea or the resigned lives of the poor, e.g., sailors, dock workers, tavern frequenters, prostitutes, and fishwives. Some believe fado began in the bows of boats before appearing on Lisbon's streets.

I discovered quickly that the beguiling musical expression of fado is a very integral part of Portuguese culture and nightlife. There are countless atmospheric restaurants or fado house venues that feature the poignant music. The fado houses are located across most of the old Lisbon neighborhoods, each with its own history, charm, and reverence. As my hotel was in the lively bohemian Bairro Alto neighborhood, I headed to popular Café Luso, which is an established favorite fado house of many tour groups. I also liked that Café Luso was a prestigious site dating to 1927 and linked to fado music. Most of the great fado singers sang here, and the restaurant was regarded as one of the finest of Lisbon's fado houses. More so, the impressive café is beautifully located in the old, vaulted wineries and stables of a seventeenth-century palace which survived the 1755 great Lisbon earthquake. In the end, it was well worth the trek up the steep cobbled streets of Lisbon. I enjoyed a fun evening at Café Luso, including a delicious Portuguese dinner and wine, haunting renditions of fado music, as well as some entertaining regional folk dancing.

Alcácer do Sal

My next stop and work destination in sunny Portugal was *Alcácer do Sal*. After a wonderful, very long day and night in the gorgeous and charming city of Lisbon there was a business conference to attend. Exhausting, educational, and rewarding bleisure travel at its best! The following morning, I traveled via my rental car from Lisbon to Alcácer do Sal. I recall it was a straightforward drive of seventy miles through sleepy rural Portuguese towns on the A2 motorway, a term I use loosely.

Alcácer do Sal is a historic medieval port town that runs along and above southwest Portugal's Sado River. Its location made Alcácer an excellent and important trade thoroughfare and military stronghold. Sitting above the river in the upper town is an ancient Moorish castle for which the town is named. Alcácer (al qasr or Al-Kassr) means "castle" or "fortress" in Arabic, and Sal refers to salt, which was an important industry in the area.[3] Salt manufacturing and fish processing were very lucrative. The castle's high-ground site provided evolving fortification for many centuries as the Muslims and Christians battled to gain control of Portugal. Though the town Alcácer do Sal has been inhabited since time immemorial, archaeologists have placed human presence here at forty thousand years, dating back to the Mesolithic period or Stone Age. The Phoenicians, who occupied Alcácer since the sixth century BC, formally established Alcácer in 7 BC. It was the Phoenicians who pioneered early Mediterranean trade and introduced flourishing Portuguese commercial colonies. Shortly thereafter, Alcácer was briefly annexed to the expanding Roman Empire. The Vikings, Moors, and thirteenth-century Crusaders would follow. The town of Al-Kassr was once the bustling capital of the Moorish province until firmly conquered by determined Portuguese forces. Under the eventual protection of the Portuguese monarchy, an influx of African slaves came to Alcácer from the sixteenth through the nineteenth centuries. Consequently, a large percentage of Alcácer's maternal lineage is sub-Saharan. And still standing dominant on the hilltop over Alcácer's river valley is the once impregnable twelfth-century Islamic Moor castle. The castle is isolated well above the town, river, and distant plains and lush green paddy fields that surround Alcácer. However, by 1570, its military importance diminished, the castle grew obsolete and became a Catholic convent. It sheltered the "Poor Clares," or Order of Saint Clare nuns, named the Poor Clares because the order followed the strict principles, including extreme poverty, of Saint Francis and Saint Clare, both of Assisi, Italy. The castle remained a convent for nearly three hundred years until it fell into disrepair and underwent major restoration. It is still ringed by its original walls. And it is exactly here in this history-laden medieval castle that my visit to Alcácer do Sal unfolds.

Today, the ancient castle is the stunning *Pousada Castelo de Alcácer do Sal*, otherwise known as the *Hotel Dom Afonso II*. The pousada (alternative hotel) is one of the thirty-four country-run pousadas of Portugal Group historic properties. "Pousada" derived from the Portuguese word "pousar," which means rest. Many of these hotel properties were formerly monasteries, palaces, convents, or castles. Each is located in a superb historical city, lively seaside, or a charming rural location. The pousadas are beautifully converted into elegant accommodations, each among the best and most unique hotels in Portugal. The corporate folks believed that the opulent

3. For information about Alcácer do Sal in this section, see Alves, "Alcacer de Sol Castle"; Wikipedia, "Alcácer do Sal"; and Visit Portugal, "Alcácer do Sal."

Hotel Dom Afonso offered a perfect site for a contained, quiet retreat and an enjoyable, productive group meeting. Dom Afonso II himself was the third king of Portugal and reigned during the Fifth Crusade's 1217 conquering of the Moors in Alcácer do Sal. The luxury hotel is billed as the perfect refuge of culture, charm, and Portuguese character. Getting to that point was not an easy task. Work on restoring the castle as a hostel began in earnest in the 1990s. Like many archeology projects throughout Europe, recovery was interrupted when an ancient Roman forum site was discovered. Consequently, and by decree, the property was taken over by the Portuguese Republic and has operated as a pousada for over twenty years. The site is both ancient and modern. For example, there is an archaeological museum in the castle's crypt that chronicles Alcácer do Sal from prehistoric times. The pousada walls also enclose the Romanesque church of Santa Maria, which features a striking Renaissance chapel doorway and exquisite Portuguese tiles. The church dates to the twelfth century and was likely built on the site of a former Muslim mosque. Originally, the fortress had twenty towers, each over eighty feet high, and a large keep tower. A keep tower is a fortified tower within a Middle Age castle that served as a fortified residence. Many of the original towers and belfries remain to be climbed and explored and offer spectacular views across the plains below. Of course, I was up for a climbing adventure and photo opportunity, which surprisingly was passed up by many of my colleagues.

One final amusing memory from my castle tour was the surprising discovery of large white birds everywhere. They were meandering around the castle grounds and nesting in large numbers in the towers. I had asked the guide what type of bird they were and, speaking little English, he said, "Cegonha, cegonha!" Looking puzzled, I pressed him further and he expounded, "Babies, babies!" A light bulb went off and I realized that the beautiful large white birds were in fact storks! I'm not sure I ever encountered storks in the wild, though they did strongly resemble the characteristic long beaked, baby-diaper-carrying birds of lore. As I understand it, over time the stork may have been conflated with the pelican species, which is associated with Catholicism, rebirth, and maternal rearing of the young. I was told that the number of storks in Portugal have increased dramatically since they've come under protection. Also, maybe attributed to climate change, many usually migratory storks no longer make the arduous journey south, overwintering in Portugal. In any event, it was very cool to see many storks. My stay at the charming Portugal pousada was very different from the contrasting hectic, energized charm of larger European city hotels, though my above account should verify it was no less memorable . . . I am blessed to have enjoyed the beautiful Portuguese countryside.

My time in Lisbon was very short but long on memories. I immediately realized why Lisbon, the charismatic capital of Portugal, is regarded as one of the most beautiful and historic cities in all of Europe. The neighboring Portuguese countryside and coastal towns were equally beautiful. The impressive architecture, narrow cobbled alleys, fantastic squares, surrounding water views, street music, and mostly the warm reception of the kind and welcoming Portuguese people all create the unique, unmistakable soul of Lisbon.

CHAPTER 10

VENICE

A realist, in Venice, would become a romantic by
mere faithfulness to what he saw before him.

—*Arthur Symons (British poet)*

The city of Venice really does not need an introduction, except to say that no matter how many times you've seen Venice in photographs, paintings, and films, the reality of seeing Italy's floating city in person is way, way more surprising and spellbinding than you could ever imagine! When asked about my favorite city, I typically characterize each city as uniquely special. Without a doubt, Venice is the most astonishing and magical city I've visited.

I visited Venice on my first trip to Italy on a weekend layover in Milan. Given I had the weekend free, I decided to book a train to visit either Venice 155 miles to the east or Florence 195 miles to the southeast. I very much wanted to see both these beautiful, historic Italian cities but had to choose. I chose Venice. However, I was very fortunate to eventually visit Florence while back in Milan on business several years later. "Bleisure" is a portmanteau for "business and leisure" travel, and Italy is the ideal location to experience both. The most popular and easy way to travel the two-plus hours from Milan to Venice is via train. Over thirty trains make that trip daily. I arose early that Saturday morning in May and boarded the train at the Milano Centrale Station on my way to Venice's Santa Lucia Station. Milan's beautiful, bustling main train station was built in the 1930s, and the gorgeous architecture reflects the city's penchant for fashion and commerce.

It's been said that renowned American architect Frank Lloyd Wright once visited Milan and declared Milano Centrale the most beautiful train station in the world. Milano Centrale is also the largest station in size in all of Europe and one of its busiest, second only to Paris. There is great comfort and peace in the rhythmic background noise of a rambling train ride, viewing the charming European countryside at eye level out the window. In this case, the train meanders through the scenic Lombardy and Veneto regions to Italy's Adriatic coast. I was also pleased to learn the train made a stop in the town of Verona, famous as the setting of Shakespeare's *Romeo and Juliet*. There's even a fourteenth-century residence in Verona with a tiny balcony overlooking a courtyard that is known as Juliet's House. But, sadly, Verona would need to be explored at another time. Arriving at Venice's 1950s Santa Lucia Train Station is a treat unto itself. The picturesque train station sits directly across the lagoon, smack on Venice's Grand Canal. Stepping outside the station for the very first time provides an impressive, amazing view of Venice's most famous canal, an unparalleled experience. Add to that children merrily playing and laughing and art students sitting on the train station steps creating last-minute sketches of the idyllic scene. My thirty-six-hours in fascinating Venice were underway.

To best describe the city of Venice, imagine this. It floats in a shallow Adriatic Sea lagoon on an archipelago of 118 small islands formed by over 150 canals and linked by 438 bridges. Venice is in the center of the Venetian lagoon, one of the largest wetlands in all of Europe. Most of the canals are just five or six feet deep, though the Grand Canal is deeper at sixteen feet. The islands of Venice have tiny pedestrian alleys and no roads (only canals). Therefore, Venice is car-free. The islands are accessible somewhat by train though mainly by boat or "vaporetto" (public water-bus), the preferred mode of transportation. The actual city of Venice is only about the size of New York City's Central Park and has a population of roughly fifty thousand residents. Conversely, the Venice metropolitan area, which includes two large surrounding cities, has a total population of 2.6 million. Venice is routinely ranked as the most beautiful city in the world and always one of Europe's most romantic cities. It's a city of incomparable beauty and charm brilliantly built on water, with all the complexities and issues that come with that.

The Venice region has been periodically inhabited since the tenth century BC. Although no historical records reveal the exact building of Venice, its traditional founding dates to March 25, 421 with the dedication of its first church. There's a school of thought that these fifth-century Venetians were forced to flee from the mainland to escape oncoming conquerors and marauders. Evidence suggests that the original population of Venice likely "consisted of refugees—from nearby Roman cities . . . as well as from the undefended countryside." The refugees were forced to flee "successive waves of Germanic and Hun invasions,"[1] raids led by Visigoth barbarians, then Attila the Hun. Building Venice on the murky, unnavigable wetlands of the lagoon wisely provided requisite safety and protection. Invaders were also unable to survive the diseases that were understood and controlled by those native to the lagoon. By the eighth century, the Venetians elected the first of their 118 doges (dukes). Doges would lead Venice over the next thousand years, though in 814, Charlemagne and the Byzantine emperor attempted to seize and recognize Venice as Byzantine territory. It was Charlemagne's son "Pepin of Italy" who sought to overtake Venice but failed and would succumb to disease. Subsequently, Byzantine influence would gradually wane. As such, Venice successfully operated as a neutral party navigating business interest between the western Roman and the eastern Byzantine Empires. Venice continued to trade with Muslim leaders in Syria and Spain while also serving as port to crusaders determined to gain control of the Holy Land from the Muslims. With an estimated thirty-six thousand sailors operating 3,300 ships, Venice maintained solid control of the Mediterranean trade routes.[2] Eventually, by the thirteenth century, Venice was "at the peak of its power and wealth" and was regarded as "the most prosperous city in all of Europe."[3] Once the Age of Discovery opened new routes across the Atlantic Ocean, Venice no longer controlled the seas. Venice shifted and grew its reputation for incredible art, music, and gaiety. Venice's ultra-wealthy leading families built the grandest palaces and supported works of the greatest, most talented Renaissance artists of the time. Eventually, by 1797, Napoleon conquered and claimed Venice. Napoleon looted Venice's valuable religious art and precious gems. Notably, the *Wedding Feast at Cana* (1563) painting by Paolo Veronese was plundered by Napoleon. The painting remains in the Louvre in Paris to this day. The story of this expansive, colorful painting, one of the most superb in the Louvre, is a fascinating story unto itself. Until recently, onlookers at the *Mona Lisa* would have their backs to this Veronese painting as it proudly hung directly across the room. Venice would continue under then-Austrian control until 1866 when it formally joined the newly formed Kingdom of Italy.

Along the way and of necessary note is Venice's all-important technological development of early printing and publishing. Whereas Germany invented the first printing press, its art and practice rapidly spread throughout

1. Wikipedia, "Venice," sec. "Origins." See also Wikipedia, "History of the Republic."
2. Italiaoutdoors, "History of Venice," para. 2.
3. Wikipedia, "Venice," sec. "Expansion."

Europe. The 1440 invention of the movable-reusable-type printing press by Johannes Gutenberg was quite significant. The press afforded the world great access to knowledge and prose and a leap in culture. The Gutenberg Bible was the first book in the world printed on a movable-type press, and many followed. Venice was an early and fervent adopter and became the inevitable center for this new craft. By 1482, due mainly to its geographic location and intellectual liveliness, wealthy Venice had become the printing capital of the world. Publishing thrived in cosmopolitan Venice due to its spirited freedom of press, a dynamic artisan and commercial environment, and its openness to forefront novelties. Additionally, a major center for quality papermaking had formed in nearby Tuscany. Add that Venice's exceptional location afforded inexpensive sea transportation. Finally, factor in that Venice was so powerful at the time that even Rome and the Catholic Church chose not to or failed to censor its publishing.

Most important, Venice's printing skills, speed, and innovations, namely those of famed-printer Aldus Manutius, led to publication of smaller, low-cost paperback and pocket books welcomed by the public. In effect, these technical innovations removed the long-standing exclusive, aristocratic character of reading and scholarship. Technology quickened the spread of literature, knowledge, and discoveries across the world. Venice also introduced illustrated books, colored inks, italic print, and standardized punctuation. The Venetian printers were the first to translate, copyright, and publish classic Greek literature. Accordingly, by the year 1500, there were over two hundred printing establishments and countless bookselling shops located throughout Venice. Millions of books were being printed and distributed. Venice is truly the city that launched today's multibillion-dollar publishing industry.

In parallel, alluring Venice has also long been a source of inspiration for poets, authors, and playwrights, both local and abroad. Consequently, there is no shortage of great literature set in the Italian city. This includes William Shakespeare's *Merchant of Venice*, Ernest Hemingway's *Across the River and into the Trees*, and Henry James's *The Aspern Papers*, just to name a few. Likewise, you may be surprised to learn that two of the most noted, historic Venetian writers were none other than Marco Polo and Giacomo Casanova. Marco Polo, the merchant explorer who set out on Orient voyages during the Middle Ages, coauthored a series of books known as *The Book of the Marvels of the World*. His writings provided important unknown knowledge of lands east of Europe. Marco Polo wrote of his twenty-four-year travels through Asia along the Silk Road, stories of the Eastern world's foreign, mysterious cultures and customs. He described the wealth and great size of China's Mongol Empire. Marco Polo offered firsthand insights into Persia,

Japan, Russia, and present-day Burma, India, Indonesia, and Viet Nam. The detailed chronicle of Marco Polo's travel experiences greatly influenced Europeans and inspired other explorers such as Christopher Columbus. That said, some have viewed Marco Polo's tales and writings with skepticism simply as romance or fable. However, historians have largely judged his referenced descriptions and chance encounters as uniquely accurate.[4]

In addition to Marco Polo, there is another unlikely Venetian author of note—namely, the adventurous Giacomo Casanova. Yes, that Casanova! He was also a prolific writer! Best known as a world-famous womanizer and lover, Casanova was also a scam artist, gambler, musician, soldier, spy, and a short-term church cleric. He fought duels and escaped from more than one prison. The scandalous Casanova is primarily remembered for his colorful autobiography, *Histoire De Ma Vie* (Story of My Life). Casanova's acclaimed French-written book is regarded as the most authentic and provocative exposés of eighteenth century European social life.[5]

Grand Canal

Venice's busiest "street," it's amazing, treasured boulevard, is the glistening, watercraft-dotted, eye-popping *Grand Canal*. The Grand Canal divides the city into two halves and curves in an inverted, serpentine *S* from Venice's central neighborhoods (train station) all the way to expansive Saint Mark's Square. The nearly 2.5-mile regal Grand Canal is flanked by 170 structures. The canal passes by fifty iconic *palazzi* (mansions) and six churches, and under four varied-era bridges. Pastel yellow, green, cream, and orange buildings unexplainably emerge from the emerald canal waters. Along its way, you pass lively markets, restaurants, and magnificently manicured gardens. Cruising the canal's bends past a bombardment of opulent thirteenth- to eighteenth-century jewel box palazzi could cause one whiplash! Don't dare blink, as you may miss one of the canal's wondrous buildings. The Grand Canal's scene-stealing backdrops are so intriguing and dramatic that they've even been featured in four James Bond films. The bustling canal is the main artery of Venice and, therefore, never ever idle. In addition to the public vaporetto, bedecked gondolas shuffle tourists about in awestruck Italian commotion that is both frightening and highly entertaining. Out of reverence to my absent wife, I did not ride a gondola, an experience I deemed best shared (or maybe it was just too expensive). Lastly, although it's a thrill unto itself, the Grand Canal also succinctly connects most all of

4. Wikipedia, "Travels of Marco Polo"; Waugh, "Marco Polo's Travels."
5. Wikipedia, "Giacomo Casanova."

Venice's top attractions. The beauty and magic of the Grand Canal waterway with its stirring reflection of grandiose mansions and churches is an image I'll never forget.

Rialto Bridge

The renowned *Rialto Bridge* is the oldest of the four bridges that span the Grand Canal of Venice. It's also possibly the most famous bridge in all of Italy due to its fascinating history and beautiful, daring Renaissance design. Completed in 1591, the Rialto Bridge was the only bridge on the Grand Canal for hundreds of years. There are three other bridges spanning the Grand Canal today, dating to 1854, 1934, and 2008. Because the Rialto Market area gained increasing importance to Venetian life in the eleventh century, a bridge was needed to provide access. First, a simple bridge made of boats and covered with planks was constructed then failed. Several other pontoon and high-maintenance wooden bridges followed, but they too dangerously failed. A new, trusted, ornamental bridge was needed. As was often the case during the Renaissance period, given no shortage of world-class Italian architects, a competition of proposed bridge designs ensued. Even the great sculptor Michelangelo is claimed to have been considered as a designer of the bridge. However, it was famed Venetian architect and engineer Antonio da Ponte and his nephew whose controversial design was ultimately chosen. The eventual winning arched design was considered so audacious that several competing architects predicted future ruin. One architect went so far to predict that the bridge would crumble even before it was finished. The over 430-year-old Rialto Bridge has certainly defied those disgruntled early critics.

The stunning twenty-four-foot stone arch bridge in the very heart of Venice wisely crosses over the narrowest point of the Grand Canal. It was deemed a very significant architectural and engineering achievement for the period. The walking bridge connected the Venice districts of San Marco and San Polo in its burgeoning commercial hub. It was also imperative to allow boat traffic to cross underneath. The Rialto Bridge was allegedly constructed from ancient stones (dating to 49 BC) of a ruined Roman theater located in the nearby city of Padua.[6] What is known is that the bridge is constructed of dense limestones from an Adriatic Sea peninsula in what is now Croatia. As was typical practice in the sixteenth century, twelve thousand wooden logs were pushed deep into the soft, marshy lagoon soil for stabilization. Over time, the logs petrified and now support the large Venetian structures. The

6. Wikipedia, "Rialto Bridge," sec. "History."

Rialto Bridge design consists of a single twenty-four-foot stone arch or span that supports a broad covered deck carrying two arcades. The deck houses twenty-four small specialty shops, selling jewelry, leather, etc., which front the bridge's three walkways. The width of the bridge is sixty-six feet while its lower chord length at the canal's narrowest point is a mere eighty-three feet. To transverse the bridge, there are six stairways with fifty-nine steps to the top of the iconic bridge. Lastly, as coded images and religious symbols were vital and largely understood, Venice sought to present itself as a divinely ordained city-state—namely, by creating a link between the birth of Christ and the birth of Venice. Venice was founded on the Roman Catholic Feast of the Annunciation in the year 421. The biblical annunciation is the moment Archangel Gabriel tells the Virgin Mary that she would conceive a son to be named Jesus. Accordingly, the Rialto Bridge depicts this link. There are several stone reliefs, one of Archangel Gabriel holding a lily and one of the Virgin Mary. At the top of the bridge arch is the Holy Spirit depicted as a dove. There are also reliefs of Saint Theodore and Saint Mark, the first and current patron saints of Venice. The reliefs were intended to send a powerful message to visiting dignitaries and everyday pedestrians.

The Rialto Bridge is central to the fascinating history of Venice. At sunset, there are few more beautiful and romantic places to be in the city. For these reasons, the bridge remains a significant tourist attraction to millions of pedestrians as well as those who are fortunate enough to pass underneath the bridge in a Grand Canal gondola.

Saint Mark's Basilica

In discussing Venice's *Basilica di San Marco* (Saint Mark's Basilica) it's probably best to start with Saint Mark himself, the patron of Venice.[7] Or perhaps I should say "the theft of Saint Mark"! Saint Mark was born in AD 12 in Cyrene, North Africa (now Libya). Known as Mark the Evangelist, he is traditionally attributed as the author of the Gospel According to Mark. Some believe Mark the Evangelist was identified as one of the disciples of Jesus sent out to proclaim and disseminate the gospel. In AD 41, the apostle Peter escaped the realm of King Herod in Judea and fled to Greece and Asia Minor. It is believed that somewhere along his travels Peter encountered Mark the Evangelist who was traveling and evangelizing with Paul and Barnabas. It followed that Mark became a travel companion and interpreter for Peter. He wrote down his powerful sermons, Peter's firsthand accounts, and composed the Gospel According to Mark. Contrary traditionalist thinking

7. See St. Mark Catholic Church, "Our Patron."

identifies Mark the Evangelist among the servants at the Marriage of Cana where Jesus turned water into wine. They also believe that Mark was among the disciples present on Pentecost, where the resurrected Jesus appeared and the Holy Spirit descended upon them. Other scholars simply believe Mark was an anonymous unknown author.[8] By AD 68, Mark the Evangelist ran afoul of pagans and was martyred and buried in Alexandria, Egypt. He left behind the Gospel According to Mark, the shortest account of the life, death, resurrection, and ascension of Jesus. Mark's gospel is a lasting treasure for believers. It was the earliest written account aiding Matthew and Luke in writing their Gospels. By all accounts, the Gospel According to Mark helped the Christian world to know that Jesus suffered and died to save us.

Now here is the "swashbuckling tale" of the theft of the supposed body of Saint Mark the Evangelist.[9] The kidnapping from Egypt was by two very brave and wily Venetian merchants. And as hard as it is to believe, the level of associated detail is astounding. In the year 828, over 760 years after the death of Saint Mark, two men decided to smuggle his body back to Venice, a scheme intended to boost the standing of their home city. The men, Buono da Malamocco and Rustico da Torcello, recently completed business in Alexandria. Before returning home, the men went to worship at a church dedicated to Saint Mark and entombing the evangelist's body. Custodians of the church sanctuary, a monk and priest, advised the Venetians that the church would soon be ransacked by Muslims who were plundering Christian churches to build mosques. The two thieves decided to remove the remains of Saint Mark and replace them with a nearby body. Buono and Rustico allegedly snuck the corpse past Muslim officers by hiding it under layers of pork and vegetables stored in barrels. In passing customs, the two Venetian merchants reported their goods as "khanzir, khanzir" (pig in Arabic). While holding their noses in disgust at the thought of pork, the excisemen quickly waved the thieves through. Unfortunately, the caper did not end there. When at sea, a storm nearly drowned the tomb raiders and their sacred cargo. It was claimed that Saint Mark himself appeared to the sea captain, telling him to lower the sails and thereby saving the ship. The body of Saint Mark reportedly arrived safely in Venice on January 31, 828, and was immediately placed in the royal Doge Palace. Thus, Venice's ninth-century Basilica di San Marco was then founded to respectfully and gloriously enshrine the stolen corpse of Saint Mark.

8. See White, "Gospel of Mark"; Wikipedia, "Mark the Evangelist."

9. L., "St. Mark's Basilica." On the theft, see also Fitzwilliam Museum, "Relics of St Mark"; Guise, "Grave Robbers in Gondolas"; and Wikipedia, "*Saint Mark's Body*," sec. "Subject."

Construction of the Basilica of Saint Mark began immediately after the kidnapping and arrival of the remains of Saint Mark from Egypt. Started in 828, the original building was completed in 836. The basilica was built specifically to revere the body of Saint Mark, the newly named protector of Venice. Initially, the incredible church was built solely as the doge's private chapel. Construction of the present-day basilica began in 1063, though remnants of the original survived. The Byzantine style basilica clearly represented the great commercial wealth and power of prosperous Venice. Its central base is in the shape of a Greek cross and includes a mixture of ancient and oriental art. The basilica was also made possible by the courage and recklessness of the many adventurous Venetian merchants and conquerors in the Mediterranean. The basilica underwent several modifications throughout the seventeenth and eighteenth centuries, resulting in a beautiful blend of architectural styles. It is here in this historic basilica, chapel of the doge (or duke), where most of the dukes of Venice were consecrated between the years 836 and 1797.

Features of the basilica first and foremost include eighty-five thousand square feet of astonishing mosaics, mostly twenty-four-carat gold leaf, completed over centuries. Just inside the church's vestibule are some of the oldest mosaics, including the nearly thousand-year-old *Apostles with the Madonna*. The gold mosaics depict complex religious concepts and Venetians' grand devotion while also conveying the great wealth and worldly political weight of Venice at the time. There are also over five hundred mostly Byzantine columns in the basilica which were pillaged from the sixth to the eleventh century. Most of the basilica's antiquities came from the Fourth Crusade, which ended in the year 1204. This is where Vatican-sent crusaders successfully conquered Constantinople (modern day Istanbul). Although their intent was to take back the Holy Land of Jerusalem, the sidetracked Crusaders conquered Constantinople, which was a Christian empire. The action was influenced by the doge since Constantinople had shown favor to Genoa and Pisa, who were Venice's enemies. The pope was not pleased with an attack on fellow Christians. The outcome: treasures such as the four ancient bronze horses, enamels of the Golden Altarpiece, crosses, chalices, and other relics were shipped to Venice for installation in Saint Mark's Basilica. Along the way, the four massive bronze horses were plundered and briefly carted to Paris by Napoleon before being somewhat rightfully returned to the basilica. Most admired is the tenth-century Byzantine Pala d'Oro altarpiece. Made entirely of gold, the altar screen is studded with 1,500 pearls, three hundred emeralds, three hundred sapphires, and four hundred garnets, along with amethysts, rubies, and topazes. There is also the 323-foot-high Saint Mark's campanile, or bell tower, built in the ninth century and bolstered and rebuilt "as was" in the early twentieth century following its collapse. Visitors to the top of this bell tower enjoy a 360-degree view of the Venice lagoon. From the bell tower, you can also share an experience with the great Galileo, who tested his telescope in the campanile in 1609. And of course, the basilica is still home to Saint Mark's tomb, located under the main altar. Decorated with bronze and marble statues, the tomb strongly symbolizes Venice's enormous pride and grand history. And it all started with that dramatic kidnapping of Saint Mark's corpse from Egypt in the year 828. Saint Mark's Basilica, known as the church of gold, is now a thousand-year-old Venice legacy known worldwide. The dazzling architecture, stellar collection of world-class mosaic artwork, centuries-old religious relics and artifacts, and its divinity make Saint Mark's Basilica the must-visit Venice attraction.

Saint Mark's Square

Piazza San Marco, *Saint Mark's Square*, was constructed in the ninth century in front of the newly built basilica. The small square was initially dotted with trees and originally separated from the basilica and Doge's Palace by a small canal. It wasn't until the end of the twelfth century that the then very wealthy doge initiated changes that created the grandiose square as we know it today. The canal was filled, land acquired, an orchard cleared, buildings razed, and new buildings and arcades constructed. At the very same time, the Byzantine architecture and art that had been plundered from Constantinople during the misguided Fourth Crusade was shipped back for the adornment of Venice's Saint Mark's Square and Basilica—a significant challenge, as the large square is 590 feet long by 230 feet wide. Considered one of the finest squares in the world, it is surrounded on three sides by stately arcades of public buildings with Saint Mark's Basilica on the fourth side.

As we know, the entire city of Venice is built on water. Further, Saint Mark's Square is built at Venice's lowest point, just three feet above sea level. Consequently, Saint Mark's Square is the first part of the city to get wet, extremely prone to flooding, and totally submerged under water on occasion (usually wintertime). Over a hundred thousand wooden piles were used to secure Saint Mark's Square. Also curious: Napoleon, who is considered the man that ended the glorious republic of Venice, was a huge fan of the city. He conquered Venice in 1797, stole most all the gold and precious stones, along with the famous bronze horses and art, and sailed them off to Mother France. Nonetheless, as testimony to his admiration, Napoleon is credited with once calling Saint Mark's Square "the world's most beautiful drawing room."[10]

Today, given its proximity to the bordering Doge's Palace and Saint Mark's Basilica and bell tower, Saint Mark's Square is a natural magnet for first-time visitors arriving in Venice. In fact, it's said that all roads, or rather all canals, lead to sweeping Saint Mark's Square. Continuously, the premiere public square (the "piazza" as it is better known) has formed the civic, social, religious, and political center of Venice. Saint Mark's Square is the place in Venice where everyone (locals, tourists, and pigeons alike) comes to see and be seen.

Doge's Palace

The Palazzo Ducale, or *Doge's Palace*, is a majestic tenth-century palace and masterpiece of Gothic architecture located next to the Basilica di San Marco.[11] The palace was initially built as a fortified core base and home for the doges, the supreme authorities of the Republic of Venice. Remarkably, it is from the Doge's Palace that 120 doges directed the amazing fate of Venice for nearly a thousand years. In the twelfth century, restructuring and expansion transformed the fort into an elegant palace. By 1342, the palace began to obtain its present appearance as an agglomeration of multiple buildings serving various purposes. The palace has three stories and extends five hundred feet long. Several devastating fires occurred throughout the next two centuries. By the early seventeenth century, a new prison was added beyond the canal and annexed to the palace by the infamous Bridge of Sighs. In 1797, after the fall of the republic to Napoleon and French, then Austrian, rule, the palace was reconditioned to merely house administrative offices. Finally, after the annexation of Venice to the Kingdom of Italy in 1866, the decaying palace underwent further restructuring until 1923 when it was designated to become a vital commemorative museum of the once powerful Venetian Republic.

With its location on the Adriatic Sea, Venice was much closer to the eastern Byzantine realm of influence than that of further-afield Rome and other settlements to the south. The Doge's Palace original architectural style was Byzantine-Venetian. And although few traces of the original ninth-century palace remain, Byzantine characteristics are evident in the

10. Civitatis, "Piazza San Marco," para. 3.

11. For information in this section, see Venice Museum, "Doge's Palace"; Wikipedia, "Doge's Palace," sec. "Doge's apartments"; Finelli, "Absolutely Ridiculous History"; and Fodors, "To Live Like a Doge."

ground-floor Istrian stone and herring-bone brick patterns. The palace's present appearance is Gothic though layered with significant building elements and ornamentation from many periods, including the Renaissance and the subsequent sixteenth-century elegant and playful Mannerist periods. Beautiful inside and out, the palace has frescoed walls, gilded ceilings, ornate furnishings, magnificent staircases, and a stunning Gothic open portico façade. Consequently, the palace's many chambers, rooms, atriums, and grand halls are an aggregate of utterly fascinating, historical, quirky opulence. A brief overview of a few of the Doge's Palace remarkable rooms follows.

Chamber of the Great Council: This fourteenth century restructured room measures an astonishing 173 feet by 82 feet, one of the largest in Europe. The incredible room is surrounded by magnificent paintings by the most famous artists of the period. The walls are decorated with facing paintings depicting Venetian history, acts of valor, and heroism with reference to The Holy Roman Empire. There are also portraits of the first 76 doges with the other 44 in an adjoining room. The 55th doge, who unsuccessfully attempted a coup d'état in 1355 and was executed and is represented by a black shroud. Most noticeable in this room is one of the largest oil paintings on canvas in history (78 x 32 feet). Domenico Tintoretto's swirling *II Paradiso* (1592) represents heaven on earth and was intended to look over the council and guide appropriate decisions.

Lastly, one other interesting fact in republic governance. The Great Council of Venice was an ancient institution and a most important political body. Amazingly, all male members of patrician Venetian families over 25 years of age, regardless of their individual status, merits, or wealth, served on the Great Council. The council, notwithstanding certain Senate restrictions, was a true bastion of political equality.

Doge's Apartments: Being a doge was not a particularly easy or rewarding job; several even refused the lifelong position to serve as Venice's ruling elite. Severe measures were taken to ensure the doge would not abuse the office. To prevent any secret alliances, the doge was forbidden to send notes to anyone, including his wife. To discourage bribery, the doge could accept no gifts beyond flowers and rosewater. The doge had to avoid social settings where he might have a chance to plot against democracy. The doge was also forbidden to engage in any money-making activities, and his garments were no more than state uniforms worn for rigid etiquette. Possibly worst of all, the doge was required to lead Venetian fleets into battle. Even a doge's poor health and old age were unacceptable excuses. The doge apartments were similarly crafted as a modest residence for the doge and his family. They were residence to 120 doges and their families in total over the millennium of their rule. Until the seventeenth century, doge apartments were quite small and considerably less comfortable than those accustomed to by wealthy families in private life. The plan was to humble the new doge and reaffirm that his foremost priority was the Republic of Venice. Each doge relied solely on furnishings from his private residence. Upon his death, next of kin would remove the furnishings and the new doge would follow. The only prestige was in the location of the apartment near Jacopo Sansovino's (1559) twenty-four-carat-gold gilt stuccowork Scala d'Oro (Golden Staircase). The honor of climbing the richest staircase in the world was reserved for the doge, illustrious visitors, and high-ranking magistrates.

Within the doge apartments was the Scarlet Chamber (scarlet colored antechamber), the Scudo Room, where he would grant audiences and receive guests, and the Erizzo Room with access to a roof garden. There was also the Priuli Room, Philosophers' Room, and Corner Room. All were adorned with incredible art but served no specific function other than the private use of the doge.

Hall of the Council of Ten: One of the most intriguing aspects in the history of Venice is the Council of Ten—a committee of ten "innermost circle" men whispering in the ears of the doge. The Ten presumably held the real power and ruled the Republic of Venice. They served as Venice's major governing body from 1310 till the end of the Republic in 1797. The Council of Ten had broad jurisdictional powers to impose policy at home, in the waters, and abroad relative to merchant guilds, taxes, and even punishments (torture and death sentences).

The *Hall of the Council of Ten* in the Doge's Palace is where secret meetings on sensitive issues of peace and tranquility, prosperity, and morality were hosted. The room is where torturous inquisitions and punishment for the crimes of political prisoners, nobles, and citizens were harshly levied. It is through the chamber's ceiling and the layout of the hall that the Council of Ten is best understood. The ceiling decoration consists of twenty-five carved and gilded compartments displaying painted images of divinities and allegories. Most notable and famous are the central oval panels by a young Paolo Veronese depicting *Juno Showering Gifts on Venice* (1556) and *Jupiter Hurling Thunderbolts at the Vices* (1554–56), the latter being a copy, as Napoleon took the original painting to the Louvre.[12] Also, still very visible in the chamber perimeter are the wooden bumps where the deputies sat and outlines of the seventeen semicircular seats of the Ten along with the doge and six counselors. As with most of the palace's judicial offices a door led to the prison via a staircase. The hall's décor is strongly intended to illustrate the absolute power of the Ten, like the court of heaven, to punish the guilty and free the innocent.

The Compass Room: The Doge's Palace was also the sheriff's office and jail in medieval Venice. The palace's Compass Room (Sala della Bussola) or Hall of the Compass was dedicated to the administration of justice. The room's name pertains to the large, elaborately carved wooden compass in the corner, which is topped by a statue of Justice.[13] The Compass Room is an antechamber to the council chambers and the powerful magistrates of justice. All rooms exercising justice were interconnected vertically to the terrible ground-floor prisons. Famed Italian Renaissance painter Paolo Veronese was again commissioned to decorate the Compass Room ceiling (1554) in pictures exalting good government. The central panel features Saint Mark descending to crown the three Theological Virtues. Thanks again to mischievous Napoleon, the original painting was pillaged and resides in the Louvre in Paris.

Bear in mind that it was relatively easy to end up in a Venice jail. Often, a single anonymous denunciation (secret accusation of illegal action) slipped into a "Lion's Mouth" postbox or complaint box was enough to get one arrested. These could be trading disputes, market fraud, or tax gripes. Often, these stone receptacles resembled the carved face of a lion with a slot at the mouth into which letters could be inserted. The earliest Lion's Mouth dating to 1618 is still intact and visible in the Doge's Palace Hall of the Compass.

The Armory: The four rooms of the palace armory contain a valuable historic collection of weapons and armaments. Many of the two thousand exhibits predate the fourteenth century. There are also later firearms, swords, crossbows, implements of torture, and even a chastity belt. Throughout the ages, the armory was historically stocked with many weapons readily available to both the palace guards and trained shipyard arsenals. The

12. Fondazione Musei Civici di Venezia, "Institutional Chambers," sec. "Chamber of the Council of Ten."

13. Fondazione Musei Civici di Venezia, "Institutional Chambers," sec. "Compass Room."

armory also contains many unique fifteenth- and sixteenth-century suits of armor. One beautiful, fitted suit belonged to Erasmo da Narni better known Il Gattamelata (Honeyed Cat). The Honeyed Cat was a poor farmer's son who became one of Italy's most famous and best-known mercenaries. The Honeyed Cat led Venice to many victories.

The Prisons: The Doge's Palace prisons and dungeons are another highlight of the museum and the culmination of tours through the palace. As noted, Venice's prisons were present from the very start of the palace, as it was the judicial center of the republic. Documents as early as the 1200s reference the crowded, unhealthy, dark, damp prison cells by specific names. There's both the original prison (pozzi), on the palace main building ground floor, and the new prison (piombi) built across the canal in the 1590s, accessible via the famous Bridge of Sighs. The cells of the newer prison were somewhat improved and reserved for less serious criminals. Amazingly, cells from the sixteenth and seventeenth centuries, still in use till a hundred years ago, are visible today. No less ornate or amazing was the new prison construction. The annexed Doge's Palace prison features an elegant façade with the Istrian Peninsula limestone and lion heads and heavy metal bar décor. However, it was the old prison that gained notoriety when, on October 31, 1756, a cunning thirty-year-old Giacomo Casanova (yes, once again, that Casanova) escaped. Casanova dedicates a chapter in his famous memoir to the adventure, telling of the conditions of prison life and the escape, though fact and fiction may be interspersed. Casanova was serving a five-year, solitary confinement sentence for public outrages against holy religion. Miserable and alone, Casanova executed a daring, cross-rooftop midnight escape. Fleeing to Paris, the young Casanova vowed to change his ways, though it wasn't long till he was again conning wealthy men out of their money and beautiful women out of their dresses. As evidenced in his memoir, Casanova's long life (he died at age seventy-four) was never boring.

There are so many more rooms, features, a beautiful courtyard, and endless astounding art associated with the Doge's Palace Museum, which makes a visit an extraordinary experience. Anyone interested in the illustrious history of Venice, the surrounding lagoon, and untold design opulence of the period will enjoy the Doge's Palace.

Bridge of Sighs

Of the more than four hundred bridges in Venice, none can quite compare with the enchanting, mysterious, white-stoned Ponte dei Sospiri, romantically nicknamed the *Bridge of Sighs*. With its dark backstory, the slender Bridge of Sighs spans the Rio del Palazzo canal. The bridge annexes the beautiful Doge's Palace complex with its notorious sixteenth-century prison. The delicate covered bridge's beauty and intrigue make it a favorite Venetian attraction. Completed in 1603 by architect Antonio Contino, the neoclassical Bridge of Sighs was intended as a narrow walkway to funnel prisoners to and from their cells and the palace magistrates. The bloodlines are interesting, as Contino's uncle was Antonio da Ponte, designer of the Rialto Bridge. Bridge of Sighs features include grimacing sculpted heads and the requisite coat of arms of the then-reigning commissioning doge. The bridge's telling feature, however, is two small square windows nearly obscured by shuttered stonework. The windows allow for only a sliver of light and just a fleeting glimpse of the outside world. It is through these windows that despairing prisoners gaze (a final glimpse for some) at the beauty of Venice's distant Grand Canal. Wearily, they would "sigh" while being led away to imprisonment or death. Thus, the bridge's romantic name . . . the Bridge of Sighs! The name was later immortalized by British poet Lord Byron in his 1812 poetic work *Childe Harold's Pilgrimage*. Lord Byron's famous quote is, "I stood in Venice, on the Bridge of Sighs; / A palace and a prison on each hand."[14] Finally, there's a belief that if you and your loved one are passing under the Bridge of Sighs and share a passionate kiss your love will last an eternity. Others raise a higher bar in that it must also be sunset and Saint Mark's bell tower must be tolling. Either way, it's quite romantic, and a good opportunity to steal a kiss!

Harry's Bar

As mentioned, I'm not one to shy away from a city's cliché, touristy landmark sites or activities. They are usually great fun and always interesting. In Venice, after a day of sightseeing, this would entail enjoying a Bellini cocktail at the legendary *Harry's Bar*. What better place given that Harry's Bar invented the Peach Bellini? It was also a frequent haunt of Ernest Hemingway and has been visited by most celebrities, including Charlie Chaplin, Katherine Hepburn, Alfred Hitchcock, Frank Lloyd Wright, Truman Capote, Orson

14. Byron, *Childe Harold's Pilgrimage*, canto 4, lines 1–2.

Welles, and George Clooney. Conveniently, Harry's Bar is situated along a canal just around the corner from Saint Mark's Square.

Harry's Bar, founded by bartender Giuseppe Cipriani, has been going strong since 1931. Its start is one of the best "pay it forward" stories going. Legend is that Cipriani was a bartender at Venice's Hotel Europa, a favorite drinking establishment of a rich young American named Harry Pickering. Cipriani had noticed that Pickering unexpectedly stopped frequenting the hotel bar. Cipriani learned that Harry was cut off financially by his wealthy family when they discovered his excessive drinking habit. As fate would have it, Cipriani lent Harry Pickering 10,000 lire ($500 at the time). Pickering returned to the bar two years later and gave Cipriani 50,000 lire. He repaid Cipriani the original 10,000 lire with a bonus. Harry Pickering then advised Cipriani that the other 40,000 lire was in appreciation of his kindness and should be used to open a bar that they would call "Harry's Bar."[15] The rest is history!

With its enduring art deco club-like atmosphere and illustrious history, Harry's Bar is now owned and operated by fourth-generation Cipriani family. It was a memorable experience to be in charming Venice at Harry's Bar sipping a cool Bellini and enjoying their signature dish of beef carpaccio with a zingy cream sauce.

Sadly, the weekend in Venice came to an end and I returned to Milan by train on Sunday. Along with a few souvenirs, I brought home a beautiful Venetian masquerade carnival mask that still hangs on the living room wall above our piano. My wife also enjoys telling the story of that Saturday night I called home from my hotel room. It was 6:00 p.m. sharp and church bells throughout the floating city chimed in unison as gondoliers merrily serenaded lovers below. Being Italian (my grandfather immigrated from southern Italy) I half-jokingly pronounced, "I am home!"

15. Wikipedia, "Harry's Bar (Venice)."

CHAPTER 11

BARCELONA

Barcelona is a fountain of curiosity, shelter of strangers, hospice to the poor, land of the valiant, avenger of the offended, reciprocator of firm friendships, a city unique in its location and beauty.

—*Don Quixote, by Miguel de Cervantes*

When I think of Spain, I inevitably think of Don Quixote . . . the Man of La Mancha. Perhaps the epic story and farcical adventures appealed to me as a child, forming my earliest images of Spain. The beautiful climate and landscape, the conquistadors, flamenco dancers, and bullfighters, the familiar colorful culture and pageantry. Years later, as a young schoolboy, my parents authorized me to paint our old brick fireplace. I chose to paint it white then replicate the stark 1955 *Don Quixote* sketch by none other than Pablo Picasso. You know the popular sketch—scribbled bold black lines of a tall, gaunt, armored Don Quixote mounted high on his horse, his short, round amigo Sancho Panza atop his donkey below, the bright sun with its rays, and several distant windmills. I never fully read Miguel de Cervantes's epic novel *Don Quixote*, released in two parts in 1605 and 1615. I know that the publication is considered both the first and the greatest modern novel in history. It is also one of the most translated books in the world and the best-selling individual book of all time. Although I, like many American kids, studied Spanish in high school, my proficiency stalled and quickly faded. So here I was, my prospects of one day visiting exotic Spain undeniably slim. At least they were slim until one day at work I received a call and an invite to attend and present at a Global Travel Management conference in Barcelona.

Global business travel is a critical component of any successful multinational corporation; it's also often the largest "indirect cost" of doing business. Among all other direct and indirect spend, I had responsibility for our company's Travel Management program. Being acquired by a large international enterprise provided countless opportunities for cooperation, spend analysis, best-practice sharing, leverage, and ultimately alignment and integration. In addition to mandated compliance with audited policies and practices, there were new travel booking and expense management tools, as well as volume-driven corporate agreements with global and regional airlines, hotels, car rental agencies, corporate credit cards, etc. Our smaller US-based corporate branch expenses were less than $5 million and appeared well managed. In contrast, the global travel expenses of the large, acquiring German corporation exceeded $100 million annually. Striving to fully leverage global travel spend and operating to "gold standards" were our primary goals. Of course, employees' overall satisfaction and safety were a given. As a gesture of good will and to aid our smaller company's timely and full compliance, the head of global travel invited me and my travel and fleet manager to join her global team for a three-day conference to be held in Barcelona. Here, we would be a part of the annual review and rollout of new supplier agreements as well as program and system innovations. We were thrilled to attend the global event and meet new colleagues. The opportunity to visit Barcelona, Spain, was merely icing on the cake. However, as usual, bleisure travel entails more business than leisure. Arrival day always provides the best independent time for sightseeing. Often, evening team-building activities and fun attraction or tour-based activities are planned. More on that later. But first I needed an overview of the incredible city of Barcelona.

A high-level snapshot of Spain is a good precursor to Barcelona's rich and varied history. Like much of Europe, Spain is a country with very profound and troubled historical roots. In fact, it is believed that the first modern humans settled in Spain over thirty-five thousand years ago.[1] Spain has been the occupied home to numerous empires over many centuries. The Phoenicians are traced to the ninth century BC, followed by the Greeks, Carthaginians, and finally the Romans in the second century BC. In due course, the Visigoths drove out the Romans who conquered the North African Moors (Muslims). Notwithstanding Christian uprisings, the Muslim culture flourished for many centuries, though in the 780s Charlemagne's armies fought to extend Frankish control and bring Christianity into

1. CENIEH, "First Modern Humans." For this section's general overview of the history of Spain, see Wikipedia, "Spain"; Wikipedia, "History of Spain."

northern Spain. The intent was to serve as a buffer territory between his empire in the north and the Muslims to the south. The privileged geographic location of Spain between the Atlantic Ocean and Mediterranean Sea made it highly coveted by all. Add to that Spain's rich agricultural and mineral resources and the international stakes were high. By the fifteenth century the Europeans, as part of the Reconquista (reconquest), regained control of Spain, profoundly impacting Christian Europe.[2] The subsequent Age of Exploration, sponsored by the Christian Monarchs Ferdinand and Isabella, led to Spain's conquest of the Americas. The Spanish monarchy represented an early but powerful modern Renaissance state. Spain was regarded as the world's most powerful country at the time. Eventually, by 1588, the British defeated the Spanish Armada in a battle of the world's two great navies. The slow decline of the Spanish Empire would follow. By 1808 Napoleon had arrived and attempted to unify Spain after crossing through Portugal. A six-year war with France followed until Spain regained independence. Unfortunately, by the late nineteenth century, many of Spain's colonies sought independence. Spain faced countless revolutions, fiscal exhaustion, and growing imperial decline. Subsequently, Spain was crippled by so many competing conflicts. Due to unrest and Cuba's proximity to America, the United States demanded Spain's immediate withdrawal from Cuba. The sixteen-week 1898 Spanish-American War followed, with fighting in both the Caribbean Sea and the Pacific Ocean. With Spain's loss, and the favorable Treaty of Paris, Spain had to relinquish sovereignty over Cuba. Spain also ceded Puerto Rico, Guam, and the Philippines to the United States. As a positive aside, it was this Spanish-American War that redefined America's post–Civil War national identity. Spanish aggression became a common enemy to America's north and south. More far-reaching, the Spanish-American War also officially marked the initial entry of the relatively new United States into global affairs, conflicts, and overall world order.[3]

Recovery of Spain's economy temporarily improved due to its neutrality during the First World War—at least until 1936, when Francisco Franco led a military coup seizing much of Spain and an intense civil war ensued. By 1939, the dictator General Franco had gained control, and forced exiles and economic hardship followed. A long cold war period followed, and a return to democracy was viewed as the only viable means of Spain's integration with Europe. Nonetheless, Franco ruled until his death in 1975. It was the long-standing, discreet, strategic reign of King Juan Carlos I (1975–2014)

2. Heritage History, "Reconquista."

3. Wikipedia, "Treaty of Paris (1898)"; Wikipedia, "Spanish–American War"; SparkNotes, "Spanish American War," sec. "Overview."

that proved critical to Spain achieving freedom, political stability, and national reconciliation, though the colorful monarch would shamefully adjudicate the crown to his son and now lives in self-imposed exile. By 1986, Spain successfully became a full European Economic Community (EEC) member. In 1992, Barcelona, Spain, was recognized worldwide and awarded to serve as the coveted host of the Summer Olympic Games.

Buoyed by the 1992 Olympic Games, considered the most hugely successful games in modern history, Barcelona made itself into one of Europe's most desirable and dynamic cities. Its once shabby waterfront along with deteriorated, poorly planned neighborhoods and mountain ranges were completely and brilliantly transformed. Today, Barcelona not only rivals Spain's capital city of Madrid but is on par with the finest cities in Europe. Yet on the other hand, in many ways Barcelona is very different than most other European cities. Cosmopolitan Barcelona is bold, modern, creative, open, tolerant, forward-thinking, environmentally aware, and unflappable. If you stop and think about it, Barcelona has everything a world-class city could possibly dream of having. Barcelona is home to the Mediterranean's busiest and most beautiful port, a large modern airport, ideal climate, white seafront beaches, and Spain's Catalan culture and cooking. You can add to that Barcelona's Modernista architecture, Roman ruins, ancient medieval alleyways, Gothic Quarter, historical monuments, prestigious universities, abstract art, and other cultural riches. Another idiosyncrasy is the region's decentralized democracy. Although there's a national parliament, each of Spain's seventeen regions operates autonomously, managing their schools, hospitals, and public services. Lastly, Barcelona is uniquely diverse; about a quarter of Barcelona's residents are of international origins.[4] Barcelona's coastal location and nearby French border have created a showcase of outside influences, including countless languages and cuisines. Finally, each evening after dark, the city's many plazas, fashionable marina, and famous promenade are reimagined with a youthful excitement among residents and tourists alike.

Barcelona is on the northeastern coast of Spain and has a city population of 1.6 million residents, though the Barcelona urban area is home to nearly five million people. The city is a major cultural and economic center, with a striking physical setting between scenic mountains and the glimmering Mediterranean Sea. Barcelona is the capital of the autonomous and naturally beautiful region of Catalonia. Barcelona, founded over two thousand years ago, had not become a city of real importance until third-century Roman times. Its history followed that of Spain's under centuries-long

4. Info Barcelona, "New Record."

control of the Romans, Visigoths, Moors, Charlemagne's Frankish armies, the Spanish monarchy, and, briefly, Napoleon (French/Austrian) from 1808 to 1813. More recently, beginning in the late nineteenth and early twentieth century, Barcelona enjoyed a few decades of prosperity. The city had a boost in strength and personality from the developing modernist movement, a movement driven by the great architect/designer Antoni Gaudí and painter/sculptor Pablo Picasso. The innovative modernist movement's underlying principle was a rejection of history and conservative values. It included experimentation with form (abstraction, shapes, lines, and colors), a moving away from the past, and a search for new forms of expression. New groundbreaking architecture, art, literature, style, and cuisine left an indelible, very apparent mark on boundless Barcelona. Modernism is on full display at the Picasso Museum and with every Gaudí-designed building. For these and other reasons, Barcelona remains one of the world's trendiest cities, with a very cool, avant-garde vibe. Here are just a few of my limited-time, off-work bleisure experiences.

Las Ramblas

Choosing the most beautiful avenue or famous boulevard in the world is a very subjective and difficult process. To fully appreciate world-renowned urban landscapes you must look beyond aesthetic beauty. Differing factors such as original atmosphere, cultural impact, historic perspective, and shared experiences must also be considered. Of course, the world's most famous and iconic avenue is the Champs-Élysées in the heart of Paris. The beautiful, high-end, tree-lined avenue is over one mile long and ends at the historic Arc de Triomphe landmark. In my view, albeit quite different, running a very close second is Barcelona's *Las Ramblas.* I'm not sure I ever experienced anything like a stroll down lively Las Ramblas. An exotic, boisterous, carnival-like atmosphere abounds. In Spain, many towns have their own "Rambla" or pedestrian promenade where people go to see and be seen—a common meeting place for family outings, fun with friends, attractions, food, and drink. It's almost a Spanish ritual. However, Las Ramblas, Barcelona's three-lined pedestrian-only thoroughfare is next level. The vibrant, three-quarter mile boulevard is adorned with mansions, endless shops, kiosks, flower stalls, street artists, theaters, markets, tarot readers, caged birds, terraced restaurants, cafés, and clubs. Think of an around-the-clock party with an abundance of tapas and sangria. Much like the Champs-Élysées with the Arc de Triomphe, Las Ramblas magnificently ends at the towering Christopher Columbus monument in Barcelona's revitalized waterfront, smack on the Mediterranean Sea!

Las Ramblas is a rite of passage for any first-time visitor to Barcelona, an ideal place to start your initial visit to the city. It's impossible to resist a stroll down the charming, though tourist-swarming, avenue. Part magnificent boulevard, part heinous tourist trap, but 100 percent must-see. Usually referred to in the plural, Las Ramblas is a series of streets. The name is derived from the Arabic word "ramla," meaning riverbed. Remember that the North African Moors controlled much of Spain in medieval times. And the boulevard's fifteenth-century origin is as a dried-up sewage-filled stream outside the city walls. The stream fed the mountain rainwaters to the sea. It wasn't till the end of the eighteenth century that Las Ramblas first gained its present form and appearance. The boulevard divides Barcelona's two very distinct centermost districts. To the east is the touristy Gothic Quarter or the heart of the very old medieval city. And to the west is the shabby chic El Raval neighborhood. El Raval evolved from religious and medical institutions to factories to an edgier area of nightlife near the port. Beyond the churches and palaces, there are several worthy attractions as you descend Las Ramblas from the top to the sea. The large Catalonia Square is at the top of Las Ramblas and is home to hotels and upscale shopping. Nearby is the ornate 1892 Canaletes Fountain. This area is the site of many FC Barcelona (soccer) fan rallies. Also, legend holds that whoever drinks the fountain water will return to Barcelona. It has not happened for me yet! Next there's Barcelona's central Sant Josep Market, or "La Boqueria" as it's better known. Dating back to the twelfth century, the city market is an ideal place to buy exotic fruits, fresh fish, and most everything imaginable. A bit further, in the middle of Las Ramblas, on the ground, is a large, circular, colorful mosaic. The commission was completed in 1976 by world-famous Spanish painter Joan Miró. Not your typical pavement art! Miró's mosaic is a priceless gift to Barcelona's citizens and visitors alike. There's also the rebuilt charming 1837 Grand Liceu Theater (Barcelona's oldest theater still in use). Reopened and modernized in 1999, "El Liceu" is regarded as one of the world's finest opera houses.

So many other palaces, museums, and attractions are on the Las Ramblas route . . . all leading to the waterfront *Columbus Monument*. Looming over the lower end of Las Ramblas, where the boulevard meets the sea is a monument to Christopher Columbus (1451–1506). Born in Genoa, Italy, the controversial explorer has been claimed by many nations, though none more than Spain. After failing to obtain expedition funding from Portugal, Columbus moved to Spain. It was Spain's King Ferdinand and Queen Isabella who, in return for discovered gold, spices, and riches, agreed to fund Columbus's voyage to the New World. Although the Leif Erikson–led Vikings entered America five hundred years earlier, it was Columbus who first established a permanent colony there in 1492. As a result, it is Christopher Columbus who is considered the first European discoverer of the continent. Columbus's mission was to find a sea route from Europe to East Asia. Failing, Columbus himself had thought he landed in India when they most likely docked on an island in the Bahamas. In the process, Columbus often oppressed and destroyed native populations and confiscated their treasures. Columbus, seeking fame and glory, was promised certain rights and ten percent of the booty. Accordingly, favorable public opinion of Christopher Columbus has greatly changed with many worldwide memorials removed. In fact, even Spanish factions have unsuccessfully attempted to have his monument removed in 2016, 2018, and 2020. And although the achievements of Columbus have certainly been significantly reframed, his indisputable influence remains. The initial voyage took ten weeks with a ninety-man crew. They spent the following five months exploring other Caribbean islands. When he returned, Columbus chose to disembark from his first trip to the Americas back in Barcelona. There he was royally received by none other than King Ferdinand himself and celebrated for discovering the New World. As a powerful reminder and in preparation for the 1888 World Exhibition in Barcelona, the Columbus Monument was later constructed. The two-hundred-foot-high monument commemorates Columbus's first voyage to the Americas. The Columbus Monument is the finishing touch to the south end and coastal façade of Las Ramblas.

The bronze statue of Christopher Columbus defiantly points to the sea. In his left hand, Columbus holds nautical charts of his route. The statue underscores Spain's and Columbus's impactful though tainted naval exploration achievements. The sculpture sits high above the sea on a column on a sculptural base. The sculpture itself proudly sits atop a supporting, inscribed stone socle or plinth which simply reads, "Tierra" (Land). The plan to construct the Columbus Monument lingered many years. It wasn't until 1881 that city approval and financing were fully secured. A seven-year construction effort commenced. Only local architects were to be used. The project was divided into three parts. The first part was the circular base with four flights of wide stairs and eight sculptures representing Spain's provinces. Added were scenes from Columbus's voyage. Each of the staircases is flanked by two powerful lions. The second part was an eight-sided polygon pedestal with allegorical sculptures. And the third part was the impressive slender cast-iron Corinthian column. Two griffins at the base of the column hold Barcelona's coat of arms. There are also "famas," winged feminine figures, offering crowns of immortality to Columbus. And there's a half world globe representation of Columbus's discovered land. Mounted on top of these three components is the twenty-four-foot bronze Christopher Columbus statue, the work of sculptor Rafael Atché. No one is quite sure where Columbus is exactly pointing. Some believe it's simply to the sea, others to the New World, and others to Columbus's Italian birthplace of Genoa. In any case, on June 1, 1888, the Columbus Monument was officially inaugurated. The event was attended by many dignitaries including Austria's Queen Regent Maria Christina, the King of Italy Umberto I, and even former United States President Grover Cleveland. A year after inauguration, an elevator was added inside the column. The lift has since been renovated and greatly modernized on several occasions. The Columbus Monument interior is now one of few global monuments using geothermal energy for air conditioning. The lift ascends from the monument's ground floor to the very feet of the Christopher Columbus statue. Obviously, the viewing platform offers incredible panoramic views of Barcelona's city center, the Olympic Marina, the castle on Montjuïc Hill, and the stunning Mediterranean Sea.

Antoni Gaudí and the Sagrada Familia

As much as anyone, *Antoni Gaudí* (1852–1926) is synonymous with Barcelona! You can hardly mention one without mentioning the other. If you are not familiar with Gaudí when arriving in Barcelona, you'll certainly know all about him before departing the city. The eccentric Spanish architect and designer created many of Barcelona's most recognized landmarks. Most notable is his labor of love, the *Basilica de la Sagrada Familia*. Gaudí's neo-Gothic unconventional Sagrada Familia (Holy Family) Basilica is the most visited monument in all of Spain and the very essence of Barcelona. Gaudí was at the forefront of Spain's art nouveau movement, and his masterpieces help define Barcelona.

Antoni Gaudí was the youngest of five children. He was born into a Catalonian family of boilermakers and was taught early on how to work and create with his hands. He learned about space and volume creating in the family workshop. Gaudí developed a special talent for designing and creating space and transforming materials. As a child in constant poor health, Gaudí also spent much time resting and enjoying outdoors. Gaudí considered nature "the supreme work of the Creator"[5] and this, too, greatly shaped his art. Largely exempt from compulsory military service due to his health, and gifted in drawing, Gaudí began formal studies as an architect in Barcelona. The eighteen-year-old paid for his studies by drawing and

5. Barcelona.com, "Gaudi Barcelona," sec. "Timeline," 1852.

collaborating with many architects as a draftsman. Gaudí was just an average student with an individualistic modern approach to architecture. He was influenced by his growing interest in nature, history, philosophy, aesthetics, and religion. So unique was Gaudí's character that upon his graduation one director commented, "We have given this diploma to a madman or a genius. Time will tell."[6] Gaudí's career gradually took off as the art nouveau movement began to spread throughout Europe. In Spain, and for Gaudí, this movement took the name of modernism. Though Gaudí's uniquely personal and incomparable organic architectural style defies any real classification. Early traits of Gaudí's genius were evident as Spain's flamboyant era gave birth to many commissions leading to several of the architect's most beautiful works. Included were palaces, churches, crypts, a park, and even the Welcome Pavilion for Barcelona's 1888 World's Fair. Consequently, by 1900 Gaudí was a renowned architect and extremely busy.

However, perhaps Gaudí's past school director was correct on both accounts. Over time, it's possible that "genius Gaudí" also began showing traits of "madman Gaudí." The youthful Gaudí was always a young dandy of gourmet taste who greatly favored Barcelona's social gatherings. Sadly, by 1915 Gaudí progressively withdrew from society to devote himself entirely to the work of his life . . . building the Sagrada Familia—the "Cathedral of the Poor," as he often referred to the church. An economic crisis had paralyzed work on the church and the following decade was difficult for Gaudí. In response, he surprisingly and fervently devoted himself to a singular religious sentiment and his intensified Catholic faith. So impactful was Gaudí's religion that he earned the nickname "God's Architect," and a cause for his canonization was subsequently opened in 2003.[7] Unfortunately, in the process Gaudí completely distanced himself from society, completely neglecting his personal appearance and fasting or eating and living very frugally. He even eventually abandoned his residence to reside inside the Sagrada Familia workshop, living as a recluse. Gaudí had lost all his remaining family and most of his friends. He took refuge in his work and the spiritual peace of his Catholic faith. In his final years, Gaudí would often take to the street to collect alms to continue his work.

On the evening of June 7, 1926, heading back to Sagrada Familia after having taken his daily walk to the nearby Church of Sant Felip Neri, Gaudí was knocked down by a passing tram and rendered unconscious. Nobody suspected that the disheveled old man in ragged, worn clothes was

6. Barcelona.com, "Gaudi Barcelona," sec. "Timeline," 1870.

7. For this and other details about Gaudí's life, see Wikipedia, "Antoni Gaudí"; Barcelona.com, "Gaudi Barcelona"; and Casa Batlló, "About Antoni Gaudí."

the famous architect, and he was not immediately rescued. Not carrying any identification papers, Barcelona's great Antoni Gaudí was initially mistaken for an anonymous beggar. With the help of passersby, Gaudí was eventually transported by taxi to the hospital, where he received only rudimentary care. The following day, Gaudí was finally recognized by the attending chaplain. Unfortunately, by this time Gaudí's condition had severely deteriorated, and on June 10, 1926, he died at the age of seventy-three. Days later, Gaudí was buried in one of the Sagrada Familia chapel crypts. Throngs of Barcelona citizens came out to bid the city's most revered architect a final farewell.

There are many older extraordinary, otherworldly, faith-shaking churches and basilicas throughout Europe. Then there's the Temple Expiatori de la Sagrada Familia. The still unfinished Sagrada Familia, Gaudí's greatest work, is Europe's most unconventional church. Welcoming 4.5 million arrivals each year, the neo-Gothic church is the unmissable symbol of Barcelona, an astounding architectural masterpiece and city highlight despite being unfinished and under construction for over 140 years and counting. Further and unbeknownst to all, construction was carried on illegally for 137 years until 2019 when a building permit was granted.[8] Sagrada Familia (Temple of the Holy Family) was originally intended as a simple Catholic church dedicated to Jesus, Mary, and Joseph. The original design was quite different when construction first started in 1882 under architect Francisco de Paula del Villar. A year later a young and fast-rising architect, Antoni Gaudí, took over the assignment and he took a very different direction. Gaudí reconceived a new, groundbreaking design, pushing the boundaries of all known architectural styles. His goal was to build a church highlighting Jesus's nativity, passion, and glory. Gaudí realized that the project was so ambitious that he would not see its completion in his lifetime. He also feared that the project would be stopped after his death if the interior worship function was completed.[9] For these reasons, Gaudí started work on the church's elaborate exterior. Gaudí was able to oversee the first of the three monumental facades, the spectacular Nativity Façade. Reaching Gaudí's great artistic heights, the façade expresses the hope and joy of life. However, the still unfinished Glory Façade is supposed to be the most monumental. There's little doubt that Gaudí considered the creation of Sagrada Familia his holy earthly mission. Gaudí would spend the final forty-three years of his life designing and building Sagrada Familia. In the latter years, he even depleted his own funds to sustain construction. At the time of Gaudí's death, the basilica was no more than 20 percent complete.

8. John, "Sagrada Familia Gets Building."
9. Lonely Planet, "La Sagrada Família," para. 9.

To that end, Gaudí is said to have often stated, "My client is not in a hurry."[10] The Sagrada Familia has always been a project by the people for the people. Despite its international renown, funding always relied purely on private contributions. Funding was scarce during the 1930s Spanish Civil War and the decades following. The basilica suffered a long period of neglect, and a great number of original plans, documents, and scale models were destroyed. Work slowly resumed in 1954 (championed by artist Salvador Dalí), and construction has continued ever since. However, again, it was the successful 1992 Barcelona Summer Olympic Games that fueled an enhanced international reputation, greatly increased tourism, and finally accelerated church funding and construction. The project was to be completed in 2026 for the centenary of Gaudí's 1926 death, though the COVID-19 pandemic has impacted that date. At this time, Barcelona is hopeful that all construction will be fully completed by 2032 in time for the 150th anniversary of Sagrada Familia.

It's nearly impossible to describe Sagrada Familia, but here goes. In a nutshell, once completed, Sagrada Familia will be an ascending feast of eighteen sky-high, spine-tingling towers. The towers are intended to represent the twelve apostles, the four evangelists, the Virgin Mary, and Jesus Christ. Each of the apostle towers is topped with Venetian mosaics. The evangelist towers contain symbols, i.e., winged bull (Saint Luke), winged man (Saint Matthew), eagle (Saint John), and winged lion (Saint Mark). The tallest tower, the recently completed spire of Jesus, is surmounted by a giant, fifty-six-foot cross and measures an incredible 565 feet high. Now that the Jesus spire is complete, Sagrada Familia is the world's tallest church building.[11] The staggering height is only slightly less than Barcelona's Montjuïc Hill, as Gaudí believed his creation should not surpass God's own. Overall, the primarily stone basilica is three hundred feet long by two hundred feet wide, with a capacity of nine thousand people. Gaudí also intended that wind-driven tubular bells be placed in the spires, driving soft sound down into the church's interior. An elevator will lead up one of the towers, or you could try the four hundred steep steps of the spiral stone staircase. The basilica's soaring interior is in the shape of a Latin cross with a roof supported by extraordinary, angled, leaning pillars. With nature as Gaudí's favorite muse, the interior effect is a magical treelike living forest. Via the many stained-glass windows, the church is splashed with calming rays of streaming yellow, blue, green, and red sunlight. Of course, there's so much more to see, including the Gaudí Museum (workshop replica), Schools of Gaudí

10. Steward, "12 Facts," sec. "Gaudí never worried."

11. Wikipedia, "Sagrada Família," secs. "Spires" and "21st century."

(for children of the basilica's workers), chapels, and the crypt where Antoni Gaudí is buried.

Picasso Museum (Museu Picasso)

Whether you admire his life and art or not, eccentric, long-living Spanish painter and sculptor Pablo Picasso (1881–1973) was the man! Famous Australian art critic Robert Hughes wrote, "To say that Pablo Picasso dominated Western art in the 20th century is, by now, the merest commonplace. . . . No painter or sculptor, not even Michelangelo, had been as famous as this in his own lifetime."[12] Consequently, Picasso is unanimously regarded as one of the most influential artists of the twentieth century. He is known for introducing the cubist movement, and he constructed sculptures, collages, and a wide variety of developed and advanced styles. He was exceptionally prolific: at the time of Picasso's death there were over forty-five thousand unsold works of art in his estate, including paintings, sculptures, ceramics, drawings, tapestries, and rugs. He was much more prolific than most artists of his era, rivaled, in my mind, only by American artist and mass producer of paintings Bob Ross. For Picasso, it was said that "work, sex, and tobacco" were his passions and addictions.[13] Many works depict the noted womanizer's sexual relationships. And while erotic emotion appeared vital to Picasso's artistic process, it was deeply damaging to the important women in his life. Nevertheless, artistic value never suffered based on Picasso's tainted character and massive work volume. Picasso's revolutionary art resulted in universal acceptance, unimaginable influence, and an immense fortune. Even today, many of Picasso's paintings rank among the most expensive in the world. In 2015, a record was set when Picasso's 1955 painting *Women of Algiers* (*Les Femmes d'Alger*) sold for $179.3 million at Christie's in New York City.[14]

Pablo Picasso was born in Malaga, Spain, though he moved with his family to Barcelona by age fourteen. Picasso's father had accepted a teaching position at the city's art academy where Picasso enrolled. The precocious Picasso had already demonstrated extraordinary natural artistic talent at a very young age. Happily, Picasso would spend his formative years and youth in Barcelona before moving to Paris. It was in Barcelona where Picasso honed his skills and passions and became a recognized artist. It was also in Barcelona where Picasso first began associating with other intellectuals,

12. Hughes, "Artist Pablo Picasso," paras. 1–4.
13. Wikipedia, "Pablo Picasso," sec. "Personal life."
14. Hickey, "Picasso Painting Breaks Record."

visionaries, and renowned artists. By the age of seventeen, Picasso would frequent the progressive Els Quatre Gats Café (Four Cats) in Barcelona's Gothic Quarter. Quatre Gats opened in 1897, at the height of modernism, in the likeness of Paris's famous "Le Chat Noir" (The Black Cat) cabaret. The Four Cats quickly became the meeting place for Barcelona's growing artistic avant-garde. The venue was a cultural showplace and center of artistic expression for all types of emerging talents, including painters, musicians, and writers alike. It was at the Four Cats Café, in 1899, that a young Picasso had his very first individual paintings exhibit. Even today, the Quatre Gats Café continues to serve as a place of inspiration for highly recognized international artists. Eventually, by his early twenties, Picasso left Barcelona for Paris only returning on a few occasions. Picasso's opposition to General Franco and the 1930s Spanish Civil War kept him in France. Most of Picasso's life was spent in the south of France, where he is buried. Nonetheless, the city of Barcelona had a very significant impact on the artist. Picasso's genius is often attributed to his modern ideas, ever-changing radical styles, and experimentation fostered first in Barcelona and then Paris. In the end, the selected location of Picasso's first museum proved that Barcelona remained in his heart and soul throughout his life.

By the 1960s, Picasso's close friend and personal secretary Jaume Sabartés conceived an idea of creating a museum dedicated to the world's greatest living artist, Pablo Picasso. Sabartés had planned to build the art museum in Picasso's birth city of Malaga, Spain. However, Picasso adamantly convinced his good friend that the museum should open in Barcelona's Old City. After all, Picasso always loved Barcelona, its people, and its culture. Picasso was ever grateful for the recognized start Barcelona provided his artistic career. In March 1963, the *Picasso Museum* (Museu Picasso as it is known) opened to the public in Barcelona. It was the first museum dedicated to Picasso's artwork. It was also the only museum created in Picasso's name during his lifetime. Since then, other exceptional Picasso museums have opened in Paris, Malaga, Antibes (France), and Münster (Germany). Additionally, many of Picasso's finest paintings, sculptures, and collections are scattered all over the world in cities such as Madrid, London, Cologne, and New York. As examples, Picasso's famous, powerful painting *Guernica* (1937) is displayed in Madrid's Queen Sofia National Museum. The painting is a dramatic anti-war personal protest of Adolf Hitler's German bombing of the Spanish town at the request of Spain's General Franco. Likewise, New York's Museum of Modern Art is fortunate to display the cubist *Three Musicians* (1921). London's Tate Modern displays Picasso's mistress in *The Weeping Woman* (1937). Finally, the *Family of Saltimbanques* (1905), a desolate circus performer, is displayed in the National Gallery in Washington, DC.

Little does any of this impact the unique magnificence of Barcelona's Picasso Museum and his largest collection of works. To begin with, the museum is located along a grand, medieval street in the edgy El Born neighborhood (also known as La Ribera) in Barcelona's Old City. Bohemian-chic El Born is regarded as the trendiest neighborhood in Barcelona. This district is full of charming old buildings, tiny pedestrian alleys, funky boutiques, upscale wine bars, music venues, Barcelona's best local cuisine, and even some medieval jousting fun. In essence, El Born is one of the best areas in all of Barcelona to wander. Deserving nothing less than this thriving location, the Picasso Museum appears in the middle of El Born. The museum is housed in five ornate, interconnected thirteenth- and fourteenth-century medieval palaces. The museum's palaces are full of Gothic archways, lavish painted ceilings, dripping crystal chandeliers, staircases, and an elegant inner courtyard. Picasso's works are wonderfully illuminated on three floors among the museum's collective thirty-five white studio rooms. The museum's refined medieval setting, in striking contrast to Picasso's outlandish twentieth-century artistic creativity, is a draw unto itself.

Even more impressive than its striking Gothic location is the incredible 4,251 works of Pablo Picasso art in the museum's extensive permanent collection. While most people know Pablo Picasso for his distorted images, the Barcelona Picasso Museum features his earlier, more controlled works. The museum's focus is the formative years of the artist, many of which were spent in Barcelona. Picasso was established as an extraordinary talent at an astonishingly young age. Consequently, on full display in Picasso's early works is the artist's otherworldly technical virtuosity and versatility. Even as a teenager, Picasso painted major works of collectible art. On display are Picasso's *Portrait of Aunt Pepa* (1896) and *Science and Charity* (1897), which he painted as a fifteen-year-old boy. Additionally, there are also many later whimsical works, including masterworks from Picasso's Blue Period and the end of his career. The museum opened in 1963 with just 574 works from the personal collection of Picasso's great friend and museum founder Jaume Sabartés. Quickly, Barcelona added gifted art already in the possession of the city's museum of modern art. Several other friends and collectors of Picasso gifted artwork as well. The museum's collection was continually expanded with personal donations. As more substantial donations were added, the museum's importance greatly grew. Sabartés bequeathed further works upon his death in 1968. Picasso personally donated many early works kept by his sister as well as graphic works left in his will. Picasso's widow, Jacqueline Roque, donated hundreds of ceramic pieces. The museum also acquired other sought-after works. In turn, the museum's physical space greatly expanded throughout the 1990s and was beautifully remodeled in

2003. It's no surprise that the Museu Picasso is one of Spain's most popular art galleries. As intended by the artist himself, the museum also deeply reveals Picasso's lifelong relationship with his beloved Barcelona.

Salamanca Restaurant

Occasionally when traveling, I'll pass a national treasure or a landmark establishment with no knowledge of what I just saw or experienced. Usually, I'll hear or read about it later and regret that I was unaware. This was the case with Barcelona's classic *Salamanca* restaurant. In this instance, it wasn't until years later that I realized I had experienced a work team dinner in one of the best long-standing seafood restaurants in Barcelona. Dinner at Salamanca provided a chance to fully enjoy the genuine regional taste of Catalan food in an unparalleled atmosphere. You see, Salamanca is in the heart of the older, posh Barceloneta (Little Barcelona) seaside neighborhood. In fact, the restaurant is located on the Mediterranean beachfront! So intoxicating is the Barceloneta beach that it is believed to have inspired writer Miguel de Cervantes over four hundred years ago. The location unofficially served as the book setting of the fight between Don Quixote and the Knight of the White Moon.

I should have realized just how special Salamanca restaurant was at the time of my visit. The walls are filled with an array of photographs and notes from Spanish and visiting celebrities prominent in the field of sports, film, and music. In fact, there was a buzz that two tall, handsome "footballers" (soccer stars) were there the night of our visit. Salamanca had both a mixed "old boys' club" mentality and a young vibe! Add to that the authentic, delectable Spanish dishes of the Catalonia region, three of which I certainly remember. The first is the restaurant's classic seafood paella. Paella is traditionally cooked in a large pot and consists of Spanish rice topped with fresh, savory, high-quality fish and seafood (or meats, vegetables, etc.). The brothy signature rice dish was brimming with local prawns, clams, cuttlefish, tender squid, and langoustines. The second dish served was simply plates of Spanish ham—not just any ham but exquisite Jamón Ibérico ham of the noble black Ibérico pig from Spain's ancient oak pastures. Many believe, my apologies to the Italians, that Spain produces the best ham in the world, an elevated prosciutto. Lastly, the third surprising dish was, believe it or not, barnacles. An expensive delicacy in Spain and Portugal. The long-necked crustacean grows along the rocky, wave-battered sea perches. As a result, barnacles are extremely dangerous to harvest. While connoisseurs greatly enjoy this supposed lobster-tasting delicacy, I had difficulty overcoming the fact that they were barnacles!

Just outside the restaurant, on the Barceloneta Beach, is the *Parc del Port Olimpic* (Olympic Park). The park was developed for the successful 1992 Summer Olympics Games hosted by Barcelona. It was a perfect spot for an "after a delicious dinner" walk. The palm-lined urban beach area remains one of Barcelona's liveliest and most attractive stretches, full of bars, restaurants, sculptures, and nightclubs. The beach promenade is also filled with parks, playgrounds, benches, Olympic flagpoles, tropical shrubbery and flowers. Of course, a bronze figure of Cobi, Barcelona's lovable 1992 Olympic Games Catalan Sheepdog mascot, is there as well. Urban beaches are always surprisingly exciting!

Ah, as evidenced above, my brief time in Barcelona, Spain, is very fondly remembered. Just as imagined, Barcelona is a historic, sun-kissed, beautiful, festive city. Barcelona's vibe is filled with a colorful, ever-present spirit of both the past (Don Quixote, Christopher Columbus, Antoni Gaudí, Pablo Picasso) and a promising future. In the end, the enduring core of Barcelona's identity is a zest for living and a deep love for having a wonderfully good time. It's a country where the people clearly get it! Spaniards passionately put equal efforts into enjoying both their lives and their work . . . perfect "work-life" balance as they say. Consequently, my envisioned Barcelona bleisure mission was easily and roundly accomplished!

CHAPTER 12

FLORENCE

Not much was really invented during the Renaissance,
If you don't count modern civilization.

—*P. J. O'Rourke*

Florence is the Renaissance city and a work of art unto itself. A visit to Florence is a breathtaking, eye-opening experience for most visitors. It's quite easy to fall in love with Florence. In the compact, concentrated, historic city center you will find some of the world's most famous frescoes, sculptures, churches, palaces, and romantic restaurants. There are even tiny fifteenth-century wine windows carved into Renaissance buildings along the cobbled streets. The obscure windows were once used by wealthy Florentine families to sell wine without spreading the plague. The windows were recently brought back into use to serve libations and gelato. Most consequential and still apparent is the "rebirth" or Renaissance that occurred in Florence over five hundred years ago—both a rebirth of man and a rebirth of classical Greek and Roman culture. Fifteenth-century Florence, with its powerful banking, textile, and artists' guilds, along with a philosophy dedicated to the welfare of the city, is considered the cradle of the Renaissance. As a result, Florence was a most exciting, thriving, prosperous place to be. Influenced by the city's Medici family, a strong humanist, cultural movement and a more productive spiritual way of living were fostered and adopted. Florence's wealthy patron families and its writers, architects, painters, philosophers, and political thinkers all propelled the model Renaissance city. Overlapping within the same fifteenth century, Florence experienced

Michelangelo, Leonardo da Vinci, Raphael, Sandro Botticelli, Donatello, Filippo Brunelleschi, and Lorenzo the Magnificent de' Medici. In Florence, you walk in the footsteps of these native sons, founding fathers and symbols of the Renaissance. They are arguably among the greatest artists and most brilliant minds of all time. All aspects of civilized life as previously known were transformed first in Florence and then throughout Europe. The Florence Renaissance changed the very way we see the world! In the process and with such steadfast extraordinary focus, the Italian city-state of Florence became, and many argue remains, the most beautiful and fascinating city in all of Europe.

Guilty . . . alright, guilty as charged! In all my work years and associated travels, I'm proud to say that I never played "hooky," skipping out of work when on a business trip . . . except this once! I was visiting our office in Milan, Italy, assigned to lead efforts to bid, evaluate, and select new office furniture for the relocation of approximately 230 employees—an approximate $1 million-plus budgeted spend. As usual, I had already obtained competitive proposals from our three Tier 1 global partners (Hayworth, Herman Miller, and Steelcase). And, as per our global strategy and the request of Milan management, I also evaluated a few local (Italian) manufacturers. A cross-functional team was formed to assist me, and we would visit various showrooms. It was not often that a local manufacturer could compete with our worldwide partners in terms of quality, lead times, and negotiated price schedules. But Milan, much like Stockholm, is a noted international design mecca, so consideration was given to a couple well-established, family-run Italian manufacturers. From the onset, Milan was set on more stylish Italian workstations. Our global procurement strategy did provide for cultural inputs and preferences as to brand and other specifications. Following an extensive review process and necessary due diligence, I formulated an executive summary of recommendations to present Friday morning. I had a return flight home on Saturday. Staying late Thursday evening, I had just finished a summary presentation as the executive team surprisingly entered the conference room. The executives requested my recommendations at that time, so I obliged. I did concede to the Italian workstations as the quality was sound and they took a clear position to sacrifice pricing (usually a poor decision). However, we had agreed to select the Herman Miller Aeron task chairs, which graded highest during showroom visits. The same chairs are used in many US offices as well as in London, Barcelona, Stockholm, Bangkok, and other international offices. The site executives accepted our plan and appreciated the diligent efforts of the team. In parallel, they canceled the scheduled Friday morning review. It was at that very moment that I decided to rise early, hop the train, and take a day trip to Florence! The city of Florence was highest on my bucket list. I had just two team calls to join with the German office but decided to make those calls from hotel lobbies in Florence. And that is exactly what I did . . . executing the plan to perfection and spending a long, beautiful, mostly uninhibited spring day in the Renaissance city!

"Florence—the city of tranquility made manifest": the words of novelist Katherine Cecil Thurston.[1] And quite noticeably, there is a predominant peaceful, calm feeling in Florence. It's as if the city has nothing to prove, that they've been there and done that, so just enjoy the city's unparalleled beauty. Accordingly, the sentiment is that you cannot imagine any situation more agreeable than Florence. While in high school, we had a wonderful Franciscan priest, Father Joseph Avella, OFM. He taught us English Literature. Father Joe became a very close family friend and even married me and my wife, Susie, after college. Once, he took a group of high school students to visit his mother and his childhood home in West Philadelphia. Yes, the same West Philly that the "Fresh Prince" escaped from to move in with wealthy Uncle Phil, Aunt Vivian, and snobby cousins Carlton and Hilary in Bel-Air. I quickly learned why as I got stabbed twice by a passing neighborhood gang during that visit. Another story for another day. . . . I survived. In any case, in preparation to serve as a priest and educator, Father Joe had studied abroad extensively. On countless occasions, Father Joe would state that Florence was his favorite city and the most beautiful city in the world. Unfortunately, Father Joe passed away at a relatively young age, but I couldn't help but think of him as I arrived in Florence. The Renaissance city casts a spell in a way that few cities can.

Florence, or Firenze in Italian, is derived from Latin derivatives conveying "good luck" or "to blossom." Thus, Florence is also known as the "Lily City." The history of Florence resembles most of Western Europe with Roman origins. Established in 59 BC and built as an army camp, Florence would serve as a colony for veteran Roman soldiers. Florence was ideally situated in the fertile Arno River valley on the main route from Rome (Via Cassia). The city quickly became an important and popular commercial center. Much like the surrounding region, Florence too faced turbulent periods, first succumbing to Germanic Gothic tribes and subsequently to Byzantine rule. Peace returned by the sixth century, though Florence was briefly conquered by Charlemagne in 774 before its independence as a city-state. Slowly, the population grew as Florence prospered. The twelfth century marked the golden age of Florentine art, a booming textile industry, rapid growth of an industrious merchant community, and international

1. Thurston, *Gambler*, pt. 3, ch. 1.

trade. Driven by powerful guilds, Florence became quite rich and economically successful, growing into one of Europe's largest cities. The long Renaissance period in Florence lasted three centuries, from 1300 to 1600. The early period of initial development of the broader Renaissance culture spread across Europe, though the true Renaissance period flourished in the fifteenth and sixteenth centuries. Even the language spoken in Florence during the fourteenth century came to be accepted as the countrywide language—Italian. Subsequently, the wealthy, noble Medici family reigned as grand dukes of Tuscany from 1569 until 1737. By 1804 Napoleon Bonaparte had gained control of France and claimed the title of Emperor of France. Shortly thereafter Napoleon renewed his Italian campaign. Conquering the Italian Republic, Napoleon also proclaimed himself king of Italy. However, in 1814, the Napoleonic regime collapsed in Italy as it did in the rest of Europe. Finally, in 1861, Tuscany and its capital, Florence, would become a region in the newly formed United Kingdom of Italy. Shortly after, Florence briefly replaced Turin as the capital of Italy, though by 1871, Rome superseded Florence, becoming Italy's third and present capital. Finally, World War II brought a year-long German occupation of Florence. Paying a severe price in battle, Florence was ultimately liberated by Allied troops on August 4, 1944. Many of the brave World War II Allied soldiers are buried in cemeteries just outside the city. Today the magnificent city of Florence has a population of over 360,000 residents, with nearly one million inhabitants in its gorgeous surrounding Tuscan metropolitan region.

I fully understand that Florence is not limited to Michelangelo's *David* statue at the Accademia, the Duomo, the Ponte Vecchio Bridge, the Uffizi Gallery, and the Arno River at sunset. But what if it were . . . as it was for me? That's more than plenty, a day well spent, as each of these must-see attractions can only be truly experienced in person. Fortunately, Florence is space-intensive, with most of its sublime art and mind-boggling sights concentrated in the small historic city center. It didn't take long to discover the magic of Florence.

Statue of David (Michelangelo)

Michelangelo's *Statue of David* is an Italian Renaissance masterpiece and one of the most famous sculpted works in the history of mankind. The original *David* is splendidly displayed in the *Accademia Gallery of Florence* (Galleria dell'Accademia di Firenze). The Accademia, founded 1563, was originally an art school where many sculptures, paintings, and prints were collected to inspire students. It is now a famous museum, and its prized *David* statue embodies and represents the city of Florence. *David* took on new political meaning shortly after its creation. Namely, David's astounding biblical image of youthful beauty perfectly symbolized Florentine strength, liberty, and blossoming civic pride. As with most "otherworldly" art, the history and story of Michelangelo's *David* is nearly as spellbinding as the amazing sculpture. The story begins long before Michelangelo. In 1296, the Florentine Republic Opera del Duomo (OPA) was founded to supervise construction of a new cathedral, Santa Maria del Fiore. OPA was the Cathedral Works Administration or "works commission." The emblem "Agnus Dei" or Lamb of God was adopted by OPA. This was to pay homage to Florence's powerful Woolen Cloth Guild, which almost entirely funded construction of the cathedral. Following completion of the Florence Duomo (cathedral), OPA acquired a giant marble block from the Fantiscritti quarry in Carrara. The marble block was brought to Florence across the Mediterranean Sea and up the Arno River on barges. The block was stored for many years. In 1460, two Florentine sculptors undertook an ambitious project to sculpt twelve figures to decorate the cathedral's exterior. The project failed and the giant marble block fell back into oblivion, stored in a warehouse. In 1501, the project resumed with the OPA evaluating artists of the time, which included Michelangelo, as well as consulting Leonardo da Vinci. By September 1501, the OPA officially commissioned Michelangelo for the project. The task was made even more arduous because the weathered marble block was flawed and too narrow. Marble is best carved fresh out of the quarry, as age and exposure increase hardness and limit artistic control. Additionally, three sculptors had previously failed to chisel the block, only worsening its condition. Even worse, the marble block had been abandoned for over forty years before Michelangelo began. Not a problem! The twenty-six-year-old genius artist isolated himself nearly three years through May 1504. And, despite all the above, Michelangelo miraculously created the colossal, six-ton, seventeen-foot-high statue of David—believed by many to be the most beautiful art object ever created by man.

Michelangelo was always a notorious workaholic. The "Divine One," as he was known,[2] labored till his death at age eighty-nine. Michelangelo "contended that he was merely liberating figures that were already existent in the stone, and that he could see them in his mind's eye."[3] This may never be truer than with his heroic *David*. Once completed, the statue was too large and beautiful to be positioned along the cathedral roofline. Following a study, *David* was positioned under roof in the civic government building, Piazza della Signoria, a symbol of secular power versus strictly religious

2. Andrews, "9 Things."

3. Wikipedia, "*David* (Michelangelo)," sec. "Process."

intent. The statue was transported a half-mile there (over four days) on fourteen greased logs rolled by forty men.[4] It was unveiled on September 8, 1504. Subsequently, as necessary to prevent any deterioration, *David* was relocated to the Accademia in 1873. In 1910, a replica was placed in the original location and remains there today.

In addition to the great size of the statue of David, what is most noticeable is Michelangelo's dramatic depiction. As known, the story of the biblical underdog hero is of a boy-warrior who defeated the giant Goliath and saved the Israelites from the Philistines. The young shepherd, using only a sling and a stone, hits Goliath in the head, felling the giant, before decapitating him. Most artists depict a victorious hero standing over the decapitated head of defeated Goliath. Conversely, Michelangelo chose to depict a wary but confident boy-warrior sizing up the giant before battle. Plus, no earlier artists had altogether omitted the giant.[5] With its incredible detail, it's easy to forget that *David* is a rigid sculpture of inert stone. What's most evident is that every masterful, chiseled inch of *David* incredibly suggests immanent movement and life. Michelangelo's *David*, as with all his sculptures, is a result of his intense anatomy studies. Each bodily muscle is exact, absent one back muscle. Turns out Michelangelo was "aware of the flaw," noting that "a defect in the marble block made it impossible to reproduce the muscle."[6] Simultaneously, David's intense facial expression and seemingly pulsating veins reveal expected tension in anticipation of a dangerous encounter. *David's* calculated gaze with piercing eyes signals deep thought and analysis of the impending battle. And, in Renaissance fashion and despite David's strong male body, it's clear that victory will not be derived from brute force but rather skill, reason, and intellectual strength.

More than five hundred years later, Michelangelo's *David* remains a very compelling image visited by 1.5 million visitors annually. And to think: among so many masterworks, Michelangelo's famous *Pietà* preceded *David*, and his painting of the Sistine Chapel ceiling followed. Though *David* is generally considered priceless, its monetary value has been estimated as high as one billion dollars.

Uffizi Gallery

As beautiful and spellbinding as the Accademia Gallery's *Statue of David* is, Florence's actual premier gallery is the Gallerie degli Uffizi, otherwise

4. Wikipedia, "*David* (Michelangelo)," sec. "Placement."
5. Wikipedia, "*David* (Michelangelo)," sec. "Interpretation."
6. Lorenzi, "Michelangelo's David Is Missing," paras. 4–5.

known as the *Uffizi Gallery*. This museum is in the very heart of Florence and home to the world's greatest collection of Italian Renaissance art. Consequently, the Uffizi is, in fact, one of the most famous and important museums in the world. And, like many of Europe's finest museums, the Uffizi Gallery is fittingly housed in an elaborate former palace (palazzo). In this instance, the Uffizi Palace, completed 1560–80, was built as administrative offices for the Medici Grand Duke Cosimo. A grand corridor connects the Uffizi with the Pitti Palace, the then-new residence of the Medici family. Shortly thereafter, the Medici family installed their personal art collection on the palace top floor. The exhibits and grandeur of the palace are unparalleled. In 1591, the Medici family opened their private art collection to friends and family (initially by request only) before creating Europe's first modern public museum. By 1743, the last Medici family heir (Anna Maria Luisa de' Medici) formally bequeathed the extensive, highly valuable art collection to the city. She conditioned that the entire collection remain intact and that it never leave Florence. Its legacy cemented, the Uffizi Gallery is a prized, everlasting wonder.

Never intending the building to serve as a museum, Cosimo de' Medici commissioned his favorite Florentine architect, Giorgio Vasari, to create a vast, grandiose, U-shaped Renaissance palace. It was to contain a long labyrinth of halls—since enlarged to forty-nine halls with art in 101 rooms. The palace fronts the enchanting Arno River adjacent to the Palazzo Vecchio, the seat of governmental power in Florence. Medici intended the palace to house the magistrates, the seats of the various powerful Florentine guilds, and other judiciary offices: thus, the name "Uffizi," which translates to "offices" in Italian.[7] After navigating the Uffizi lines and entry process, you ascend two Renaissance-era stairways to the gallery entrance. Then, unveiled in dramatic fashion are the stunning frescoed ceilings and ornate décor of a historic medieval palace and the most amazing collection of art.

Exploring the glory of past masterpieces is always a special and memorable experience. Doing so in amazing Florence at the venerable Uffizi Gallery is next level. The gallery is home to works by most Renaissance-period masters, including Botticelli, Michelangelo, Caravaggio, Filippo Lippi, Leonardo da Vinci, Raphael, Rembrandt, Giotto, and many other European artists. The gallery's corridors also boast invaluable Medici collections of ancient Roman statues and busts. If you're not an entrenched, hardcore museum enthusiast, or if you're pressed for time on business travel, relax and take it easy. My strategy is not to enjoy all the paintings, frescoes, and sculptures on view. Rather, I leisurely enjoy a few predetermined, designated favorites.

7. Wikipedia, "Uffizi."

Usually, the most noted exhibits are readily known, or you could obtain a complete guide to current collections at a newsstand. I've also discovered that late afternoons or evenings, as available, are favorable visiting times. Often, arriving just an hour or two before closing provides ease of access. Somehow, with a little luck and persistence, I was able to obtain a ticket and visit the Uffizi Gallery after just a short wait in line that afternoon. I was personally hopeful to view, at minimum, da Vinci's *Annunciation*, as well as Sandro Botticelli's *Primavera* and *Birth of Venus*, Michelangelo's *Doni Tondo*, Raphael's *Madonna of the Goldfinch*, Rembrandt's *Self-Portrait of an Old Man*, and Caravaggio's *Bacchus*.

Each artwork tells a fascinating story of unimagined images and centuries past, stories of the world's greatest idiosyncratic geniuses captured in paintings at the zenith of their documented lives. Each unthinkable painting is steeped in astounding symbolism of literature, classical mythology, or otherworldly spirituality. Add to that centuries of historical importance and tales of intrigue, survival, and restoration. One of my favorite fiction authors is Daniel Silva, who has an ongoing series of books relative to lead character Gabriel Allon.[8] Mr. Allon is of German heritage, his mother a survivor of a Nazi death camp. He grew up in an Israel kibbutz and performed his mandatory service in the Israeli Defense Forces (IDF) with distinction. Mr. Allon is also an accomplished artist and art restorer. He had enrolled in the Jerusalem School of Art at the time of the 1972 Munich Olympics massacre. Recall that eleven Jewish athletes were brutally murdered. In response, Gabriel was promptly recruited as a skilled assassin by his country. His task was to avenge these deaths ("Operation Wrath of God"). Mission completed, Gabriel worked throughout Europe, under an alias, as a famed Venetian-trained art restorer. Concurrently, he would oftentimes excuse himself from projects to continue important work for the IDF, eventually advancing to office director. Many of his thrilling books blend exciting, page-turning tales of world travel, espionage, terrorist plots, and usually world-class art. Included are storyline references to famous Renaissance artists and their respective masterpieces. Amazingly, the actual stories behind many of these world-renowned paintings are equally, if not more, fascinating.

An example are the two large panel "star paintings" at the Uffizi Gallery by Sandro Botticelli. Dating to 1480, *Primavera* and *The Birth of Venus* are among the most written about, controversial paintings in the world. No paintings other than *Primavera* bring together a group of classical mythology figures in allegory to the lush growth of spring. Included are Venus, Zephyrus, Chloris, Mercury, Cupid, and the Three Graces (sisters). The

8. See gabrielallon.fandom.com for information about Daniel Silva and his books.

painting reflects a rare deep knowledge of philosophy, ancient poetry, and classical literary sources. Add to that pastoral scenery that includes five hundred identified plant species and nearly two hundred flowers that can also be specifically identified. Although the painting's meaning is argued, it is thought to represent an idealized love. In 1482, talented Botticelli followed these masterworks by adding paintings to the Sistine Chapel. These and other paintings were temporarily moved from the Uffizi Gallery to a castle south of Florence to protect them during World War II.

Another interesting example from the Uffizi Gallery is Raphael's *Madonna of the Goldfinch* (1506). Raphael, too, was oftentimes commissioned by the Vatican and has glorious paintings in the Sistine Chapel. The *Madonna of the Goldfinch* has its own fascinating story. The painting recently completed a ten-year restoration process, during which time an antique replica hung in its place. The painting depicts a young, beautiful Madonna with Christ and John the Baptist as young babies. John holds a goldfinch, with Christ reaching out to touch the bird. The goldfinch sadly symbolizes Christ's crucifixion. Legend is that the goldfinch's red spot was born at the crucifixion as the bird flew above Christ's head and removed a thorn from the crown.[9] The goldfinch was sprayed with a drop of his red blood. Raphael had given the beautiful Madonna painting as a wedding gift to a friend. Several years later (1548), the family home where the painting was displayed was destroyed by a landslide. The painting broke into seventeen pieces. Quickly and hastily salvaged, the painting was reassembled; nails though the seams remained quite evident. It wasn't until 454 years later (2002) that a famed art restorer (Patrizia Riitano), much like the fictional Gabriel Allon, was given the task of major restoration. Utilizing X-rays, CAT scans, lasers, and infrared photography, the lengthy process was completed. Previous quick-fix restoration layers were first distinguished and stripped, and centuries of dirt and grime were cleaned (with degraded colors restored). The sixteenth-century landslide damage was now properly repaired to reveal a true brilliant Raphael painting. In 2008, the *Madonna of the Goldfinch* was rightfully returned to its longtime home in room 26 at the Uffizi Gallery where it remains today.

When visiting Florence, it's imperative to plan a day around a visit to the Uffizi Gallery, the crown jewel of Florence. Over two million people visit the museum annually. And once you've seen your share of priceless, mind-blowing Renaissance art, head to the rooftop café or terraced hanging garden. Here you can leisurely enjoy Florence's fragrant air and spectacular

9. Wikipedia, "Madonna del Cardellino," sec. "Painting."

views from the very location that the Medici family enjoyed musical performances from the piazza below.

Ponte Vecchio

Another surefire way to capture the alluring beauty of Florence is a walk across picturesque and historic *Ponte Vecchio* (literally "Old Bridge" in Italian). Florence's oldest bridge, initially a rickety wooden structure, dates to the tenth-century Roman era. It was followed by a twelfth-century bridge also destroyed by flooding. Consequently, the current Ponte Vecchio, utilizing some original stones and piers, dates to 1345. Many scholars attribute the medieval bridge's current design and construction to Dominican friar Giovanni da Campi.[10] The Dominican friars rebuilt several other structures following the devastating 1333 flood. What is known is that whoever designed Ponte Vecchio was very skilled in architectural design and mathematics, with a keen sense of proportion.[11] Specifically, Ponte Vecchio is built harmonically upon three aesthetic stone arches. The bridge's segmented arches wisely allow for floodwaters and debris to easily pass underneath. The newest up-to-date fourteenth century engineering principles and only enduring materials were employed in the medieval design. Ponte Vecchio also included four towers for defensive purposes. The cobbled, pedestrian bridge is 328 feet long and 104 feet wide and sits at a natural fording point over the beautiful Arno River. Moreover, Ponte Vecchio connects the old historic city center to Florence's vibrant Oltrarno (literally "beyond the Arno") neighborhood just across the river. Within the bridge's many shops is a large prominent piazza in the center. Ponte Vecchio's reflection bounces off the glorious Tuscan sun across the Arno River. The forceful brick and stone piers contrast greatly with the soft yellow façade housing the ramshackle shops above. On one side of the bridge is the famous cathedral (Duomo), Uffizi Gallery, and the Piazza Vecchio. And on the other side, the aristocratic Medici family (Pitti) palace with its grand (Boboli) gardens, sculptures, and fountains. Lastly, the "secret" bridge reveals many interesting mysteries of ancient Italy and the medieval past of Florence.

Fans of Dan Brown's best seller *Inferno* were treated to rare insights of Ponte Vecchio's secret hallway (otherwise known as the Vasari Corridor), the book's escape route for its adventurous characters. As known, Mr. Brown also famously wrote *The Da Vinci Code* and *Angels and Demons.* With a shadow of intrigue, royal-select painters, writers, and architect

10. Through Eternity, "7 Fascinating Facts," sec. 2.

11. Flores, "Ponte Vecchio."

Giorgio Vasari were commissioned by Cosimo de' Medici in 1565 to create the half-mile passageway. The passageway was completed in just five months in preparation for the wedding of Cosimo's son Francesco I to Joanna of Austria. The intent was to provide direct access from the Palazzo Vecchio government offices, across the Arno River, to the Medici family residence at Palazzo Pitti, which was deemed necessary so as not to endanger himself or Medici family members and guests along the streets.[12] It was a period of great mystery and murder plots. The corridor also served as a separate spectacular art gallery with precious paintings and busts of famous Florentines, of which Cosimo considered himself one! The Vasari Corridor is hardly visible as it soars through the existing private palaces and tower homes, past the Church of Santa Felicita, and discreetly over the many shops of the Ponte Vecchio. The corridor's splendid, elevated archway ends in the Uffizi Gallery. There was even a balcony stop in the Church of Santa Felicita so the Medici family could attend Mass without the need to walk the streets. It's hard to imagine a secret covered corridor connecting two palaces by running through houses, a church, and over a bridge! The corridor offered a way for Cosimo de' Medici to get freely from home to work and back without fear of surprise attack. Unfortunately, a visit through the secret corridor with all its exquisite and extraordinary art is exclusively reserved by advance appointment only. Guess I'll need to watch the movie!

In medieval times, with space in Europe's urban centers sparse, it was not uncommon to see merchants selling their goods at the unavoidable river crossings. This was true in Venice, London, and Florence. In fact, the high costs associated with building the bridges were offset with municipal commercial rental fees. Leaving the bridge's thoroughfare open, the shops are suspended over the river. For centuries, it was Florentine butchers, fishmongers, and leather artisans who peddled their trade across the Arno River and Ponte Vecchio. The tanners, operating alongside the butchers, competed for high quality, discarded animal hides, with the river legally treated as a bloody sewer. The rivers were favored over city centers on hygiene grounds. However, by 1593, the rank stench and industrial waste created by the bridge's trades finally became too much for the Medici family, who crossed above on the Vasari Corridor daily. By decree, seeking to elevate the prestige of Ponte Vecchio, Medici Grand Duke Ferdinando I promptly expelled all the butchers, fishmongers, and tanners. In their place, the grand duke invited the city's goldsmiths and jewelers to set up shop along the Ponte Vecchio. A higher rent was made possible as well. It was the final stage of the Medici long-term plan to improve the long-standing, pungent, less-than-enjoyable

12. Visit Florence Italy, "Ponte Vecchio Bridge."

commute across the Arno River. In quick fashion, hanging legs of lamb, ominous pig heads, and barrels of fresh-caught prawns were all gone, and the bridge completely transformed. It has remained that way for over four hundred years through today. There are still forty-eight Ponte Vecchio shops, mostly goldsmith and jewelry shops selling fine, expensive gold and gems to locals and worldwide visitors. A bit out of my price range, though I recall my middle daughter purchasing a beautiful Italian leather jacket on her subsequent visit.

The Ponte Vecchio is also special for being the only Florence bridge crossing the Arno River that was not destroyed during World War II by the fleeing German Nazis in 1944. Instead, the Germans chose to demolish several medieval buildings on each side of the river, thereby blocking access to Ponte Vecchio. Rumor is that the führer himself (Adolf Hitler) became taken by the charms of Florence when on a state visit with fascist ally Benito Mussolini in 1938. In fact, the bridge's windows were enlarged to provide Hitler better views of the Arno River. Further rumor has it that Hitler crossed the Vasari Corridor with Mussolini and developed a fondness for the amazing artwork that lined the secret passageway.[13] In any event, German diplomate Gerhard Wolf had directly counseled Hitler not to lay waste to Florence bridges. Nonetheless, on August 3, 1944, with Allied troops nearing Florence, all the Arno River crossings except Ponte Vecchio were blown sky high and destroyed. A small plaque commemorates Herr Wolf's humanity in possibly preserving Ponte Vecchio during the Germans' wartime occupation. Just downriver, west from Ponte Vecchio, is the bridge Ponte Santa Trinita (Holy Trinity) designed and originally built in 1567, possibly from earlier sketches by Michelangelo. Ponte Santa Trinita was among the bridges destroyed by the retreating Germans but was painstakingly recreated after the war in 1958. Several original stones and monuments were raised from the Arno River, and others were taken from the same quarry. Preserved Florentine archives were examined in the process. Many young lovers also enjoy this romantic bridge for its beautiful views of the city and river. Thankfully, the venerable and iconic Ponte Vecchio continues to proudly serve as an everlasting symbol of Florence.

The Duomo (Florence Cathedral)

There are beautiful cathedrals, then there's the *Florence Cathedral*, also known as *Duomo di Firenze* or the *Cattedrale di Santa Maria del Fiore*. "Saint Mary of the Flower" alludes to Florentia (Florence) as the blooming

13. Through Eternity, "7 Fascinating Facts," sec. 6.

"city of flowers." Florence's decorative pink, white, and green marble Gothic cathedral dominates the skyline rising tall over the city. The cathedral is the fourth largest in the world, outsized only by Saint Peter's (Rome), Saint Paul's (London), and the Duomo in Milan. With nearly ninety thousand square feet of floor space, the cathedral is five hundred feet in length, as wide as three hundred feet, and 376 feet tall. Built as a basilica, the cathedral's plan forms a Latin cross in shape. Its astonishing size, heart-of-the-city location, and distinct mix of colorful polychrome marble panels renders the Florence Cathedral one of the most recognizable cathedrals in the world. Among the majestic cathedral complex, you can also climb 414 steps to the top of Giotto's slender, freestanding 278-foot bell tower, visit the ornate octagonal baptistery (of Saint John), or ascend the 463 stairs to the top of Filippo Brunelleschi's magnificent dome.

Construction of the vast Florence Cathedral began in 1296. At the time, architect Arnolfo di Cambio was commissioned to design and build "the loftiest, most sumptuous edifice human invention could devise,"[14] and that he did. The cathedral is built on the site of the seventh-century Church of Santa Reparata, whose building remains are still visible in the crypt. Saint Reparata was a fourth-century French saint martyred in the Roman province of Palestine. That church was built on top of the even earlier fourth century Basilica of San Lorenzo, consecrated by the influential Saint Ambrose (Bishop of Milan) in 393. The Florence Cathedral itself was not structurally completed for nearly 150 years. It wasn't until the unimaginable vaulted dome was added that the cathedral was consecrated by Pope Eugene IV on March 25, 1436. Statues of the many devoted architects, including Cambio and Brunelleschi, can be found outside the cathedral where they are able to admire their stunning work for all eternity. With limited time to tour, I was struck by the immensity of the cathedral. Relatively stark, the church is full of giant pillars, Gothic arches, and forty-four beautiful stained-glass windows. The floor is decorated in inlaid mosaic marble completed by the grand ducal workshops. Many consider the pavement, resembling mosaic carpet, a main attraction.

Though most of the Cathedral's original best-known art has been relocated to nearby museums, several significant artworks remain. Most notable is Giorgio Vasari's *Last Judgement* on the dome's interior. There are also two towering equestrian frescoes honoring past soldiers. Most interesting is Domenico di Michelino's mystical *Dante Alighieri with Florence and the Realms of the Divine Comedy* (1465) depicting a famous portrait of Dante Alighieri, Italy's favorite poet. The gifted Florentine poet was exiled from the city for

14. Destinology, "Florence Things to Do," sec. "Florence Duomo."

political reasons in 1302. Subsequently, while in exile, Dante completed his epic poem, *The Divine Comedy* (1321). Nonetheless, though he never returned to Florence, Dante had remained greatly famous and was roundly reclaimed by his birth city. Even today, there are engraved marble slabs with quotes from the *Divine Comedy* located throughout the city. Also of interest, just above the main cathedral door is a bizarre-looking seven-foot-diameter 1443 clock by Florentine watchmaker Angelo di Niccolò. It's the only clock of its kind in working order anywhere in the world. The one-handed clock runs counterclockwise with Roman numerals from I to XXIIII. The confusing clock measures Italian, Bohemian, or Julian time (promulgated by Julius Caesar), which begins and ends at sunset. This was problematic as even today the clock must be reset weekly to varying seasonal times of sunset. The dial of the clock is a fresco painted by the great Renaissance artist Paolo Uccello. Thus, the famed clock is better known as "Uccello's clock." It is both a fascinating timepiece and an astounding work of art.

The real enchanting glory of the Florence Cathedral, and ingenious engineering feat, is architect Filippo Brunelleschi's unmatched dome, or cupola. After his death in 1446, Brunelleschi was buried in the cathedral's crypt under the dome that he masterfully built brick-by-brick (over four million in total). Constructed between 1420 and 1436, the six-hundred-year-old dome remains the largest masonry vault in the world. The dignity and grace of the octagonal cathedral dome, so large and so high above ground, is visibly felt throughout the city. The innovative architect was tasked with creating a dome absent reinforcements in wood since none would ever sustain a cupola of this size and weight. As a result, all traditional methods of dome construction, including wooden centering and scaffolding, were abandoned. Newly designed equipment and novel building methods were required of Brunelleschi. First, the architect creatively built not one but two ribbed domes, one inside the other to lessen the crushing weight of the dome. It's between the two domes that the 463-step stairway to the dome's lantern was added . . . a climb not for the faint of heart. Regretfully, I was unable to schedule a tour of the dome. The weight of the seventy-foot white marble lantern is skillfully used by the architect to counterbalance the thrust force of the internal dome. A bronze cross set atop a bronze ball tops the dome's lantern. Meanwhile, the visible outer dome exterior is covered in beautiful terra-cotta tiles. Brunelleschi also employed new scaffolding and new self-supporting bricklaying methods (Roman herringbone pattern). The end result is an absolute masterpiece of art and one of the world's great engineering breakthroughs. Most of Europe's later dome designs, including Michelangelo's Saint Peter's in Rome, employed Brunelleschi's innovative methods. Accordingly, from the very moment of its creation, the cathedral dome became the symbol of Florence, much like the Eiffel Tower symbolizes Paris—so much so that a popular phrase for "homesick" Florentines is "nostalgia del cupolone" (homesick for the dome).[15]

The Florence Cathedral and dome are part of the larger monumental complex of Santa Maria del Fiore. As noted, there's also the baptistery and the bell tower, along with a museum, remnants of the prior seventh-century church, and the crypt.

Baptistery of San Giovanni

The *Baptistery of San Giovanni* (Saint John) was constructed between 1059 and 1128, making it older than the cathedral and one of Florence's oldest buildings. It was consecrated by Florentine Pope Nicholas II in 1059 and has the status of a minor basilica. Until 1935, Saint John's Baptistery was the only place that Florentines were baptized. Consequently, Dante Alighieri, Amerigo Vespucci, and members of the Medici family were all baptized there. That said, the octagonal baptistery is probably most famous for its three sets of ornate, artistically important bronze doors added during the Renaissance. Most notable are the seventeen-foot-tall, three-ton east doors. Based on their grandeur and remarkable beauty, these doors were subsequently dubbed by Michelangelo as truly worthy to be the "gates of Paradise."[16] The doors, *Gates of Paradise* as they subsequently became known, were designed and sculpted by Lorenzo Ghiberti. Ghiberti was widely recognized as an outstanding celebrity artist, showered with commissions from many including the pope. Ghiberti and his workshop painstakingly toiled for twenty-seven years until 1452 to complete the door's ten panels, each depicting figural, narrative scenes from the Old Testament. Ghiberti's imagery, artistic genius, approach, techniques, and tenacity are on full display. The east doors are described by fellow artists as "undeniably perfect in every way, ranking them among the finest masterpiece ever created.[17] Unfortunately, in 1990, the originals were replaced with modern replicas and relocated to the cathedral museum. Presently, the *Gates of Paradise* are gradually being expertly restored and preserved following over five hundred years of exposure and damage.

15. Fodor's Travel, "77 Best Sights," sec. "Duomo."

16. Wikipedia, "Florence Baptistry," para. 5.

17. Fong, "Masterpieces of the Renaissance," quoting Giorgio Vasari; see also Lubow, "Gates of Paradise."

Giotto Bell Tower

Finally, sitting in front of and apart from the cathedral is the majestic, free-standing *Giotto's Bell Tower* (campanile). I was first struck by the attachment of Giotto's name to the structure and the fact that the bell tower rises above the cathedral looking down upon Brunelleschi's illustrious dome. It's not often an artist's first name is used to identify architecture, so why? The commission was originally with Arnolfo di Cambio, the architect of the beautiful cathedral itself. After his death in 1302 and a long interruption, the project was assigned in 1334 to the famous Florentine master Giotto di Bondone. Giotto, as he is widely known, was already considered one of the most important painters in art history. His works changed the course of artworks by blending long-standing religious antiquity with emerging concepts of humanism and empathy. Giotto broke from centuries of Byzantine-style painting to depict his subjects accurately and three dimensionally, drawing from nature and according to life. Also, by depicting space and perspective, Giotto introduced a fresh sense of authenticity. The same authentic exquisiteness was applied to Giotto's construction of the tower. A bell tower was needed to complement updated cathedral plans and expand Florence's religious center. An obvious case in point as to perspective is the fact that the windows of the tower's upper floors gradually increase in size, brilliantly done to create an impression that the windows are all the exact same size when observing from ground level. However, as typical with such daunting projects, only the early stages of construction (first floor) were completed during Giotto's lifetime. The artist died in 1337. In fact, the tower's construction outlasted two of the three devoted project architects. Giotto's apprentice completed the second floor before his death. The final three floors were completed by Francesco Talenti, who stuck to Giotto's original vision and plan. Fortunately, Talenti made one change, adding a large projecting rooftop terrace. Giotto himself designed the tower to match the cathedral, selecting and purchasing the tower's white Carrara marble, the green Prato quarry marble, and the rare Maremma red marble. Each floor featured relief-carved, hexagonal panels by various artists of the time. The first tier, taken from Genesis, depicts the creation of man. The second tier depicts planets, virtues, and the seven sacraments. The upper tiers feature sculpted prophets and sibyls—though, again, all the incredible original reliefs, replaced with replicas in the 1960s, have been moved to the cathedral's museum.

Completed in 1357, the result is a soaring, slender, multicolored marble structure considered to be one of the finest campaniles in the world. Square in plan, the five horizontal floors measure forty-seven feet and collectively rise 280 feet tall. Giotto's Bell Tower rules the Florence city skyline. The bell tower features seven large cast bells added throughout later centuries; the musical partners all have special names related to the Virgin Mary. As is well-known, the number seven holds special biblical meaning, symbolizing perfection. The 414-step climb to the bell tower terrace rewards you with staggering, sweeping views of the city and an extremely up-close look at the cathedral dome next door. Though he never lived to see his completed bell tower, Giotto can rest assured knowing that his seven-hundred-year-old Florentine masterpiece is one of the most iconic landmarks in all of Italy.

If you are not on bleisure travel and you're given several days or a week in Florence and Tuscany, there is obviously plenty more to see and do. In the historic city of Florence, there is the Gothic *Basilica Santa Croce* (Holy Cross). Santa Croce is best known for the famous Florentines buried there, including Michelangelo, Vasari, Galileo, Machiavelli, composer Rossini, and a monumental grave for the exiled poet Dante. There are the beautiful *Boboli Gardens* and the lesser known, tranquil *Bardini Gardens*, both with their exquisite trees, fountains, statues, ponds, and grottoes. On a distant hill above the city is the *Piazzale Michelangelo* offering panoramic city views and a replica of the *David* statue. For a pleasant market atmosphere and noted Tuscan culinary specialties, visit the *Mercato Centrale* (Food Hall). Enjoy a refreshing Italian gelato! There's even a fun contemporary *Galileo Museum* dedicated to the renowned scientist and astronomer Galileo Galilei. Further afield, *day trips* to many beautiful Tuscan cities, including Siena, Luca, Pisa, and Cinque Terre are all possible. Finally, of course, there are also the stunning, idyllic Tuscan lakes to visit. Think *Under the Tuscan Sun*!

Unfortunately, I suspect that it's only through personal experience that one can truly appreciate the city of Florence, to understand just how Tuscany's largest city excitedly buzzes with unmatched, high-born history, art, and romance. Even a very short visit provided me a unique glimpse into Florence's cultural legacy and artistic mastery. Add to that the city's unparalleled cultural significance, its invention and timeless testament to human achievement, modern civilization, and rebirth. Little wonder that for centuries Florence has captured the imagination of so many fortunate travelers.

CHAPTER 13

BRUSSELS

Life is short, eat more Belgian chocolates.

—*Unknown*

You've got your brussels sprouts, Belgian waffles, French fries, numerous Belgian beers (Stella Artois), and, of course, world-famous Belgian chocolates, e.g., Godiva. Beyond that, there was very little I knew about Belgium or its capital city, Brussels. Yet I found myself quickly passing through quirky Brussels on three different occasions. When sourcing supplies to develop, test, manufacture, and sell world-class medical devices, best-in-class suppliers and plant locations from all corners of the world must be considered. Consideration includes research, references, proposals, site visits, quality audits, and further extensive due diligence. This is particularly true when ramping up production to support a significant, ever-growing global market share. In one instance, I recall, our US-based chemical supplier could no longer meet our supply needs. They shared that their larger Belgium plant could also produce the required resin, and in greater volumes both to support our European requirements and offset the looming US shortfall. You can imagine that there is considerable work to qualify and deploy such a strategy relative to a critical medical product raw material. Although the supplier plant was in the historic city of Ghent to the north, it was a quick and easy day trip from Brussels. The second visit occasion was also to evaluate a newly proposed partner to a key supplier of ours who performed plastic injection molding. This supplier produced tens of millions of syringes. The syringes were used to support CT and MRI medical imaging scanning procedures in hospitals throughout the world. More specific to the visit, an integral part of this process is precise, affordable, sophisticated tooling. For various reasons, including recent reliability and lead-time issues, our supplier was proposing a change from their Chinese toolmaker to one located outside Brussels, Belgium. Again, these decisions are paramount to securing assurance of supply with world-class quality while also pursuing needed cost reductions. Both trips were very quick, highly beneficial, and timed to correlate with already planned visits to neighboring Germany to the east. Any time you can meet face-to-face with key supply partners, often friends, is wonderful and always productive. The third visit was with my beautiful wife on the lone occasion that she joined me on multicountry business trip to Europe. My wife, an elementary school teacher, was unavailable to travel with me except for the summer months. From a mere business need, and with that being the slow holiday season throughout Europe, very few of my trips occurred in June through August. However, on this one occasion, I had business in the Netherlands (Maastricht and Amsterdam) and Germany (Cologne), and we also briefly visited France (Paris) and Belgium (Brussels). I loved the opportunity, albeit whirlwind, to visit Europe with my wife, and we made wonderful memories. I also recall that it was a very successful business visit with DHL Logistics in Amsterdam. All that said, my time in Brussels was brief, and these bleisure visits were much more business than leisure. Nonetheless, Belgium has a unique historical perspective, and there are a few beautiful and interesting sights and fun experiences I want to share.

By no means should tiny Brussels (with an inner-city population of just two hundred thousand) be shortchanged. It's seriously quite a big deal! As the seat of the European Communities (since 1958)—now the European Union (EU)—Brussels is widely regarded as the "capital of Europe." Being the center of Europe's international governance and daily business, Brussels has accordingly grown as a widely recognized global city, a status shared with major metropolises the likes of New York, London, and Tokyo. Today, Brussels serves as both the significant host of the EU as well as headquarters of the North Atlantic Treaty Organization (NATO). Brussels, along with its so-called European Quarter, is also the regional capital city of Belgium. A post–World War II economic boom first brought laborers from throughout the Mediterranean region. A significant number of immigrants from beyond western Europe, including Africa, shortly followed. Along with these groups came increased ethnic and religious diversity. With increased growth, like most cities, Brussels faces ongoing social and logistical problems. Residents feel that national and international interests oftentimes take precedence over local needs, resulting in high taxation and unequal economic development.

Also, in some regards, the city is a bit polarized by its industrial old neighborhoods and the evolving new EU district. Adding to that is the fact that Brussels is multilingual, with fluent Flemish, French, and even German and English, used interchangeably, though due to societal pressure and prestige, French is now the city's preferred and predominant language, with Flemish still favored beyond Brussels throughout the country. Nonetheless, Brussels remains a major, flourishing, busy European tourist and cultural attraction. And despite all the significant integral changes, multicultural Brussels has further evolved to become the vibrant, cosmopolitan city it is today.

The exact history and origin of Belgium is quite debatable. In fact, its history is better defined by a few significant, relatively recent nineteenth-century events.[1] It is believed that Belgium's name is attributed to third-century BC Germanic or Celtic tribes living in what was then known as Gaul.[2] Eventually, Julius Caesar overpowered these uniquely brave and daring tribes. Even with the fall of the Roman Empire, the land that forms Belgium remained part of the diminishing Holy Roman Empire through the Middle Ages and into the twelfth century. Over the centuries, the region segregated into small medieval or feudal states, and urban areas such as Brussels, Gent, and Bruges began to develop. Consequently, until the nineteenth century, present-day Belgium was controlled by the Dutch, Spanish, and French. A series of events would lead to the creation of a new country out of the remaining part of Europe. The first was the defeat of Napoleon and the First French Empire at Waterloo (near Brussels) in 1815. Subsequently, the triumphant forces of Austria, Britain, Russia, and Prussia met in Vienna to redistribute jurisdiction in the region. The most important French regions were added to the United Kingdom of the Netherlands. This miscalculated decision resulted in considerable religious and linguistic unrest between the southern Catholic (French language) and northern Protestant (Flemish language) regions. In turn, the decision led to the 1830 Belgium revolution. In dramatic fashion, the revolt started inside the Brussels opera house as a small protest targeting attending Dutch ruler Willem I. The uprising quickly expanded into the streets. As a result, the Vienna Congress had no choice but to ratify Belgium's independence from the Dutch. Therefore, it was not until July 1831 that Belgium is said to have formally come into existence.

From the twelfth century onward, with enterprising merchant families, guilds, and craftsmen, Brussels was a major town within the contested region. Its economic mainstay was the manufacture of luxury fabrics exported to fairs in Italy and France. It was the city of Brussels that played

1. See Wikipedia, "Belgium."

2. Wikipedia, "Belgians," sec. "Etymology."

a major role in the uprising and in Belgium gaining independence from the Kingdom of the Netherlands. During my brief visits to Brussels, I was able to visit a few of the better known historic, beautiful, and occasionally intentionally quirky attractions.

La Grand-Place

The *Grand-Place*, French for "Grand Square," is the beautiful central square of the city of Brussels. Also officially named *Groote Markt* in

Flemish, the square is often pronounced the *grand plus*. The Grand-Place is "surrounded by the opulent Baroque guildhalls of the former Guilds of Brussels," as well as the city's "flamboyant" neo-Gothic Town Hall and the King's House, or Bread House, home of the Brussels City Museum.[3] The Grand-Place is known for its decorative aesthetic wealth and is considered one of the world's most beautiful public squares. I've heard that French writer Victor Hugo himself declared it such during an 1852 visit. Accordingly, in 1998, the Grand-Place of Brussels was registered on UNESCO's World's Heritage List. This designates the Grand-Place as a special cultural landmark with outstanding universal value.[4]

As a large, prestigious venue measuring 223 by 361 feet, the charming, central, cobbled Grand-Place frequently hosts festive and cultural events. This includes concerts, fairs, folklore tales, summer flower carpets, and the Christmas nativity scene. The Grand-Place's story began as an eleventh-century market square. Gradually, the square was filled with wooden houses and halls. The stunning Gothic Town Hall and splendid trade guilds were later installed in the fifteenth century. The square was largely complete by the seventeenth century. However, in 1695, during the Nine Years' War, most of the square was destroyed during the bombardment of Brussels by French troops. Only the façade and the tower of the Town Hall and some stone walls survived. As the long-standing central nerve of Brussels, the houses and guilds surrounding the Grand-Place were swiftly rebuilt. This time construction was in stone, giving the square its current baroque appearance. With subsequent ongoing renovation campaigns, the square's heritage value was proudly rediscovered in the mid-nineteenth century.

The most beautiful and impressive building in the Grand-Place is easily the majestic Town Hall of Brussels (Hôtel de Ville de Bruxelles). Brussels's Town Hall, whose first stone was laid in 1401, is a world-renowned jewel of Gothic Revival architecture. The Town Hall was completed in 1455. With over three hundred sculpted statues on the façade and a 315-foot tower, the gorgeous Town Hall is one of the most emblematic buildings in the Belgian capital. The landmark Town Hall is Brussel's only remaining fifteenth-century medieval building constructed in Gothic style. The Town Hall, the tallest building in Brussels's Grand-Place, functions today as the mayor's office and includes an underground railroad. Throughout the Town Hall's sumptuous corridors and richly decorated chambers, you'll discover tapestries, paintings, Gothic woodwork, and the guilds' coats of arms from era to era, encompassing six hundred years of history. Not to be missed is

3. Wikipedia, "Grand-Place," para. 1.

4. UNESCO, "About World Heritage."

the Town Hall's original, imposing fifteenth-century Gothic-style lantern tower. Climb the spiral staircase of two hundred narrow steps, starting in the courtyard, to the tower's medieval balcony. Those reaching the top are rewarded with unique, breathtaking, panoramic views of Brussels. Additionally, at the tower's summit is a spire supporting a nine-foot gilt metal statue of archangel Saint Michael, the city's protector. Brussels's patron saint is depicted valiantly slaying a dragon.

Through the ages, the Grand-Place market square has endured a hive of activities and many dramatic happenings, some sadly murderous. This includes gruesome public executions, the Catholic Inquisition, an exiled Karl Marx penning the Communist Manifesto, German occupation, IRA bombings, and more. For a period during World War I, the Town Hall even served as a makeshift hospital for fleeing refugees who flooded Brussels. Nonetheless, the sheer beauty of the cobbled Grand-Place rectangle, the social heart of Brussels, is sure to halt you in your tracks. The square's gilded facades, extravagant flowered lampposts, inviting outdoor cafés, tiny specialty shops, and sweet-smelling chocolatiers offer a charming respite for locals and visitors alike.

Manneken Pis

Just a short five-minute walk from the Grand-Place you can find the most famous, best-known Belgian, *Manneken Pis*. The name is Dutch for "Little Pissing Man." Full disclosure, the Manneken Pis is but a zany twenty-two-inch bronze fountain sculpture depicting a naked little boy urinating into a fountain basin. Though its early existence dates to 1452, the bronze statue as known today was put into place in 1619. From its inception during the fifteenth century until the nineteenth century, the fountain played an essential role in the distribution of Brussels's drinking water. The exquisite system was even well-known throughout Europe. Surviving the 1695 French bombardment of Brussels, Manneken Pis has been celebrated and enjoys ever-growing glory. Symbolizing the rebellious, self-mocking spirit of Brussels, Manneken Pis is the very essence of Brussels folklore.

There are many unsubstantiated legends behind the origin of Manneken Pis.[5] One dates to 1142 when the troops of a two-year-old lord were in battle. To give themselves courage, the troops hung the infant lord from an oak tree in a basket. Just as hopes were fading, the two-year-old lord rose from his hanging basket and urinated on opposing troops below . . . spurring his troops to victory. A second legend attest to a fourteenth-century

5. For details discussed below, see Doezema, "Manneken-Pis."

little boy spying on an invading foreign power about to place explosive charges in Brussels's city walls. The small boy is said to have urinated on the burning fuse, saving the city! Yet a third tale tells the story of the beloved son of a visiting wealthy merchant who went missing. A search party was formed, and the small boy was eventually found merrily urinating in a small nearby garden. As a gift of his great gratitude, the merchant had the city's fountain and Manneken Pis sculpture built. Who really knows? Though any of these stories is befitting the enigmatic landmark.

Throughout the years, many Manneken Pis misadventures occurred, including it being stolen and recovered at least seven times. Finally, in 1965, matters were more serious as the statue was broken by the thief, leaving only his feet and ankles behind. An anonymous tip signaled that the Manneken Pis "body" was in a nearby canal.[6] Fortunately, divers were able to find the statue in the large canal and it was returned and professionally restored. At wits' end, a replica of the statue was commissioned and installed in the outdoor fountain location in place of the original. The original 1619 version is now displayed and guarded on the second floor of the Brussels City Museum in the Grand-Place. In fun fashion, the Manneken Pis statue is dressed in varying amusing costumes. This custom dates way back to 1698. Even today, an association reviews hundreds of costume design submittals and publishes a schedule of dress on the fountain railing. Manneken Pis's wardrobe consists of over a thousand costumes, many of which are also on display in the Brussels City Museum. Manneken even got a "little sister" named Jeanneke Pis in 1987. Toss a coin in Jeanneke's fountain and you are promised fidelity in your love life. Admittedly, the Manneken Pis is one of the quirkiest attractions I've seen, though it's certainly memorable to me and my wife.

The Statue of Everard t'Serclaes

Much less known compared to Manneken Pis is *Everard t'Serclaes*. However, nearly impossible to miss on the walk from the Grand-Place to the Manneken Pis fountain is a sculpted monument to the rebellious fourteenth-century patriot. Everard's story takes place in 1356 after Flemish troops, failing to accept the ruling Duke family succession, occupied Brussels. One night, scaling the city walls, brave Everard and a small group of patriots led a rebellion. Everard recovered Brussels, forcing the Flemish to flee. Power was restored to the rightful rulers. Unfortunately, years later, as an old man,

6. Wikipedia, "Manneken Pis," secs. "History: Origins" and "History: 20th century–present."

our hero was beaten to death in further defending the city. It wasn't until 1902 that a Belgian artist sculpted a shining bronze monument to commemorate Everard t'Serclaes. The monument depicts a reclining corpse of Everard overlaid on bas-reliefs of the liberation of Brussels. Initially, most people, including myself, mistakenly believe the beautiful statue depicts an angel or known saint. Interestingly, locals believe that the statue of Everard brings good fortune and grants wishes to all who touch it. For this reason, the monument is a popular attraction, with many passing tourists gathering around to rub the statue. There is often a queue to approach the memorial. Folklore is that a touching of the arm ensures a return visit to Brussels. Ironically, the constant specific touching of the face, hand, arm, and leg result in a daily polishing. This in turn keeps those parts shiny gold contrasted to the rest of the statue. However, once again, the original sculpture was replaced in 2016 by a bronze copy and has been relocated inside the Town Hall. With all its superstitions, the Everard t'Serclaes memorial is an interesting, fun stop.

Belgian Chocolate

Belgians love their chocolates as do its visitors. Dating to 1635, chocolate production in Belgium has greatly flourished since the nineteenth century. With massive expansion and a gained international reputation, Belgium's chocolate production has evolved into a major industry and a vital component of its economy and culture. This may seem odd because most raw materials used in chocolate production, namely cocoa, originate in Africa and Central and South America. But by 1900, large quantities of cocoa were imported from the Belgian Congo, making chocolates very affordable to the Belgian working class. Today, there are over two thousand chocolatiers in Belgium, all established connoisseurs of fine chocolate. Belgian confections are divided into two categories: (1) soft-shell truffles filled with buttercream and (2) hard-shell pralines containing many varied fillings. A few of the favorite chocolate producers include Neuhaus, Wittamer, Maison Pierre Marcolini, Mary Chocolatier, Laurent Gerbaud, and of course iconic Godiva. Neuhaus is the oldest of the group operating since 1857. In fact, Swiss confectioner Jean Neuhaus claims to have invented what he named the "praline" in Brussels in 1912.[7] Mary (Marie) Delluc of Mary Chocolatier, Brussels's first woman chocolatier, started in 1919 and quickly gained favor with the royal family. Mary's chocolates are hand produced and packed in chic, recognizable vintage boxes. Probably best known is Godiva, founded

7. Neuhaus Chocolates, "Our Story."

in Brussels in 1926. Inspired by Lady Godiva, the company is named in her honor, promising a bold, pioneering spirit. Since 1968, Godiva has been named the official chocolatier of the royal court of Belgium. Godiva is sold in over a hundred countries and has opened international boutiques in New York City, Paris, and Tokyo. It's little wonder that Brussels International Airport is the largest chocolate-selling point in the world.[8]

Brussels, the noted capital of chocolates, is full of inviting shops with creative, heavenly treats. Around the Grand-Place and throughout the city, you can find the classic renowned confectioners, artisan craftsmen, and the exciting rising stars. Few visitors miss the opportunity for a fix of decadent Belgian chocolate. The national delicacy did not escape my wife's eye, and we had fun exploring several of the eye-popping shops along our way.

The one word visitors often use to describe Brussels is "quirky." It differs from the traditional European capitals in that it simultaneously feels a bit more whimsical and modern. Brussels also has a surprising fun, eccentric undercurrent. It's a city where you can certainly eat well, drink well, and mix with plenty of interesting international visitors and friendly locals. The city of Brussels, particularly the Grand-Place is like a giant park where a proud sense of community is uniformly promoted.

8. Brussels Airport, "Belgian Chocolate House."

CHAPTER 14

OSAKA and KYOTO

In Osaka, every day is a festival, and
every meal is a celebration of life.
—*Actress Tetsuko Kuroyanagi*

"We're not in Kansas anymore," is all I could think of as I sleepily deboarded the plane at Kansai International Airport in Osaka, Japan. For one, I realized I was stepping into Asia, a continent with clear and striking cultural differences and norms from the other visited continents. Asia is far and away the most populous continent, with the oldest recorded civilizations. It comprises 60 percent of the world population. Asia is also home to many of the ancient religious systems, steeped in myths as well as civility, ethics, and morality. Japan is no exception . . . with 40 percent of the population of the United States, it's a country not quite the size of Montana.[1] Consequently, space is at a premium and cleanliness is paramount. Additionally, the archipelago string-of-islands country of Japan is naturally and massively homogeneous in race and language. I unexpectedly learned the hard way that Japanese do not speak English any more than Americans speak Japanese. Likewise, all signage is solely in Japanese. And strangely, at just six feet in height, I was eerily the rare tall white guy. I discovered another significant difference even before landing. Specifically, following the 6,300-mile, eighteen-hour flight from Chicago to Osaka, I spotted Japanese land only to learn that Osaka has the world's first ocean airport. Built in 1994, the $40 billion, 2,600-acre Kansai International Airport is an artificial island built

1. Wikipedia, "Asia."

offshore in the middle of Osaka Bay. That was very different! All that said, I felt great excitement and gratitude for the first-hand opportunity to experience a new intriguing world. Once inside the airport, I immediately felt and appreciated the unique Japanese culture and amazing diversity of humanity.

Let's step back and I'll first explain the business need for me and my colleague to visit Japan, the Land of the Rising Sun! As previously mentioned, my company, which manufactured medical imaging equipment was becoming the fast-growing star of Pittsburgh. The company had built a commanding worldwide market share and opened both a European and Asian headquarters to keep pace. The Asia subsidiary was in Osaka, Japan. Throughout the early years, the Osaka office was relatively small and operated independently. With growth, it was time to align the global offices with the overall business on a national, regional, or global basis, wherever possible. Namely, there was a need to properly leverage obvious synergies, processes, key supply partners, and best practices. At the time, my team managed worldwide indirect spend. A business's indirect spend typically includes all expenditures unrelated to manufacturing the direct end products. Examples of "indirect costs" include travel, fleet, utilities, computers and telephones, logistics, marketing, facilities management, catering, credit cards, legal, professional services, office supplies, and more. Collectively, indirect costs comprise a significant, often overlooked overall expense for businesses. As you can surmise, there are countless opportunities to consolidate spend for volume discounts, improved quality, and very meaningful requisite cost savings. This was the case in Japan with what we refer to as "low-hanging fruit" . . . easy, welcomed changes with clear, measurable cost savings.

An initial spend analysis generally points the way to utilization of existing global agreements with airlines, hotels, an office supply company, and freight and telecommunications carriers. Other regional suppliers compete for awards, resulting in local agreements. All this was accomplished in Osaka in a matter of four days and subsequent follow. The most memorable Japanese meeting was with Nissan Motors relative to our fleet management program. There were approximately sixty vehicles in our Japanese fleet with others in surrounding countries. Included in a corporate fleet are company cars for designated executives and the sales team as well as trucks for those working in the service area. All vehicles were already being leased through Nissan Motors, though absent any substantial negotiations or an agreement. Manufacturers are thrilled when they supply corporate vehicles and will offer outstanding discounts and incentives for the privilege. This was not occurring and was properly corrected. Nissan Motors agreed to provide retroactive rebates and improved terms moving forward. The fear of switching to a new manufacturer is ever present. The meeting was highly successful and quite unique in that it was the only time I negotiated with a supplier through an interpreter. This same process was employed in several other countries with similar success, resulting in great appreciation and recognition.

Osaka and Kyoto are a pair of mind-boggling cities within near proximity (twenty-seven miles) of one another. Even better, Japan's Shinkansen "bullet train" provides a comfortable, inexpensive, fifteen-minute lightning-fast trip between the cities. Despite their neighboring location, Osaka and Kyoto could not be any more different. Osaka brings exuberant energy while, in striking contrast, Kyoto offers serene, traditional Japanese culture. Luckily, the two cities together provide both glitzy urban edge and rich nostalgic charm . . . a perfect "CliffsNotes" introduction to Japan. Osaka and Kyoto provide an easy way to experience Japan's spectacular highlights, culinary delights, and heritage (as best as possible, given just a few days of bleisure travel). We were able to visit Kyoto on our day of arrival prior to visiting the office the following morning, while Osaka was reserved for a couple lunches and evenings, including attending an exciting Japanese professional baseball game with our coworkers.

As historical background, it is reliably believed that modern humans first arrived in Japan as far back as 36,000 BC.[2] This is described as the Japanese Paleolithic period (a period predating the development of pottery). Additionally, it is claimed that Japan reached self-sovereignty in 660 BC, which under that criterion possibly makes Japan the oldest nation in the world. However, the first written historical perspective of Japan (provided by the Chinese) did not appear until AD 100. Gradually immigrants across Asia migrated to Japan, bringing an agricultural civilization. Eventually, between the fourth and ninth centuries, Japan's many kingdoms and tribes slowly unified under the emperor of Japan. Much internal conflict followed in medieval Japan. Finally, by the sixteenth century, Portuguese navigators reached Japan and significantly westernized the country. Following the Western European model and with great determination, Japan became a great global power leading up to World War II (1945), where they were overextended and defeated. With significant post-war growth, Japan quickly rebuilt and remains a world power, so much so that Japan has the world's third-largest economy, trailing only the United States and China. Nonetheless, bordering China, Russia, North Korea, South Korea, and Taiwan, Japan remains in an increasingly dynamic and volatile political environ.

2. Wikipedia, "Japanese Paleolithic," sec. "Archaeology of the Paleolithic period."

More specific to the present and my visit, the buzzing metropolis of Osaka, with a population of 2.7 million, is the third most populous city in Japan. The lively urban phenomenon is recognized for its standout eclectic food (commonly tagged "the kitchen of Japan"), energetic, neon-lit nightlife, and an abundance of fun, taking a top-notch food scene and fun to another level! Osaka is the tenth largest urban area in the world with nearly twenty million friendly inhabitants. Early on, Osaka developed into an important regional port and was known as Japan's economic hub. Osaka even served as Japan's imperial capital during the seventh and eighth centuries. The city had long been considered a busy, vital port for the rice-brokering feudal lords and the merchant class. In fact, a rice exchange and the world's first futures market were established in Osaka back in 1697. Because of its attractive location, Osaka is likely one of the first settlements of Japanese inhabitants. The city's favorable geological conditions, fresh water, lush vegetation, and defensible position against military attack were highly advantageous.

Likewise, the city of Kyoto served as the next capital of Japan for over a thousand years, from 794 through 1869. Kyoto remains Japan's serene cultural capital and the country's ninth largest city, with 1.5 million inhabitants. Surrounded by rich natural beauty, traditional Kyoto is laid out with picture-postcard old-town streets and spacious avenues. Kyoto is famous for its dazzling Buddhist temples, Zen rock gardens, imperial palaces, Shinto shrines, wooden houses, delectable cuisine, and possible geisha sightings. Kyoto's history is marked by many key events and conflicts. The city was ravaged by fourteenth-century feuding warlords and subsequently restored in the sixteenth century. During World War II, the understood cultural significance of Kyoto enabled the city to be spared from major destruction. In 1994, seventeen of Kyoto's preserved historic temples and gardens were designated as UNESCO World Heritage Sites. If there are any doubts about this popular bucket-list destination, bear in mind that Kyoto is consistently rated by Condé Nast as one of the world's best cities.[3]

KYOTO

While in Osaka on business, visiting nearby *Kyoto* is a must. Incredibly exhausted from the 6,300-mile, halfway-around-the-earth flight, I was most thankful that we took the afternoon to visit this memorable city. Surely we did not get to properly absorb Kyoto; however, what we did see in a matter of several hours was entirely fascinating on another level. The short bullet train ride from Osaka station, adjacent to the Ritz-Carlton, was an experience

3. Kyoto Travel, "Kyoto Ranked Second."

unto itself. After dropping off our bags and a quick refresh, we were off to Kyoto's Imperial Palace Park.

Nijō Castle

After a short walk from the Kyoto train stop, our first stop was *Nijō Castle* which, due to its historical importance, is one of the best-known castles in all of Japan. Specifically, Nijō Castle represented the power the shogun warlords gained over the emperor of Japan during the Edo period (1603–1867). The castle was built in 1603 as the Kyoto residence of the first Edo shogun, Tokugawa Ieyasu. Western Japan feudal lords, at the request of the shogun, funded construction of the Nijō Castle. Completed in 1626 by the shogun's grandson, Nijō Castle was purposely constructed overlooking the Imperial Palace to mock the weakening emperor. Also, in contrast to the palace's stark design, Nijō Castle featured showy intricate wood carvings and luxurious decorative panels as a further sign of the shogun's great importance and wealth.[4]

The first impression is that Nijō Castle is a very real castle. The castle is fortified with double high walls, two wide moats, and various watchtowers. On the massive sixty-eight-acre castle grounds are palaces, support buildings, and several Japanese gardens. The buildings themselves occupy an impressive eighty-six thousand square feet of space. The fortified inner and outer wards of protection are only accessed through a few elaborate Chinese-style gates. Ninomaru Palace is the main attraction, behind the second line of defense, and served as the highly protected residence and office of the shoguns during their Kyoto visits. The palace remains original and is comprised of multiple separate but connecting buildings. Inside, the large open rooms feature decorated ceilings and beautifully painted sliding doors and are covered with tatami sleeping mats. Notwithstanding its grandeur, my favorite feature of Nijō Castle and the Ninomaru Palace were the so called "nightingale floors." The outdoor corridors of the palace's buildings were constructed with wide, wooden nightingale floors. While dry boards naturally creak under pressure, nightingale floors are built in such a way that the floor nails rub against a clamp to create chirping noises. The chirping is likened to that of the Japanese bush warbler (nightingale), a common Japanese songbird. Legend is that the floors are used as a security measure to reveal intruders. Nijō Castle is considered home to the most famous example of a Japanese nightingale floor!

4. For these and other details in this section, see Wikipedia, "Nijō Castle."

Lastly, in an ironic story twist, after 264 years the emperor finally got his revenge. In 1867 at the end of the Edo period shogunate, it was precisely at Nijō Castle where restoration of power to Japan's emperor was proclaimed.

Golden Pavilion (Rokuon-ji Temple)

The most widely recognized image and poster child of Kyoto is unequivocally the *Golden Pavilion.* The Zen temple's top two floors are completely covered in gold leaf, resulting in its popular name of Kinkaku (Temple of the Golden Pavilion). The Golden Pavilion is officially the Rokuon-ji Temple. The famous Golden Pavilion is a pagoda made to store the sacred relics of the Buddha. The Golden Pavilion land was once home to a powerful Japanese aristocrat's villa until the late fourteenth century. The villa caught the attention of the third Ashikaga period shogun, who purchased the site to build his retirement complex. The impressive Golden Pavilion structure was built overlooking a large pond, and is the only building left of the shogun's former complex. Each floor of the three-story Golden Pavilion evokes a different and distinct architectural style, namely Shinden, Samurai, and Zen. The roof is thatched with shingles topped with a large, golden Chinese phoenix. The Golden Pavilion structure is strategically placed in a Japanese strolling garden, which extends below and surrounds the pavilion. I overheard that the pavilion grounds were built in a minimalistic approach, as Buddhists seek to illustrate harmony between heaven and earth. The palace also provides an excellent example of fourteenth-century classic Japanese garden design. Correlation between buildings and their settings were greatly emphasized during this period. The temple's gardens and architecture were said to evoke paradise on earth, and the site was the destination of many esteemed visitors, including Japan's emperor. The shogun and site were also central in promoting trade relations with neighboring China and importing aspects of Ming-dynasty Chinese culture into and throughout Japanese society. Following the shogun's death in 1408, according to the shogun's will, the villa was turned into a Zen temple by his son. The Golden Pavilion is not open to the public; visitors happily view and photograph the temple from across the pond, walk the landscape rock gardens, visit the tearoom, and grab souvenirs.

Sadly, the Golden Pavilion was burned down numerous times throughout its history, including twice during Japan's civil war that destroyed much of Kyoto. Most recently, the Golden Pavilion was set on fire by a fanatic twenty-two-year-old novice monk in 1950. The present forty-foot-high pavilion structure was rebuilt in 1955. The reconstruction is said to be a close copy of the original, although I've heard that some have questioned its comparative, extensive gold-leaf coating. During a period marked with the visual excess of shoguns, gold was an important addition to the original and rebuilt pavilions. The underlying meaning of gold leaf was intended to mitigate and purify negative thoughts and feelings towards death. Being highly covered in gold, framed in pine trees, the breathtaking Golden Pavilion is a visually striking scenic delight. Further, in the Kyoto sunlight, the reflection of the Golden Pavilion beautifully glistens on the pristine mirror pond. This lasting memory was captured in one of my favorite travel photos.

Kyoto Imperial Palace

A short walk from the Golden Pavilion is yet another highly regarded piece of Japan's cultural heritage . . . the *Kyoto Imperial Palace*. The palace resides in the spacious twenty-seven-acre Kyoto Imperial Park, a welcoming park in the center of Kyoto. The imperial park features wonderful broad gravel paths, ample lawns, and decorative groves of trees. The Japanese cherry trees were in final bloom during our mid-April visit. As noted, Kyoto was the capital of Japan for an incredible period of over a thousand years. The palace complex was built in 794 and served as the residence of Japan's imperial family until 1868, when the emperor and capital moved from Kyoto to Tokyo. Historically, the residences of retired emperors and high court nobles were grouped close together around the palace within the surrounding walled area. When the capital was eventually moved to Tokyo, the residences of the court nobles were demolished. Most of Kyoto's Imperial Palace is now a park open to the public. The grounds can be entered and explored freely without joining a tour and without any prior arrangements. Visitors can see the palace buildings and gardens, though none of the buildings can be entered. On the day of our visit, I noticed many groups of young schoolchildren in uniforms who were bussed to the educational site. I obtained another favorite *personal* photo with a group of young schoolchildren who were seemingly giving the peace sign (V-sign). I later learned that the sign is a common gesture used in photos and informal greetings in Japan to express gracefulness and happiness, or to simply say "hello" or "cheese." That photo always makes me smile!

The palace, stark in comparison to the shoguns' Nijō Castle, is situated in a large rectangular enclosure nearly a mile long and a half-mile wide. The complex is enclosed by long walls and consists of several gates, halls, and gardens. It also contains the Sento Imperial Palace and gardens, the Kyoto State Guest House, a remaining mansion, shrines, a pond, and a few other historic sites. The palace, like many of the oldest historic buildings in Japan, was destroyed by fire, moved, and rebuilt eight times over the centuries. The version presently standing was completed in 1855, with an attempt at reproducing it in the original palace architectural style.

The current Imperial Palace has been officially located in this area since the late twelfth century. The enthronement ceremonies of several latter emperors were held in the palace's main hall. It's not every day you get to enjoy historic Japanese imperial palaces!

Gion (Kyoto Geisha District)

The last stop in Kyoto was a walkthrough of the city's timeless *Gion* district. Gion is one of Kyoto's most beautiful and picturesque districts and dates to the Middle Ages. Located along the bank of Kyoto's Kamo River, charming Gion is renowned for its narrow, winding streets, lantern-lit courtyards, traditional wooden houses, relaxing teahouses, and exquisite Japanese cuisine served in elegant townhouse restaurants. Gion emanates historic ambiance straight out of a fairy tale that harkens back to Japan's yesteryear. Though, above all else, the Gion district is best known as Japan's most famous "geisha" neighborhood. Geisha are very strongly associated with Japan's ancient capital of Kyoto and its Gion district. In fact, geisha are one of the most sought-after sights in the district. In deference to the geisha, "no photography" and "no trespassing" signs are scattered throughout Gion's private streets where geisha live and work. Better known as *geiko* in Kyoto, geisha are high-class, well trained, highly respected female entertainers who perform traditional arts and provide hospitality. Both *geisha* and *geiko* have similar meanings that loosely translate to "person of the arts." Geisha, incredibly charming by nature, are trained a minimum of five years in conversation, music, dance, parlor games, flower arranging, calligraphy, and more. Further, they continue to train throughout their careers. Geisha attend dinners and gatherings as companions where they entertain guests with their beauty, glamour, charm, and honed skills. Oddly, even today, geisha must leave the profession to date or marry. Only around a hundred fully-fledged geisha are thought to remain in Kyoto today.[5] An evening with an authentic geisha could cost several hundred or even thousands of dollars.

Geisha were more recently popularized by the book and subsequent Rob Marshall–directed, Steven Spielberg–produced American movie *Memoirs of a Geisha*. Geisha are widely recognized in their elegant kimonos, smooth white makeup, and bright red lipstick, with a classic demure look—though many women walking the streets of Gion dressed in kimonos and makeup are often just tourists playing dress-up. The imposters look the part and happily pose for photographs. Fortunately, after spotting a couple genuine Gion geisha in full dress, we understood the significant difference and were thrilled with the rare, exciting Japanese experience. We also begrudgingly honored the "no photography" requests.

With imperial palaces and castles, a golden temple, classic Zen gardens, Buddhist shrines, intoxicating cuisine, and mystical, enchanting geisha, Kyoto is a fascinating step back in time. It is no wonder why Kyoto, Japan, is universally ranked as one of the best and most beautiful cities in the world.

OSAKA

After a day visiting Kyoto, time in Osaka was primarily dedicated to the work objectives at hand. We had just a couple of fun off-hours activities to enjoy. Our proud Japanese hosts and colleagues generously gave us their time and were most excited to share Osaka experiences.

Shopping Street

In addition to being a food and fun haven, Osaka is foremost a shoppers' paradise. The city is ideal for shopaholics who enjoy bustling streets, vibrant shops, and retail adventures. Streets are full of merchants selling daily essentials, produce, world-class street food, international brands, and plenty of quirky local Japanese souvenirs. The mere magnitude of stores and illuminating advertising create a sensory overload. That said, one common denominator in many Japanese towns is a major shopping street, closed to traffic and covered under a high-vaulted roof. This Japanese-style "shopping street" is known as a *shōtengai*. A shōtengai is much more than a shopping street; it's also a meeting point. It's where the daily services and needs of locals are provided and a place where many community activities are held. While in Osaka we visited and discovered the *Tenjinbashisuji*

5. Inside Kyoto, "Kyoto Geisha," sec. "Kyoto is Geisha Central."

shopping arcade. Stretching over 1.5 miles in Osaka's oldest merchant area, Tenjinbashisuji is the longest shōtengai in all of Japan. With over six hundred stores, Tenjinbashisuji offers an incredible shopping experience. It was the perfect starting place to immerse yourselves in day-to-day Japanese life. Among its many shops, you can purchase books, household goods, handicrafts, clothes, kimonos, croquettes, and most everything else. I purchased Anna Sui–designed "Hello Kitty" jewelry and traditional Japanese fans for my daughters and a cultured pearl from Osaka Bay for my wife. Beyond shopping, the covered street also provides a cool nostalgic atmosphere and contains many excellent traditional restaurants. We were able to enjoy a delicious, authentic Japanese lunch with our colleagues. I sampled *korokke*, the Japanese adaptation of the Western bechamel croquettes made with chopped meat with mashed potato. A perfect, enjoyable meal while exploring the lengthy, lively arcade and breathing in the local flavor.

Japanese Baseball Game

On the final work night of our time in the Osaka home office, our colleagues arranged for us to attend a *Japanese professional baseball* game at the indoor Osaka Dome. I was excited to compare the atmosphere of a baseball game in Japan to one back home. We learned that it was not a game with the hometown (Osaka) Orix Buffaloes but rather a game between the Yakult Swallows and Yomiuri Giants, the two Tokyo teams. It hardly mattered, as the stadium was packed with boisterous die-hard baseball fans. Now I enjoy baseball, even played at the high school and college levels. I love our local Pittsburgh Pirates team and our beautiful downtown ballpark. I've seen Major League Baseball games in many other American cities, including Boston, Los Angeles, Miami, Seattle, Houston, San Diego, Dallas, Cleveland, San Francisco, and Cincinnati. I've also visited several fun minor league parks throughout the country. You would think that baseball is baseball, whether played in America or in Japan. You'd be very, very, very wrong . . . I quickly learned that baseball in Japan is next-level, serious business!

That night, I learned there's nothing quite like watching a baseball game in Japan. It's their national sport. The game had an electrifying atmosphere, spirit, and vibe more like a major college football rivalry game or an international soccer match. First, most fans turn out in team colors and gear, even beyond what you would see at a Pittsburgh Steelers football game. And Pittsburgh is a town where fans commonly wear their jerseys to church on a Sunday game day! Likewise, both cities couple that enthusiasm with plenty of beer drinking. In Japan, fans can purchase concessions or are even permitted to bring their own food and beverages. Second, the cheering and noisemaking are nonstop at a Japanese baseball game. Fans bring or purchase plastic boom sticks and bang them incessantly in unison throughout the game. Third, fans from both teams are separated and bring their own marching pep bands and flag wavers to lead and accompany the cheering. The home team provides dancing cheerleaders, zany mascots, beer girls, and even more entertainment. Fourth, there is continuous pep band and fan base drumming and trumpeting, which replaces the traditional piped-in stadium organ music of American ballparks. Fifth, home players don't get individual "walk-up" music as they approach the plate . . . they get special personalized chants or cheers known and sung together by all fans. Additionally, with clapping noisemakers loudly clamoring, fans stomp their feet every time a player is up at bat. Although the crowd sang in Japanese, it made for a fun, entertaining environment. The fans were fully engaged the entire game rather than passively spectating or roaming the stadium's corridors. The noisy contraptions, constant cheers, chanting, and dancing admittedly seemed a bit chaotic, though the fans' vocal support of their respective teams was most impressive.

The history of the Japanese Baseball League is very interesting. The first professional baseball team in Japan was founded by a Japanese media mogul in 1934. The founder named the team the Dai Nippon Tokyo Yakyu Kurabu, which translated to the "Great Japan Tokyo Baseball Club." This team was created to match up with a team of visiting American All-Stars that included Babe Ruth, Jimmie Foxx, and Lou Gehrig among others. The Tokyo team then spent the 1935 season barnstorming in the United States and winning an astonishing ninety-three of 102 games. More impressive, they played against solid semi-pro and Pacific Coast minor league teams. According to one historian, the only drawbacks to the Japanese team's popularity in the States were the cumbersome Japanese team's name and the uniform's Chinese-script characters.[6] In a smart marketing move, the team quickly resolved that issue by renaming themselves the Tokyo Giants and adopting uniforms and colors identical to the then New York Giants, now the relocated San Francisco Giants.

As to the game itself, I was excited to see the mighty Yomiuri (Tokyo) Giants, though the Yakult Swallows won the game 8–2. Most hardcore baseball fans are aware that the Tokyo Giants are the oldest and most successful sports team in Japan. They have won a collective thirty-one Japan Series titles in the evolving twelve-team league since the 1930s. Many regard the Yomiuri Giants as the "New York Yankees" of Japan. Much like the Yankees,

6. NPB Card Guy, "Uniforms."

the Giants' major Tokyo location, widespread popularity, and great success has a polarizing effect on the nation's fans. That night, it was two American players with multiple hits who had a big hand in the Swallows win. Each Japanese team was then allowed two international players, now expanded to four players. In total, over six hundred professional American players have played in the Japanese league, though the great majority for just a single season. Conversely, more than sixty Japanese star professional players have signed and played American Major League Baseball.[7] The most notable examples are Hideo Nomo of the Los Angeles Dodgers, Ichiro Suzuki of the Seattle Mariners, Hideki Matsui of the New York Yankees, and current mega-superstar Shohei Ohtani of the Los Angeles Dodgers. Ohtani recently led the Dodgers to 2024 and 2025 World Series championships and was named unanimous league MVP. He also recently signed the major league's highest paid contract of $700 million for ten years. It's clear that Japan's cultural passion for baseball along with very strong youth development programs are producing more and more world-class ballplayers. Consequently, Japan is also enjoying great success in international competition. Case in point: just outside our Osaka high-rise office building, I briefly watched a high school baseball team practice on a field below. At least in this instance, the observed highly rigorous structure, approach to fundamentals, and great discipline of that practice far outpaced the American model.

What a fun night it was! Knowing how the Japanese tend to put a fun twist on most everything, I should have foreseen that we were in for a treat. I am extremely grateful that our colleagues arranged for an evening at the ballpark. Every American fan should be fortunate enough to experience a professional baseball game in Japan!

Kaiseki (Japanese Cuisine)

I was aware that Japan's fantastic and exotic cuisine—traditional dishes such as ramen, sushi, and tempura as well as more unusual dishes such as sea urchins—is highly esteemed worldwide. Neither my colleague nor I are serious "foodies" or even very adventurous eaters. Nonetheless, when in Rome (or in Japan in this instance), do as the locals do! For that reason, when possible, I make it a point to visit a landmark or fashionable restaurant and sample local delicacies. On our final evening in Japan, I suggested just that. I spoke with the hotel staff, and they recommended the wonderful world of *kaiseki*, a must-try genre of dining that inspired nouvelle cuisine. The kaiseki style of seasonal fine dining, consisting of multiple "chef's choice" (omakase)

7. Wikipedia, "American Expatriate Baseball Players."

small dishes served one by one, is steeped in centuries of Japanese tradition. The kaiseki haute cuisine menu typically includes an appetizer, soup, sashimi, a grilled dish, a steamed course, and dessert. Regarded as one of the world's most refined styles of cooking, each course is meticulously prepared and exquisitely served. Even the pottery and ceramic tableware elements are selected to enhance the overall culinary experience. Kaiseki is considered a delicate balancing act of flavor, texture, and color . . . a feast for both your eyes and taste buds. The style features only peak available ingredients and provides a demonstration of Japan's amazing culinary prowess. Kaiseki creates the perfect synergy between haute cuisine and artistic expression, the epitome of Japan's formal dining experience.

While kaiseki-style cooking is better associated with imperial Kyoto, the seasonal fine dining style is slightly varied and often referred to as *kappo* in Osaka. The kappo meal tends to be a bit more casual, flexible, and less structured than kaiseki. However, it's a difference likely indiscernible to the average first-time visiting diner. Both styles provide a special Japanese treat of the most sublime, incredibly fresh and flavorful dishes you're likely to encounter anywhere. Oftentimes, watching the artistic chefs create these dazzlingly creative dishes is an exciting part of the appeal. The kaiseki set-course meal is selected by the chef to highlight a specific seasonal theme rooted in nature. Springtime may be represented by a budding sakura, the Japanese cherry blossom in full bloom, whereas kaiseki celebrated in autumn would feature the rich, earthy flavors and colors of fall's seasonal ingredients such as mushrooms, chestnuts, persimmons, and pumpkins. Chef-choice menus are aimed to familiarize visiting diners with Japan's local specialties, peak seasonal ingredients, and long-established cooking methods. The dishes are then beautifully arranged and garnished with real leaves and flowers as well as edible garnishes designed to resemble plants and animals. Such themes highlight the superior quality of the meal's natural ingredients and are carried forward by the restaurant's subdued lighting and calming atmosphere. What the heck, we thought, let's give it a try!

I am not quite sure what we were thinking! Or what we ate the evening of our kaiseki-style meal in Osaka (accompanied by a round or two of sake, Japanese rice wine)! Admittedly, kaiseki or kappo may not be for everyone, particularly those accustomed to and favoring heartier, informal, less costly dining. I do not recall much except for the grilled fish. Flavored fish is chosen and stocked for seasonal flavor and varies widely according to the time of year—possibly rosy seabass from Tsushima Island, Wakasa-style grilled sea bream, freshwater eel, Pacific saury, etc. The fish is typically garnished with salt and seasoned overnight before a charcoal-roasted grilling with a light coating of soy sauce. The result is a fluffy, tender texture with aromatic skin. However, what I recall most is the Japanese preparation of the fish still seemingly alive (ikizukuri method). The head remains wholly attached so the diner can see continuing gill movement, intended to denote the freshness of the fish. That was quite disconcerting; I am certain the chef was disappointed and annoyed with our ignorance and less-than-enthusiastic reception. For the most part, I enjoyed all the colorful, seasonal flavors and the unique kaiseki-style dining experience. However, my colleague gleefully stopped at the local McDonald's on the walk back to our hotel! Though quite a different meal, I would not have traded the one-of-a-kind cultural dining experience for anything.

It doesn't take long to understand why Japan is a special, magical place . . . the "Land of the Rising Sun." Geographically located in East Asia, Japan stretches out into the Pacific Ocean. Because of Japan's location east of China and Korea, it is one of the first places in the world to witness the sunrise each new day. The nickname symbolizes Japan's unique position in the world and is a source of great pride to the Japanese people. A rising sun represents renewal, hope, and a forward-looking perspective. I saw firsthand that Japan is a country with both a fascinating history and a vibrant progressive culture. Japan is a country known for its rich cultural heritage, natural beauty, ancient iconic landmarks, modern innovation and technology, and world-famous culinary excellence. I'll long remember my unique bleisure visit to Japan.

CHAPTER 15

SYDNEY

If Paris is a city of lights,
Sydney is the city of fireworks.
—*Baz Luhrmann*

There's yet another very-far-away, must-visit destination I will never forget. This one is the striking, vibrant, cosmopolitan harbor town of Sydney, Australia. Most everyone is quite familiar with Sydney's iconic landmark attractions and its stunning beaches. However, exploring Sydney firsthand—one of the most beautiful, safest, and most livable cities in the world—is a whole new exciting experience. Many consider Sydney's amazing climate, beach-culture lifestyle, and its overall high quality of life the envy of the world. And, as noted, Sydney is literally the city of fireworks! Each year, over 1.5 million visitors are attracted to Sydney Harbour's New Year's Eve "world's best" fireworks celebration.

Back at work, rumor was quickly spreading that we were looking to acquire a small like-minded medical device manufacturer located in Sydney, Australia. I was always very proud that our work culture was one of utmost collaboration and outstanding teamwork. Accordingly, I learned that a cross-functional team of department heads—Operations, Quality, Procurement, Legal, and Finance—would be engaged in the matter. We, me included, were tasked to visit and evaluate the target company to rapidly complete requisite due diligence. Further, in this instance, the relatively small, privately held company was elated to potentially be acquired by a world-recognized international healthcare enterprise. The niche Australian company similarly and primarily produced and sold contrast injection systems and consumables for that region's radiology market. Such devices are routinely used to inject contrast dye and saline flush through the body during millions of annual MRI and CT imaging procedures. Unlike our established full-feature, hospital suite products (85 percent worldwide market share), this company's basic injectors were specifically designed to be compact, mobile, and more economical. In automobile terms, these reliable injectors were lower-cost subcompacts, principally marketed and sold in the Oceania region of the world. Given the application of our award-winning designs, production, marketing, sales, and service bandwidth, these compact injectors provided a very attractive complementary option for many Asian countries. I can report that we did subsequently acquire the innovative Sydney manufacturer and it remains a very successful subsidiary company.

Traveling to Australia is an adventure . . . duration of flights westbound through San Francisco or elsewhere can surpass twenty-four hours. It's essential to approach the flight with an understanding, positive, fun-loving attitude. Nearly ten thousand distant miles to Sydney, actual air mileage is far beyond the 6,300 miles to Japan. The reason is that Australia is in the southern hemisphere, well below the equator and quite south of Japan. To make matters worse, I decided to forego the initial rest day and join the group at work a day later immediately upon landing in Sydney. This allowed me to attend my youngest daughter's high school soccer team's Senior Night. I was glad to delay travel, as I made it a point not to miss family events. Unfortunately, there was a cost to be paid: I could barely stand and keep my eyes open on the tour through the site that day. In any event, I was thrilled to be experiencing a new fascinating continent. Another pleasant surprise was our well-located hotel in the harbor on the bay. Further, I learned that there were both water ferries and taxis from the harbor's nearby Circular Quay up the Parramatta River estuary directly to Rydalmere Wharf. This river is the main tributary of Sydney Harbour. Exiting the water taxi, it was just a short walk to the plant site located in the suburb of Rydalmere. The cherry on top . . . the taxis went directly past the world-famous Sydney Opera House and under the engineering marvel that is the Sydney Harbour Bridge. What an easy, beautiful, relaxing, and fun way to travel to work!

The history of Sydney is really a tale of two cities, or rather two tales of one city.[1] For a documented thirty thousand years, though possibly sixty or seventy-five thousand years, Sydney was initially inhabited by people who had migrated to Australia from southeast Asia. Radiocarbon-dated

1. For the historical information that follows, see Mbantua Gallery, "Aboriginal Culture"; Wikipedia, "Sydney"; and Wikipedia, "Australian Aboriginal Culture."

evidence indicates existence of human activity in that period.[2] These inhabitants, known as Aboriginal Australians, subsisted on fishing, hunting, and the gathering of plants and shellfish. They are considered the oldest known civilization on Earth. There were twenty-nine known Aboriginal clan groups in the Sydney metropolitan area. These traditional early Aboriginal owners of the Sydney area are referred to as the *Eora* people. Naturally, coastal clans were more reliant on seafood while the hinterland clans relied on forest animals and plants. Aboriginal clans enjoyed rich ceremonial lives and, despite language and cultural barriers, would convene to foster trade, intermarry, and build necessary clan alliances. All was going well until April 1770 when British explorer Captain James Cook voyaged to Australia and claimed the land for the British crown. It was here that Captain Cook initially encountered the Aboriginal clans. This was the first recorded European contact with the eastern coastline of Australia, and the clan understandably opposed the landing party. At this time there were an estimated eight thousand Aboriginal people living in the greater Sydney region. Cook and his British crew explored the surrounding area collecting water, timber, fodder and botanical specimens. They unsuccessfully sought to establish relations with the Aboriginal population and quickly departed after a week.

In addition to Australia, Captain Cook was famous for several other voyages. He courageously sailed thousands of miles across largely uncharted areas of the known world. Captain Cook's fame grew from his superior seamanship, surveying, and cartographic skills. He mapped new lands and recorded islands and coastlines on European maps for the first time. Captain Cook left a legacy of scientific and geographical knowledge. Along the way, during his third and final voyage in the Pacific, Captain Cook encountered the Hawaiian Islands. Sadly, he was killed during a dispute with a Hawaii chief. Notwithstanding his courageous and impressive feats, Captain Cook is often criticized for his violent encounters with Indigenous people and his part in subsequent British colonization.

Australia, and specifically Sydney, was significantly redefined in 1788 when it first became a British prisoners (convict) settlement. Prior to this date, beginning in 1615, the British used the American colonies as penal colonies. British convicts were sentenced to seven-year terms and transported to America. The convicts were usually poor, from larger industrial cities, and often convicted of minor petty crimes such as stealing. Though most British prisoners were from England, many others were from Ireland and Scotland. These convicts were known as "His Majesty's Seven-Year

2. Wikipedia, "Prehistory of Australia," sec. "Dating of sites."

Passengers"[3] and put to work in agriculture (primarily tobacco). In Virginia and elsewhere, the prisoners were auctioned off to British plantation owners, tradesmen, and shipbuilders. Effectively, the convicts were the white slaves of America. About fifty thousand British convicts, or one quarter of British settlers in the 1700s, were sent to colonial America. And although most colonists opposed the practice, the British convicts were very instrumental in America's early development. The American Revolutionary War quickly ended this practice, forcing Britain to establish penal colonies elsewhere.

By 1783, shortly after Britain lost the American colonies, English jails were again overflowing. In response, Britain decided to transport its prisoners to Australia, the land claimed by Captain Cook years earlier. Britain's proponents of colonization understood the strategic importance of a new base in the Asia-Pacific region; namely, its potential to provide necessary timber and flax (food and linens) for the British Navy. As a result, in 1788 under the command of British Captain Arthur Phillip, the first fleet of eleven ships arrived in Australia. Captain Phillip triumphantly raised Britain's Union Jack. The initial fleet comprised over a thousand settlers, including 736 British convicts. The arrival of the British fleet at the safe harbor of Sydney Cove marked the beginning of the European colonization of Australia. And with that was the start of a new British penal colony. Waves of convicts were transported to Australia for eighty years until 1868, over 150,000 prisoners in total. It was Captain Phillip himself, appointed the first governor of New South Wales, who named the cove Sydney after Britain's home secretary. British officials increasingly referred to the township as Sydney, and it was formally declared a city in 1842. Colonization was initially very difficult for the British, with conflicts and starvation rampant. More importantly, British colonization sadly changed forever the lives of the Aboriginal (Eora) people. The effects on the original Aboriginal owners of the land in Sydney were devastating for decades. Thousands of Aboriginals died in conflicts with British settlers and from newly introduced transported diseases such as smallpox. The Aboriginals' great suffering was further compounded by the loss of long-standing cultural traditions and languages. Nonetheless, over the years and despite great hardships, plagues, wars, and economic depressions, Sydney gradually developed and prospered. By 1901, Australia became a self-governing British Empire dominion. Australians valiantly fought with the British during both world wars. Rapid growth after World War II established Sydney as a very attractive major tourist destination. It was only quite recent, March 3, 1986, that Britain officially relinquished its remaining power over Australia.

3. Roller, "Out of Sight," para. 5.

Sydney is located on Australia's southeast coast and is the most populous city in Australia. Greater Sydney consists of over six hundred unique suburbs with an estimated population of 5.45 million. Despite being one of the most expensive global cities, Sydney consistently ranks in the top ten most livable cities in the world.[4] Sydney is classified as a highly integrated Alpha+ city. It is a city with worldwide influence that complements the needs of London and New York City within the Pacific/Asia region. Today, the largest proportion of Sydney's citizens remains of British and Irish descent. However, post–World War II, Australia (primarily Sydney) took in large numbers of immigrants from numerous European and Asian countries as well as New Zealand. Many of the inner suburbs have a proud, distinctly ethnic character and a broad variety of ethnic restaurants. There also remains a small community of Aboriginals who still live under somewhat depressed conditions. Consequently, Sydney exudes a genuinely international atmosphere amidst a blend of its British heritage and its South Seas locale. Sydney is both a thriving metropolis and a laid-back beachside city with a relaxed coastal vibe and a ready "no worries" attitude. It's a vibrant down-under city situated on a spectacular bay with innumerable water inlets and coves. Millions of tourists visit Sydney each year to enjoy the beaches, nature reserves, parks, and landmarks. Beyond that, the two major tourist attractions remain the Sydney Harbour Bridge and the World Heritage–listed Sydney Opera House.

Sydney Harbour Bridge

As brilliant and recognizable as San Francisco's Golden Gate Bridge and London's Tower Bridge is the *Sydney Harbour Bridge*. The Sydney Harbour Bridge is an engineering masterpiece completed during the technical revolution. The bridge was a pivotal step in modern Sydney's overall development. Built in 1932, the bridge is one of Australia's most famous landmarks, second only to the Sydney Opera House. Oddly enough, it was a convict architect in 1815 who first proposed a bridge over Sydney Harbour. Only after another century did the bridge idea become reality. A workable design was finally submitted in 1916. It would be a majestic arch bridge with an integrated transport system, including an extensive network of rail and roadways leading to the bridge. By 1924, a contract with a bridge-building firm from England to build the iconic structure was finalized. Construction started that year. It took over two thousand men eight years to complete the landmark bridge. The skilled workforce was necessarily multinational

4. Wikipedia, "Sydney," para. 3; Dorn, "10 Most Livable."

though mainly comprised of Australians. Sadly, as was too often the case in the early industrial age, sixteen men died during the bridge's construction phase. Likewise, nearly eight hundred families (469 buildings) living in the bridge's footprint were abruptly relocated without compensation. The incredible feat of engineering required fifty-three thousand tons of steel and six million hand driven rivets. The Sydney Harbour Bridge ascends 440 feet above the waters of Sydney Harbour, still the tallest steel arch bridge in the world today. The bridge was also the world's widest long-span bridge at 160 feet, and today is second widest only to a bridge in Vancouver, Canada. In terms of commitment and stick-to-itiveness, completion of the bridge in the 1930s coincided with the darkest days of the Great Depression. Accordingly, the Sydney Harbour Bridge opening was a joyous and momentous occasion drawing one million people. Proud Australians triumphantly celebrated and commemorated the bridge made by Australians for Australia. Due to its forward-looking design, the bridge carries rail, vehicular, bicycle, and pedestrian traffic. The main roadway across the bridge is the Bradfield Highway, which is a mere 1.5 miles long and one of the shortest highways in all of Australia. Pedestrians can easily walk across the incredibly scenic bridge in just thirty minutes or so. There is also a four-lane tunnel under the Sydney Harbour Bridge called the Sydney Harbour Tunnel. The tunnel greatly reduces traffic congestion by providing an alternate route across the bay. A second tunnel is currently under construction.

I am still not quite certain whether this was a *bummer* or a *blessing*. However, those up for a high adventure can complete a three-hour, thousand-step *BridgeClimb* experience. Due to me trailing my work colleagues by a day, they all went ahead and did the amazing Sydney Harbour BridgeClimb before I arrived. Believe me . . . I heard all about it! The bridge climbing experience was an outgrowth of the occasional reports of illegal climbers who had scaled the bridge by night. Since 1998, it became possible for tourists to legally climb the bridge. Each climb begins on the eastern side of the south end of the bridge. Once the group ascends to the summit, they cross over to the western side of the arch for the descent back to the start. This experience did not happen by chance. This initiative involved numerous years of collaboration with Australian state and local government bodies and community groups. Various safety, logistics, media, heritage, and conservation experts were also heavily consulted. After nearly a decade of research and development, BridgeClimb Sydney was officially launched, becoming the world's first tourism operator to offer bridge climbing as an experience. Specifically, groups of climbers are provided protective clothing and are given a thorough orientation briefing before climbing. During the climb, attendees are always safely secured to the bridge by a wire lifeline. As a nod to finally reaching the summit, climbers are rewarded with stunning views of Sydney from the bridge's top arch. It's the perfect spot for a selfie as well! Couples have the option to get married on the bridge, and the experience has also attracted many famous actors, musicians, and royals. The list of climbers includes Oprah Winfrey, Robert De Niro, Justin Timberlake, Will Ferrell, Matt Damon, Prince Harry, Nicole Kidman, Will Smith, and Cameron Diaz, just to name a few. Many have left behind autographed photos that are on display.

Sadly, I missed this unique BridgeClimb opportunity. However, motoring directly beneath the Sydney Harbour Bridge in the bay offers another worthwhile though very different perspective. From below you a get a sense of the ingenuity and magnitude of the towering, iconic bridge. Thankfully, my daily water taxi and ferry commutes from Sydney's Circular Quay to the suburb of Rydalmere and elsewhere did just that!

Sydney Opera House

The *Sydney Opera House* is Sydney's world-famous performing arts facility and best-known landmark. The opera house is one of the most photographed buildings in the world and is known for its unique use of a series of gleaming white sail-shaped shells as its roof structure. The Sydney Opera House sits prominently on the bay's Bennelong Point named after Woollarawarre Bennelong, a senior Aboriginal man and liaison at the time of the arrival of the British in Australia back in 1788. The opera house's original design was submitted by a Danish architect in an international competition sponsored by the government in 1956. Construction began in 1959, with the opening of the opera house originally planned for Australia Day (January 26) in 1963. However, due to the innovative nature of the facility's design, a variety of problems arose, including unplanned structural engineering difficulties, outrageous cost overruns, and major delays. Much like Paris's Eiffel Tower, the project grew controversial and public opinion turned against it at the time. Numerous design iterations and architect resignations occurred. Some even feared that the opera house might never be completed. It was so problematic that construction continued for an added ten years until September 1973. Construction, expected to take four years, took fourteen years and involved ten thousand construction workers. Consequently, the original Sydney Opera House cost estimate of $7 million had ballooned to a final cost of $102 million. On a positive note, the opera house's astounding costs were largely paid for by the New South Wales State Lottery. The Sydney Opera House was completed and finally had its grand opening on October

20, 1973, with none other than Queen Elizabeth II presiding. Her Majesty rightly noted that the Sydney Opera House had captured the imagination of the world. She further stated, "The human spirit must sometimes take wings or sails, and create something that is not just utilitarian or commonplace."[5]

The Sydney Opera House features a modern expressionist design wildly accentuated by a series of large concrete "shells" that form the fourteen roofs of the structure. The original architect had stated that the design of the Sydney Opera House was inspired and guided by nature, its forms, functions, and colors. Specifically, the architect's expressive roof design was influenced by shells, bird wings, clouds, walnuts, and even palm trees. However, the architect claims that the final design of the shells or sails was ultimately inspired by peeling an orange.[6] Many others view the shells as magnificent sails! The design of the roof was one of the most difficult and costly aspects of the opera house's build. The shells are composed of 1,056,006 tiles, manufactured by a Swedish company, in both glossy white and matte cream. Apart from the roof tile and the foyer's glass curtain walls, the building's exterior is largely composed of pink granite. From conception to completion, the opera house saga greatly tested the then-limits of engineering, construction, and modern design. A significant though "worth-it" price was paid for such an architectural breakthrough. The building itself covers 4.5 acres of land and is six hundred feet long and nearly four hundred feet wide at its widest point. The roof's highest point rises twenty-two-stories above sea level. The opera house is also wonderfully surrounded by substantial open public spaces. In fact, the stone-paved forecourt area with its adjacent monumental steps is regularly used for outdoor performances. Lastly, you can rest easy, as the opera house was significantly wind-tested and is safely supported on 588 concrete piers sunk as far as eighty feet below sea level.

The multipurpose Sydney Opera House performing arts facility features two primary large theaters. The largest venue is the 2,679-seat concert hall, which hosts symphony concerts, choir performances, and popular music shows. The second largest indoor venue with a seating capacity of 1,507 is the Joan Sutherland Theater, home to Opera Australia and the Australian Ballet. Up to seventy musicians can be accommodated in the theater's orchestra pit as well. This theater is proudly named after Sydney's hometown girl and world-renowned, award-winning operatic soprano. Finally, there are also three flexible theaters of various sizes for stage plays, film screenings, and smaller musical performances. With nearly 350 annual

5. Google Arts and Culture, "Sydney Opera House," sec. "1973: The Grand Opening."

6. See Sydney Opera House, "Our Story" and "Architecture Meets Nature."

performances, the Sydney Opera House is one of the busiest performing arts centers and community meeting places in the world. A few other interesting facts include a 1960 visit from American singer and civil rights activist Paul Robeson. Long before construction was complete in 1973, Mr. Robeson climbed the scaffolding and sang "Ol' Man River" to the construction workers as they ate lunch. This is considered the very first performance at the Sydney Opera House. A second interesting fact is that, with temperature and humidity critical to ensure that musical instruments stay in tune, the symphony concert hall must be continuously maintained at 72.5 degrees Fahrenheit. Lastly, in terms of sustainability, the Sydney Opera House heating and cooling are directly powered using circulated seawater taken directly from the bay.

The Sydney Opera House is a global architectural masterpiece and vibrant, prestigious performance venue. With programming spanning so many arts forms, the opera house began a new era of cultural discovery when it first opened over five decades ago. As its aspirational mission and idealistic quest, the opera house project was launched to mold a better and more enlightened community. Mission accomplished! Today the opera house is Australia's leading tourism destination with nearly twelve million visitors annually. In 2007, the beautiful Sydney Opera House was added to UNESCO's World Heritage List, designated a cultural landmark with outstanding universal value. Due to time constraints, I was not able to attend a performance or enjoy one of the guided tours. Nonetheless, I had a wonderful time visiting the Sydney Opera House's open public space, retail shops, and café and simply mingling with all the international visitors.

Bondi Beach

After a successful workweek, I had come to my final day in Sydney. The others had flown home Sunday morning, though I was scheduled to return Monday. Thus, I had Sunday in Sydney all to myself. Usually, I would probably rent a car and feverishly explore the country from dawn to dusk. However, the late work nights and dinners, Saturday meetings, and a serious fifteen-hour time difference had exhausted even me. Also, it was mid-October, when Australia was slowly transitioning into Spring. The weather was sunny and pleasant but chilly (think March in the United States). A decision was made. I had enjoyed a few of Sydney's city charms and now I would explore its seaside life. Fortunately, just a mere fifteen-minutes from Sydney Harbour is Australia's iconic *Bondi Beach* neighborhood. More than just a beach, Bondi is known as the jewel of Sydney's laid-back beach lifestyle. Bondi Beach is an internationally recognized symbol of Australia's surf culture and the country's vast global appeal.

The sweeping white-sand crescent of Bondi Beach, just four miles from the heart of Sydney, attracts millions of visitors every year. Surfers are drawn to its reliable waves, walkers and joggers enjoy the scenic cliffside coastal walk, locals swim in a historic year-round ocean pool, health-conscious Sydneysiders head to laid-back cafés, and hip traveling backpackers frequent the area's many casual pubs. Several Australian celebrities visit or live in the Bondi Beach neighborhood, and even Wolverine himself (Aussie actor Hugh Jackman) owns a stunning beach penthouse. All that said, Bondi Beach is regarded as a somewhat dangerous, lifeguard-patrolled beach. The ever-present riptides, occasional great white and gray nurse shark sightings, and seasonal jellyfish (bluebottles) require utmost safety and adherence to warning signs. There's a long-running Australian hit television series called *Bondi Rescue* that depicts real-life rescue scenarios. Believe it or not, there are nearly five thousand rescues, many involving inebriated swimmers or unaware tourists, each summer. On busy days, the "Bondi blue"–clad lifeguards may save up to a hundred people. Consequently, locals take beach safety very, very serious. Much like the residents in Amsterdam receive cultural bicycling training, the world's first surf lifesaving club was founded at Bondi Beach in 1907. The *Bondi Surf Bathers Life Saving Club* educates on ocean dangers and excels at rescue and resuscitation and many other icons of lifesaving. The club is the recipient of many gold medals for their successful efforts. In fact, the chilly morning I visited, I witnessed dozens of red-and-gold-dressed instructors working on the shore with over a hundred young children. Lastly, much like California's famed Manhattan Beach, Bondi Beach hosts many major beach volleyball competitions. When Sydney hosted the universally acclaimed 2000 Summer Olympics, a temporary ten-thousand-seat stadium, a smaller stadium, warm-up courts, and training courts were all constructed on Bondi Beach.

My Sunday in Sydney would include early Mass (twelve years of Catholic schooling), a good relaxing brunch, and a leisurely visit to Bondi Beach. As I commented earlier, sometimes you just luckily stumble into good fortune . . . and that was the case with brunch. It was only recently that I learned that superstar Taylor Swift's first stop in Sydney, direct from the airport, is usually the buzzy neighborhood restaurant known simply as *Bills* (no apostrophe). Turns out Bill Granger, who sadly passed away from cancer Christmas Day 2023 at the young age of fifty-four, was a self-taught celebrity chef, food writer, and restaurateur. At the age of twenty-four, Bill opened his first restaurant in Sydney. There are now nineteen Bills throughout Sydney, London, Hawaii, Japan, and South Korea. None of this was known to me at the time. However, what I do recall is the restaurant's famed, creamy-to-a-fault scrambled eggs. The recipe appears to be equal parts eggs and heavy whipping cream, producing soft, smooth, amazing scrambled eggs. Bill Granger's scrambled eggs are often cited as the best scrambled eggs in the world. Among his many other remarkable achievements, Bill is also credited as the "godfather" of avocado toast.[7] The very first recorded sighting of smashed avocado on toast was at one of Bill's Sydney restaurants in 2016. By all accounts, the charmingly modest, talented chef was a fun, enthusiastic, ambitious, and endlessly generous family man. Bill Granger was a devoted husband and father whose founding spirit continues with his wife and their three daughters. Looking back, I'm very happy that I experienced a wonderful brunch at Bills.

Following brunch, I headed over to Bondi Beach for Sydney's most iconic walking trail, a 3.5-mile path known as the *Bondi to Coogee Coastal Walk*. Best described as an urban coastal cliff-top walk, it has stunning views of several beaches, parks, bays, and cliffs. All the while you are passing by charming neighborhoods of specialty shops, cafés, and restaurants. Probably the most amazing site I saw was an Olympic-sized sea pool and restaurant club seemingly built into the ocean at the southern end of Bondi Beach. Turns out that it's the landmark *Bondi Icebergs Swimming Club*, which was established in 1929. The club was founded by a dedicated band of local lifesavers seeking to maintain their fitness during Sydney's cooler winter months of June to August. The Bondi Icebergs "Winter Swimming Club" even drew up a constitution with a well-defined rule. Namely, it is mandatory that swimmers compete on three Sundays out of four for five years to maintain membership. The Bondi Beach ocean pool is also open to the public for casual swimming throughout the year. Recently, famed Aussie actress Margot Robbie promoted her critically acclaimed, blockbuster movie *Barbie* at the Bondi Icebergs pool. The scenic pool sitting over sandy Bondi Beach is always an Instagrammer's dream!

Bleisure travel is truly a double-edged sword with both good and bad aspects. This was particularly true in visiting Sydney, Australia. The *good*, and I'm truly grateful for it, is that I got to travel to Australia, something I was probably unlikely to otherwise do in my lifetime. Further, business trips are essentially "all expenses paid." You also travel with wonderful colleagues

7. Wilson, "Bill Granger Obituary."

and share experiences with many interesting business companions. The *bad* is that a four-day trip to Australia, or anywhere internationally, is obviously very insufficient to experience a country. It always leaves you wanting more and hoping to someday return. Australia is the sixth largest country in the world, only slightly smaller than the United States. As such, visiting Sydney for a few days is comparable to a brief visit to Miami or Los Angeles. Lastly, the "both good and bad" aspect is that after a few days, as the excitement diminishes, you begin to sorely miss your family. You wish so much that they could be with you. Then, inevitably, you are always happy to return home! The trip to spectacular Australia will long be remembered; a return will just have to wait.

CHAPTER 16

MEXICO CITY

Mexico is more a symbol than a country, a country not at all defined by its ideological bent or its citizens or rulers but by the spirit of its people.

—*Jack Kerouac*

I ONCE HAD A business trip to beautiful Mexico City in our neighboring, often wrongly beleaguered, country of Mexico. There was no sightseeing or any visits to attractions this time. This trip was entirely business versus true bleisure travel, though I was able to somewhat explore the neighborhood and briefly experience the city's amazing people and colorful culture. It's these sentiments I, nonetheless, want to share. I had little awareness of Mexico's unique mix of cultures and landscapes or the fact that the ancient, populous country is so dominated by its capital, Mexico City . . . the sixth largest metropolis in the world. The city is also the oldest capital of the New World. Mexico remains a very traditional country still extremely centered on family, religion, sports, and the arts. I suppose for these reasons, visitors are very welcomed and readily accepted. In a way, the experience sweetly differed from other countries I visited. Lastly, and I'm embarrassed to admit, I was not exactly sure where Mexico City was located relative to the popular, better-known seaside resort towns of Cancun, Cozumel, Cabo San Lucas, Puerto Vallarta, and Acapulco. In fact, and unbeknownst to me at the time, Mexico City is situated in a large valley in the high plateaus of south-central Mexico. Comparatively, Americans all know about our Mile High City of Denver, Colorado. Denver reaches exactly one mile (5,280 feet) above sea level. What I did not know is that Mexico City sits 7,350 feet above sea level.

Further, it's surrounded by mountains and volcanoes that reach astonishing elevations of sixteen thousand feet, or over three miles high!

In addition to being the highest metropolis in the North American continent, Mexico City is also the oldest, as it was founded in 1325 by the Aztecs. It served as the capital of the Aztec Empire. And if that's not enough superlatives, Mexico City is also the most populous city in the western hemisphere, with a population of twenty-two million. Further, Greater Mexico City is also the largest Spanish-speaking city in the world. Lastly, it's one of only two capital cities founded by Indigenous peoples, Quito, Ecuador being the others. The city itself is divided into sixteen boroughs, which are in turn further divided into many neighborhoods. Of course, the climate of Mexico City is influenced by its high elevation and mountainous surroundings. The mean annual temperature, with only minor seasonal variances, is sixty degrees Fahrenheit. In terms of Mexico itself, the country is approximately one-fifth the size of the United States, rendering Mexico the thirteenth largest country in the world by land mass (the United States is third, behind only Russia and Canada). The country of Mexico is slightly larger than the United States' largest state of Alaska, which is more than double the size of Texas, the second largest state. The overall population of Mexico exceeds 130 million, which is more than the states of California, Texas, Illinois, and New York combined.

The history of ancient Mexico City is both furious and fascinating. The oldest signs of human occupation date to the finding of a woman's skeleton (the Peñon woman) placed at 12,700 years old. The Peñon woman constitutes one of the oldest examples of remains discovered in the Americas. What's unclear is her origin, being either Asian, European, or Aboriginal Australian. Most important, by the eighth century, the area of Mexico City became a migration destination that would give rise to various Indigenous Mexican cultures, most notably the Aztecs. It was the Mexica peoples or Aztecs who first arrived by the fourteenth century to settle in the valley. In 1325, they built the city on a group of islands in Lake Texcoco and named it Tenochtitlan. All was going well until 1521 and the Spanish conquest of the Aztec Empire. With it came the fall of its capital city of Tenochtitlan and Aztec civilization. The contributing event was the earlier arrival of Hernán Cortés, a Spanish nobleman who arrived with a fleet of conquistadors. Notwithstanding astounding internal politics and numerous clashes and growing tensions with Mexico's Indigenous people, Cortés marched forward. The situation and relations between the Spaniards and Aztecs continued to rapidly deteriorate, leading to revolt. Initially, Cortés was forced to flee and rebuild his alliances with the many local, subjugated enemies of the Aztecs. Returning with a vengeance, the siege of Tenochtitlan lasted from

1519 to 1521. Playing a critical role in the siege was smallpox. With the Spanish having mostly acquired immunity against smallpox, the disease greatly struck the Aztec natives. Many died from the plague and from hunger resulting from the inability to farm and hunt. Battles raged in merciless and vicious fashion, and several peace overtures failed. Eventually, the Aztec forces were destroyed, Tenochtitlan was nearly razed, surrender was gained, and brutal documented atrocities followed. The city was eventually rebuilt to Spanish urban standards, and in 1524 the municipality of Mexico City was formally established. Consequently, Mexico City played a major role in the early Spanish colonial empire. By 1821, following years of armed conflict, military triumph, and a collapse of the Spanish royal government, the Declaration of Independence of the Mexican Empire solidified Mexico's independence from Spain. Though Mexican independence was never an inevitable outcome, timing was surely on their side. Fortunately for Mexico, a simultaneously invasion of Spain by Napoleon Bonaparte in 1808 had set into motion Spain's bigger crisis. Internal war had greatly impacted their oversea possessions. Today, with its historic, persevering character richly shaped, Mexico City remains the independent capital of Mexico, also known as the Federal District.

A business need for travel to Mexico City was twofold. It's particularly advantageous when business trips can address multiple unrelated needs and provide opportunities to network with numerous key colleagues and supply partners. This was absolutely the case in Mexico City; I was fortunate that they coincided. First, we were relocating the Mexico City headquarters to a new "greenfield" site in the city's prestigious Polanco neighborhood. Polanco is widely considered one of the richest and most affluent neighborhoods in Mexico City. For my company, with nearly 4,500 employees located in administrative and production sites throughout Mexico, the country represents a long-standing, most important foreign subsidiary. A new exciting headquarters was needed to house over three hundred corporate employees. Support was needed to coordinate construction efforts and assist with office design and furnishing decisions. Working with a cross-functional team of employees and local authorized suppliers proved most beneficial. All actions were well conceived, documented, and planned in accordance with the Real Estate Global Office Sourcing Strategy. The detailed, approved strategy considers essentials such as branding, safety, ergonomics, technology, cost, and more, including local cultural needs and preferences. Second, in addition to a new office, a visit to Mexico City provided an ideal opportunity to meet with *Office Depot de Mexico* (a foreign joint venture of Office Depot/Office Max, headquartered in Boca Raton, Florida). The Mexican group is owned by Grupo Gigante, whose model is to expand United States commercial chain business throughout Central and South America. Office Depot was our global office supplies partner, with support already in thirty worldwide countries throughout Europe as well as the United States, Australia, Brazil, Canada, and China. The opportunity to roll in Office Depot de Mexico would extend to Mexico as well as Chile, Panama, El Salvador, Costa Rica, the Dominican Republic, and Columbia. The best-practice, gold-standard value of having a single global supply partner is immeasurable in terms of enhanced performance, quality, cost savings, standards, innovation, automation, reporting, and overall management.

In the end, both the above visit goals were successfully accomplished, though not so easily, in Mexico. Specifically, visits to Mexico (as well as Brazil) are taxing and almost exclusively business. First, the time difference is marginal; Mexico City is only two hours behind Eastern Standard Time. Consequently, travel is somewhat routine, with quicker visits. Second, and more restrictive, corporate policy at the time prohibited free travel throughout Mexico. Due to added safety precautions, a designated corporate driver was assigned to always escort us. Although it never felt particularly dangerous, it was very evident that many individuals and groups had adopted similar safeguards, even though we were in one of the city's safest neighborhoods. For these reasons I can only expand on just a couple interesting experiences. For certain, I was still pleased for the opportunity to briefly visit beautiful Mexico City.

Polanco

While there are hundreds of neighborhoods (*colonias*) in the huge, chaotic, overpopulated metropolis of Mexico City, in the center of the city is the very upscale neighborhood of *Polanco*, perfect base location and home to both the existing Mexican headquarters and the planned relocation project. Turns out Polanco is an ideal base location for any visitors wishing to explore Mexico City, enjoy world-class shopping, and frequent some of the best restaurants not only in Latin America but in the world. Often referred to as the "Beverly Hills of Mexico City," the affluent Polanco neighborhood is renowned for it's upscale shopping boutiques, incredible fine dining, lively art scene, museums, diversity, and cosmopolitan vibe. Many of Mexico City's celebrities and politicians live in Polanco. Being in Polanco, it is quite easy to temporarily discard detractors who profess the city's many problems, drawbacks, and acknowledged dangers. The contrast in neighborhoods is significant. Also, although you don't typically think of cultural diversity in foreign countries, Polanco is home to one the largest Jewish and

Lebanese communities in Mexico. Immigrants fled Lebanon in the early twentieth century and later Poland and Germany during the 1930s. In fact, there are several noticeable synagogues in the wealthy neighborhood. In parallel, the presence of Polanco's numerous international embassies and consulates assures some added safety measures. Many streets throughout Polanco are named after famous writers, philosophers, statesmen, and scientists, including Oscar Wilde and Miguel de Cervantes. However, the defining avenue in Polanco is the posh *Avenida Presidente Masaryk*, or simply Avenida Masaryk. All the top designers are represented on Avenida Masaryk, the most expensive street in Mexico. The street was named in 1938 by Mexico's then president after the death of the Republic of Czechoslovakia founder and its first president, Tomáš Masaryk. Czechoslovakia is the only central European country that proudly remained a democracy during the interwar period. The avenue honors the president and reflects Mexico's vital international relations.

In addition to shopping, there are food tours to explore the culinary delights and many flavors of Mexico. Many restaurants are within the confines of Polanco's elegant mansions, parks, and picturesque landscapes. Polanco was initially developed in the 1930s and largely consisted of upper-class single-family mansions, gardens, and tree-lined streets. For those interested in world-class dining, celebrated Quintonil earned a two-star Michelin rating and was recently named the best restaurant in all of Mexico. In 2025, the restaurant was ranked number three on the William Reed "World's 50 Best Restaurants" list.[1] Pujol is another well-established Polanco two-star Michelin-rated restaurant and is rated one of the world's best. Unfortunately, I did not have an opportunity to visit either of these exclusive eateries. Another Polanco site I passed is the beautiful Parque Lincoln. Named after Abraham Lincoln, the park is a welcome sight for strolls, picnics, and other lively community affairs. Several of Polanco's favorite cocktail destinations also offer a welcomed break. Lastly, a cultural oasis in the heart of Polanco is the architecturally stunning Museo Soumaya.

It was easy to understand why Polanco is where Mexico City's rich live and come to play. With the highest land costs in Mexico, Polanco apartment pricing starts at $15 million. Polanco certainly represents the good life in Mexico City. Though, admittedly, I realize that by staying in Polanco I experienced Mexico City through rose-colored glasses.

1. William Reed, "World's 50 Best Restaurants."

Soumaya Museum

Just a couple blocks from our Mexican corporate headquarters, also in the affluent Polanco neighborhood, is a futuristic, shapeless, shimmering building known as the *Museo Soumaya*. The building is composed of sixteen thousand hexagonal aluminum tiles and somewhat resembles a giant silver cocoon. Amazingly, the *private* museum is entirely sponsored by the Carlos Slim Foundation and is named after his late wife Soumaya. Both Carlos and his wife are children of Lebanese parents who had immigrated to Mexico at young ages. If you are not familiar with Carlos Slim Helú, think Elon Musk, Bill Gates, and Jeff Bezos. Like these entrepreneurs, business magnates, investors, and philanthropists, Mexican billionaire Carlos Slim was also once *Forbes*'s richest person in the world (2010 through 2013).[2] Presently, with a net worth of $125 billion, Carlos Slim is the richest person in Latin America and the sixteenth richest person in the world.[3] Unlike his American counterparts, and being in a country where nearly 20 percent live in poverty, Carlos Slim's massive fortune represents an astounding percent of Mexico's gross domestic product. Nonetheless and to his credit, Slim has always expressed and exhibited strong support for philanthropy. He is consistently on *Forbes*'s list of the world's most generous philanthropists outside the United States.

The Polanco Museo Soumaya was designed by Fernando Romero, famed Mexican architect and the son-in-law of Carlos Slim. The museum first opened in 2011 and holds over sixty-five thousand pieces of artwork, including religious relics, documents, and Spanish coins and viceroys. In addition to works by Leonardo da Vinci, Claude Monet, Vincent van Gogh, Pablo Picasso, and Pierre-Auguste Renoir, etc., the museum houses the largest collection of Auguste Rodin sculptures outside France, including *The Kiss*, and a large Salvador Dalí collection. The museum boasts an impressive collection, including everything from pre-Columbian sculptures to the European masterpieces. Most of the museum's permanent pieces are from Carlos Slim's private collection. The da Vinci painting *Madonna of the Yarnwinder* is believed to be the collection's most valuable work of art, valued at $200 million. Total value of the collective Museo Soumaya art exceeds $700 million.

The six-story, 170,000 square-foot (museum) building is 150 feet high and cost Carlos Slim $70 million to build. Each of the six floors is uniquely shaped and made of high-quality marble imported from Greece. Of course,

2. Dolan et al., "Decade of Billionaires."

3. Mexico News Daily, "More Mexicans Than Ever."

the exterior hexagonal aluminum tiles were supplied by a company owned by Carlos Slim. Incredibly, public admission to the Museo Soumaya is completely free of charge, and all operating costs are graciously covered by Slim's great fortune. In addition to the art galleries, the museum includes a library, a restaurant, and a large auditorium. Carlos Slim the businessman has oftentimes been criticized for the opulent museum. However, Slim has maintained that since most Mexicans cannot travel to Europe to view art collections, it was important to bring them to Mexico City. Generally, it appears that the museum is either loved or hated, with few opinions in between. A second beautiful museum location also exists in the southern part of Mexico City. With over one million annual visitors, the Museo Soumaya is the most visited museum in Mexico, and there are nearly seven hundred of them throughout the country. The museum also ranks as the thirtieth most-visited art museum in the world.[4]

My time in Mexico City was very limited but the memories are lasting. And it truly is the spirit of its people that is most memorable. Never, ever before or since have I been greeted at a business office with more enthusiasm and more genuine caring than on my visit to Mexico. Not only are you greeted with smiles, but it was also not uncommon at that time for you to receive a kiss on the cheek. Sounds a bit unusual now, but it was routine in Mexico. For these reasons, despite a limited, atypical bleisure visit, I'm happy to share a few impressions of beautiful, colorful, vibrant, and undoubtedly hectic Mexico City!

4. Wikipedia, "List of the Most-Visited."

CHAPTER 17

GERMANY

Germany has become a country that
many people associate with hope.

—*Angela Merkel*

To me, in more ways than one, Germany is a complete *dichotomy*. First, Germany is an idyllic, scenic nation of beautiful meadows, dense forests, jagged mountains, moseying rivers, fairy-tale castles, quaint villages, apple strudel, wiener schnitzel, steins of beer, cuckoo clocks, and oompah music. In contrast and in relatively short order since its humiliating near destruction during World War II, Germany founded and sits solidly at the forefront of the European Union. A relentless proponent of peace, unity, and tolerance, Germany is the most populous European Union country, with its biggest economy. Astoundingly, as a country not quite the size of the state of Montana, Germany has prospered to become the fourth largest industrial power in the world. Despite its small structure, and with a population of eighty-four million, Germany creates a gross domestic product that is 20 percent that of the entire United States. Consequently, in contrast to its imagery and spectacular scenery, Germany is about leading-edge human progress and high technology. Germany is a country blessed with numerous shimmering, very efficient industrial cities. The second dichotomy is even deeper and cannot be ignored. The German colleagues I've met in business are some of the finest people I've known. The Germans are very proud, progressive, highly responsible, intelligent, hardworking, bilingual, and possess a cosmopolitan worldview. They also have very cool names like

Dieter, Axel, Heinrich, Astrid, Birgit, and Lina. However, again in complete contrast, it is impossible for most visitors to dismiss Germany's association with its dark Nazi past and the resultant horrific war crimes. It is hard to comprehend. Today, there is a strong feeling that Germans remain utterly remorseful and determined to learn from the past. Still evident decades later is that Germany remains a country in perpetual national penance for its Nazi crimes. Since the war, Germany has continued to redress crimes and commemorate the victims to the best of their abilities. In the capital of Berlin, there is an outright block-long *Memorial to the Murdered Jews*, which serves as a haunting reminder of the atrocities committed against the six million Holocaust victims. Looking forward, Germany's location at the very heart of Europe will continue to shape history—it's essential. More than any other European country, Germany borders nine varied neighbors: the Netherlands, Belgium, Luxembourg, France, Switzerland, Austria, the Czech Republic, Poland, and Denmark. Germany must serve as a country of hope!

Germany's roots run very deep and complicated. Germanic-speaking people have lived in and ruled much of western Europe north of the Alps for millennia. Humans first settled in northern Europe following the end of the last Ice Age about ten thousand years ago. Consequently, although Germany is an ancient land, the nation of Germany as known did not come into being until the nineteenth century. Germanic tribes first moved south from Scandinavia and northern Europe. It was Julius Caesar himself who referred to the unconquered area east of the Rhine River as Germania. By the ninth century, Germanic territory was consolidated under the post-Roman barbaric Frankish Empire. Otto the Great eventually became both German king and Holy Roman emperor ruling the then Kingdom of Germany. Over the following centuries, much social and political change ensued. Most specifically, in 1517 a humble priest and professor of theology named Martin Luther started the Protestant Reformation against the powerful Catholic Church. Luther's reformation movement rocked Catholicism and greatly influenced Western and Christian history. By the seventeenth century, disparity and grievances between the two churches intensified, leading to Europe's most destructive *Thirty Years' War*. The war, with estimated deaths of eight million people, turned the entire Holy Roman Empire into a bloody battlefield. In parallel, the powerful Prussia kingdom state continued to expand and amass land. By 1806, German feudalism all but ended, the Holy Roman Empire dissolved, and Napoleon Bonaparte (France) briefly seized the area, which then fell to the Austrians. Germans continually revolted. Finally, by 1871, a politician named Otto von Bismarck consolidated the patchwork of German-speaking small states, kingdoms, principalities, and cities to officially form a unified German Empire. Otto von Bismarck became the first (Iron) Chancellor of the German Empire. As known, World War I, World War II (Nazi Germany), a Cold War, and finally German reunification in 1990 leads us to the present time and the Federal Republic of Germany as we know it.

Business took me to Germany on many occasions and for a multitude of reasons. By far, Germany is the country I visited the most and grew to greatly enjoy. There were many cities that I visited throughout Germany, northernmost to the stormy Baltic Sea and southward to the soaring Swiss-Austrian Alps. For this reason, unlike the previous chapters, this chapter broadly covers a few of my most memorable German cities and related bleisure experiences.

BERLIN

Everyone agrees, *Berlin* is a world-class capital city packed with great energy and edge. It's both glamour and grit in the best of ways, simultaneously bustling and chilled. Berlin is a city that has experienced upheaval and renewal like no other. Consequently, Berlin's tangible sad historic past sits literally alongside its tangible booming present. Berlin is a very large city, nine times the size of Paris, comprised of many chic neighborhoods. The population is 3.7 million within its city limits. It's really two ever-changing reborn cities in one with two of most everything and even three opera houses. Berlin is noticeably Germany's greenest city, with beautiful leafy boulevards, forests, sprawling parks, lakes, and river beaches. Yet Berlin is still largely defined by the World War II years, the East-West divide, and the Cold War that followed. In 1961, the East German government, to prevent escapes, surrounded West Berlin with the infamous concrete Berlin Wall, a wall that painfully encircled the free sectors of Berlin. The wall sadly remained in place until 1989 and the country's subsequent reunification. Today, Berlin remains a city of great contrasts albeit one with a fun, vibrant cultural scene and plenty of exceptional landmarks. Lastly, I remember Berlin for our entertaining team-building activities. Beyond dinners and occasional clubbing, I enjoyed an educational city scavenger hunt, a river Spree boat tour (passing alongside many of Berlin's attractions), and a guided tour of Berlin's historic Reichstag (German Parliament) Building.

Brandenburg Gate

The quintessential symbol of Berlin is undoubtedly the magnificent, iconic, neoclassical *Brandenburg Gate*. Completed in 1791, Berlin's majestic gateway structure was modeled on the Acropolis entrance in Athens, Greece. Most noticeably, the gate is crowned by a quadriga, a bronze four-horsed chariot, driven by the goddess Victoria. The gate reflects Germany's turbulent story like no other landmark. Through the centuries, armies from Prussia's King Frederick William II to France's Napoleon Bonaparte to Nazi Germany's Adolf Hitler have all marched through the emblazoned entrance. The gate was one of few structures that predominantly survived World War II though it quickly adorned a Russian flag in 1945. During the Cold War (post–World War II), Germany was divided into occupation zones, with East Berlin falling under Soviet control and West Berlin being divided up between the British, French, and Americans. The Berlin Wall, erected practically overnight in 1961, came to symbolize the Iron Curtain between Europe and the Eastern Bloc. For nearly three decades, the Brandenburg Gate sat inaccessible between East and West Berlin (obstructed within the Berlin Wall). Until the wall's fall in 1989, the gate was a somber marker of the city's division. The Berlin Wall was outside the site of President John F. Kennedy's impassioned anti-Communist "Ich bin ein Berliner" (I am a Berliner) speech in 1963. In 1987, President Ronald Reagan, standing at the Brandenburg Gate, bravely proclaimed, "Mr. Gorbachev, open this gate. Mr. Gorbachev, tear down this wall."[1] Both speeches were squarely aimed at the Soviet Union. The Brandenburg Gate will forever be a symbol of Germany's tumultuous past. However, today and recognizing Germany's 1990 reunification, the Brandenburg Gate is also an everyday symbol of Berlin's rejuvenated capital, representing European peace and unity.

In the eighteenth century, under the triumphant Frederick the Great, the Kingdom of Prussia was one of the great expanding states in Europe. By 1786, Frederick William II of Prussia (nephew of Frederick the Great) ascended to the throne. Frederick William II was determined to establish Berlin as a major cultural center comparable to Vienna, Paris, and London. Consequently, Frederick William II summoned the best German architects to design and build a significant neoclassical, sandstone, Greek-style "peace gate." He sought to build a "new Athens" on Berlin's Spree River.[2] Unfortunately, after the French defeat of Prussia in 1806, it was Napoleon who first used the Brandenburg Gate for a triumphal procession. Worse yet, Napoleon dismantled and confiscated the gate's bronze quadriga sculpture

1. Reagan, "Remark on East-West," para. 12.
2. Wikipedia, "Brandenburg Gate," sec. "18th-century reconstruction."

with the goddess Victoria and took them to Paris as spoils of war. The theft was short-lived as Prussia defeated Napoleon in 1814, occupied Paris, and rightfully restored the quadriga to Berlin's triumphal arch. In defiance to the French, the quadriga was skillfully redesigned clearly representing the Roman goddess Victoria, the personification of victory. The goddess was now equipped with a Prussian eagle and iron cross on her lance as well as a laurel wreath of oak leaves.

The Brandenburg Gate is in the western part of Berlin's city center within the swanky Mitte neighborhood. It sits in Pariser Platz (Paris Square), one of Berlin's most visited and beautiful squares. The gate marks the start of Berlin's busy boulevard Unter den Linden (named after the linden trees that line the avenue). I always made time to visit the historic area and the many surrounding attractions. Nearby is the glass-domed Reichstag Building (home to the German parliament), the lush Tiergarten Park, the former Prussian City Palace, Berlin Cathedral, the Memorial to Murdered Jews of Europe (Holocaust Memorial), the United States embassy, and the historic ritzy Hotel Adlon Kempinski. The 2004 Holocaust Memorial is merely a somber 2,711 concrete slabs arranged in a grid on a sloping hill. The design is purposely puzzling, intended to create an uneasy, confusing atmosphere likened to a loss of human reason. Its underground info center holds the names of three million Jewish Holocaust victims as provided by an Israeli museum. In stark contrast, the Hotel Adlon directly faces the Brandenburg Gate and opened in 1907. Hotel Adlon is Berlin's most prestigious hotel. Notable early guests included industrialists Thomas Edison, Henry Ford, and John D. Rockefeller. The "Golden 1920s" brought Charlie Chaplin, Mary Pickford, Albert Einstein, Josephine Baker, Enrico Caruso, and Marlene Dietrich. Presidents Franklin Roosevelt and Herbert Hoover were also once guests at Hotel Adlon, though the most "infamous" guest was surely pop star Michael Jackson. It was Michael Jackson in 2002 who, while blowing kisses to fans from the hotel's presidential suite balcony, recklessly dangled his infant nine-month-old son Prince Michael over the balcony's edge. Onlookers were horrified and backlash was plenty. As for me, Hotel Adlon was out of my expense budget. I was plenty grateful to oftentimes stay at the wonderful nearby Westin Grand Berlin. The Westin Grand was the very recognizable filming location of *The Bourne Supremacy* (2004) with Matt Damon portraying former CIA assassin Jason Bourne. Also, there were always elaborate hotel parties for opera or museum groups that I was occasionally and unexplainably invited to attend as the American guest.

Checkpoint Charlie

As mentioned, post–World War II (1945), Berlin was divided into four sectors between the Soviets, United States, British, and French. Through the 1950s, movement across Berlin sectors was relatively easy. However, due to extremely harsh conditions in Soviet-controlled East Germany, many of its citizens were fleeing to the West. By 1961, over three million East Germans (20 percent of their entire population) had emigrated. Most emigrants were young, well-educated, skilled professionals. The exodus greatly damaged the political and economic viability of East Germany. That said, crossing specifically through West Berlin was the primary way or main route for the East Germans to reach the West. This forced the Soviets to increasingly and abruptly end emigration in Berlin. In August 1961, the border between East Berlin and West Berlin was completely closed with roadblocks, barbed wire, and the *Berlin Wall.* The concrete Berlin Wall (two separate walls) was ninety-six miles long and thirteen feet high. To slow escapes, the walls were separated and heavily guarded with mined corridors and channels of ploughed earth in between, an area known as the "death strip." In parallel, to facilitate any remaining movement between the west and east, checkpoints were set up along the wall. Passing was necessary and open for foreigners, military personnel, journalists, diplomats, and other dignitaries. The most famous and internationally recognized of the Allied checkpoints was *Checkpoint Charlie.* Checkpoint Charlie would become the scene of numerous escape attempts; some succeeded while others sadly failed. Established in 1961, the name "Checkpoint Charlie" came from the NATO phonetic alphabet (Alpha, Bravo, Charlie, Delta). Accordingly, Checkpoint Charlie was the third checkpoint opened by the Allies in the Berlin area. These checkpoints were the final line in the sand between East and West. Checkpoint Charlie was designated as the single crossing point for any foreigners and members of the Allied forces crossing by foot or car. Contrary to the East German side, the Allied authorities never erected a permanent building; the original checkpoint was a small, simple wooden shed surrounded by barriers, sandbags, signage, and a flag. Situated at the checkpoint as a popular viewing place for Allied officials, armed forces, and visitors was the famous Café Adler (Eagle Café).

On a much more serious note, Checkpoint Charlie became world-famous through a single frightening event in October 1961. Construction of the Berlin Wall had already set off alarms and condemnation. Shortly thereafter, at the Checkpoint Charlie sight, a confrontation between the United States and Soviet superpowers came to a head. Despite an agreement that there was to be free movement for Allied forces in all of Berlin, the

East German border guards had stopped a United States diplomat headed to East Berlin to attend the opera. This seemingly minor personal inconvenience quickly escalated into an international crisis. Several days later, ten Soviet and an equal number of American tanks menacingly squared off just a hundred yards apart on either side of Checkpoint Charlie. Iconic photos of the precarious event were broadcast around the world. It was then Attorney General Robert F. Kennedy who helped negotiate an agreement with Soviet intelligence to reduce tensions and peacefully withdraw the tanks.

Wow! Is it any wonder why Checkpoint Charlie has been the glamorized setting for many thrilling movies and spy novels? Of course, my favorite spy, James Bond, even appeared at Checkpoint Charlie in *Octopussy* (1983). It is at the famous border crossing where 007 enters East Germany. Bond is seeking Octopussy, a beautiful heroine who operates a smuggling ring under the guise of a traveling circus playing in East Berlin's Karl-Marx-Stadt.

Thankfully, Checkpoint Charlie was removed on June 22, 1990, shortly after the Berlin Wall fell in November 1989. Today, a copy of the small original guard house is built on the site of Checkpoint Charlie. Remaining is a large, chilling sign that reads, "You are leaving the American sector." Near the guardhouse is the *Haus am Checkpoint Charlie* (Checkpoint Charlie Museum). Though cramped and dated, the museum gives added context to the Berlin Wall and border crossing. The museum's most interesting exhibits connect to the East Germans' brave, ingenious escape attempts. There are secret compartments built into cars, hot-air balloons, specially constructed suitcases, and even a mini submarine. Checkpoint Charlie is an interesting, easy place to visit and a very popular tourist location for photo opportunities. For any curious historians, Checkpoint Charlie is a must-see while in Berlin.

POTSDAM

Bordering Berlin is the independent, beautiful, aristocratic city of *Potsdam*. Serving as Berlin's holiday retreat, Potsdam was the opulent eighteenth-century countryside playground of Frederick the Great. Filled with ornate palaces and a royal park, Potsdam is one of Germany's most interesting cities, beaming with Prussian history. Barely outside West Germany, Potsdam's Havel River became the natural border between the Soviet and United States sectors of Berlin. Potsdam, with a bedroom community population of 170,000, sits on a lake where its lakeshore was once bordered by the Berlin Wall. So naturally, Potsdam is also home to a couple very important Cold War sights. An annual Global Procurement Meeting took us to a stunning neighboring lakefront village and the Resort Schwielowsee. The resort was in a sleepy, scenic town next to the cultural city of Potsdam. Unfortunately, a full work schedule limited any team bleisure activities and I experienced just a couple very interesting, memorable attractions from a historic American perspective in passing.

Potsdam Conference

I suppose most every generation on occasion feels it's the end of the world as we know it. That things have never been worse. That our problems are too insurmountable to solve. Certainly, that was the sentiment in the spring and summer of 1945. And for good reason. There was a raging global conflict between two powerful coalitions with worldwide political balance clearly at stake. World War II revealed an uncertain future and mobilization of resources for and by nearly all the world's countries. However, on May 7, 1945, Germany's unconditional surrender to the Allied forces occurred. Just nine weeks after the German surrender and prior to the subsequent Japanese surrender on September 2, 1945, the government heads of Britain, the United States, and the Soviet Union met in July 1945. The location was a sprawling Potsdam villa in the layout of an English-country-style manor. It was here that these leaders officially drew the map of Europe, soundly punished Germany, and "unintentionally" set the stage for a forty-five-year protracted Cold War.

Driving through Potsdam you will come to an early twentieth-century palace named *Cecilienhof.* Prime Minister Winston Churchill, President Harry S. Truman, and Soviet leader Joseph Stalin, with entourages, convened at Cecilienhof, from July 17 through August 2, 1945, for what is known as the *Potsdam Conference.* Although Mr. Churchill was replaced by newly elected Britain Prime Minister Clement Attlee mid-conference. Earlier, Churchill, Stalin, and President Franklin D. Roosevelt had all agreed to meet in Germany to primarily determine post-war borders. While the Allies were still committed to fighting Japan, the Soviet Union was not. This led to difficulties gaining post-war consensus on Europe's reconstruction. The group was also wary not to make the same mistakes of World War I and the Treaty of Versailles, which may have led to the rise of Nazis.

Despite many disagreements, the significance of agreements reached at the Potsdam Conference were massive. Specifically, Germany would be demilitarized and disarmed and occupied by American, British, French, and Soviet quadrants. Germany's educational and judicial systems would be purged of Nazi influence, and war criminals would be hunted down, tried, and punished. German society was to be reshaped; however, the reconstitution of the country as a sovereign state was postponed indefinitely (only occurring forty-five years later in 1990). A desire to end the positions of Germany's wartime allies Italy, Bulgaria, Hungary, Romania, Finland, and related African colonies was also agreed upon. This was subsequently completed in Paris the following year. And reparations, how best to punish Germany for dragging Europe through another devastating war, were also roundly debated. Though it was the post-war fate, resettlement of a democratic Poland, and the expulsion of millions of ethnic Germans that proved to be the biggest stumbling block. In the end, Poland was compensated large areas of Germany.

Despite being President Truman's first major appearance on the world stage, and his having to succeed President Franklin D. Roosevelt, Truman proved masterful. It was in Potsdam that Truman advised Stalin that the United States possessed a "new weapon of unusual destructive force" with no specific mention of the atom bomb. There is no doubt that the Soviet leader was already very aware of the bomb through the extensive Russian spy network. Stalin merely responded that he hoped that the United States would make "good use of it against the Japanese."[3] What a most historic time it was at the Potsdam Cecilienhof countryside villa.

Bridge of Spies

Driving through Potsdam, we came across an old, relatively small, though scenic, plain steel bridge. Crossing the Havel River, the bridge connects Potsdam to bordering Berlin. At first glance, the *Glienicke Bridge* (glee-na-ka) doesn't appear like anything special. The bridge is quite easy to pass by without giving it a second thought. That would be shortsighted as it's a small bridge with a very BIG history. You see, during the 1960s, the Glienicke Bridge was chosen by the Cold War superpowers (Russia and United States) as the perfect location for several spectacular exchanges of captured spies—an isolated, high-profile location between the Eastern Bloc and the West. Consequently, in popular culture, the Glienicke Bridge earned the epithet "Bridge of Spies." And even though the rather mundane looking bridge has retained little historical association, it's not hard to vividly imagine the legendary bridge's historical significance. Of course, we took the opportunity to briefly admire and stroll on the infamous Bridge of Spies.

The Bridge of Spies' notoriety and role in history has inspired various artists to make the bridge the subject of countless spy stories, music, books,

3. United States Department of State, "Foreign Relations," para. 2.

and movies. However, it was the 2015 Hollywood blockbuster film *Bridge of Spies* that brought the bridge's historical significance to a global audience. The film was masterfully directed by none other than Steven Spielberg and starred the great Tom Hanks. The critically acclaimed *Bridge of Spies* earned six Oscar nominations including Best Picture. The film is based on the Cold War's most notable exchange of prisoners. Consequently, the movie propelled the bridge into the international spotlight. The specific date was February 10, 1962. The Soviet Union exchanged captured American CIA U-2 pilot Francis Gary Powers for convicted Soviet spy Rudolf Abel. In the movie, Tom Hanks portrayed James Donovan, the Soviet spy's appointed legal counsel in 1957. At the time, Donovan was a private practice insurance lawyer burdened with the task. Many other American attorneys declined to represent the Soviet spy. Nonetheless, Donovan was committed to providing a vigorous defense, refusing to unfairly settle with the CIA or to violate his client's confidentiality. Although the Soviet spy was ultimately convicted, Donovan convinced the judge to spare Abel's life, arguing he could prove useful for a future prisoner exchange. Of course, because he so strongly represented the Soviet, Donovan and his family faced serious harassment.

Meanwhile, back in the Soviet Union, Powers was sentenced to ten years in a Russian prison. In the movie, when Donovan mysteriously receives a letter from East Germany, the CIA recognizes the communication as a back-channel Soviet message hinting at a prisoner swap of Powers for Abel. Donovan is then tasked with going to Berlin to negotiate the exchange. In a twist, when the Soviets want to release another prisoner (American student), a defiant Donovan insists on both prisoners, including Gary Powers. In the end, both United States prisoners were surprisingly exchanged for Abel. The film shows Powers and Abel suspensefully passing each other on, you guessed it, the Bridge of Spies. Donovan's courageous, skillful negotiation is publicly acknowledged by the government. Accordingly, in heroic fashion, Donovan's badly tainted American public image was rightfully and fully rehabilitated. The historic telling of the dramatic true story, with Hollywood flair, proved to be box-office gold. Even German Chancellor Angela Merkel visited the film set at the Glienicke Bridge, taking the opportunity to meet the talented cast and production team during the movie's filming.

The Glienicke Bridge was closed to citizens during the entire Cold War period, used as another checkpoint shielded by the Berlin Wall. However, on the evening of November 10, 1989, just one day after the fall of the Berlin Wall, the bridge was reopened to pedestrians. Shortly thereafter, with 1990 German reunification, barricades and border fortifications were dismantled and free travel between Berlin and Potsdam resumed. By all appearances, the pretty 1907 Glienicke Bridge, over a hundred years old, is a simply designed bridge crossing. However, this span is much more than its physical structure. The iconic Bridge of Spies is a lasting symbol of intrigue, espionage, service, bravery, diplomacy, and basic humanity forged in the beautiful German countryside.

COLOGNE

One of my favorite German cities is Cologne. Cologne's location very near our global headquarters rendered it my most visited German city and a welcoming and familiar international destination. Germany's fourth largest city, with one million inhabitants, boasts reconstructed medieval flair, winding cobblestone alleys, lively squares, and a generally joyous attitude. The urban metropolis on the river Rhine also exudes an endless party spirit rooted in a thriving music and art scene. Add to that cozy rustic pubs and brew houses serving Cologne's signature Kölsch beer, the world-famous Cologne Carnival, shopping, an authentic festive German Christmas market, and, of course, the hallmark Cologne Cathedral. And smack in the middle of all this is the beautiful, convenient nineteenth-century Cologne Central (Railway) Station with nearly three hundred thousand daily travelers. Fun fact . . . Cologne is also famous for its Eau de Cologne, the scented toilet water developed by an Italian chemist, which has been produced in the city since 1709. As known, "cologne" has become the lasting recognizable generic term. In any event, the daily hustle and bustle of Cologne are palpable. Moreover, everything is in easy walking distance in the compact area known as Cologne's Altstadt (Old Town).

Cologne, called Colonia, was founded and established as a German territory by the Romans two thousand years ago in the first century. By the fourth century, Constantine, the first Christian emperor, established Cologne as an important cultural and religious center. Constantine opened the city as a Jewish community to dispersed Jews following the Siege of Jerusalem. By the late eighth century, the emperor Charlemagne established Cologne as an important seat of a Holy Roman Empire archbishop. The city maintained high standing throughout the Middle Ages and beyond. By the twentieth century, in retaliation for the German bombing of London, the British would bomb and destroy 90 percent of Cologne during World War II. Today, the quickly reconstructed modern post-war city is a prosperous commercial and cultural center with a rich historic past.

Work has taken me to Cologne on many occasions. Most visits were filled with routine train commutes to and from our always exciting sprawling global campus. Much like home, workdays were filled with early starts and late evenings. The opportunity to meet and work with so many German corporate colleagues, teams, and management was always enjoyable and extremely beneficial, albeit exhausting at times. Of course, your everyday responsibilities were always present each evening. Consequently, bleisure time in Cologne was mostly limited. That said, having so many wonderful major attractions just outside the hotel made the visits easy and fun as well. It was unnecessary to venture much beyond the Old Town area, which extended a few blocks from the train station, the cathedral, and the river. Unlike much of modern Cologne, this walking area was largely rebuilt in its original medieval style with premier hotels and a multitude of restaurants, pubs, and music venues. Lastly, the pedestrian shopping streets, carnival, and Christmas market were also fun happenings just steps from the hotel entrance.

Cologne Cathedral

When it comes to Cologne, there's simply no better place to start than the colossal Gothic *Cologne Cathedral* . . . the heart and soul of Cologne whose towering spires shape the cityscape. To Cologne residents and frequent visitors alike, the sight of the cathedral (known also as the Dom) says you are home. At first site, Cologne Cathedral will likely leave you speechless. With twin towers that rise 515 feet above the city center square, the cathedral appears too large for earth. The cathedral is highly visible for miles from air and from incoming railways and as a barometer throughout the city. I have seen many notable cathedrals from around the world. However, to me, the Cologne Cathedral eclipses in size and grandeur most other sites. Cologne Cathedral, Cathedral Church of Saint Peter, belongs to the Catholic Church and remains the seat of the archbishop established by Charlemagne. It is Germany's most visited landmark, attracting six million people a year. Cologne Cathedral is the world's tallest twin-spired church and the third tallest church of any kind in the world. The two huge spires give the cathedral the largest façade of any church in the world. At the time of its completion, Cologne Cathedral was even believed to be the world's tallest structure, a distinction held until 1884 when the Washington Monument was completed. With eight thousand square meters of floor space and ten thousand square meters of stained-glass windows, the cathedral can hold more than twenty thousand visitors. In total, over three hundred thousand tons of stones were used in the cathedral's construction. Even today, nearly a hundred masonry craftsmen work every day to conserve the cathedral at a daily maintenance cost of more than €30,000. The incredible 140-foot-tall interior ceiling is another reminder of the cathedral's ambitious, looming size. And, although priceless, because the cathedral is unsalable, the national treasure maintains a dated book value of a mere €27.[4]

Often cited as the perfect cathedral, Cologne Cathedral has a *legendary* construction period that extends from 1248 to 1880. Cologne's medieval builders planned an imposing structure to house the reliquary of the three kings and to create a grand place of worship for the Holy Roman emperor. However, by the sixteenth century, funds evaporated and construction was halted. The cathedral sat unfinished for three hundred years. Attempts to complete construction only resumed in earnest in 1842 when the project was properly funded. The powerful ruling Prussians decided to fund speedy completion of the glorious cathedral to promote German unity. By 1880, going full speed for thirty-eight years, seven hundred dedicated workers amazingly finished the church to its original medieval Gothic plan. The majestic Cologne Central Railway Station was simultaneously and wisely built adjacent to the towering cathedral. Today, even after 632 years of construction, work on the Cologne Cathedral (jokingly referred to as "God's eternal building site") continues. Consequently, there is a saying and strong belief in Cologne that "when the cathedral is finished, the world will end."[5]

Cologne Cathedral harbors many fascinating items, mysteries, stories, curiosities, and legends. For these reasons, the medieval cathedral remains a most important pilgrimage site for many pious Catholics as well as anyone interested in religion, art, and culture. One big mystery is why wasn't the cathedral more severely damaged during World War II as was most all of Cologne? Hit by at least fifteen British bombs, the cathedral only flexed but remained standing. In anticipation, the cathedral's glass and art were previously sheltered and preserved. By lucky coincidence and contrary to standard practice, the rafters of the cathedral's roof were not made of wood (as for example those of Notre Dame in Paris) but of iron. It was the largest steel structure in the world in 1860, thirty years prior to the Eiffel Tower, and saved the cathedral from serious war damage. To this day, the iron truss securely carries the cathedral's heavy vaulted roof.

Lastly, for fit and bravehearted visitors, consider climbing upward to the cathedral's tower. It rises 318 feet skyward and is reached only by climbing 533 narrow, slippery steps to the top. There is no elevator, and space can be tight as you encounter descending visitors. Halfway to the top of the tower you'll come across Saint Peter's Bell, also called "Decker Pitter" (Fat Peter). Fat Peter, cast in 1923, is over ten feet in diameter and weighs nearly

4. Cologne Tourism, "Cologne Cathedral," para. 1.

5. Cologne Tourism, "Cologne Cathedral," para. 2.

fifty-three thousand pounds. Until 2016, it was the largest bell in the world swinging on a straight yoke. The bell's clapper alone weighs 1,300 pounds. Saint Peter's Bell still rings today but only on special occasions and major German holidays. Be sure to keep climbing the steps. Once you've arrived at the tower you will be rewarded with panoramic views of Cologne's city center, the Rhine River, and beyond.

Shrine of the Three Kings

Here is another fascinating cathedral mystery, curiosity, and legend all wrapped in one! In the Middle Ages, religious relics were a very big deal. Prized relics were often justified as a rather ironic Christian symbol of the king's medieval secular power. Recall that the Cologne Cathedral's vision originated with the acquisition of the bones of three kings in the late twelfth century. Yes . . . those three kings of Christmas carol fame. The first to recognize and worship the baby Jesus as Savior of the world, they are often referred to as the three wise men, astrologers, or magi. The legendary background story is naturally fascinating. In 313, Emperor Constantine the Great issued an edict declaring Christianity legalized across the Holy Roman Empire. Devout Empress Helena, mother of Constantine the Great, was an avid collector of holy relics. She traveled widely and sought out all objects related to Jesus of Nazareth. Helena is even believed to have located the tomb of Jesus and the Holy Cross of the crucifixion. It was also Helena who originally located and brought the relics of the magi back to Constantinople (Istanbul) in the early fourth century. In 314, entrusted to her son Constantine, the relics were painfully transported by oxcart to Milan. Eight centuries later, in 1164, the conquered Holy Roman emperor relinquished ("gifted") the relics to the archbishop of Cologne as spoils of war. Aiming to gain fame, the archbishop understood that treasured biblical relics had great value to pilgrims. The valuable three kings relics were guardedly transferred to Cologne. In Cologne, a golden *Shrine of the Three Kings* was completed in 1225 to safely house the relics. The shrine (or reliquary) was installed in a small predecessor cathedral. The shrine has attracted a steady stream of pilgrims, many hoping for miracles, ever since. The influx of pilgrims justified construction of the large, magnificent Cologne Cathedral. The massive, gilded reliquary is a masterpiece of medieval goldwork and ranks as one of the largest in the Western world. The shrine now sits prominently behind the Cologne Cathedral high altar. Shaped like a basilica, the wooden shrine is eighty-seven inches long, sixty inches high, and forty-three inches wide. Covered in decorative gold and silver overlay, the splendid shrine is decorated with over a thousand jewels and beads. High relief images of prophets, apostles, and evangelists further decorate the shrine. Lastly, there are gold figures of the three kings (Melchior, Caspar, and Balthasar) offering their respective gifts of gold, frankincense, and myrrh to Mary holding the infant Jesus. The Shrine of the Three Kings is encircled by offertory candles, twenty-four lamps, and a grand chandelier symbolizing the star on that heavenly Jerusalem night. Accordingly, the appropriate theme of the Cologne Cathedral has forever remained that life is a pilgrimage, a search for God.

It wasn't until 1864, under the guidance of experts, that the shrine was finally opened in Cologne. Inside the shrine were eleventh-century coins, bandages, aromatic resins, and the relics of the Magi. The relics included numerous bones of three males that could be assembled into nearly complete bodies. Their skulls were adorned in gold crowns. As to the question of whether these are really the remains of the mysterious three kings, there are conflicting legends and a few intriguing clues. By most appearances, outright forgery can be ruled out. First, the opened shrine revealed the skulls of a young man, a middle-aged man, and an old man; this is consistent with some accounts of the magi. Also, the revered bones were wrapped in valuable silk fabrics from Palmyra (Syria) that date back to Helena's late antiquity period.[6] However, as a spokesperson for the Cologne Cathedral's Builders' Works put it, the question of whether they really are the three wise men is "ultimately a matter of faith."[7] The gold shrine has been resealed and unopened since 1864. However, the front end of the reliquary is partially opened for viewing each January 6 (the Feast of the Epiphany). On the feast day, it is possible for all Cologne Cathedral visitors to view the three skulls.

Pubs and Breweries

Cologne, Germany, and especially Cologne's Old Town hub, has a variety of cozy pubs, outdoor restaurants, and breweries hidden in quaint cobblestoned alleys and bustling, fun-filled medieval squares. However, across Cologne, it's all about the city's unique and popular signature ale and lager hybrid *Kölsch* beer. Kölsch is an unassuming delicate beer with dialed back hops (less alcohol) and subtle aromas of apple, peach, and wheat bread. The crisp, light, effervescent beer is as clear as a bell and very refreshing on the palate, even for a non–beer drinker such as myself. Adding to its allure, the glass of choice for serving Kölsch beer is miniscule at just six ounces. The theory behind the small glasses is that the Kölsch stays cold and never goes

6. Cords, "How the 'Three Wise Men,'" sec. "A matter of faith."
7. Cords, "How the 'Three Wise Men,'" sec. "A matter of faith."

flat. When passing through Cologne, I would usually enjoy a Kölsch at two lively, favorite spots.

The first spot is the *Früh Brauhaus*, which is the most popular biergarten (beer garden) in Cologne. Früh Brauhaus is also known as *Früh am Dom* due to its convenient central location very near the Cologne Cathedral. Opened in 1904, Früh is Cologne's quintessential Kölsch Brauhaus. A stop is pretty much mandatory for any beer drinkers visiting Cologne. This is not your typical pub! With room for 1,500 guests, Früh is the second largest brewery pub in all of Germany, second only to the famous Hofbräuhaus in Munich. Every year, an astounding 2.5 million guests stop by the Früh Brauhaus for a meal and/or a Kölsch or two. The vast pub is spread across three floors in a rambling collection of discreet spaces and back rooms reminiscent of an imagined medieval banquet hall. Some rooms are dark, others brightly sunlit through large stained-glass windows, and the pub also opens out onto the quaint square. With cold Kölsch served by a brash Köbes (waiter), the process is very simple. Start by taking a table and a Köbes will immediately greet you with a tray of beers. Small talk is limited. Give a quick nod that it's beer you're after and you're all set until it's time to settle the bill. From there, endless beers are delivered lightning quick in the hope that your speed of drinking is equally fast. Once you're anywhere near the end of a glass of beer, nonstop replacements are delivered. The only way to stop the influx is to symbolically place your beer mat on top of the glass. At this point, the brusque Köbes counts the pencil marks they've inscribed on your beer mat and charge accordingly. Note that I only know this from observing my work colleagues! Früh Kölsch is ideal for large groups and for socializing in true German fashion. A cold Früh Kölsch after a busy day can be a real treat. I even introduced my wife to the fruity Kölsch beer at the Früh Brauhaus . . . the face of Kölsch worldwide.

Each of Cologne's breweries has their own unique character. In addition to the Früh Brauhaus, my other favorite and a frequent dinner stop was *Peters Brauhaus*. Located in the heart of Old Town on a beautiful quiet street in a beautiful building, Peters Brauhaus was more recently established in 1994, though the new brewery occupies the spot of an old, beloved, historic Cologne brewery and tavern. In addition to their own Kölsch beer, Peters Brauhaus is also a very popular restaurant for locals and visiting diners alike, serving delicious traditional German food. Aromas of roasted meats and rich sauces greet you immediately upon entering. The brewery's many packed rooms provide great ambience and a wonderful German feel. The interior features beautiful wrought iron windows, stained-glass ceilings, an elaborate chandelier, warm wooden floors and paneled walls, ceramic tile work, many photos, old paintings, and numerous awards. Peters Brauhaus is a just an enjoyable, comfortable place to enjoy authentic, sophisticated German cuisine and hospitality. The menu features classic German home cooking such as potato soup, schnitzel, pork knuckle, sauerkraut, cabbage and dumplings, and even apple strudel. In some rooms, guests are seated at large communal wooden tables intended to promote interactions and a whole lot of fun. On one visit, when I noticed that there was an American man seated next to me, we began to talk only to discover that we were from the very same hometown of McKeesport, Pennsylvania. Seems that after high school, he was awarded a football scholarship to attend Vanderbilt University. The gentleman ended up marrying a southern girl, stayed in the south, and built a very successful career in sales. For these reasons and more, Peters Brauhaus is the kind of local German pub you could easily spend a few hours enjoying.

MUNICH

Munich (München in German), or "Home of the Monks," is the third largest city in Germany after Berlin and Hamburg. Munich, with a population of 1.5 million, is the capital of Bavaria (state) located in beautiful southern Germany. The city traces its eighth-century origins to a Benedictine monastery. However, Munich was only first mentioned in 1158 as a Catholic stronghold that politically resisted the Reformation, resulting in the Thirty Years' War. By 1806, the Kingdom of Bavaria was established and Munich, despite its landlocked location, fast became a major European center of arts, culture, and science. After the Nazis' rise to power, Munich was reluctantly tagged as a capital of the movement. And like most major German cities, Munich was heavily bombed during World War II, though most of the old town and thirty thousand citywide buildings survived. After the war, there were great increases in Munich's population and economic power. Subsequently, Munich was ceremoniously named host city of the 1972 Summer Olympic Games. It was the first time since 1936 that Germany hosted the Olympics. Today, Munich has risen to a global center of technology, finance, business, and tourism. The city is home to centuries-old architecture, wonderful museums, and, of course, beer halls and the annual Oktoberfest celebration. Munich was named the world's most livable city in 2018 for its high standard and quality of life.

I arrived in Munich to attend a meeting of six major German companies who had formed a large Procurement Alliance. Wherever possible, our group of international enterprises would consolidate category spend to achieve beneficial global supply agreements. Beyond work, my downtime in

Munich was very limited to just the day and evening of my arrival. Unable to truly "bleisure" Munich, I decided to simply walk around, visit Munich's sports-themed Olympic Park, and enjoy dinner at the famous Hofbräuhaus.

Olympiapark (Olympic Park)

Olympic Park, a sprawling 210-acre park, was created for the 1972 Olympic Games. The impressive, aging neighborhood park remains a popular place to enjoy recreation, a variety of sports, nature, spectacular events, festivals, and concerts. Most of Munich's Olympic venues are now history. However, sites like the Olympic Stadium, the world-famous tent roof, Olympic Hall, and the 620-foot-high Olympic Tower with its viewing platform remain. And there's still an abundance of activities underway, from swimming to ice skating, tennis, paddleboats, golf, biking, jogging, and plenty of picnicking.

The park is an enjoyable place to visit, though I could not help thinking about the Munich terrorist attack and massacre that occurred during those 1972 Summer Olympics. Sadly, during the Olympics' second week, eight members of the Palestinian militant group Black September, disguised as athletes, infiltrated the Olympic Village. The village was specifically constructed to accommodate the athletes attending the games in apartments and bungalows, all within easy walking distance of the competition area. Prior to this horrific event, Munich's concept for a sports quarter in a green area with short distances between venues and no cars had proved a roaring success. However, it was ultimately within the Olympic Village that the terrorists killed two members of the Israeli Olympic team. Nine other Israeli team members were taken hostage and later killed during a botched West German rescue attempt. The event was televised worldwide. As a result, many questions were raised relative to the Olympic Games' preparation, growing safety concerns, prior tips, a significant lack of heavy security, internal involvement, and overall accountability. Shortly after the massacre, an Israeli committee chaired by then Prime Minister Golda Meir authorized a covert assassination campaign named Operation Wrath of God. The mission was to exact justice with the assassination of everyone involved in Black September. The group spent twenty years tracking down and successfully killing those suspected of planning or participating in the Munich massacre. Of those believed to have planned the massacre, only the massacre's alleged architect Abu Daoud is known to have lived and died of natural causes. Until his death in 2010, Daoud remained unrepentant and evaded extradition while traveling under assumed names and diplomatic immunity. At his death, he is believed to have stated, "Today, I cannot fight you [Israel] any more, but my grandson will and his grandsons too."[8] Over fifty years later, very sadly and prophetically this likely has proven all too true.

Relative to the Munich Olympic Village, life moves on even under the direst situations. The city's experimental 1970s approach to urban development remains relevant even today. In 1973, the former male section of the Olympic Village was transferred into a residential neighborhood. The apartments and bungalows of the village's female section were developed to accommodate university students. Today, over six thousand people live in the highly coveted Munich neighborhood of extensive green spaces and easy, excellent transportation to the city center. And just like the Olympic Park, the village's parkland area had been landscaped to recreate the Alpine foothills. The Olympic Village area is regarded as one of the most popular residential areas in all of Munich. I'm certain I might have better spent an afternoon in beautiful Munich. However, on that given day, I was intrigued and happy to stroll the Olympic Park and reflect on bigger, ever-present world events. I even debated discussing the Munich massacre except from a relative historical perspective.

Hofbräuhaus

Whew! On a much, much lighter note, I happily transitioned to a German beer hall that evening. And not just any beer hall but the most famous, largest, and most boisterous one in the world, complete with plenty of German oompah music! I'm referencing none other than Munich's Hofbräuhaus. Touristy, for sure, but still a whole lot of fun, and half the daily guests are locals. For good reason, this traditional beer hall in the heart of Munich is recognized worldwide as the embodiment of Bavarian beer culture. Add to that the Hofbräuhaus historic charm and communal seating and you've got a very vibrant and festive atmosphere. The Hofbräuhaus was founded back in 1589 by the Duke of Bavaria, founded as the brewery to the old Royal Residence. Hofbräuhaus (HOAF-broy-howz) translates to "court brewery" or "royal brewery." While most Europeans drank wine, beer was not readily available in sixteenth-century Germany, and the cost to import beer was high. Thus, the need for a royal brewery. Not caring much for average dark and heavy brown beers, the royals requested a light wheat beer. Once it was developed, they forbade other breweries from brewing the light beer, thereby creating a monopoly. Clearly the nobles and servants of the court greatly enjoyed the royal beer. Only after centuries of producing "royals

8. Wikipedia, "Abu Daoud," sec. "Death."

only" beer was the brewery opened to the public in 1828, accomplished by decree of Bavarian King Ludwig I. This decree was much to the chagrin of Munich's private brewers, who rightfully feared losing customers. Hofbräuhaus quickly became the center of Munich's public and political life. In 1852, ownership was officially transferred to the Kingdom of Bavaria. Still to this day, Munich's Hofbräuhaus is owned by the Bavarian state government. So popular was the expanding Hofbräuhaus that prominent beer lovers such as Wolfgang Amadeus Mozart, the Austrian Empress Elizabeth, and Vladimir Lenin and his wife were all stopping by. Adolf Hitler paid a visit to Hofbräuhaus in 1920 for his first public speech. There, Hitler announced to over two thousand guests the official platform of the Nazi Party. At the time, Hitler was propaganda chief, though he was quickly elected führer of the Nazi Party in July 1921 at another Hofbräuhaus meeting. Other subsequent famous patrons included John F. Kennedy, Louis Armstrong, Thomas Wolfe, and Mikhail Gorbachev.

Today at its current location (last expanded 1897), Hofbräuhaus is enormous. The pub can serve up to five thousand people at a time. That said, high demand for beer and good times in Munich still make it difficult to find an empty table. The elaborate three-story building includes a ground-floor beer hall with a music podium featuring endless brass bands. Oddly, it's very common to hear John Denver's catchy "Take Me Home, Country Roads" blaring as most everyone sings along. Over a thousand guests can easily fill the ground-floor hall. There's also a quieter café on the ground floor favored by the locals. On the top floor is the large Festival Hall where folk singers and music groups perform. The Festival Hall is also a popular venue for folk dancing. Lastly, on a warm day or evening, be sure to head through the imposing arch and snag a shady spot in the outdoor beer garden. It's always an endless party at the Hofbräuhaus.

Post–World War II, many American soldiers stationed in Munich brought home their beer mugs with the famous Hofbräuhaus "HB" logo. Thanks in part to these returning American soldiers, Munich's Hofbräuhaus quickly became and has remained a major tourist attraction. Consequently, demand for Hofbräuhaus beer halls in other parts of the world, and throughout Germany, took hold. Today there are twenty-nine Hofbräuhaus locations in Germany and another eight locations throughout the world. To my personal amazement, a lively Hofbräuhaus was opened in my hometown of Pittsburgh in 2009. The pub's structure and ambience are very similar to the Munich location, albeit smaller scaled. Still, the Pittsburgh South Side site is a fun venue where we have enjoyed several group meetings and celebrations!

LEIPZIG

Leipzig (lipe-zuhg) is known as one of Europe's top musical cities and the music capital of Germany, with music, education, and industry as its claims to fame. With a rich musical heritage, Leipzig is the birthplace of Richard Wagner and was home to many other famous composers, including Mendelssohn, Schumann, and most notably Johann Sebastian Bach. Leipzig is also home to the world-renowned Gewandhaus Orchestra, the Leipzig Opera, and the famous eight-hundred-year-old Saint Thomas Boys' Choir. No other city can boast of such acclaimed musical tradition. Educationally, the University of Leipzig dates to 1409 and built its outstanding reputation through luminaries such as Martin Luther, Goethe (the "German Shakespeare"), and alumni Richard Wagner, Friedrich Nietzsche, and Angela Merkel. Third, from an industry perspective, underrated Leipzig is known for its relentless entrepreneurial spirit in areas such as mining, textiles, printing, and piano making. Leipzig has been a major trade city since the time of the Holy Roman Empire. Just over an hour south of Berlin in Saxony (state), culturally rich Leipzig has moved far beyond East Germany's Iron Curtain. Since the 1989 fall of the Berlin Wall, Leipzig has healed and transformed into a vibrant hub. Today, Leipzig (population 630,000) is considered one of Germany's coolest cities, a hot spot for creative people, with hipster hangouts galore. Arriving in Leipzig by train is a treat unto itself. *Leipzig Hauptbahnhof* is breathtaking and Europe's largest central railway station. Under the station's six towering stone arches and two cavernous mirror-image arrival halls are two stories of shopping with hundreds of stores. In 2021, Leipzig Hauptbahnhof was ranked the best railway station in Europe.[9]

Historically, two important events occurred in Leipzig. The first event was the 1813 *Battle of Leipzig* between the Napoleon-led French and an allied coalition of Prussia, Russia, Austria, and Sweden. Prior to World War I, this was the largest ground battle in Europe. The alliance defeated France and ended Napoleon's presence in Germany. Napoleon was forced to abdicate his throne and was briefly exiled to Elba before escaping. The war had a major impact in stimulating German nationalism, though Leipzig managed to balance its interests between Prussia and France. A *Monument to the Battle of Nations* was completed in Leipzig in 1913 to commemorate the hundredth anniversary of the defeat of Napoleon's French army. The second event is the *Peaceful Revolution*. The Peaceful Revolution started seven years prior to the fall of the Berlin Wall. In 1982, parishioners of Leipzig's Saint

9. Oliver, "Revealed."

Nicholas Church gathered each week to pray for peace and a better world. This practice continued for years, building to a few hundred protesters. Finally, on October 16, 1989, it would be *Decision Day*. In organized fashion, over fifty thousand pamphlets were distributed, strongly urging protesters to remain nonviolent. Suddenly, the streets of Leipzig were filled with seventy thousand protesters, with thousands of others poised throughout East Germany. Fearful yet unyielding, the protesters marched while chanting, "Wir sind das Volk" (We are the people)! An estimated eight thousand armed forces, prepared for a violent crackdown, met the protestors, awaiting orders to shoot. However, by now the peaceful protesters had swelled to a hundred thousand strong, which stymied any marching orders for massive bloodshed. All of Germany, aware that there would be a mass demonstration in Leipzig, waited anxiously for news. When the police wisely failed to intervene, the successful demonstration ended peacefully. Two young protesters climbed the church tower and began ringing the bells signaling to East Germans that Leipzig was safe and that it was time for them to join the movement. It was just a couple weeks later that the Berlin Wall came down. Today throughout Leipzig, there are sites with '89 plaques denoting the Peaceful Revolution. Rightfully, the heroic residents of Leipzig remain proud of their nonviolent role in ousting the Communists. A few years later, it was President John F. Kennedy who famously said, "Those who make peaceful revolution impossible will make violent revolution inevitable."[10] No doubt that JFK was very aware of Leipzig.

Today, fierce and versatile Leipzig simultaneously thrives on its amazing past while delighting in its lively present scene and relaxed way of life. Leipzig's famous *Auerbachs Keller* (Auerbach's Cellar) restaurant is celebrating five hundred years. The cellar owes its long-standing reputation to writer Goethe's great tragedy *Faust*. As his favorite wine bar, it is the site where the student Goethe received his inspiration to write the masterpiece. The cellar is also featured in *Faust*. A bronze statue of Faust and Mephisto, representing good and evil, adorns the cellar's entrance. As to the present, the dynamic, most livable city has over 150 musical events planned for the upcoming *Leipzig* Bachfest. And, each winter, the three-hundred-stall-strong beautiful *Leipzig Christmas Market*, dating back to 1458, returns.

I had a brief two-day visit to Leipzig to attend an annual Global Procurement Conference. Turns out that Leipzig is a very popular location for business gatherings. The city appeared filled with more business travelers than tourists. With just a day to explore the city, I focused on a cluster of Leipzig's historic and fascinating Johann Sebastian Bach sights. Then, one

10. Kennedy, "Address," para. 28.

evening, we had an interesting and informative team event that included a group dinner and factory tour at the Porsche Experience Center Leipzig. Though, reflecting on the many team events over the years, I am not sure anyone enjoyed them quite as much as I did. With jet lag and never-ending demands of work, it's understandable. Many business travelers simply crave a quiet dinner and a good night of rest and relaxation in a comfortable hotel room.

Johann Sebastian Bach

Surpassing even Vincent van Gogh, the great composer *Johann Sebastian Bach* (1685–1750) just might be the most talented, prolific, intriguing, sorrowful, creative, faith-filled, and misunderstood genius in history. Bach was born into a musical family as the youngest of eight children and orphaned at age ten. He was raised by an older brother to age fifteen, at which time he left home for school after having secured a place in a select choir of poor boys. There Bach continued his formal music education. At age eighteen, Bach commenced work as a professional musician in the Protestant churches of various German towns and for a longer period in royal courts where he expanded his organ repertory, engaged in baroque chamber music, and continually developed. In 1723, Bach was appointed as cantor of Saint Thomas School in Leipzig. His duties also entailed serving as director of music for the four principal churches in the city of Leipzig. Bach also directed and composed secular music for the university's student ensemble *Collegium Musicum*. By some accounts, Bach was not the city council's first or even their second choice for the prestigious role.[11] Nonetheless, the industrious Bach took it upon himself to write a new sacred cantata for every Sunday and holiday service throughout the church year. He also had to provide performers for all four churches. Finding strength in his great faith, Bach would start each composition with the initials J.J. (Jesu Juva), translated to "Lord Help Me," and sign each completed manuscript S.D.G. (Soli Deo Gloria), translated to the "Glory of God Alone." To Bach, music was divine prayer. At Saint Thomas School, Bach's responsibility included shepherding students and the famous 50–100 member boys' choir (ages eight to eighteen). Meanwhile, crowd-pleasing performances by the university student musicians drew considerable attention to Bach's secular opera and chamber compositions. These no-fee performances occurred regularly at Leipzig's finely appointed Café Zimmermann coffeehouse. Along the way, Bach incredibly had twenty children with his two wives—seven with Maria Barbara

11. Braw, " When JS Bach."

and thirteen with Anna Magdalena. He endured great loss and heartbreak when his first wife died unexpectedly while he was away. More sadly, ten of his children never reached adulthood, and he buried an eleventh child. In any event, Bach spent the final twenty-seven years of his life in Leipzig frantically and tirelessly working to barely keep his large family and the beloved Saint Thomas Boys' Choir afloat. Following botched eye surgery and a period of failing eyesight, Bach died from a stroke in 1750 at the age of sixty-five. The great composer was initially buried in an unmarked grave in a humble graveyard and quickly forgotten.

Far and away, it was in Leipzig where Bach experienced his most astonishingly productive period. During this period, Bach wrote a mind-blowing 226 surviving cantatas, the famous *Magnificat*, two great *Passions*, and many other sophisticated, highly studied sacred and secular pieces across a variety of instruments. During his life, Bach was respected though unknown and not particularly popular outside Leipzig or Germany. Bach's symphonized baroque style was overlooked. At the time of his death, Bach was viewed merely as the church cantor, a teacher, and a piano restorer. It wasn't until 1829, an astonishing seventy-nine years after Bach's death, that the "Bach Revival" began. It was Jewish composer Felix Mendelssohn who had received a copy of Bach's *Saint Matthew's Passion* from his grandmother and performed it in Berlin. Bach's *Passion* was wildly received and an instant sensation. With a newfound understanding and appreciation of Bach's expressive genius, his overdue fame rapidly spread throughout Germany, Europe, and the world. Many subsequent composers have readily adopted Bach's innovative composing techniques. Mozart, Haydn, and Beethoven have all acknowledged that Bach had a profound influence on them. Beyond classical music, Bach has had multigenerational influence on jazz artists and a "who's who" list of contemporary musicians. They range from Bobby McFerrin, Dave Brubeck, Nina Simone, Paul Simon ("Bridge Over Troubled Water"), the Beatles ("Blackbird," "Penny Lane," "All You Need Is Love"), Procol Harum ("A Whiter Shade of Pale"), the Beach Boys, Eminem, and Lady Gaga.[12] Today, the overworked and undervalued Leipzig church cantor is often considered the greatest composer the world has ever known. In Leipzig, it is possible to visit Saint Thomas Church, the tomb of Bach, and a museum dedicated to Leipzig's favorite composer.

12. See Macdonald, "15 Pop Songs"; Cherry Classics, "Brubeck."

Saint Thomas Church

Located in Leipzig's central district is the historic *Saint Thomas Lutheran Church*. A church has been located on this site since the twelfth century, and by 1212 an earlier structure became the Church of Saint Thomas (college of Augustinian canons), which later became the core of the University of Leipzig founded in 1409. Also in 1212, the internationally known Saint Thomas Boys' Choir (Thomanerchor) was founded. The choir exists to this day and still performs at the very church. With a flow of wealth from silver mining and a thriving Leipzig, the church had been continually rebuilt over the centuries and was eventually replaced in 1496 by the current Saint Thomas church with its neo-Gothic hall and clean, uncluttered, Protestant aesthetic. All subsequent repairs and renovations emphasized the Gothic character of that building. Don't let the church's stripped-down appearance fool you. It was in Saint Thomas Church where reformer Martin Luther preached in 1539. It was there where several prominent composers visited and performed, including a touring Wolfgang Amadeus Mozart in 1789. It was there where the great composer Richard Wagner was baptized and mentored. And it was in Saint Thomas where Napoleon's French army established a munitions depot and a military hospital during the Battle of Leipzig. However, above all, Saint Thomas Church will forever and properly be best associated with Johann Sebastian Bach. Bach served as the church's director of music (Thomaskantor), and taught at its affiliated school, from 1723 until his death in 1750. The site holds immense significance, as it was in the adjoined school cantor's residence where Bach and his family lived (since demolished in 1902). The site is also where the prolific composer created his most iconic works and is buried today.

Tomb of Bach

In front of the Saint Thomas Church altar is the *Tomb of Bach*—at least we think so? Recall that the unappreciated Bach was hastily laid to rest in an unmarked grave on July 30, 1750. Few detailed specifics were recorded or captured by the über-busy Bach during his lifetime. Still today, little remains known of Bach the man versus Bach the genius. Only one modest though insufficient portrait had survived and was available as reference. Inexplicably, the composer of *Saint Matthew's Passion*, *Toccata and Fugue in D Minor*, *Jesu, Joy of Man's Desiring*, and countless other transcendent masterpieces had been long forgotten. Bach even harmonized my favorite Easter hymn, *O Sacred Head, Surrounded*. Fortunately, on the heels of the Bach Revival, the public became immensely interested in the whereabouts of Bach's remains. It became clear that the remains of Leipzig's now-favorite son must be located and moved to a prominent final resting place. Guided by archival documents to look for an oak coffin at a spot "six paces in a straight line from the church door," the excavators began to search. On October 22, 1894, nearly 150 years after his burial, the earthly remains of Johann Sebastian Bach were *believed* to be found. The bones were examined by a team of local and Viennese medical experts and declared authentic. Wisely, the director of the group summoned the local sculptor (Carl Seffner) to reconstruct and preserve Bach's facial expression from the alleged skull. The bones were initially placed in a stone crypt in Leipzig's Saint John's Church before their transfer to Saint Thomas Church. The new grave in the church sanctuary with a bronze cover was sponsored in 1949 by the Leipzig cultural officer of the then-ruling Soviet Army. The fitting grave was inaugurated on July 28, 1950, exactly two hundred years after the death of the great composer.

Bach Statue

Outside the Saint Thomas Church sits the large, beautiful, bronze *Bach statue*. Located just outside the west entrance, Bach is positioned standing in front of his favorite instrument, the pipe organ. A donated Bach stained-glass 1895 church window, created in Munich, is strategically located directly behind the monument. The statue was only later created by Leipzig's Carl Seffner and dedicated in 1908. The memorial is a remarkable tribute to Leipzig's legendary composer. Seffner used his copy of Bach's alleged skull to create the statue. The imposing statue measures eight feet in height and sits atop a ten-foot socle or base. The statue depicts Bach in action grasping a rolled-up music roll as a baton in his right arm, raised to conduct. He is working hard, as usual, with his left hand just released from the organ manual. His long state coat is wildly opened with his vest jacket unbuttoned as a slot to shove the sheet-music baton into and free his hand. Lastly, his bare jacket pocket is turned out, as he tirelessly advocated and scrounged for needed funding. The surrounding square continues to serve as a gathering place for music enthusiasts to perform. In the summertime, "Monday Concerts by the Bach Statue" are held. The Bach Statue is a popular object of veneration by Bach pilgrims.

Bach Museum

Across the beautiful courtyard outside Saint Thomas Church is the relatively small *Bach Museum*. The museum is housed in the sixteenth-century Bose House in Saint Thomas Square. The house was the residence of the Bose family, affluent gold and silver merchants and close friends of the Bach family. Today the building houses the Bach Museum and Bach Archive. Here, the extraordinary story of the life and work of Johann Sebastian Bach is told across twelve thematically structured exhibition rooms. Visitors can explore sheet music, documents, artwork, period furniture, documentary footage, and musical instruments. Also displayed is the Bach's family tree, a group of more than fifty musicians and composers of great importance to the history of music over two hundred years. The museum's exciting interactive features give visitors the chance to actively play period instruments and experiment with sounds. A research lab teaches and enables visitors to date Bach's works, while the permanent exhibition provides fascinating insights into Bach research and his genius. Among the most interesting exhibits is an organ console that Bach himself played in the year 1743. There's also a double bass that was part of his orchestra and a recently discovered iron cash box saved from the Bach household. A special highlight of the museum is the treasure room, home to original Bach manuscripts and other rare items on display. Seeing the great complexities of these handwritten compositions for various instruments, painfully copied by associates and family, was mind-blowing. On top of all that, visitors can relax in the museum's garden, its listening studio, a baroque courtyard, a gift shop, and a café. Baroque music concerts are oftentimes performed in the Summer Hall.

The Porsche Experience

Shifting gears (no pun intended) . . . the German people love music, but they also have a deeply ingrained love for cars. The passion is rooted in the German culture and the country's strong luxury automobile industry. Start with the beauty and precision engineering of German car brands like Mercedes-Benz, Porsche, BMW, and Audi. Add the world-famous German Autobahn (a network of high or unlimited speed roads) that allows drivers more freedom to responsibly enjoy quality performance cars. I learned that in Germany, cars are not just a mode of transportation—they are a way of life. Cars are a lifestyle choice deeply and proudly embedded in Germany's national identity. But why? It may be that many German towns are more walkable. Europeans also have outstanding access to commuter trains. So, possibly, the primary utility of cars in Germany is longer trips needed to experience nearby cities and bordering countries. Recall that Germany borders nine different countries. Or is it just that Germans are technology-driven, sustainability-conscious, and fiercely competitive? Whatever the case, I too enjoy the driving experience of upscale German-made cars. Mercedes . . . "The Best or Nothing!" BMW . . . "The Ultimate Driving Machine!" For this reason, and being a former General Motors employee, I was very excited to learn firsthand about their industry with a planned visit to a Porsche automotive assembly plant.

Leipzig proved to be an ideal, relaxed location for our global meeting. The city was convenient for German travelers and a relatively easy destination for those traveling from abroad. As for team-building, organizers considered the German affinity for both lean manufacturing and automobiles. A short distance from town, in the Leipzig countryside, was a large, state-of-the-art, dynamic Porsche factory. The Leipzig factory was the second Porsche production site after the company's headquarters in Stuttgart, Germany. Employing over 4,600 employees, the factory is obviously a very important economic driver and employer in the Leipzig region. In fact, the sports car manufacturer supports numerous regional projects relative to education, culture, social issues, sports, and the environment. Within the Leipzig factory, all the worldwide four-door Porsche Macan and Panamera models are built. The factory is also home to the *Porsche Experience Center*, which includes a gourmet restaurant and meeting space with panoramic views as well as a motorsports-certified track and off-road course. Unfortunately, the co-driving experience was not a part of our package. However, after an educational introduction and delicious team meal, we were given an exclusive, behind-the-scenes factory tour. While not explicitly "one day builds," many Porsche models are built to order in that time frame. We were told that many royals and eastern cultures request unusual color combinations. Also, many Porsche enthusiasts often purchase two Porsches at once, one to drive and one to collect.

Based on Porsche's ultra-efficient, resource-sparing, smart, lean, and green processes, we followed the Macan and Panamera on their way through production, watching a highly demanding interaction between man, eight hundred robots, and machine. From cycle to cycle, as it should be with a world-class sports car manufacturer, timing of operations was precise to the second. Assembly was an incredible example of lean production with a high degree of complexity. I was impressed with the "just in time" delivery of components and tires, with many required Porsche suppliers located within a mile of the factory. As opposed to concrete, the work area floors of the spotless factory were hardwood (mahogany) ensuring an ergonomic environment for employees.

The production process was unbelievably lean and smart. First is the body line, the birthplace of every Porsche. This is the station at which the car is given its "birth certificate," a transponder with a specific identification code. The code contains all details and specifications of the car build. Next up is the paint shop. The car's body is cleaned, degreased, and dipped in a zinc phosphate solution that ensures optimum adhesion of corrosion protection. Three different coats of paint are applied, with the final coat being the color selected by the customer. Once dried, a clear varnish seals the paint coats. In less than two minutes, two robots scan the entire body, take a hundred thousand photos, and identify even the tiniest paint irregularities. Final assembly follows, with installation of the windshield, rear window, headlights, and seats. Doors are also refitted to the body, and the Porsche crest is attached. Then it's the fully automated merging of the body with the completed power train. Lastly, work is concluded by filling the car with fuel, brake fluid, coolant, and window cleaner. The wheels are also fitted at this point. However, the baptism of fire for every Porsche is a final inspection and a test drive on the factory's own circuit. The cars are then delivered all over the world as Porsche dreams become reality.

From my enthusiasm, you can deduce that the Porsche factory tour was a memorable, educational, inspiring event. Consequently, I was not at all surprised to learn that the Leipzig Porsche factory was recently named Factory of the Year. Approximately one hundred factories from all over the world had submitted bids for the renowned auto industry award.[13]

KIEL

Unlike Berlin, Cologne, Munich, and even Leipzig . . . there's a very good chance that you've never heard of *Kiel, Germany*. In retrospect, Kiel (KEEL) was one of the most interesting and fun bleisure cities I encountered in Germany—with emphasis on "leisure," even if only for a day. Kiel is a spectacular coastal city and maritime hub located in Northern Germany approximately fifty-six miles northeast of the famous port city of Hamburg. With a population of 250,000, Kiel is the largest German city on the Baltic Sea. The city's strategic port serves as a vital link between the Baltic and North Seas. Undoubtedly, water is the dominant element of Kiel; the Baltic Sea has forged a path into the very city center of Kiel. This has created a magical maritime atmosphere. Kiel is widely and best known for its variety of international sailing events. And, of course, *Kieler Woche* (Kiel Week), the biggest sailing regatta in the world. The German-hosted 1936 and 1972

13. Porsche Newsroom, "Porsche Plant in Leipzig."

Summer Olympics sailing competitions were even held in the Bay of Kiel. Home to the German Navy's Baltic fleet, as well as the University of Kiel, founded in 1665, Kiel is also a high-tech shipbuilding center. And, located just sixty-five miles from Denmark, Kiel is a gateway to Scandinavia. Lastly, Kiel serves as a popular Baltic Sea cruise ship destination and an important transfer hub. From Kiel, you can board passenger ferries to many countries, including Sweden, Norway, and Lithuania. In parallel with all the above, the port city of Kiel is easily characterized by its modern urban flair, vibrant student scene, and laid-back lifestyle.

You're probably wondering what brought me to such a relatively unknown, distant, off-the-beaten-path place. As driven by the "voice of the customer" interactions, there was a need for a European-based supplier capable of producing glass prefilled syringes. Medical imaging suite throughput is in high demand and expensive. Syringes already prefilled with contrast are very beneficial. Absent prefilled syringes, technicians are pressed to perform millions of procedures, each routinely requiring tedious, time-consuming, messy filling of plastic molded syringes with contrast. It was recognized that a move to prefilled syringes would be most welcomed. That said, the ability to produce prefilled syringes is not a capability many manufacturers possess. A supplier is needed to manage the process from soups to nuts. The process entails molding, prefilling, packaging, sterilizing, and shipping glass syringes. There weren't a lot of suppliers with this capability and, more so, capacity to support a large demand. After failed efforts, our search took us to meet a relatively small family-owned manufacturer in Hamburg, Germany. The group was coincidentally presently adding manufacturing capacity and was ever so eager to discuss the prospects of working with a large, international, highly recognized enterprise. My thought was that this just might work. With a team in hand, we undertook extensive due diligence. The team even visited their planned new plant location in Neumünster (north of Hamburg), which was under construction. One of the best parts of international business travel is often the wonderful and interesting people you meet. In addition to the owner brothers, the brilliant head of operations was a former judoka (practitioner of judo) who competed for East Germany in the 1980 Moscow Summer Olympics. Following several days and an indication to preliminarily move forward, the supplier requested we enjoy our final day. Insisting that we get out of the office, our hosts were excited to entertain us with a visit further north to Kiel . . . and it just happened to be Kiel Week!

Kiel Week

What started out in Kiel as a ship racing championship in 1882 has long since become a very large festival. Held annually the last week in June, the nine-day *Kiel Week* usually attracts around five thousand sailors, two thousand ships and yachts, and over three million visitors each year. In parallel, there are hundreds of live, open-air concerts and various stage performances playing on public venues throughout the city. I never experienced anything quite like this festival—the largest summer festival in Europe! The festival provides an extraordinary international atmosphere and is an assault on your senses by sea, air, and land!

By sea, the world's largest competitive sailing regatta attracts sailors from all over the world, with over fifty countries represented. The event is for every kind of boat, from one-man dinghies to astounding tall ships. It's regatta sailing at the highest level. Admiring spectators excitedly watch as ships and boats compete. Most larger ship races begin at Kiel's Olympic Harbor. The harbor serves as the center of most sporting activities during Kiel Week. Kiel Week is also one of the largest tall ship conventions in Germany, attracting many worldwide traditional sailing ships. The majestic tall ships spend the week providing day tours out of Kiel, berthing in view of the festival visitors. Then, usually on the regatta's second Saturday, hundreds of traditional ships and yachts participate in the *Tall Ships Parade* (*Windjammerparade*). The spectacular, two-hour parade tops off the highly competitive nautical week. The parade was first held in 1972 and was organized in celebration of that year's Summer Olympic Games. The initial parade was the first large gathering of multiple-mast tall ships. The parade's great success led to the annual Kiel Week parade. Watching the races and seeing the tall ships is truly an exciting experience. The esteemed winner of the sailing championship is announced on the final day of the festival. Simultaneously, Kiel Week ends in celebratory fashion on the final Sunday at eleven o'clock at night. The week ceremoniously ends with an enormous late-night fireworks display visible throughout the maritime city and across the Bay of Kiel.

Next, by air and attracting thousands of hot-air balloon enthusiasts, is the Kiel Week International Balloon Sail. Colorful balloons of many different shapes and sizes fill the sky. It's a vibrant spectacle of hot-air balloons and airships with mesmerizing Night Glows and dazzling, synchronized-music firework displays. With all that's going on throughout Kiel, just in front of the balloon setup is one of the large concert venues. Here, you might just see the likes of Sting performing. Attendees can even embark on captivating balloon rides during Kiel Week.

Lastly, by land, the old-fashioned festival offers a huge variety of events off the water, suitable for young and old. The festival's packed schedule of cultural events and music includes over three hundred free concerts where international stars, newcomers, and locals all get a chance to shine. Performances by children's singers are also very popular and offered for young families. There are amazing puppet performances by theater companies from across the globe, including seventeenth-century *Punch and Judy* shows. Of course, there are plenty of dancing and jazz events. There is a huge range of activities for kids—from painting and learning to simply playing. Then there's the countless food and drink stands featuring exotic culinary specialties from many different countries. I kept encountering Kieler Sprotten (Kiel sprats), a popular small fish dish smoked over beech wood. Of course, I had to try the sprats. Lastly, there were games of chance, magicians, and plenty of rides, many seemingly from another era—and a few games that I imagined would never be OSHA safety approved. The whole festival had the feel of a wonderful circus event from a much earlier time. There were so many international visitors and a multitude of nautical servicemen and women enjoying the festival. As the child of the Cold War, it was very strange to encounter a group of young Russian soldiers—then quickly realizing that, like everyone else, they are just young kids with their own hopes and dreams.

I couldn't think of a better way to enjoy a summer day, relax, and leave everyday life behind than a trip to Kiel Week's long-standing festival. The day was a perfect way to understand, live, and celebrate Kiel's renowned sailing regatta, their culture, cuisine, and proud maritime heritage. It was a day I'll long remember.

BAD NAUHEIM

A second somewhat quirky, unknown German town I briefly visited and fondly remember is *Bad Nauheim* (bud-no-hime). Bad Nauheim, with a population of just thirty-two thousand, is conveniently located twenty-two miles north of metropolitan Frankfurt. Turns out that Bad Nauheim is a world-famous resort, noted for its salt springs, which are used to treat heart and nerve diseases. As with other German town names, the "Bad" (bath) indicates that it is a spa town. Likewise, Nauheim translates to "effervescent." Bad Nauheim's famous carbon dioxide bubble bath was one of several types used in the early 1900s during the heyday of hydrotherapy. Accommodating his ailing father, the young future President Franklin D. Roosevelt traveled to Bad Nauheim. FDR attended school in Bad Nauheim for a short two-year period in the 1890s. However, real fame came to Bad Nauheim when an American soldier named Elvis Presley came to town in 1958. His presence had an electrifying effect on Germany and remains felt today nearly seventy years later.

I visited Bad Nauheim to attend one of our annual Global Procurement Conferences. Unfortunately, I never visited a spa or even saw the town's large, famous bathhouse. That's one of the occasional understandable downsides of visiting exciting cities while on business. Nonetheless, I would have surely welcomed some bubbly hydrotherapy!

Elvis Presley

By 1958, Elvis Presley had ascended to unprecedented rock and roll fame. Elvis was at the height of his fame and widely regarded as the most well-known name in the world of entertainment. Nonetheless, in December 1957, Elvis was drafted to serve two years in the United States Army as an active-duty soldier. Millions of Elvis fans around the country were outraged. Conversely, many parents, religious leaders, and teachers' groups, who viewed Elvis as a gyrating menace to society, were ecstatic. Based on his enormous fame, Elvis was offered numerous chances to enlist in Special Services, where he could simply entertain troops. The navy offered Elvis a chance to simply perform in Las Vegas and live in private quarters, while the army offered Elvis an opportunity to tour worldwide army bases to boost morale. Even the Pentagon proposed an offer. Elvis realized a "celebrity wimp-out" would rightfully anger many Americans.[14] As such, Elvis declined any special treatment, opting to serve as a regular soldier. The decision earned Elvis the respect of his fellow soldiers, worldwide fans, and even the American groups who previously viewed him in a very negative light. Further, Elvis donated his entire Army pay to charity, provided television sets for the post, and bought everyone in his outfit an extra set of fatigues. Upon completing basic training in Fort Hood, Texas, Elvis was assigned to serve overseas in the Tank Battalion at Ray Barracks in West Germany.

In October 1958 Elvis Presley first arrived in Friedberg, West Germany. Granted permission to live off base, Elvis rented the second floor of the Hotel Villa Grunewald in neighboring Bad Nauheim. Elvis stayed, lived, and served in West Germany for nearly eighteen months, completing his remaining military service overseas. It was in Bad Nauheim where "The King" met his great love and future wife, then fourteen-year-old Priscilla Beaulieu. Priscilla was the American stepdaughter of an Air Force serviceman also

14. Wikipedia, "Military Career of Elvis," sec. "The draft."

stationed in West Germany. Still, Elvis was far from a regular soldier; he served with an entourage. Just one week after Elvis's arrival in Germany, his father, Vernon, his grandmother, Minnie Mae, and his two best friends and bodyguards arrived in Bad Nauheim for initial support. Not surprisingly, the hotel's room number 10 (the Elvis Room) is still in its original 1950s state and can be booked for special occasions.

Even today, traces of Elvis are found everywhere in Bad Nauheim—though I was unaware that Elvis was stationed there until I arrived and saw for myself. Just outside the Hotel Villa Grunewald in Elvis Presley Square is an Elvis stele (stone slab) commemorating Elvis Aaron Presley's former residence. The popular memorial is visited by fans from all over the world. Flowers and messages, in many languages, are placed there by Elvis's adoring fans. Bad Nauheim boasts an Elvis Walk of Fame, and there's also a more recent bronze statue of Elvis on the town's renovated Usa Bridge. Years after the rock 'n' roll star's death, fans in Germany and worldwide still can't help falling in love with "The King." Lastly, memories of Elvis are displayed throughout Bad Nauheim's cafés, restaurants, bakeries, barbershops, jewelers, and cigar bars. It appears that Elvis was gracious enough to leave many Bad Nauheim establishments a signed GI photo and a positive endorsement. Photos of a youthful, handsome Elvis were found proudly hanging in most every locale I visited.

Lastly, every August, around the anniversary of Elvis Presley's death, fans from all over the world flock to Bad Nauheim to celebrate their idol at the annual *Elvis Festival*. Women and men alike, styled in 1950s, 1960s, and 1970s fashion, attend. There's a classic car parade with plenty of Cadillacs and other vintage motorcars. The festival is highlighted by live concerts, a fan market, music contests, and its many special guests including close associates and musical companions of the late Elvis Presley himself. Attending bands and big stars thrill the large returning crowds with their iconic Elvis and oldies music.

There are many reasons to love Germany and, absent time away from my family, I greatly enjoyed my numerous visits there. Most of all, I enjoyed the German people. As noted, the major German cities are consistently ranked among the most livable in the world. Germany's rich cultural heritage, vibrant towns, historic sites, and connection to nature make Germany a jewel.

CHAPTER 18

IRELAND

There are no strangers here,
just friends that you haven't yet met.

—*W. B. Yeats*

Ireland, the Emerald Isle, Éire, the Land of Saints and Scholars, is different, it's special. With a relative lack of urbanization and a distinct identity rooted in the ancient Gaelic language, the lush green island with the world's friendliest people has forged a unique character. At first, I failed to get it, looking instead for the bustling flair of a metropolis London, Barcelona, or Paris. However, with each subsequent visit, my appreciation of the beautiful country with the greenest of landscapes and quaint villages of thatched cottages, churches, castles, pubs, and sheep rapidly expanded. Consequently, I have saved Ireland as my book's final chapter. The associated reason is threefold. First, I visited and experienced Ireland on business ten times. All were done in the coordination of one of the single most interesting, challenging, exciting, and fulfilling projects of my career. Second, I parlayed my business travels to Ireland into an incredible, surprisingly successful, week-long Ireland family vacation. And once word of the Ireland trip circulated, there were twelve family members, ranging in ages from twenty-three to eighty-three, tagging along. And third, I am unapologetically biased in my inbred love and admiration of the Irish. You see, I am proudly half O'Neil, and my wife is proudly half O'Grady, both on our mothers' sides. Like over 10 percent of all Americans, our ancestral roots are easily traceable to the Emerald Isle. Irish ancestry is a significant ongoing part of our and America's identity.

I was on an exciting project that started in a somewhat clandestine morning meeting at the renowned Mayo Clinic. The project would then take me to Manchester, United Kingdom, to Vienna, Austria, and primarily to Ireland, where we worked with a catheter manufacturer in Limerick as well as the University of Galway National Centre for Laser Applications. At the Mayo Clinic Cardiology Center in Rochester, Minnesota, our team initially met with a leading cardiologist at six o'clock in the morning before his rounds began. The brilliant cardiologist had invented a procedure in his garage to treat thrombosis, a serious condition of a blood clot blocking blood flow. His process involved a catheter-directed thrombolysis to break up and flush the blood clot from the vein or artery. Typically, this could not be done through small catheters with fluids at very high psi (pounds per square inch). What would occur is a potentially dangerous, whipping "firehose effect" with the catheter. The cardiologist had experimented and determined that if six hundred micro-sized laser holes were inserted in the catheter's tip (which was the size of a pencil tip), the fluid could be gently dispersed even at high psi. The doctor's dilemma was how to fully develop such a device and bring it to market in volumes. Knowing that we recently acquired a Minnesota-based thrombosis medical device company, he called us to discuss. He noted that the procedure could more safely be done on an out-patient basis, saving everyone involved significant time and expense. I recall the cardiologist excitedly telling the group that development of such a product would be a "grand slam." The idea was carefully advanced in stages with a selected Limerick-based manufacturer—the only identified manufacturer possessing sufficient capacity to take on such a project. That supplier enlisted the University of Galway research center to address required micro-laser capabilities. We even secured a €25,000 grant from the country of Ireland to pursue the project. The winding sixty-mile trip from Limerick to Galway became commonplace. From there, the search for the required specialized laser took us to Britain, while the need for a dedicated injection molding machine led us to Austria. With considerable effort over many months, the catheter was successfully developed and briefly manufactured. Realizing that such a product was probably beyond our niche capabilities and interests, we eventually sold the product line to a large company directly dedicated to comparable medical solutions.

The family vacation came about when I had promised my wife, Susie, who was battling non-Hodgkin's lymphoma, that we would visit Ireland once she was fully recovered. Somehow this became a promise or commitment to not only take my wife but also her two sisters, her so-called "inner circle" of supporting caregivers, though I assuredly do not recall that part of the deal. Thanks be to God, following treatments, chemotherapy, as well as a few impactful Healing Masses, Susie miraculously achieved complete remission. She subsequently published a wonderful spiritual memoir, *Love Was There: A Testimony of Faith*. The autobiographical book documents her faith-filled life, cancer battle, and the great power of prayer. Several years later, with our three daughters finishing up college, we were ready to take that trip to Ireland. We decided that by inviting her sisters, it would be the perfect way to honor the *alleged* commitment. However, that invite ballooned into further invites and soon there were twelve of us headed to Ireland! I was happy to accommodate the group and even developed a thoughtfully planned itinerary. The objective was simple: provide an adventurous, fun time, share lots of laughs, and ensure a fitting overview of magical Ireland. All in just one week's time! With the help of our oldest daughter, Bridget, and her husband—two of our expanded traveling entourage—mission wildly accomplished. Though I'd be remiss if I failed to mention our knowledgeable and personable driver, Flan Kelly, and the new, rented coach with ample captain seats. Flan truly made the trip a wonderful, memorable experience. Consequently, the many Ireland business trips, along with the fantastic 2019 family vacation, are the basis of this final chapter.

Irish history is long and complex and the connection between the Irish people and their homeland is incredibly strong. Notre Dame University is referred to as the "Fighting Irish" for good reason, as most of Ireland's history revolves around the fight for independence and the right to self-govern. Irish playwright George Bernard Shaw may have said it best: "Ireland, sir, for good or evil, is like no other place under heaven, and no man can touch its sod or breathe its air without becoming better or worse."[1] Many people think of Ireland merely as an enchanted land, though more than most nations, Ireland has been among Europe's poorest regions and beset with serious perennial concerns. Through it all, and I've seen firsthand, the Irish people are known for their incredible resiliency, a reputation for thriving even through great adversity and sorrow. The Irish have endured and overcome significant challenges, such as economic crises, pandemics, and social inequalities. It's the Irish cultural identity, strong sense of community, and spirit of optimism that have seen them through. Also helpful, though perhaps a bit of stereotype: the Irish people, with the "gift of gab," are known for their wealth of folklore and storytelling. Consequently, Ireland is indeed also an enchanted land of tiny leprechauns with hidden pots of gold,

1. Shaw, "Ireland."

legendary Saint Patrick ridding the island of snakes, and the three-leaved Christian Trinity shamrock.

The Republic of Ireland is an island nation in the North Atlantic Ocean closely separated from Great Britain to the east predominantly by the Irish Sea. In addition to emigration, another of the serious perennial concerns in Ireland is geopolitical relations with Northern Ireland. Ireland, at least for the time being, is a divided nation. The island's thirty-two counties are separated into the Republic of Ireland and Northern Ireland. The Republic of Ireland (Ireland) is a sovereign state of twenty-six counties covering five-sixths of the island. Conversely, Northern Ireland is comprised of six counties and remains part of the United Kingdom. The population of the entire island is 7.2 million, with 5.3 million in Ireland and 1.9 million residing in Northern Island.[2]

Ireland is an ancient land. It is believed that Ireland had been occupied since the end of the last Ice Age.[3] Once the ice receded, the Scottish people first arrived by boat, providing a farming existence until the Bronze Age when the warrior Celts arrived in 500 BC. The Celts left a lasting influence on the Irish. Christianity arrived in Ireland in the fifth century. And by the late eighth century, the Norse Vikings arrived. With the Vikings came commerce, violence, and slavery. The Norse ruled until 1014, when they were defeated by the Irish feudal kings. The next seven-hundred-year period was constant fighting between the Irish kings and expanded control of Britain in Ireland. During this period, Catholic landholders were displaced by English and Scottish Protestant settlers. Many settlers were assigned powerful positions in the Irish Parliament. Draconian conditions were placed on Ireland's mostly Catholic population, and by 1800 Roman Catholics were banned from government. What followed was a group of brave, ambitious "rebels" who entered the Irish legal and political scene. The rebels vigorously fought British rule seeking Catholic emancipation, followed by the Irish right to self-govern and a free unified nation independent of Great Britain. These included heroic men like Daniel O'Connell, Michael Collins, and Éamon de Valera. Though they eventually succeeded, the emergence of Ireland as an independent nation is a very recent reality. It was in 1920 when the island was first partitioned with six counties as Northern Ireland. And it was not until 1949 that Ireland's twenty-six counties gained sovereignty as the Republic of Ireland.

I was thrilled to visit the ancestral homeland often on business and on a wonderful, expanded family vacation. Every chance to experience the

2. Wikipedia, "Historical Population of Ireland."

3. Wikipedia, "Ireland," sec. "Prehistoric Ireland."

people of Ireland, its green-hued landscapes, and the magnificent coastline along the 1,600-mile Wild Atlantic Way is welcomed. Accordingly, this special final chapter briefly covers just a few of the most memorable Irish cities and villages I visited and some related fun bleisure experiences.

ADARE

Adare is a beautiful village in County Limerick located just twenty-seven miles from the Shannon International Airport on the western coast of Ireland. Shannon Airport is the westernmost international airport in Europe, the easiest commute from the States. Adare is not just any Irish village but rather a designated heritage town, consistently celebrated as the prettiest village in all of Ireland. The tranquil, quintessential Irish village is adorned with charming, thatched cottages, boutiques, award-winning restaurants, churches, and pubs featuring traditional Irish music. Adare overlooks the fording tidal point of the village's picturesque Maigue River, a feature from which Adare, meaning "The Ford of the Oak," derives its name. First mention of Adare as a market settlement is traced back to 1226.[4] Along with the ruins of three medieval monasteries, you can also find Adare's thirteenth-century Desmond Castle. The cherry on top: also located in picture-perfect Adare is the five-star Adare Manor. To me, Adare is the very best of enchanted Ireland, a real-life manifestation of the Ireland of your imagination.

Adare Manor

In the very heart of picture-perfect Adare village, on the fast-flowing river and surrounded by medieval ruins, is a stately world-renowned 840-acre fairy-tale Irish manor. With its walled French gardens, fairy-driven forest paths, a Michelin-star restaurant, and a bucolic world-class golf course, *Adare Manor* has reached the global stage. Need further convincing? Adare Manor was recently named the "number one resort in the world" by *Condé Nast Traveler*.[5] Other manor amenities include a sports complex, glass-walled swimming pool, La Mer skin spa, wellness center, shooting ranges, chocolate shop, movie theater, and an underground speakeasy or "Tack Room" serving a multitude of Irish whiskeys favored by my son-in-law.

The present neo-Gothic structure was built in the early nineteenth century, retaining elements of the earlier seventeenth-century manor. In a fortunate stroke of luck, the building of Adare Manor provided needed

4. Adare Village, "Geoffrey De Marisco."
5. Ryder Cup, "Adare Manor."

employment for the surrounding villagers facing Ireland's great potato famine, a period of mass disease and starvation in Ireland that occurred from 1845 to 1852. The soft gray granite manor features a total of 365 leaded windows, fifty-two chimneys, twelve exterior doors, seven pillars, and four towers (one of just a few so-called calendar houses). Inside, there are 104 lavishly appointed guest rooms. You may be wondering how I could ever afford to stay at majestic Adare Manor in the blissful Irish countryside . . . I couldn't! However, there are also four-bedroom (private baths) manor lodges located on the property near the Carriage House. The lodges provide full access to the manor, the grounds and activities, its restaurants, and the Tack Room! On several occasions, four of us work colleagues would opt to stay here when working in nearby Limerick. Prior to recent manor renovations, the lodges were a reasonable alternative and acceptable business expense. Recognizing such, when I finally took my family (arriving in Shannon), the lodges at Adare Manor served as an ideal home base the first two days. Adare also served as the perfect gateway to our destination, southwest Ireland's *Wild Atlantic Way* coastline. My goal was to provide an incredible, stylish, top-notch introduction to Ireland . . . and I couldn't think of a better way than a stay at Adare Manor.

The expansive property and recent extravagant two-year renovations are credited to the Adare Manor owner, Irish billionaire and local Limerick-boy-made-good, J. P. (John Patrick) McManus. It's not uncommon to see Mr. McManus, also a racehorse owner, arrive at the manor via his helicopter, as my family experienced. Undoubtedly, the prize jewel of his efforts is surely the manor's new, Tom Fazio–reimagined championship golf course. The esteemed course has hosted numerous tournaments, and Adare Manor has won the bid to serve as host venue of the prestigious 2027 Ryder Cup.

Adare Manor should be on most serious travelers' bucket lists. And for those of us who have been fortunate enough to have visited Adare Manor, it's staying on the list for a return visit.

LIMERICK

Limerick is more than a short, humorous verse or naughty poem (e.g., "There once was an Irish city . . ."), though the associated term "limerick" is derived from the melodic chorus of eighteenth-century Irish soldiers singing "Will You Come to Limerick?"[6] *Limerick*, straddling the gray-blue estuary of the Shannon River, is the third-largest city in Ireland. The ancient western Irish city has a population of 102,000. Archeologists can trace

6. Britannica, "Limerick."

human evidence in Limerick, Stone Age tombs and circles, back to 3500 BC. Like most of Ireland, the Celts first arrived in 500 BC, establishing kingdoms. Christian monasteries and churches were established in the fifth century, though it was the Norse who attacked in AD 812 (Viking Age) and formally established Limerick in 922. Through the years, over four hundred medieval castles were built in Limerick. Eventually, it was French Norman explorers who redesigned Limerick in the twelfth century, creating a grand feel with notable architecture such as King John's Castle.

Limerick was known as a rough-and-tumble, blue-collar town with a reputation for hardship, petty crime, and neglect. Case in point: Limerick was the dire setting of local teacher and author Frank McCourt's chilling childhood memoir *Angela's Ashes*. The popular book was also adapted into a film. The town's *Frank McCourt Museum* is housed within his former school and contains artifacts from the memoir. Also hailing from Limerick is my favorite Irish actor and singer, the hell-raising Richard Harris. Harris was a critically acclaimed, award-winning actor who starred as King Arthur in the 1967 film *Camelot*. He reprised the role in the 1981 award-winning Broadway musical revival. As a chart-tracking singer, Harris recorded the seven-minute hit song, one of my favorites, "MacArthur Park." In the Limerick city center stands a six-foot bronze statue of Richard Harris depicting King Arthur in his famous role from the movie *Camelot*. Today, it's safe to say that conditions in Limerick have improved and there's a growing sense of positivity and an optimistic Irish spirit.

Nonetheless, I felt at home in gritty Limerick; it reminded me of my hometown of Pittsburgh and its rivers. Other than a few stays in Adare (eleven miles apart), Limerick served as our base as we tirelessly worked with the local catheter manufacturer to develop and produce our innovative medical device. Limerick's proud main attraction is clearly King John's Castle. However, just a short walk from our riverfront hotel was my all-time favorite Irish eating and drinking establishment, Dolan's Pub and Restaurant. In fact, Dolan's was the very first place that I took the "family tour" for a taste of Irish "pub grub" and a cold pint of Guinness.

Dolan's Pub and Restaurant

Dolan's Pub is not only one of Limerick's best traditional Irish pub and seafood restaurants, but also a meandering award-winning music venue filled with incredible Irish charm, hospitality, and unbelievable atmosphere. Even its Dock Road location on the dodgy, industrial docklands of Limerick City adds to the experience. Dolan's prides itself on being a haven for traditional

Irish music and an array of high-quality Irish dishes. Dolan's Pub and Restaurant was the perfect stop after a busy day of work. Family-owned Dolan's main pub, with capacity for one hundred guests, provides that authentic Irish feel and features live traditional Irish music every night throughout the year. As musicians stumble in for the evening performance, the pub takes on a genuine, welcoming family environment. In addition to the pub, Dolan's also houses the restaurant and three other distinct live music venues that cater to students, professionals, locals, and seasoned music enthusiasts. Limerick was home to the incomparable Dolores O'Riordan of the Cranberries alternative rock band and, accordingly, the music scene at Dolan's spans many genres. Take it from me that there's a lot going on at Dolan's nightly! Dolan's Pub and Restaurant is an integral piece of Limerick's culture and nightlife.

King John's Castle

In the heart of medieval Limerick City sits the thirteenth-century stronghold *King John's Castle*. To add to its intrigue, the Norman castle is named after the villainous, tyrannical king from Robin Hood folklore who ruled England from 1199 to 1216. John was self-proclaimed Lord of Ireland after having claimed the land. King John was also the brother of the popular Richard the Lionheart, the preceding King of England. Turns out that beleaguered King John was a very complex, unpopular antagonist who faced many challenges, even beyond legendary Robin Hood and his Merry Men. Consider that King John battled internal rebellions, fought with the pope, lost territories to the French, and was eventually forced to sign the famed Magna Carta in 1215—the very document that greatly limited the power of the British monarchy. Consequently, there are stories aplenty surrounding ruthless King John and Limerick's King John's Castle. In all my visits, I never toured the castle until the family vacation. I still recall when my niece Maura briefly disappeared to mysteriously ascend one of the ancient castle towers. The towers offer spectacular views across the roaring Shannon River over the Limerick rooftops.

Built to defend against river crossings, with five drum towers and impressive curtain walls, King John's Castle is an imposing site. Shortly after King John and the Normans arrived in Limerick, the castle was built between 1200 and 1212, although the castle site dates to 922 when the Vikings arrived and first constructed a large, high-ground, earthen defense. Over the subsequent centuries, the castle was repaired and expanded often. Remains of the prior Viking settlement, including houses, pots, and jewelry were all uncovered in 1900 during archeological excavations at the site. Other excavations have revealed King John's officers' quarters, the castle mint (King John minted his own coins), mines, a period pistol, and a seventeenth-century soldier's diary recounting the horrors of a castle siege. There were numerous sieges, most notably the traumatic 1642 siege against Protestants who occupied the castle after having fled the Irish Rebellion. The many castle remnants are reminders of the fearful atmosphere and the devastation of those medieval times.

More recently, the castle has undergone extensive redevelopment and state-of-the-art upgrades, including the visitor center, interactive activities and exhibitions, computer-generated animations and projections, and a café. The enhancements capture the castle's dramatic history, bringing the castle's story and colorful characters to life. Today, the large castle courtyard also serves as a live music venue hosting summer concerts of popular artists such as Van Morrison.

Very near King John's Castle, just a short walk down the river past an old potato market, is the oldest continuous-use structure in Limerick. *Saint Mary's Cathedral*, founded in 1168, features numerous fascinating items of interest. There's a roof-high monks' walk, seventeenth-century cannonball damage, marked stones used by soldiers to sharpen their swords and arrows, and a "leper's squint" (small opening in the cathedral wall through which lepers in medieval times could hear Mass). In 1651, after having captured Limerick, Saint Mary's was even briefly misused by England's Oliver Cromwell as an army horse stable. Today, over 850 years later, Saint Mary's Cathedral remains a living church (Anglican Community of the Church of Ireland) where daily services are offered.

Cliffs of Moher

A bit further afield from Limerick, fifty miles northwest and beyond the rocky plateau of County Clare's savage Burren region, are the breathtaking *Cliffs of Moher*—perhaps Ireland's most remarkable natural feature, and there is no shortage of those. The Cliffs of Moher represent where the black shale and limestone Burren plateau, stretching five miles wide, plunges a harrowing seven hundred feet into the sea below. Even when buffeted in mist and ocean gales, the cliffs are an unforgettable experience. If blessed with a rare clear Irish day, the distant Galway Bay Aran Islands and Connemara mountains come into view. The cliffs are the most visited tourist site in Ireland with over 1.5 million visitors annually. Most visitors start the visit at the official hillside visitor center. At the cliff's highest point, and worth a climb, is O'Brien's Tower. The observatory tower was built in 1835 and initially served as a teahouse. There's also an eleven-mile cliff walk for those so inclined, with little safeguards along the cliff's edge. I had the pleasure of visiting multiple times with colleagues while traveling from Limerick to Galway on business. And I assuredly added a visit to the Cliffs of Moher to the family itinerary. My eighty-three-year-old mother-in-law even made the climb up the hillside to O'Brien's Tower as a few other daring relatives rested precariously close to the edge!

Ireland is a land known for roadside shrines, mysticism, folklore, sacred spots, and over three thousand holy wells. One of the oldest and most famous wells in Ireland, rumored to have healing powers, is *Saint Brigid's Well* in the village of Liscannor, County Clare. Knowing we were passing by the well on the way to the Cliffs of Moher, and that Bridget, the oldest of our three daughters, was on the family tour, a brief stop was certainly in order. Coincidentally, in Irish folklore Brigid and her two sisters were known as a triple goddess. Brigid is the patron pagan goddess of the Druids, who existed in pre-Christian times. She is believed to have possessed strange supernatural powers to foresee the future, perform miracles, and heal diseases. Visible signs of Druid language and worship can still be seen in Saint Brigid's Well. There are few documented historical facts about the very popular Saint Brigid, mostly anecdotes and tales rooted in pagan folklore. In any event, it appears that Christendom had little choice but to name Brigid the foster mother of Jesus and patron saint of Ireland. Brigid was officially canonized a saint in the fifth century. Even today, Saint Brigid's symbolic woven cross remains popular and is seen throughout the world. The mystical cave-like well is in the grotto of a tiny stone house on the Irish roadside. With the faint sound of centuries-old running water, Saint Brigid's Well offers a cathartic space for devotion. The well provides a tangible connection to Irish folklore and long-standing traditions. There's an ancient cemetery on the hillside above the stone house. It is believed to be the resting place of several of Ireland's mythical kings and clan leaders. The whole experience was very Irish!

KINSALE

The seaside town of *Kinsale* is a favorite of the Irish, and I believe Kinsale was my mother's favorite place in all of Ireland. My mother visited Ireland on several occasions and often spoke highly of Kinsale, possibly because Kinsale resides in County Cork, which is where my mom's ancestral family originated. Consequently, having to spend a rare weekend in Limerick on business, I decided to drive the eighty miles down to Kinsale for a Saturday overnight stay. I was not disappointed and better understood my mom's connection. Originally a medieval fishing port, Kinsale is fabled far and wide for its natural beauty and historical importance. *Condé Nast* recently hailed fashionable Kinsale as one of Ireland's most beautiful towns. With its captivating waterfront setting and oak forest backdrop, Kinsale is nestled between the shoreline and hills. Kinsale is a vibrant, picturesque town of narrow, winding streets, famously brightly colored buildings, and lingering medieval influences. The safe, picturesque harbor sits at the mouth of the Bandon River and defines the town now known for yachting, sea angling, whale watching, seafood, and golf. Because of its reach as a popular tourist attraction and a reputation as the culinary capital of Ireland, Kinsale is occasionally referred to as "Ireland's Riviera." Kinsale has even been twinned with other renowned seaport towns such as Newport, Rhode Island. Scenic Kinsale is also just fifteen miles from the city of Cork and serves as the southern gateway to the start or finish point of the Wild Atlantic Way. Relative to our family vacation, I made Kinsale the second stop after Adare with plans to travel the Wild Atlantic Way and the Dingle Bay Peninsula on the way there. The third and final stop of the family vacation would be Dublin, the metropolitan capital of Ireland.

The name "Kinsale" means "headland of the sea" in Irish. Due to its highly strategic port location, Kinsale first became a popular trading post way back during the Bronze Age. There is also evidence of sixth-century monasteries. However, again, it was the tenth-century Vikings who established the first permanent settlement, as evidenced by the many ancient ring forts found in the area—though current Kinsale is more reminiscent of a twelfth-century Anglo-Norman settlement. In any event, historic Kinsale has been an important Irish foothold and center of commerce, trade, and fishing far beyond memory and record. In earlier centuries, whoever controlled the port of Kinsale could gain control of Ireland. For this reason, Kinsale easily claims a place among Ireland's most historically significant towns. Until the early seventeenth century, Catholic Gaelic lords substantially controlled Ireland and, outside of Dublin, the English Tudor claim to the country was largely in name only. With England exerting increasing control, the Gaelic lords allied with Catholic Spain and rebelled. Spain was already locked in a continental land war with England. Unfortunately, the 1601 Battle of Kinsale between Spanish-backed Ireland and England would be a turning point in Irish history. The English crown's quick and decisive victory over the Irish forces and the last Spanish Armada would lead to the complete English conquest of Ireland.

Unlike my solo direct-line visit from Limerick to Kinsale, the Griswold-style family vacation[7] route from Adare Manor to Kinsale was purposefully quite a bit more circuitous. Although we ensured that Grandma was safely in the van! Our route included the Dingle Peninsula, a significant and popular section of the Wild Atlantic Way. The day was reserved for some serious sightseeing in what the *National Geographic* once called "the most beautiful place on earth."[8] The breathtaking Dingle Bay stretches thirty miles into the Atlantic Ocean and is one of the westernmost points in Ireland. Thank God for our trusted, experienced driver, Flan Kelly! Our first stop before fully encountering the peninsula was the friendly Bohemian town of Dingle itself. Sad that we merely passed through the charming harbor town famed for its colorful shops, restaurants, and many pubs. The town even has a bottlenose dolphin named Fungie as its mascot. Fungie the dolphin has lived in the warm gulf stream waters of Dingle Bay since 1983. He is a beloved figure in the community. Of course, we made time for a delicious seafood chowder lunch at welcoming John Benny's Pub, followed by Murphy's Ice Cream. Now our group of twelve was fully prepared to experience the spectacular, rugged County Kerry coastline. I could never properly describe Dingle Peninsula, which is why it's listed in Tripadvisor's "top 100" places to see in the world.[9] The driving horseshoe route features steep, craggy sea cliffs with pounding, rippling blue ocean waves below. Add swirling, fast-racing skies, salty winds, jutting emerald-green headlands, an occasional sandy beach, rolling hills, lots of sheep, and spine-running mountain ranges. It all adds up to one of the world's most magnificent coastlines.

Knowing how to show us the best of Dingle Peninsula, Flan Kelly headed out of Dingle on *Slea Head Drive*. This spectacular narrow pass weaves and twists around the Irish southwest coast along one of the highest mountain roads (Conor Pass) in Ireland. Making several stops to enjoy the scenery, we first encountered *Fahan Beehive*, which boasts a good collection of medieval stone houses (clochán) with domes shaped like hives. Though thousands of years old, the surviving prehistoric dry-stone beehive huts were built as early as the sixth century. They were likely first inhabited by hermit monks. These amazing structures may look familiar to Star Wars fans as the beehive huts were featured as Luke Skywalker's hideaway in *Star Wars: The Last Jedi*. A second unexpected stop was the *Cross at Slea Head*. Along a small roadside stop was a gorgeous, towering white alabaster crucifixion scene set against jagged gray-black rocks—a perfect stopping point

7. The Griswolds are the family in *National Lampoon's Vacation* (1983) film series.

8. Dingle Peninsula Tourism Alliance, "Dingle Peninsula."

9. Dingle Peninsula Tourism Alliance, "Dingle Peninsula."

to also sit on the sky-high hillside overlooking the ocean and the haunting, uninhabited Blasket Islands in the distance. A third stop along Dingle Peninsula was award-winning *Inch Beach.* The expansive beach features stunning scenery and stretches three miles. Inch Beach is a favorite spot for avid surfers, walkers, and nature enthusiasts seeking outdoor activities. Of course, my fun-loving sisters-in-law insisted on running down the sandy beach to soak our bare feet in the cool Atlantic Ocean water, an Irish baptism of sorts. Finally, exiting Dingle Bay and headed inland, we arrived in *Killarney* to the tune of the Irish lullaby "Too-Ra-Loo-Ra-Loo-Ral." The popular tourist town has many attractions that we were able to briefly visit, including Killarney National Park and the moody *Lakes of Killarney.* The lakes are dotted with castles and abbeys. Within the park was the *Muckross House*, a fabulous imposing Victorian mansion with stunning gardens. The group even climbed the stone steps of Friars Glen wooded hillside in search of the cascading sixty-foot *Torc Waterfall.* After the brief unplanned stop, we were back on our way. I'm confident that the group will forever remember the magical September day we spent touring beautiful Dingle Peninsula on our way from Adare to Kinsale.

We were excited to arrive in the quaint seaport town of Kinsale. Kinsale is a small, intimate community with a lively punch. With its harbor and maze of narrow streets, you're never far from the water, which provides a tranquil atmosphere. My initial visit, I stayed at Acton's Hotel which prides itself as a harborside boutique hotel haven. For the family group, we stayed the two nights at the award-winning Old Bank boutique Georgian townhouse in the heart of Kinsale. I was very aware that Kinsale and the surrounding area offered grand landscapes and plenty to do in town and beyond. With that in mind, the following day was open for the group to choose their own activities. And boy did they! My daughter booked a salmon fly fishing expedition on the *Blackwater River* for my son-in-law, an avid fisherman. The villagers claim that Munster Blackwater is the centuries-old "birthplace of fly fishing." Several others set out to tour Kinsale's seventeenth-century star-shaped *Charles Fort.* Completed in 1682, the awe-inspiring military installation has fifty-two-foot-high outer ramparts that offer spectacular views of Kinsale Harbor. Built to protect further English attacks after the Battle of Kinsale defeat, ironically, the fort continued in military use by the British Army until 1922. That group chose to walk there and back and got quite a workout. Two other avid golfers with (apparently) dispensable cash went golfing at world-famous *Kinsale's Old Head Golf Links.* Old Head is a spectacular, unparalleled world-class golf course. The course occupies a stunning headland jutting over two miles into the powerful, surrounding Atlantic Ocean. With Kinsale's celebrated lighthouse, crashing waves over three hundred feet below, and fragrant hydrangea and rosa rugosa, Old Head is golf real estate like none other. A third group stayed in town to shop and pamper themselves before several of us headed by van to nearby Cork and Cobh for the "authentic" *Titanic Experience.* Both evenings in Kinsale, the entire group found "common ground" ending the evenings in the *Armada Bar and Guesthouse*, a charming and lively Irish pub in the heart of Kinsale. I suppose the pub's name pays homage to their former ally and the Spanish Armada, which tried but failed to protect Irish forces from the English during the 1601 Battle of Kinsale. The Armada bar provided an opportunity to immerse into the local culture and proved to be the ideal spot to unwind in the tiny coastal town. Nightly live traditional Irish music by the Ferrymen filled the Armada and spread out onto Market Street. Fortunately, the Armada was just a short walk from our Old Bank B&B. Spurred by a few too many Baileys Irish Creams—"the mother's milk," as my son-in-law termed the liquor—it wasn't long before the group had the locals and visiting tourists partying. There was even a tango line going out the door with our new friend Flan Kelly joining in the fun and dancing with Grandma.

Kinsale, much like Ireland itself, is a place that grows ever fonder in your heart with separation after returning home. It's also easy to overlook Kinsale's incredible historical significance and strong links to Spain, Britain, and even France and America, though many of the buildings, forts, churches, and pubs of centuries ago remain in the picturesque town. A final thought . . . Kinsale, quietly nestled between those oak forest hills and the shoreline, is every bit the gem my dear mom claimed.

DAY TRIPS TO CORK AND COBH

The Bells of Shandon

On my first visit to Kinsale, traveling alone, I took the opportunity to explore my Irish roots. That involved a quick visit to bordering *Cork City* to find the *Bells of Shandon*. My point of reference was that my great-great-grandmother Maggie O'Connell was from Cork and was, I understood, married "under the bells of Shandon." It did not take me long to learn that Shandon was a district on the north side of Cork. Sitting on the river Lee high above Cork is Shandon's eighteenth-century Church of Saint Anne, built in 1722. In fact, the three-hundred-year-old church and its tower's "Shandon Bells" and "Four-Faced Liar Clock" are the most iconic parts of Shandon. The clock is aptly named by locals as the four-sided clocks are rarely in agreement with each other. I had a chance to climb the tower, though I was unable to ring the bell that afternoon.

> On this I ponder, where'er I wander,
> And thus grow fonder, sweet Cork, of thee,
> With thy bells of Shandon,
> That sound so grand on
> The pleasant waters of the river Lee.[10]

I'm not sure of the fate of Maggie O'Connell, though I'm certain she long remembered the Bells of Shandon—a wedding story passed down through many generations. It is likely Maggie O'Connell fled Ireland after the Great Potato Famine or worse. I couldn't help thinking of the saying that "you are the result of a thousand love stories before you." That evening, I thought of a beautiful, young Irish bride named Maggie O'Connell, and I toasted her!

Titanic Experience Cobh

On April 11, 1912, the final 123 passengers came to the bustling harbor of Queenstown, Ireland (now the city of Cobh) to board the ill-fated *RMS Titanic*. The *Titanic*'s cross-Atlantic maiden voyage originated in Southampton, England bound for New York City. Four days later, as infamously known, one of the world's most tragic maritime disasters occurred. An estimated 1,517 of the 2,206 total passengers and crew aboard died in one of the deadliest peacetime sinkings of a single ship. The nearly nine-hundred-foot-long *Titanic* was the world's largest floating vessel in service at the time. The *Titanic* carried some of the wealthiest people in the world as well as many third-class emigrant dreamers seeking a new life in the United States and Canada. The town of Cobh (pronounced Cove) is a small island located in the Cork City harbor. Cobh is best known as the *Titanic*'s last port of call. Consequently, a unique visitors' experience has been created in Cobh. The *Titanic Experience Cobh* is an emotive, themed attraction and educational experience located in the original, historic White Star Line Building, the very place from where the *Titanic*'s last 123 passengers departed in 1912.

At the Titanic Experience Cobh, you are expertly guided through the *Titanic*'s tragic tale in intimate and personal detail. The guide outlines the class differences and amenities, showcases cabin reconstructions, shares amazing stories from the brave survivors, and discusses many original artifacts on display. Details on just how the allegedly indestructible *Titanic* met

10. Mahony, "Bells of Shandon," lines 5–9.

its tragic end at the hands of a massive iceberg are also illustrated. More so, in Cobh's historic White Star Line building, you can follow in the footsteps of the last 123 passengers to board the *Titanic* at the historic White Star Line building. You'll receive a boarding card for one of the travelers who came to the ticket office at this very spot. At the conclusion, you learn of your assigned fate (the passenger's fate) on the tragic voyage that occurred over 110 years ago. Spoiler alert . . . if you were a third-class passenger, your odds of reaching a lifeboat and surviving were not very good.

The story of the *Titanic* has captured the hearts of millions worldwide. The fascinating though tragic well-known story of the *Titanic* has been told over and over. Interest in the doomed ocean liner flourished after the 1985 discovery of the wreckage at a depth of over twelve thousand feet. What followed was the 1997 James Cameron film *Titanic*, starring Leonardo DiCaprio (as Jack Dawson) and Kate Winslet (as Rose). The epic romantic film grossed an overall $3.2 billion and catapulted interest in the *RMS Titanic* to an all-time high. That movie had great emotional impact on my oldest daughter, then fourteen years old, and we still mercilessly tease her about it to this day. That same daughter, and the rest of us, greatly enjoyed the Titanic Experience Cobh.

Saint Coleman's Cathedral

Following the Titanic Experience and before returning to Kinsale for a final night, we briefly stopped by *Saint Coleman's Cathedral*, Cobh's most iconic building. Construction of the Gothic Revival church began in 1868 with Saint Coleman's completed and consecrated in 1919. A smaller church had been on the site since 1769. The cathedral features a towering, highly visible 312-foot-high spire. The steeple and the cathedral's stunning setting on the Cork coastline, behind colorful homes and overlooking the Atlantic Ocean, make Saint Coleman's one of Ireland's most scenic churches. The church tower includes a forty-nine-bell carillon, one of the largest in Europe. The joyful bells can be heard on Sundays and special occasions. An automated system also chimes every hour and on fifteen-minute intervals. The beautiful Roman Catholic cathedral continues to hold Mass and religious services and often hosts recitals featuring world-famous choirs.

DUBLIN

The third and final stop of our whirlwind, one-week Ireland family vacation was *Dublin*. I sought to give the group a good contrasting overview of this beautiful, amazing country. Accordingly, we spent two nights in the Adare countryside, two nights in the seaport town of Kinsale, and the final two nights in metropolitan Dublin. No trip to Ireland is truly complete without a visit to its capital city. Having before visited Dublin on business, I had a pretty good lay of the land. Unlike other larger European capitals, ever-vibrant Dublin is a compact, super walkable city with a wealth of attractions and über-friendly, down-to-earth charm. It was a perfect final base to explore and connect Ireland's traditions, its culture, its history, and the incomparable Irish spirit.

Situated on the mouth of the Liffey River, Dublin is Ireland's largest city, with a population of nearly six hundred thousand and a suburban population of 1.3 million residents.[11] Despite Ireland's high birth rate, rugged rural Ireland remains relatively unpopulated. But Dublin is a bustling city, where Ireland's hard-working, well-educated, easygoing, youthful attitude to life is on full display. The name "Dublin" is derived from a Gaelic word that translates to "Blackpool," in reference to a dark tidal pool on the site of the Dublin Castle gardens that feeds the river.

Like most of northeast Europe, there is evidence of prehistoric human habitation in the Dublin Bay area as far back as six thousand years.[12] During construction in Dublin, excavated fish traps from that period have been discovered. It is believed the Scottish Gaels established a settlement in the area by the seventh century. The Vikings followed in the ninth century, and by the twelfth century, Dublin area was the principal settlement of the Anglo-Normans.[13] However, the Irish government recognizes 988 as the year the city of Dublin was settled and celebrated its official millennium and revitalization in 1988. Following independence of the Irish Free State in 1922, Dublin was named its capital city, remaining so after the country was renamed the Republic of Ireland in 1937.

Again, unlike my prior solo visits to Dublin, the final family vacation route from the seaport of Kinsale to Dublin was also purposefully more circuitous. We trusted our outstanding, very knowledgeable driver, Flan Kelly, to share the best of Ireland's eastern counties and get us safely to Dublin by late afternoon. In typical Irish folklore fashion, the first stop entailed ancient kings, patron saints, the devil, and, of course, Ireland's trademark stunning scenery. In its dramatic historical location high above a plain in Cashel, County Tipperary, sits the *Rock of Cashel*, also known as Saint Patrick's Rock. According to long-standing legend, the Rock of Cashel originated nearly

11. For this and other details in this section, see Wikipedia, "Dublin."

12. Wikipedia, "Dublin," sec. "History."

13. Wikipedia, "Dublin," para. 2.

twenty miles from Cashel in Devil's Bit Mountain. In the fifth century, Saint Patrick banished Satan from a mountain cave. It is believed that the angry devil took a bite from the mountain and spat it back out, and that it landed in the middle of Tipperary's countryside, becoming the Rock of Cashel. The site is also where Saint Patrick converted an Irish king to Christianity. Subsequently, an Irish clan built a fortress on the rock, ruling the area for hundreds of years. Finally, in 1101, the king donated the fortress on the rock to the church. With a character all its own, the remarkable medieval complex is one of Ireland's most spectacular attractions. Among the clustered monuments, sitting above surrounding lush green fields, is a round fortress tower, a high cross, the Romanesque Cormac's Chapel, Roman frescoes, an abbey, and an ancient cemetery. Several tombstones with our various family surnames were even located. If only the castle walls could talk!

Excitedly continuing up Ireland's eastern coast to Dublin, we encountered County Wicklow, the rugged *Wicklow Mountains*, Glendalough's beautiful "valley of two lakes," and a monastic site. It was hard to believe such beautiful, exhilarating wilderness was less than an hour's drive from our destination, Ireland's capital city of Dublin. The Wicklow Mountains are so wild, rugged, and empty that they were historically used as safe havens for Irish war lords and rebels fleeing the English Crown. Sally Gap, surrounded by bogs, pools, and streams, was the most remote pass through the mountains. In 1800, the British built a circular military road to improve access to the mountains and the rebels' hideaways. The scenic mountainous area of rocky glens, lush forests, and colorful heather remains thinly populated today. Driving through the mountain wilderness, it's easy to be utterly immersed in God's nature. Located in Wicklow Mountains National Park, en route to Dublin, was *Glendalough* ("valley of two lakes"). The stunningly beautiful glacial valley is situated between two lakes in County Wicklow. Glendalough is renowned for its monastic settlement, founded in the sixth century by Saint Kevin. Remains of the monastic city are dotted across the open glen. The medieval ruins include a 110-foot round tower, a roofless cathedral, the ruins of other churches, a priest's house, Saint Kevin's granite cross, the saintly monk's beehive home and kitchen, and Saint Kevin's man-made cave bed. Many very colorful legends surround the charismatic Saint Kevin who is said to have died in 618 at age 120!

So stunning are the Wicklow Mountains and Glendalough landscapes that the county has been dubbed "Europe's Hollywood." Beyond its beautiful nature, Wicklow is also home to two world-class film studios, experienced crews, and very favorable Irish tax breaks. Many films such as *Braveheart*, *Vikings*, *P.S. I Love You*, *Leap Year*, *Enchanted*, *Ella Enchanted*, *King Arthur*, *Excalibur*, *My Left Foot*, and *Brooklyn*, just to name a few, were filmed in

County Wicklow. Continuing travel to Dublin, there were a few major attractions that I first encountered on business travel, and desired to share with my family during our two-day stay.

Trinity College Dublin

Situated in the heart of Dublin is one of the most prestigious universities in Ireland if not the world. Beautiful, sprawling *Trinity College* is one of the seven pre-1600 "ancient universities" of Great Britain and Ireland. Trinity College was founded in 1592 by Queen Elizabeth I. By royal charter, Trinity College was modeled after Oxford and Cambridge universities. As a condition for its establishment, Trinity College was a Protestant university often associated with social elitism. The idea was to support learning to strengthen the Protestant Reformation in Ireland. For centuries, graduation from Trinity College required taking an oath, which was objectionable to Catholics. Seeing the university as thoroughly Protestant in ethos, Catholic bishops even implemented a general ban on Catholics attending Trinity College. It was not until 1970 that the Catholic Church lifted the ban for Catholics to attend the college (without dispensation). Trinity College followed in kind with the appointment of on-campus Catholic chaplains. Women were fully admitted to Trinity College in 1904 following an earlier visit to Dublin by Queen Victoria. Throughout the eras, the "Harvard University of Ireland" with over eighteen thousand undergraduate students has contributed to the flourishing of Irish literature and nurtured some of the best minds in philosophy, science, economics, music, medicine, and law. A few notable Trinity College Dublin alumni include Jonathan Swift (author of *Gulliver's Travels*), the flamboyant, witty playwright Oscar Wilde (author of *The Importance of Being Earnest*), Bram Stoker (author of *Dracula*), and poet and playwright Samuel Beckett (*Waiting for Godot*).

Notwithstanding gorgeous Trinity College itself, most visitors to the Dublin university come for the *Book of Kells Experience* and to visit the Long Room, one of the world's most beautiful, comprehensive libraries. On display as part of the experience is the university's greatest and most precious cultural treasure, a 1,200-year-old ancient manuscript known as the *Book of Kells*. The book's backstory includes ninth-century Columban monks, pillaging Vikings, Oliver Cromwell, and a remote abbey in the British Isles—namely, the Abbey of Kells, located on an island on the west coast of Scotland. Though it is unknown exactly where the Book of Kells was produced, it is estimated that it took seventy-five years to complete the glorious, early Christian illuminated manuscript of the four New Testament gospels:

Matthew, Mark, Luke, and John. The large, beautifully hand-lettered and painted lavish book, as survived, has 680 pages. Each page is filled with great symbolism, portraits, and Celtic knot motifs. The pages are vellum, calfskin tanned to paper-thinness. Smaller decorative details are so intricate as to be nearly invisible to the naked eye. What is evident is that no expense was spared in the book's production. Exorbitantly expensive gold pigments and rare blue lapis lazuli mineral paint, found only in the Middle East, were used. The book remained at Kells for centuries until 1654 when Oliver Cromwell's army arrived there. Knowing Cromwell was viciously anti-Catholic, the townspeople sent the treasured manuscript to Dublin for safekeeping. Subsequently, in 1661 the Book of Kells was given to Trinity College, where it first went on public display in the nineteenth century. On a royal visit to Dublin in 1849, Queen Victoria and Prince Albert signed the Book of Kells, though it was signed on an inserted modern page and subsequently removed during rebinding.[14] The well-preserved though fragile book has only left Ireland on four occasions in over 350 years. For visitors of the Book of Kells Experience, only a double page (two pages) is on display at any given time. The inspiring manuscript is quite simply an unmatched masterpiece for the ages. For admirers of history, religion, art, and architecture with time to spare, Dublin's Trinity College is a very beautiful and fascinating place to visit.

The Guinness Storehouse

Shifting gears, though the location is not very far from Trinity College, we turn to the Saint James Gate area and the *Guinness Storehouse*. The twelfth-century medieval gate into the then-walled city of Dublin was demolished long ago in 1734. In its place on Saint James Street, figuratively, is a nearly-as-famous, fourteen-foot-high gigantic black door with gold lettering that reads "Guinness." The imposing, popular tourist attraction symbolizes the brewery's longtime devotion to Dublin and the reciprocal success of Ireland's national beer. Guinness, also referred to as "the black stuff," is famous the world over. In 1759, an enterprising brewer named Arthur Guinness took out a low-rent nine-thousand-year lease on the existing brewery, which has been the home of Guinness ever since. By 1838, Guinness was the largest brewery in Ireland, and by 1886, with annual output of 1.2 million barrels, it was the largest brewery in the world, a title it no longer holds.[15] In 2000, at the dawn of the new millennium, the Guinness Storehouse opened and quickly

14. Study.com, "Did Queen Victoria Sign."

15. Grand European Travel, "History of Guinness Stout," paras. 2–4.

became Ireland's number one non-nature tourist attraction. The converted brewing factory building is now a gleaming, seven-floor Guinness museum and multimedia exhibition outlining the history of Guinness production. Discussed and exhibited are stout ingredients, craft brewing equipment and techniques, storage devices, and retro advertising. The whole experience is topped off with a pint glass of Guinness in the 360-degree-view Gravity Bar on the top floor. Be sure to toast and enjoy the wonderful creation of Arthur Guinness. Lastly, although you cannot see Guinness being brewed in the storehouse, there are vantage points where you can spot activity just outside. All the Guinness Draught (a dry stout beer) in the world is still brewed in the 1759 Dublin Guinness Brewery. Other locations produce only seasonal and special brews.

Kilmainham Gaol

Visiting the largest, cruelest prison in Europe—long-deserted and unoccupied and now serving as a museum—is far from an uplifting experience. However, if you're looking for poignant, albeit harrowing, insights into the history and lives of the Irish people, the hardships they endured, and their fight for independence, a visit to the *Kilmainham Gaol* (British for jail) is the best place to start. A tour of the imposing gray prison assures a dramatic, chilling recounting of the brutal conditions and momentous events at the forbidding jail.

Kilmainham Gaol was opened in 1796 and remained operational until 1924. Those years saw many major uprisings, rebellions, wars, and famine in Ireland, all part of the Kilmainham Gaol's sad story. For over 125 years, the prison held thousands of men, women, and children, most being common criminals. Crimes ranged from minor petty offenses to those highly impactful to the history of Ireland. Additionally, Kilmainham Gaol acted as a transportation point for an estimated four thousand prisoners being sent to Australia (Britain's nineteenth-century penal colony). Many of these prisoners, most guilty only of minor offenses, would never return home to Ireland.

Prison life conditions in Kilmainham Gaol were brutally harsh and inhumane. Small cells intended for one inmate often housed five inmates. Overcrowded cells were particularly commonplace during the Great Famine (1845–52) when food was so scarce that people deliberately committed crimes in search of imprisonment and regular rations. It was also a period when there was no segregation within cells by gender and most of the prisoner's time was spent in the cold and the dark. Only a single candle, intended to last two weeks, was provided for light and heat. And in the earlier years, gruesome public hangings took place outdoors in front of the prison.

More notable, most of Ireland's foremost political figures who bravely fought for Irish independence passed through Kilmainham Gaol—those associated with the 1798 rebellion through those associated with the 1916 Easter Rising. Included amongst those prisoners were Robert Emmet, Anne Devlin, the Fenians, Charles Stewart Parnell, Countess Markievicz, President Eamon de Valera, and the leaders of the 1916 Easter Rising. Many of the group were detained and executed in the jail. This sadly included fourteen from the 1916 Easter Rising who were executed by firing squad in the jail's Stonebreaker's Yard. One of those, Gifford Plunkett, got married in the jail only hours before. Another, James Connolly, too badly wounded to stand, was shot in a chair. The jail closed in 1924, remaining largely abandoned until 1966 when it was reopened as a museum. Since, Kilmainham Gaol has been preserved as a national monument. Consequently, a tour of the haunting former prison provides an evocative journey through the long, dark history of Irish nationalism. Kilmainham Gaol has played an important role in virtually every rebellious step of Ireland's painful path to independence in 1921.

All my trips to Dublin were very limited in time; however, if given an opportunity, there are many other uniquely Dublin attractions you should not miss. There's *Saint Patrick's* and *Christ Church Cathedrals*, a striking pair of ancient cathedrals built beside a well where it is said Ireland's patron saint had baptized converts. Then there's the award-winning, state-of-the-art *EPIC: The Irish Emigration Museum* where you can delve into your family's past. Of course, there's King John's thirteenth-century *Dublin Castle*, a key target of the 1916 Easter Rising. And it does not stop there. There are plenty of free museums in Dublin, including the *National Museum of Ireland* and the *National Gallery of Ireland*. Those so inclined can tour Dublin's *Jameson Bow Street Distillery* for cocktail-making classes and a premium whiskey-tasting session. Or spend the day or evening relaxing in Dublin's many beautiful public parks, such as city center gem *St. Stephen's Green* or *Phoenix Park*, where you can seek out the Oscar Wilde statue. Finally, cross the Liffey River over the *Ha'penny Bridge*, Dublin's oldest pedestrian crossing. Or, my favorite, simply visit the vibrant *Temple Bar* riverside neighborhood for live folk music, quirky boutiques, and packed pubs.

As you can see, Ireland's rich cultural heritage is every bit as interesting as its idyllic lush green landscapes and dramatic coastlines. Although in just one visit you understand exactly why mystical, magical Ireland is called the "Emerald Isle." There's also an ease in exploring Ireland's most iconic destinations and serene countryside, driving the captivating Wild Atlantic Way, or simply stumbling upon charming towns as if in a Hallmark movie. In the end, it's the warmth and friendliness of the Irish people that sets the country apart from others. With an atmosphere of lively pubs and traditional Irish music, the Irish are admired most for their hospitality and love of *craic* (fun)! Whether in a pub or coasting down the highway, I can't recall exactly how many times our group broke into a chorus of well-known traditional Irish tunes.

I recall two sayings about Ireland that really hit home with me, although I'm unsure of their origins. First, "Ireland doesn't rush, it hums. The pubs feel like old songs and the rain feels like memory." And, finally, "What if you didn't come to Ireland for the sights . . . but to feel something again?"

CONCLUSION

Travel is fatal to prejudice, bigotry, and narrow-mindedness. Many of our people need it sorely for those reasons. Broad charitable views of the world can't be gained by staying in one place.

—*Mark Twain*

As stated at the onset, I imagine most everyone dreams of visiting exciting and exotic locations . . . and I was no exception. Consequently, I am extremely and forever grateful for the great privilege and opportunity to have visited five continents and over twenty countries on business travel. The meaningful business impact of these travels was always clear, convincing, and rewarding to me. In our small way, we leveraged and advanced medical imaging science throughout the world. Though, beyond that, it was *bleisure*, a blending of business and leisure, that added the necessary "spice of life" to these travels—the interactions, connections, collaborations, and lasting friendships outside work that proved most inspiring and memorable, the place where work-life boundaries inevitably blur into one another. True living is chasing dreams, taking risks, staying hopeful, and giving it all you've got to near exhaustion. More so, it's the associated tangential caring, laughter, experiences, memories, and love and joy along the way that give meaning to travel. For these reasons, I would recommend that you always remain culturally curious and opportunistic, escape your comfort zone, embark on new activities, and really value the journey.

There are countless accounts of international travel benefits. Of course, foremost, cultural exposure significantly broadens your worldview perspective. International travel also expands open-mindedness and increases tolerance and acceptance. It also teaches patience, grows confidence, relieves stress, and deepens appreciation and gratitude. Additionally, business travel aids both your professional and personal development. I cherish having met so many wonderful colleagues and business acquaintances from around the world. With each introspective trip abroad, I strongly believe that I returned a slightly different person, hopefully a slightly better person. The vast experiences and time away from home naturally leads to serious, increased exploration of your inner self. The corresponding memorable experiences shape your personality and, hopefully, make you more interesting and richer. It's impossible to stare at the Sistine Chapel or, conversely, a Holocaust memorial and feel or learn nothing. To remain unchanged.

I enjoyed visiting so many wonderful cities and had to omit a few other favorites, including São Paulo, Brazil, Montreal, Canada, Basel, Switzerland, and San José, Costa Rica, to name a few. In turn, I hope you enjoyed my first-hand recollections, fun facts, and insights into a few of the world's greatest locations, amazing sites, and universal treasures offered from my unique "bleisure" point of view.

ABOUT THE AUTHOR

EDDY GUARASCIO earned a JD from the Duquesne University School of Law, an MBA from the University of Pittsburgh, and a BS from the Pennsylvania State University. During his career, Eddy visited many countries on business. His teams contracted for and procured goods and services totaling over five billion dollars, including everything from naval nuclear reactors to worldwide office supplies to innovative medical devices. In association, Eddy's teams were formally recognized for saving over $250 million. Born in the Naval Hospital in Oakland, California, and raised in McKeesport, Pennsylvania (outside Pittsburgh), Eddy lives in North Huntingdon, Pennsylvania with his wife, Susie. They enjoy spending time with their three adult daughters and their grandchildren.

Bibliography

Adare Village. "Geoffrey De Marisco and Adare." https://www.adarevillage.com/history/history-historic-sites/geoffrey-de-marisco-adare/.

Alves, Pedro. "Alcacer de Sol Castle." Archaeology Travel. https://archaeology-travel.com/europe/portugal/alentejo/alcacer-de-sol-castle/.

Ancestry.com. "Tracing Your Heritage: A Historical Expedition into the Mayflower's Legacy." *Ancestry Blog*, Oct. 17, 2023. https://www.ancestry.com/c/ancestry-blog/tracing-your-heritage-a-historical-expedition-into-the-mayflowers-legacy.

Andrews, Evan. "9 Things You May Not Know About Michelangelo." History.com, Mar. 6, 2015. https://www.history.com/articles/9-things-you-may-not-know-about-michelangelo.

Angier, Natalie. "Michelangelo, Renaissance Man of the Brain, Too?" *New York Times*, Oct. 10, 1990. https://www.nytimes.com/1990/10/10/arts/michelangelo-renaissance-man-of-the-brain-too.html.

Barcelona.com. "Gaudi Barcelona." https://www.barcelona.com/barcelona-attractions/antoni-gaudi-barcelona.

Bond, Michael. *A Bear Called Paddington*. New York: HarperCollins, 2014. Google Books. https://www.google.com/books/edition/A_Bear_Called_Paddington/piUoAwAAQBAJ.

Braw, Elizabeth. "When JS Bach Came to Leipzig." *Engelsberg Ideas*, June 16, 2023. https://engelsbergideas.com/notebook/when-js-bach-came-to-leipzig/.

Britannica. "Limerick: Poetic Form." https://www.britannica.com/art/limerick-poetic-form.

Brussels Airport. "The Belgian Chocolate House." https://www.brusselsairport.be/en/passengers/at-the-airport/shopping/the-belgian-chocolate-house.

Byron, Lord. *Childe Harold's Pilgrimage*. Project Gutenberg, 2004. https://www.gutenberg.org/files/5131/5131-h/5131-h.htm.

Camus, Aude. "Sublime of the Beautiful." Bentley, Apr. 17, 2024. https://blog.bentley.com/insights/sublime-of-the-beautiful/.

Casa Batlló. "About Antoni Gaudí." https://www.casabatllo.es/en/antoni-gaudi/.

CENIEH. "The First Modern Humans in the Interior of the Iberian Peninsula Were Expert Hunters." CENIEH News, Sept. 5, 2025. https://www.cenieh.es/en/press/news/first-modern-humans-interior-iberian-peninsula-were-expert-hunters.

Cherry Classics. "Brubeck." https://cherryclassics.com/pages/brubeck.

Civitatis. "Piazza San Marco." https://www.introducingvenice.com/piazza-san-marco.

Cologne Tourism. "Cologne Cathedral." https://www.cologne-tourism.com/arts-culture/sights/detail/cologne-cathedral.

Cords, Suzanne. "How the 'Three Wise Men from the East' Ended Up in Cologne." Deutsche Well, Jan. 6, 2025. https://www.dw.com/en/how-the-three-wise-men-from-the-east-ended-up-in-cologne/a-67770427.

Destinology. "Florence Things to Do." https://www.destinology.co.uk/destinations/italy/florence/things-to-do.

Dieterle, William, dir. *Portrait of Jennie*. 1948. Santa Monica: MGM Home Entertainment, 2004. DVD.

Dingle Peninsula Tourism Alliance. "Dingle Peninsula, Corca Dhuibhne." https://dingle-peninsula.ie.

Doezema, Marie. "Manneken-Pis: The Real Story Behind the Iconic Statue." *Brussels Times*, Aug. 5, 2015. https://www.brusselstimes.com/34280/manneken-pis-the-real-story-behind-the-iconic-statue.

Dolan, Kerry A., et al. "A Decade of Billionaires: 2010–2020." *Forbes*, 2020. https://www.forbes.com/decade-of-billionaires.

Donnelly, Brandon. "The $1.3 Billion Secret: How Nobu Turned Restaurants into a Real Estate Empire." *Brandon Donnelly*, Dec. 2, 2025, https://brandondonnelly.com/the-dollar13-billion-secret-how-nobu-turned-restaurants-into-a-real-estate-empire.

Dorn, Andrew. "The 10 Most Livable Cities in the World in 2025." *The Hill*, June 18, 2025. https://thehill.com/blogs/blog-briefing-room/5355863-top-livable-cities-global/.

Druckman, Bella. "The Story of 'Paddington Bear' Was Inspired by the Kindertransport Children." *Moment Magazine*, Oct. 13, 2021. https://momentmag.com/paddington-bear-kindertransport.

Duggan, Bob. "Can We Ever Restore Leonardo's 'Last Supper'"? *Big Think*, Nov. 16, 2012. https://bigthink.com/articles/can-we-ever-restore-leonardos-last-supper/.

The Economist. "Vienna Remains the World's Most Liveable City." Sep. 4, 2019. https://www.economist.com/graphic-detail/2019/09/04/vienna-remains-the-worlds-most-liveable-city.

Factum Foundation. "The Tomb of Raphael, The Pantheon." Factum Foundation for Digital Technology in Preservation. https://factumfoundation.org/our-projects/3d-sculpting/the-tomb-of-raphael-the-pantheon/.

Finelli, Sean. "The Absolutely Ridiculous History of Doge's Palace in Venice." *The Tour Guy*, Nov. 17, 2022. https://thetourguy.com/travel-blog/italy/venice/doges-palace/the-absolutely-ridiculous-history-of-doges-palace-in-venice/.

Fitzwilliam Museum. "The Relics of St Mark." https://fitzmuseum.cam.ac.uk/explore-our-collection/highlights/context/stories-and-histories/the-relics-of-st-mark.

Flores, Lourdes. "Ponte Vecchio: An Everlasting Symbol of Florence." Visit Florence. https://www.visitflorence.com/florence-monuments/ponte-vecchio.html.

Floris London. "Our History." https://us.florislondon.com/pages/our-history.

Fodor's. "To Live Like a Doge." *New York Times* (archive), 2006. https://archive.nytimes.com/www.nytimes.com/fodors/top/features/travel/destinations/europe/italy/venice/fdrs_feat_163_7.html.

Fodor's Travel. "77 Best Sights in Florence, Italy." https://www.fodors.com/world/europe/italy/florence/things-to-do/sights.

Fondazione Musei Civici di Venezia. "The Institutional Chambers on the 2nd Floor." Palazzo Ducale. https://palazzoducale.visitmuve.it/en/layout-and-collections/institutional-chambers/2-floor/.

Fong, Wallace. "Masterpieces of the Renaissance: 'The Gates of Paradise.'" *Sublime: An Arts and Science Blog*, Feb. 19, 2021. https://thesublimeblog.org/2021/02/19/masterpieces-of-the-renaissance-the-gates-of-paradise/.

Frank, Anne. *The Diary of Anne Frank*. Rev. ed. Edited by David Barnouw and Gerrold van der Stroom. New York: Doubleday, 2003.

Google Arts and Culture. "The Sydney Opera House: A Brief History in 5 Stops." https://artsandculture.google.com/story/the-sydney-opera-house-a-brief-history-in-5-stops/GwWRxVoNwSL1uA?hl=en.

Grand European Travel. "The History of Guinness Stout and How to Pour the Perfect Pint." https://www.getours.com/expert-travel-advice/history-traditions-celebrations/the-history-of-guinness-stout-irelands-famous-beer.

Guise, Lucien de. "Grave Robbers in Gondolas: How the Remains of St. Mark Came to Be in Venice." *Aleteia*, July 10, 2019. https://aleteia.org/2019/07/10/grave-robbers-in-gondolas-how-the-remains-of-saint-mark-came-to-be-in-venice/.

Heritage History. "Reconquista." https://www.heritage-history.com/index.php?c=resources&s=war-dir&f=wars_reconquista.

Hickey, Shane. "Picasso Painting Breaks Record for Most Expensive Artwork Sold at Auction." *The Guardian*, May 12, 2015. https://www.theguardian.com/artanddesign/2015/may/12/pablo-picasso-work-sets-record-for-most-expensive-artwork-sold-at-auction.

Hughes, Robert. "The Artist Pablo Picasso." *Time*, June 7, 1998. https://time.com/archive/6598161/the-artist-pablo-picasso/.

Info Barcelona. "New Record: 26.4% of Barcelona Residents Are Foreign Nationals." Barcelona.cat, Mar. 6, 2025. https://www.barcelona.cat/infobarcelona/en/new-record-264-of-barcelona-residents-are-foreign-nationals_1523360.html.

Inside Kyoto, "Kyoto Geisha." https://www.insidekyoto.com/kyoto-geisha.

Italiaoutdoors. "History of Venice and the Republic: Golden Age of the Venetian Republic." Italiaoutdoors Custom Vacation Planner and Guide. https://www.italiaoutdoors.com/index.php/history-of-italy/738-regions-of-italy/italy-veneto-region/the-venice-venezia-province-italy/venice-history/1102-republic-of-venice-from-1400-to-1600.

Jeske, Lee. "Q&A: Ruth Brown." *Rolling Stone*, Apr. 19, 1990. https://www.rollingstone.com/music/music-news/qa-ruth-brown-229481/.

Jet, Johnny. "Are Bleisure Trips Becoming More Common? This Study Says Yes." *Forbes*, Oct. 25, 2018. https://www.forbes.com/sites/johnnyjet/2018/10/25/are-bleisure-trips-becoming-more-common-this-study-says-yes/.

John, Tara. "Sagrada Familia Gets Building Permit After 137 Years." CNN Travel, June 10, 2019. https://www.cnn.com/travel/article/spain-sagrada-familia-permit-intl.

Kennedy, John F. "Address on the First Anniversary of the Alliance for Progress." Washington, DC, Mar. 13, 1962. The American Presidency Project. https://www.presidency.ucsb.edu/documents/address-the-first-anniversary-the-alliance-for-progress.

Kracklauer, Beth. "A Parisian Tradition: How the Bistro Got Its Name." *Saveur*, Nov. 18, 2010. https://www.saveur.com/article/Travels/A-Parisian-Tradition/.

Kyoto Travel. "Kyoto Ranked Second in Condé Nast Travelers' 'The Best Cities in the World' List." Sept. 14, 2025. https://kyoto.travel/en/news/kyoto-second-condenast/.

L., Elena. "St. Mark's Basilica: Kidnapping, Treasures, and Other Secrets." Walks of Italy. Updated Jan. 22, 2025. https://www.walksofitaly.com/blog/art-culture/6-fascinating-facts-about-st-marks-basilica.

Laeger, Brittany. "Did You Know? *Mamma Mia!* Edition." *Center Blog*, Aug. 6, 2024. https://www.kennedy-center.org/our-story/blog?p=did-you-know-mamma-mia-edition.

Le Carré, John. *The Honourable Schoolboy*. New York: Bantam, 1978. Google Books. https://www.google.com/books/edition/The_Honorable_Schoolboy/ZEujODlWCNUC.

London City Hall. "Parks and Green Spaces." https://www.london.gov.uk/programmes-strategies/environment-and-climate-change/parks-green-spaces-and-biodiversity/parks-and-green-spaces.

Lonely Planet. La Sagrada Família. https://www.lonelyplanet.com/points-of-interest/la-sagrada-familia/374867.

Lorenzi, Rossella. "Michelangelo's David Is Missing a Muscle." ABC Science, Oct. 18, 2004. https://www.abc.net.au/science/articles/2004/10/18/1222193.htm.

Lubow, Arthur. "The Gates of Paradise." *Smithsonian*, Nov. 2007. https://www.smithsonianmag.com/arts-culture/the-gates-of-paradise-174431341/.

Macdonald, Kyle. "15 Pop Songs You Didn't Know Were Inspired by J. S. Bach." Classic FM, May 17, 2021. https://www.classicfm.com/composers/bach/inspired-pop-rock-rap-songs/.

Mahony, Francis Sylvester. "The Bells of Shandon." In *The Sunny Side of Ireland*, by John O'Mahony and R. Lloyd Praeger, ch. "Cork." Project Gutenberg, 2006. https://www.gutenberg.org/files/19329/19329-h/19329-h.htm.

Mbantua Gallery. "Aboriginal Culture." https://mbantua.com.au/aboriginal-culture/.

Merlin Entertainments. "London Eye 25th Anniversary." London Eye. https://www.londoneye.com/25th-anniversary/.

Mexico News Daily. "More Mexicans Than Ever Made the 2026 Forbes Billionaires List." *Mexico News Daily*, Mar. 12, 2026. https://mexiconewsdaily.com/business/mexican-billionaires-forbes-2026/.

Midgley, Emma. "Paddington Bear 'Inspired by Evacuees' Says Author Bond." *BBC News*, Feb. 13, 2012. https://www.bbc.com/news/uk-england-berkshire-16964890.

National Park City Foundation. "London National Park City." https://nationalparkcity.london/.

Neuhaus Chocolates. "Our Story." https://www.neuhauschocolates.com/en_US/our-story/ourstory.html.

NPB Card Guy. "Uniforms." *Japanese Baseball Cards*, Nov. 5, 2012. https://japanesebaseballcards.blogspot.com/2012/11/uniforms.html.

Oliver, Huw. "Revealed: This Is, Officially, Europe's Greatest Train Station." *Time Out*, Mar. 24, 2021. https://www.timeout.com/news/revealed-this-is-officially-europes-greatest-train-station-032521.

Pinsky, Robert. "Labor Pains: Michelangelo's Poem About the Awkward Parturition of the Sistine Chapel." *Slate*, Jan. 26, 2010. https://www.slate.com/articles/arts/poem/2010/01/labor_pains.html.

Porsche Newsroom. "Porsche Plant in Leipzig Receives 'Factory of the Year' Award." Mar. 15, 2024. https://newsroom.porsche.com/en/2024/company/porsche-leipzig-factory-of-the-year-35524.html.

Reagan, Ronald. "Remarks on East-West Relations at the Brandenburg Gate in West Berlin." June 12, 1987. Ronald Reagan Presidential Library and Museum, National Archives. https://www.reaganlibrary.gov/archives/speech/remarks-east-west-relations-brandenburg-gate-west-berlin.

Roller, Sarah. "Out of Sight, Out of Mind: What Were Penal Colonies?" History Hit, Dec. 17, 2021. https://www.historyhit.com/a-short-history-of-penal-colonies/.

Ryder Cup. "Adare Manor Named #1 Resort in the World by Coveted Condé Nast Traveler Readers' Choice Awards." Oct. 5, 2022. https://www.rydercup.com/news-media/adare-manor-named-1-resort-in-the-world-by-coveted-conde-nast-traveler-readers-choice-awards.

Shaw, George Bernard. "Ireland, sir, for good or evil, is like no other place under heaven." AZQuotes. https://www.azquotes.com/quote/845254.

Sidhu, Harmeet Kaur. "Welling Up Outside the Room of Tears—The Sistine Chapel, Vatican City." *Huffpost*, Sept. 22, 2015. https://www.huffingtonpost.co.uk/harmeet-kaur-sidhu/the-sistine-chapel-vatican-city_b_8152766.html.

SparkNotes. "The Spanish American War (1898–1901)." https://www.sparknotes.com/history/american/spanishamerican/.

Spectrum News. "'The Mousetrap': The Longest Running Play in the World." July 20, 2023. https://ny1.com/nyc/all-boroughs/on-stage-episodes/2023/07/20/-the-mousetrap—-the-longest-running-play-in-the-world.

Steward, Jessica. "12 Facts You Need to Know About Gaudí's Sagrada Familia, Barcelona's Most Visited Attraction." My Modern Met, May 26, 2017. https://mymodernmet.com/sagrada-familia-facts-gaudi/.

St. Mark Catholic Church. "Our Patron: St. Mark the Evangelist." https://www.stmarkwheaton.org/our-patron-2/.

Study.com. "Did Queen Victoria Sign the Book of Kells?" https://homework.study.com/explanation/did-queen-victoria-sign-the-book-of-kells.html.

Suit Century. "Beau Brummell's Revolution: The Rise of the Modern Men's Suit in the 19th Century." *Suit Century Blog*, Sept. 11, 2023. https://suitcentury.com/blog/beau-brummells-revolution-the-rise-of-the-modern-mens-suit-in-the-19th-century.

Sydney Opera House. "Architecture Meets Nature." https://www.sydneyoperahouse.com/schools/architecture-meets-nature.

———. "Our Story: The Spherical Solution." https://www.sydneyoperahouse.com/our-story/the-spherical-solution.

Thingstodoinlondon.com. "Buckingham Palace Facts." https://www.thingstodoinlondon.com/attractions/buckingham-palace/facts/.

Through Eternity. "Bernini's Fountain of the Four Rivers in Piazza Navona." Rome Travel Guide. https://www.througheternity.com/rome/bernini-fountain-of-the-four-rivers-in-piazza-navona.

———. "7 Fascinating Facts About the Ponte Vecchio in Florence." Florence Travel Guide. https://www.througheternity.com/florence/7-fascinating-facts-ponte-vecchio-florence.

Thurston, Katherine Cecil. *The Gambler*. Toronto: Revell, 1905. Project Gutenberg, 2010. https://www.gutenberg.org/cache/epub/33490/pg33490-images.html.

UNESCO. "About World Heritage." UNESCO World Heritage Convention. https://whc.unesco.org/en/about/.

United States Department of State. "Foreign Relations of the United States, Diplomatic Papers, The Conference of Berlin (The Potsdam Conference), 1945, Volume II: Editor's Note." Office of the Historian. https://history.state.gov/historicaldocuments/frus1945Berlinv02/d710a-97.

USA Today. "10 Most Beautiful Places in America." Sept. 30, 2013. https://www.usatoday.com/story/life/weekend/2013/09/30/the-10-most-beautiful-places-in-america/2754657/.

Vasa Museum. "Skeletons from Vasa." Updated Oct. 12, 2025. https://www.vasamuseet.se/en/explore/research/skeletons.

Venice Museum. "Doge's Palace." https://www.venice-museum.com/doge-palace.php.

Visit Florence Italy. "Ponte Vecchio Bridge in Florence." https://florencetips.com/ponte_vecchio_bridge.html.

Visit Portugal. "Alcácer do Sal." https://www.visitportugal.com/en/NR/exeres/30D0D346–4A2F-4413-B0BE-56968ADA12A7.

Waugh, Daniel C. "Marco Polo's Travles: Myth or Fact?" *Expedition Magazine* 52.3 (2010). https://www.penn.museum/sites/expedition/marco-polos-travels-myth-or-fact/.

White, L. Michael. "The Gospel of Mark." *Frontline*. PBS. 1998. https://www.pbs.org/wgbh/pages/frontline/shows/religion/story/mark.html.

Wikipedia. "Abu Daoud." https://en.wikipedia.org/wiki/Abu_Daoud.

———. "Alcácer do Sal." https://en.wikipedia.org/wiki/Alc%C3%A1cer_do_Sal.

———. "American Expatriate Baseball Players in Japan." https://en.wikipedia.org/wiki/American_expatriate_baseball_players_in_Japan.

———. "Antoni Gaudí." https://en.wikipedia.org/wiki/Antoni_Gaud%C3%AD.

———. "Asia." https://en.wikipedia.org/wiki/Asia.

———. "Australian Aboriginal Culture." https://en.wikipedia.org/wiki/Australian_Aboriginal_culture.

———. "Beau Brummell." https://en.wikipedia.org/wiki/Beau_Brummell.

———. "Belgians." https://en.wikipedia.org/wiki/Belgians.

———. "Belgium." https://en.wikipedia.org/wiki/Belgium.

———. "Brandenburg Gate." https://en.wikipedia.org/wiki/Brandenburg_Gate.

———. "Chair of Saint Peter." https://en.wikipedia.org/wiki/Chair_of_Saint_Peter.

———. "*David* (Michelangelo)." https://en.wikipedia.org/wiki/David_(Michelangelo).

———. "Doge's Palace." https://en.wikipedia.org/wiki/Doges_Palace.

———. "Dublin." https://en.wikipedia.org/wiki/Dublin.

———. "Florence Baptistery." https://en.wikipedia.org/wiki/Florence_Baptistery.

———. "Giacomo Casanova." https://en.wikipedia.org/wiki/Giacomo_Casanova.

———. "Harry's Bar (Venice)." https://en.wikipedia.org/wiki/Harry%27s_Bar_(Venice).

———. "Historical Population of Ireland." https://en.wikipedia.org/wiki/Historical_population_of_Ireland.

———. "History of Japan." https://en.wikipedia.org/wiki/History_of_Japan.

———. "History of the Republic of Venice." https://en.wikipedia.org/wiki/History_of_the_Republic_of_Venice.

———. "History of Spain." https://en.wikipedia.org/wiki/History_of_Spain.

———. "History of Sweden." https://en.wikipedia.org/wiki/History_of_Sweden.

———. "Ireland." https://en.wikipedia.org/wiki/Ireland.

———. "Jimmy Scott." https://en.wikipedia.org/wiki/Jimmy_Scott.

———. "Justa and Rufina." https://en.wikipedia.org/wiki/Justa_and_Rufina.

———. "List of Jamestown Colonists." https://en.wikipedia.org/wiki/List_of_Jamestown_colonists.

———. "List of Most-Visited Art Museums." https://en.wikipedia.org/wiki/List_of_most-visited_art_museums.

———. "Madonna del Cardellino." https://en.wikipedia.org/wiki/Madonna_del_Cardellino.

———. "Manneken Pis." https://en.wikipedia.org/wiki/Manneken_Pis.

———. "Mark the Evangelist." https://en.wikipedia.org/wiki/Mark_the_Evangelist.

———. "Military Career of Elvis Presley." https://en.wikipedia.org/wiki/Military_career_of_Elvis_Presley.

———. "The Mousetrap." https://en.wikipedia.org/wiki/The_Mousetrap.

———. "Nijō_Castle." https://en.wikipedia.org/wiki/Nijō_Castle.

———. "Pablo Picasso." https://en.wikipedia.org/wiki/Pablo_Picasso.

———. "*Pietà* (Michelangelo)." https://en.wikipedia.org/wiki/Piet%C3%A0_(Michelangelo).

———. "Prehistory of Australia." https://en.wikipedia.org/wiki/Prehistory_of_Australia.

———. "Rialto Bridge." https://en.wikipedia.org/wiki/Rialto_Bridge.

———. "Sagrada Família." https://en.wikipedia.org/wiki/Sagrada_Família.

———."*Saint Mark's Body Brought to Venice*." https://en.wikipedia.org/wiki/Saint_Mark%27s_Body_Brought_to_Venice.

———."Spain." https://en.wikipedia.org/wiki/Spain.

———. "Spanish–American War. https://en.wikipedia.org/wiki/Spanish-American_War.

———. "St. Peter's Baldachin." https://en.wikipedia.org/wiki/St._Peter%27s_Baldachin.

———. "Sydney." https://en.wikipedia.org/wiki/Sydney.

———. "The Travels of Marco Polo." https://en.wikipedia.org/wiki/The_Travels_of_Marco_Polo.

———. "Treaty of Paris (1898)." https://en.wikipedia.org/wiki/Treaty_of_Paris_(1898).

———. "Uffizi." https://en.wikipedia.org/wiki/Uffizi.

———. "Venice." https://en.wikipedia.org/wiki/Venice.

William Reed. "The World's 50 Best Restaurants." https://www.theworlds50best.com/list/1–50.

Wilson, Bee. "Bill Granger Obituary." *Guardian*, Dec. 31, 2023. https://www.theguardian.com/food/2023/dec/31/bill-granger-obituary.

www.ingramcontent.com/pod-product-compliance
Lightning Source LLC
LaVergne TN
LVHW020536100826
845148LV00010B/1490

* 9 7 9 8 3 8 5 2 7 1 1 4 6 *